FROM SOCIAL SCIENCE TO DATA SCIENCE

T0375734

Sara Miller McCune founded SAGE Publishing in 1965 to support the dissemination of usable knowledge and educate a global community. SAGE publishes more than 1000 journals and over 800 new books each year, spanning a wide range of subject areas. Our growing selection of library products includes archives, data, case studies and video. SAGE remains majority owned by our founder and after her lifetime will become owned by a charitable trust that secures the company's continued independence.

Los Angeles | London | New Delhi | Singapore | Washington DC | Melbourne

FROM SOCIAL SCIENCE TO DATA SCIENCE

Bernie Hogan

Los Angeles | London | New Delhi
Singapore | Washington DC | Melbourne

Los Angeles | London | New Delhi
Singapore | Washington DC | Melbourne

SAGE Publications Ltd
1 Oliver's Yard
55 City Road
London EC1Y 1SP

SAGE Publications Inc.
2455 Teller Road
Thousand Oaks, California 91320

SAGE Publications India Pvt Ltd
B 1/I 1 Mohan Cooperative Industrial Area
Mathura Road
New Delhi 110 044

SAGE Publications Asia-Pacific Pte Ltd
3 Church Street
#10-04 Samsung Hub
Singapore 049483

Editor: Jai Seaman
Assistant editor: Hannah Cavender-Deere
Production editor: Ian Antcliff
Copyeditor: Richard Leigh
Proofreader: Richard Walshe
Marketing manager: Ben Griffin-Sherwood
Cover design: Shaun Mercier
Typeset by: C&M Digitals (P) Ltd, Chennai, India
Printed in the UK

© Bernie Hogan 2023

Apart from any fair dealing for the purposes of research, private study, or criticism or review, as permitted under the Copyright, Designs and Patents Act, 1988, this publication may not be reproduced, stored or transmitted in any form, or by any means, without the prior permission in writing of the publisher, or in the case of reprographic reproduction, in accordance with the terms of licences issued by the Copyright Licensing Agency. Enquiries concerning reproduction outside those terms should be sent to the publisher.

Library of Congress Control Number: 2022938266

British Library Cataloguing in Publication data

A catalogue record for this book is available from the British Library

ISBN 978-1-5297-0749-6
ISBN 978-1-5297-0748-9 (pbk)

At SAGE we take sustainability seriously. Most of our products are printed in the UK using responsibly sourced papers and boards. When we print overseas we ensure sustainable papers are used as measured by the PREPS grading system. We undertake an annual audit to monitor our sustainability.

BRIEF CONTENTS

CONTENTS

LIST OF FIGURES AND TABLES

FIGURES

TABLES

DISCOVER THIS TEXTBOOK'S ONLINE RESOURCES!

This book is supported by a wealth of online resources for both students and lecturers to aid study and support teaching, which are available at **https://study.sagepub.com/hogan**

For students (freely available on GitHub)

Jupyter notebooks with the headers and code blocks from the book help you follow the processes step by step.

Additional exercises for each chapter help you practice your skills and develop project ideas using the code in the book.

Author videos for each chapter show you how to work through some of the examples in the book and help you get to grips with key concepts.

Links to data resources, articles, videos and further reading help you take your knowledge further.

For instructors

PowerPoint decks featuring figures, tables, and key topics from the book can be downloaded and customized for use in your own presentations.

Multiple-choice questions containing questions related to the key concepts in each chapter can be downloaded and used in class or for homework and exams.

ABOUT THE AUTHOR

 Bernie Hogan (he/him/*) is a Senior Research Fellow at the Oxford Internet Institute and the current Director of the University of Oxford's MSc programme in Social Data Science. Bernie's work specialises in how to leverage computational tools for creative, challenging, and engaging methodologies to address social science research questions about identity, sexuality, and community. His favourite work in this area focuses on the capture and analysis of personal social networks, using both pen-and-paper tools and the recent free open-source application Network Canvas (https://www.networkcanvas.com). He has published over 40 peer-reviewed articles and presented at over a hundred conferences, including several keynotes. His most famous work reconsidered Goffman's offline stage play metaphor of self-presentation for online life as exhibition and 'algorithmic curation' (Hogan, 2010).

Before working at the University of Oxford's Oxford Internet Institute (https://www.oii.ox.ac.uk) he completed his undergraduate and graduate degrees in Canada. His first degree was in Sociology and Computer Science at Memorial University in St. John's, Newfoundland, Canada. His graduate work was in Sociology and Knowledge Media Design at the University of Toronto. During that time Bernie interned at Microsoft Research. Bernie lives in Oxford, UK with his husband and their sprawling vinyl record collection. He tweets (and collects vinyl) under the moniker @blurky. Most of his research is available from his departmental homepage (https://www.oii.ox.ac.uk/people/profiles/bernie-hogan/), his own homepage (https://berniehogan.me), and/or his GitHub (https://www.github.com/berniehogan).

ACKNOWLEDGEMENTS

I was hired to help design and teach the first MSc programme at the Oxford Internet Institute way back in 2008 and somehow I've been there ever since. More recently I've been responsible for directing our second programme, an MSc in Social Data Science, taking over from the first director, my wonderful colleague Scott Hale. While this book is broadly meant to be an introduction to the field of social data science, it is most closely linked to the introductory course I teach in that programme, 'Fundamentals of Social Data Science'. It shares some debt with other courses I teach, particularly 'Data Wrangling' and 'Interpreting Social Networks'. It is to these courses, the students in them, and the department that has supported this training over the last decade that I owe the greatest debt of gratitude.

I first want to acknowledge the teaching assistants (TAs) of these classes. Your patience and collaborative nature has also improved the code, provided insight into where these lessons might be going astray or need a little extra, and helped identify systematic issues that need consideration or gaps that need plugging within such a short amount of time. Thanks so much to those TAs who have worked with variations of the notes herein: Linda Li, Dragos Gorduza, Christine Sheldon, Patrick Gildersleve, Siân Brooke, Elle Yang, Siddhartha Datta, and Luca Mungo.

My students always been a source of collaboration and inspiration. The first to mention undoubtedly is Wojciech Gryc. Wojciech's generosity in helping fellow students apply solutions in Python convinced me the department needed to systematically direct resources to this coding back in 2010. These resources became first a workshop, then a course ('Introduction to Python'), then a bigger course ('Digital Social Research', with Jonathan Bright), and the first core programming course for my department's Social Data Science MSc.

Other former students (supervisees or otherwise) to thank out loud include Joshua Melville, Bruce Etling, Slava Polonski, Karim Elmehairy, Liam Bekirsky, Amadea Turk, Alex Amari, Jack LaViolette, Bethan Charnley, Adam Turowski, Kassie Scott, Hannah Kirk, Paulius Rauba, Lisa Oswald, Momin Malik, Devin Gaffney, Ryan Den Rooijen, Graham Gannon, Louis Elton, Patrick Savoie, Gaoyu Du, Sarah Ball, Ran Jiang, Victor Maimone, Michael Collyer, Yixin Chen, Annabel Ngien, Danica Radovanović, Cailean Osborne, Anna George, and, definitely not least, Freya Lily Griffiths.

This all happened at the intellectually vibrant Oxford Internet Institute. I hesitate to provide a roll call, but specifically in relation to the work and ideas in *this* book, I could not go by without mentioning the contributions of some of my peers at the University of Oxford past and present (in rough order of appearance): Victoria Nash, William Dutton, Helen Margetts, Ralph Schroeder, Eric Meyer, Tom Snijders, Alison Powell, Ian Brown, Sandra Gonzalez-Bailon, Scott Hale, Grant Blank, Mark Graham, Greg Taylor, Jonathan Bright, Bertil Hatt,

Mason Porter, Johan Koskinen, Andy Przybylski, Felix Reed-Tsochas, Sandra Wachter, Cohen Simpson, Taha Yasseri, Ahmed Medhat, Vili Lehdenvirta, Patrycja Stys, Per Block, Brent Mittelstadt, Chico Camargo, Charles Rahal, Christine Bunyan, Renaud Lambiotte, Xiaowen Dong, Janet Pierrehumbert, Min Chen, Peaks Krafft, Adam Mahdi, Fabian Stephany, Fabian Brasesemann, and Luc Rocher. I also want to singularly highlight the Network Canvas team at Northwestern, including core members Michelle Birkett, Gregory L. Philips II, Patrick Janulis, Joshua Melville, Kate Banner, associates on the project Elizabeth McConnell, Noshir Contractor and Brian Mustanski, as well as Steve McKellar from development team. The software is not featured directly in this book, but I cannot overstate its role in my academic life over the last decade.

Among the wider academic world, I want to express support for those whose worked and conversed with me about programming and computational social science over the years. Some of these conversations were just fun and energising but others were deeply influential, sometimes in ways I would only discover much later. Some even became collaborations. Some thanks in alphabetical order by first name: Adam Kalai, Alice Marwick, Anatoliy Gruzd, Brent Berry, Brent Hecht, Brian Keegan, Christian Sandvig, Cliff Lampe, Conor Hayes, danah boyd, Daniele Quercia, Danyel Fisher, Elisa Bellotti, Emre Kiciman, Eric Gilbert, Eytan Adar, Fernanda Viégas, Filip Agneessens, Jessica Vitak, jimi adams, John McLevey, Jose Luis Molina, Jure Lescovec, Kate Crawford, Lada Adamic, Lorien Jasny, Marc Smith, Mark McCann, Martin Everett, Matt Salganik, Meeyoung Cha, Miranda Lubbers, Munmun De Choudhury, Nicole Ellison, Paola Tubaro, Phoebe Moore, Rochelle Côté, Tom Baird, Ulrik Brandes. And I know there are so many more I have forgotten (I'm so sorry but thank you regardless)!

The first person to teach me to code was a librarian who volunteered at the Boys and Girls Club in Gander, Newfoundland, in the late 1980s. And speaking of forgetting names, it pains me to say I forget her name now. But I wanted to mention her, even if only anonymously. The second person would have been my uncle, Tony Norman, himself an IT educator for schoolchildren. He first introduced me to IBM computers, which effectively became the modern Windows computers. I have had many teachers in computing and programming since then, but one in particular deserves considerable thanks. In 2002 the instructor for the humbly named 'vocational languages' course, Prof. Ron Byrne, decided to feature Python for the first time rather than the reigning champ in text processing, Perl. He took a risk to keep his course fresh, and for me the benefits were profound. The fact that so much of the world has since shared this love of Python and created such a marvellous ecosystem is so gratifying. This book was written in markdown and coded in Jupyter Lab, auto-processed by pandoc into LaTeX using some custom scripts, and from there sent to Sage for processing. These technologies are themselves open source and effectively free due to considerable labour from many volunteers.

Other former teachers, educators, and programming mentors to note include Barry Wellman, Marc Smith, Jason Nolan, Bonnie Erickson, Stephen Riggins, Todd Wareham, Marion Blute, Blair Wheaton, Ben Shneiderman, Bill Dutton, and Ron Baecker.

Among my friends and family, I wanted first to thank my husband, James. You were the first person to use the tears of joy emoji with me and are still my favourite person ever. I've also been supported by a wide and wonderful support network of friends and family. Some names who have really helped along the way include James Smeaton, Dan Axel Sundelin, Patrick Lavelli, Alessandro Crillo, Angela Murray, and my always supportive parents, Jack and Cheryl

Hogan.

And finally, at Sage, I want first to thank Jai Seaman. Jai wanted me to write a book for Sage over a decade ago when I was first showing off all the fun things we can (no longer) do with Facebook data. She accepted a manuscript proposal about four years ago, and expected a book a couple of years ago. A wise old man once said a wizard is never early or late, they arrive precisely when they mean to. I'm not sure I have a right to say the same for this book, but it still feels magical to be at the end of the road. I thank Jai and her colleagues, Hannah Cavender-Deere and Charlotte Bush. They have been patient and generous, while seeing the potential for students and researchers in computational social science. To Ian Antcliff and Richard Leigh, thank you for your careful eye and attention to detail. I learned more in copy-editing than I anticipated. To the reviewers, your suggestions and feedback were considerate, generous, and encouraging. You clearly share the same passion and hope for computational methods in the social sciences. I hope this book has a small part in realising that ambition.

PROLOGUE

 Scaling up: Thinking about programming in the social sciences

The social world is all around us, in how we talk, act, and dress, but also in where we live, how our dwellings are built, how cities are planned (or not), and how life is organised around the clock. It exists in populations, in networks of kin, and vast social movements. The social world increasingly exists in networks of people known solely or primarily online. Each account or user might refer to someone from anywhere around the world (or sometimes no one, as the account could be a bot or organisation). But their behaviour is constrained by the platform, its logic, and its affordances (a.k.a. design features). It is now almost cliché to remind people that the online world and the offline world are both the same world. For example, one might remark that the offline life is also constrained, with customs, laws, road signs, etc. Of course! What is different about the online world is not so much *what* we do, but *how* we do it. And how we do things online is to be mediated, which really means to encode our actions, sentiments, and selves and send that as data to someone (or something) else.

It is no coincidence that in the examples featured in this book, social media data figures heavily. I will be drawing on examples from Twitter, Reddit, Wikipedia, and Stack Exchange. Meta is notably missing, but a lot of the skills used here can certainly transfer over to looking at Instagram or Facebook, although you might be surprised about how limited your options are for collecting and managing data on Meta's platforms. The same might be said for TikTok, Snapchat, WhatsApp, or Telegram. These platforms do not necessarily figure heavily in the book, but they still are powered by the underlying Internet and generate considerable data. My goal in this book is to show some of the key common ways we can question data, so that you can take some of the insights about one domain and apply it to the study and the platform of interest to you.

Despite the profusion of data from social media, I want to suggest that this work is not *about* social media. Rather social media permits easy access to social life *as* data. There are nevertheless many other ways that social life is encoded. Most countries have some office of statistics. Third parties like the World Bank do an extensive job of providing cross-national data in consolidated tables. Commerce generates huge transactions, as does sensor data from vehicles, people, and stationary sites. More recently, there has been the profusion of public health statistics related to the grim reality of Covid-19. Governments around the world have been reporting in timely and granular ways how this virus has shaken the world. And that data has spawned vast amounts of writing in epidemiology and social science. News media, governments, and scientists have worked overtime not only to analyse the virus itself, but also to convey the risks to the world. This has led to a profusion of data, charts, and claims in just about any venue – some better updated, more usable, or more granular than others.

Social life has always been social, but only recently has so much of it been *mediated*. This mediation represents an opportunity but also a challenge. Not all of the data is used with the same care. It is sometimes politicised, withheld, censored, or doctored (Vicario et al., 2016). Some assert that algorithms have led to both filter bubbles of misinformation (Pariser, 2011) and echo chambers (Bechmann and Nielbo, 2018; Dubois and Blank, 2018). The evidence is mixed but few doubt that platforms can exert some effects, if only over the shape of the social networks produced on the site (Malik and Pfeffer, 2016). In this space, key questions remain about how to examine users and their data, often combined with issues of social influence, identity, misinformation, health, and well-being. Answers to these questions often involve data about the sites themselves rather than just statistical analyses of existing surveys or tables.

The techniques in this book mainly focus on how to describe data. There is much to be learned simply by showing a distribution, network, or set of keywords. And given the challenge in sculpting data down to a form that can be used, filtering out unwanted or extraneous data, and identifying the interesting patterns, this is often enough when done with care. Yet often the most effective claims in social science (and in science generally) are when the data we observe helps us update our beliefs about what to expect in the world. Those expectations can be informed by prior work (e.g. we *expect* so many comments to use a certain kind of speech); they can be informed by statistical properties (e.g. we expect distributions to be independent so strong correlations might be important signals); or they can be informed by normative values (e.g. maybe we want to identify and flag hostile speech or maximise discussion about diverse topics).

By considering the gulf between expectations and observations, data can both reveal unfairness and be unfair. Revealing unfairness is a common approach in social science dating back well before the Internet. But for data to 'be unfair' has lately become considerably more noticeable. In many cases, this falls under questions of algorithmic fairness and what constitutes legitimate deployment of artificial intelligence. For example, in a modern classic, Buolamwini and Gebru (2018) demonstrate how then-state-of-the-art facial recognition algorithms were considerably better at uniquely identifying white male faces than black female faces. They noted how the subsequent use of such algorithms for everything from policing to commerce could further disadvantage one group who have historically been marginalised.

Yet, somewhere between these papers and introductory courses on Python, Stata, or R, is something missing: a book on how we actually think about that data, handle it coming in one form and then representing it in a different form. Downloading a set of threaded conversations from Kaggle is one thing, but knowing how to turn the raw data into a network, and what kind of network, is another matter. How might we get that data from Twitter over the right time period or with the right additional metadata? When we compare two distributions, how do we know that the differences are really worth considering (i.e. what does it mean to classify or say whether something is statistically significant)? The nuances of how we do any of these tasks could and should fill multiple volumes. But I mean practically. How does one go about doing these things with tools and real data? For the most part this involves programming. Code is a way to handle data as well as scale up investigations so that local intuitions can transform into potential scientific claims. Code is not the only way this happens, but it is an awfully useful one, and one that appears to endure when more clever approaches with apps and software come and go.

While many books consider the techniques for engaging in this work from a more conceptual or descriptive point of view (e.g. Hogan, 2017) or from a more traditional social scientific point of view (e.g. Marres, 2017), there still remains a need for books from a more practical point of view. Examples, of course, are emerging rapidly. One excellent case is McLevey's *Doing Computational Social Science: A Practical Introduction* (2021). His book is similar to mine in many ways, but goes into greater depth in a variety of domains later in machine learning, while not emphasising the direct workflows of cleaning data in quite the same way. Another example would be *Mining the Social Web* by Russell and Klassen (2019), with clear workflows for collecting and processing social media data. However, it comes less from a social science point of view than a practical and often industry-oriented perspective.

Given that state-of-the-art algorithms and popular social media platforms ebb and flow, it has taken me quite some time to consider what ought to go into a book that might have at least a few years of shelf life. So in this book I focus on some of the main skills in getting data from an unstructured shape to a place where it can be an object that represents some meaningful aspect of social structure. Thus, the actual advanced analytics in this book are pretty limited. The goal is to feel comfortable with every aspect of these approaches as you advance. Then you will find that when you venture out into more complex territory you will hopefully consider the introductory tutorials on areas like data reduction techniques, computer vision, word embeddings, or geocoding much less formidable.

With social media moving so rapidly, it is hard to anchor a book on any given platform, particularly a commercial platform. It is with some trepidation that I even mention things like the 'latest Twitter API' or 'Google Colab', as these technologies tend to ebb and flow. Yet, I have found that once I appreciated many of the commonalities featured in this book, like how to handle date stamps, extract URLs, or link users in a 'network graph', I was able to help students with research projects on a variety of platforms, including ones I only just encountered. So I hope that the topics, however brief (as they need to be in such an introductory book), help inspire your curiosity about how to generate, describe, and critique data, online or elsewhere.

 ## Who is this book for?

This is a book demonstrating strategies and skills for gaining insight from data, particularly online social and behavioural data. It is written using the Python programming language and is tied closely to many features of Python. This book is meant for students with limited (but not zero) experience with computer science or programming. Below I will clarify the prerequisites, but essentially it is an introduction to Python course, as most courses tend to cover the same material.

This book is not exclusively a programming text, though many chapters are very skills oriented. Rather, it is meant as an introductory statement on the interdisciplinary paradigm of social data science (or comparably, computational social science) with a focus on online sources of data. Senior social science, information science, and business undergraduates and graduate students, market analysts, user experience professionals, working academics looking to see what Python can offer, and anyone with a curiosity for the subject matter are all welcome to engage with the book and the related online materials.

This is not a traditional book in social science statistics, *but with Python!* Inferential statistics will play only a minor part in the first half of the book (and only a supporting role in the rest). Surveys will be almost entirely absent. Instead, the book will focus most intently on programming skills and how to translate these to meaningful questions using the vast amount of social and behavioural data available, particularly on the web. To that end, we will definitely use statistical approaches to consider whether what we observe aligns with our expectations and some reasonable baselines. However, here we will be thinking more about how to collect, shape, organise, and clean data for social science research. This is a task that often remains mysterious to students and researchers, leading to a reliance on fragile out-of-the-box solutions, like apps that will archive a site with a single click, but have limited customisation or archiving features.

If I were to make an analogy to the world of cookery, I might say I aspire to emulate Nosrat's wonderful *Salt, Fat, Acid, Heat* (2017). This book focuses more on how to consider the different key elements of every dish (its salt or sweetness, how fat reacts, how heat transforms or stabilises, etc.) than on a hundred ways to cook chicken. In the computational social science world, Twitter is like the chicken, with many books showing recipes for collecting data from this vast platform. In fairness, I feature Twitter's thorough v2 API in Chapter 7, but I hope that it is written in a way that teaches you about APIs more broadly.

This book will infuse this programming with a number of concepts from social sciences, particularly sociology, but also economics, communication, political science, and psychology. You do not need to be an expert in any (or even one) of these fields. The concepts are often used because for me at least they can make some phenomena about the world clearer and can help us codify patterns of behaviour. But I hope they help enliven the concepts and give a sense of purpose to why I chose these specific strategies and skills from a large and expanding toolkit.

I have organised the book into four parts: 'Thinking Programmatically', 'Accessing and Converting Data', 'Interpreting Data: Expectations Versus Observations', and 'Data Science in Practice: Four Approaches'. Below I give a summary of the chapters in each of these parts. You will notice I do not include an introduction to Python section in this book. I discuss this first below.

0.3 Why Python (and not R, Stata, Java, C, etc.)?

To do work in data science of any flavour really requires the use of a programming language. Even if you are very adept at using Microsoft Excel, eventually you will still need to get acquainted with something like Visual Basic in order to automate some tasks. When it comes to learning a computer language, I share many people's feeling that the language Python is very useful. It has a relatively gentle learning curve, it is widely supported with libraries for many data science tasks (from getting and analysing data to rendering tables and plotting graphics), and it has a very large user base leading to many online resources containing useful tips and answers.

One of the main hurdles in the adoption of Python is that people are generally familiar with something else. In social science departments, statisticians commonly use SPSS and Stata, fully fledged paid-for applications. Sometimes you see the use of SAS, often in economics and health statistics. More recently there has been a real uptake in the use of open-source tools and languages. Python is one of them. Generally speaking, open-source projects are free to use and permit outside contributions. This allows for open collaboration to improve and extend existing projects. So not only are we making use of Python, but also of many libraries created by third parties, again all freely available.

Another open-source language is R (https://www.r-project.org/). It is also commonly used for data science, particularly in social science academia. R is now so prevalent that you will see me discuss resources related to R as they are now often the best place to go next, if you cannot do something in Python. Generally with computer languages, once you get familiar with one and some of the key concepts related to it, it is possible to reach out to others more easily. Many programmers will know one language well and a handful of additional languages in a hacky but sufficient way. To that end, I avoid thinking of this sort of work as Python versus R, but as Python then R and JavaScript and Stata, etc. for any specific task at hand.

0.3.1 How much Python should I already know?

To get the most out of this book, it is useful to have at least toyed around with Python as a programming language. As one of the world's most popular programming languages, there are a whole host of resources for learning the introductory skills. What's more, these skills do not vary considerably between disciplines. So Python for data science or Python for embedded devices, web development, or text processing all tend to start in the same place.

If you do not have any Python skills, I can recommend my free book-as-worksheets, *Introducing Python* (Hogan, 2022), or an equivalent text such as *Whirlwind Tour of Python* (VanderPlas, 2016a). The latter is similarly a free online book that precedes a larger text introducing data science. There are also a variety of online courses, though I hesitate to recommend any for pay with such a profusion of *YouTube* video series teaching the basics. Where the basics end, a lot of applied work begins. That work can really vary depending on the discipline and the subject matter. That is why I start this book with some strategies for how to simplify and focus *what* you should code (thinking both in terms of what to measure and how to optimise the code itself) and then introduce the main tool for data science in Python, the `DataFrame`.

Therefore, to fully appreciate these discussions, being familiar with the following concepts is especially helpful:

- primitive data types (`string`, `float`, `int`);
- the main basic collection types (`list`, `dict`, `set`);
- how to print and format a `str` variable (e.g., `f"A result: {var}"` or `"{}".format(var)`);
- how to import a library/module and make use of it;
- how to use `for` loops, `while` loops, and `if-else` statements in order to control the flow of a program;
- how to write a simple function of your own;
- what is an object in Python is and how can we create our own instance of an object.

One thing I would like to emphasise is that you really do not need to feel a sense of mastery with these topics before starting this book. When I suggest you should know how to write a function, I mean with a default parameter and a return statement such as:

```python
def makeoutput(values):
    if type(values) is list:
        return "_and_".join(values)

makeoutput(["Kermit","Piggy","Gonzo"])

'Kermit_and_Piggy_and_Gonzo'
```

I say you should not wait because otherwise we have a 'chicken and egg' problem. The basics of Python are incredibly important and are really worth practising. Yet, they are so basic that practising just means repetition rather than comprehension, which gets boring quickly. How many ways can you print `hello world`, anyway? Fortunately, these intro Python guides can usually be completed in an afternoon or a couple days of dedicated study at most. Getting really good might take a few weeks or months, but I think it is best to just get a working familiarity and then to dive right in.

The code in this book is meant to be very lean and clear, using mainly conventional libraries and practices. And it shows how we can take data from the world and turn it into an object for our analysis, which to me is pretty interesting. Once you can start to wrangle and describe the data I show herein, it should pique your curiosity about the world and about comparable data for your own research interests. This is where it becomes easier to motivate practising Python. Thus, this book starts where introductory Python ends.

Notably, we do not immediately begin the book with Python. Instead we begin by laying some conceptual groundwork for data science. This includes both thinking about how to program and what we mean by data. We then dive into the Python in Chapter 2.

0●4   What version of Python?

For this book and the associated online learning resources, I recommend that you download and install the most recent version of the Anaconda data science distribution (https://www.anaconda.com/products/distribution). The individual version of Anaconda is free and it includes most of the libraries and tools I use in the book. Other things to install I will mention as they come up in the text. This book was written in Python 3.9, though I am pretty sure everything should work for Python from version 3.7 upwards. This was the most recent version of Anaconda as of mid-2022.

The Anaconda distribution comes with an application called Jupyter Lab. This book was written in Jupyter Lab, the online resources are Jupyter Lab notebooks, and the best way to follow along with the code is to run the Jupyter Lab notebooks on your own computer. The online repository for the book (https://www.github.com/berniehogan/fsstds/) will primarily consist of Jupyter notebooks. There I have instructions for downloading the notebooks so you can run them locally. You can also run them online as well. Look for the 'open in Colab' and 'open in Binder' buttons:

Once you have installed the Anaconda distribution, you can launch Jupyter Lab in two ways. The first is to use the application *Anaconda Navigator*. When you launch that application it should load up a panel of data science applications to launch. From here you can select Jupyter Lab and run it. The second (my preference) is to run Jupyter Lab from a command line. On a Mac, launch the *Terminal* app and type `jupyter lab`. In Windows, use the search bar to search for 'Anaconda Powershell', which is like the regular Windows command line but has some additional features for Anaconda. From here type `jupyter lab`. In all cases, the program should launch your default web browser and navigate to `localhost:8888`. Jupyter then becomes like a desktop environment within a browser. My one trick from here is that I use Firefox and the 'Popup window' extension. Clicking on this extension turns the current browser window into a popup with no address bar or tabs. So now your whole browser window is dedicated to Jupyter Lab.

0.4.1 Part I. Thinking programmatically

Chapter 1 begins with a discussion of data, what it means, and how to think about it. I sidestep a definition of data science by focusing on data as a distribution of measurements and then reflect on a theory from information visualisation called DIKW. I then talk about how we operationalise measurements to create data. I suggest that computers can help us do this efficiently. I focus first on some ideas on how to get the most out of programming and not sweat the major details. I introduce the FREE mnemonic to help think about ways to structure your coding. I then introduce the three core tools in data science in Python: the `Series`, the `DataFrame`, and the array. The `Series` and the `DataFrame` are tools that come from the Python library `pandas`. The array come from a separate (lower-level) library called `numpy`, but these libraries all work together well.

Chapter 2 introduces the `Series`, which is how `pandas` stores a distribution of data. A `Series` represents a distribution and so it makes sense that it is the first key skill. If you want to arrange multiple `Series` together, these can be combined in a `DataFrame`, which I discuss in Chapter 3. We can use a `DataFrame` to compare measurements across distributions or groups. For example, a `DataFrame` of tweets might have one column from one `Series` that represents the number of likes, another column to represent the number of retweets, etc. A `DataFrame` is also conventionally known as a 'table', but we use a `DataFrame` to refer to tables as stored in Python using the `pandas` library. As an advanced topic I also mention arrays, which are the equivalent to a matrix in linear algebra. I do not go deep into linear algebra, nor does the book generally, but `numpy` arrays are pervasive in Python and are worth encountering and demystifying.

0.4.2 Part II. Accessing and converting data

Most of the data that we can make use of from the web was not created as data for the purpose of analysis, it was created simply as a part of participating on the platform or site. A Reddit post exists to be on Reddit, a tweet exists to be sent via Twitter. Nevertheless, it is feasible for us to convert this data into a form that we can use to make claims. Reddit does not use a proprietary format, nor does Facebook or Google. Instead, they almost always send data using a small number of standardised formats such as CSV (comma-separated values), JSON (JavaScript Object Notation), and XML (Extensible Markup Language). So if we learn how to get CSV, JSON, and XML into a `DataFrame`, then this really opens up a multitude of sites for us to collect data, and not just one that we introduce specifically.

Chapter 4 introduces many kinds of file types that we can make use of in Python. The first one is CSV, which is the most akin to a `DataFrame`. Then we look briefly at Microsoft Excel documents, which also look like a `DataFrame` in that they are tabular and have rows and columns. We then look at hierarchical formats with data nested inside other data, like XML and JSON. These could be collections of comments or search results nested inside a listing. I then finish with a small section on temp files that you can store during your work.

In Chapter 5 we look at concatenation, merging, and grouping as ways to combine data from multiple `DataFrame` objects. In the last third of this chapter, I introduce one final data type: SQL data. I saved SQL until after merging because SQL really shines when thinking about merging tables, so it is good to have the concepts in hand before seeing SQL syntax.

The next two chapters involve how we collect data from the web. Chapter 6 considers open data on the web that we can collect just by asking for it. This is primarily through the `requests` library in Python, which consolidates and simplifies a lot of earlier syntax. We will explore GET requests, look at some good habits for data collecting and end with some discussion of the ethical challenges inherent in big data (Mittelstadt and Floridi, 2016; Puschmann and Burgess, 2014). The final chapter of Part II looks at what happens when we need permission to access data. Here we explore the use of APIs and authentication. I demonstrate how to keep your API keys out of your working code, how to use a library to collect data from Reddit and Twitter, and I introduce some working code for Twitter's new v2 API. I conclude with some reflections on how limits of data access can constrain and steer our research.

0.4.3 Part III. Interpreting data: Expectations versus observations

The previous chapters were pretty technical in the sense that we were learning about how to collect and shape data. But the important part really comes down to making claims with this data. In that sense, we need to focus on the difference between what we expect to find and what we actually observe. We will explore this key difference across two chapters. The first is a short chapter on research questions. I thought it would be prudent here to add my own spin on the topic as well as emphasise some key considerations that occur when doing work in computational spaces, particularly helping to untangle a number of different ways to make claims with online data.

The next chapter twins visualisation and statistics. Typically, chapters on visualisation can be dry affairs that list all the different ways you can represent data. Similarly, introductory statistics chapters tend to start by building up formulae from basic maths. Yet in computational social science and data science, much of what we are doing with visualisation is really presenting a way for someone to appreciate how a distribution or set of distributions differs from what we might expect. So in this chapter I focus on visualising expectations. What is an expectation? It is a way of predicting some value from some other value.

In this way, we will see statistics and visualisations as both part of the same goal: to interpret the difference between what we might expect and what we observe. To kick this off I visualise three common distributions: *uniform*, *normal*, and *exponential*. These represent three different ideal types in data. So, I use a distribution that *should* be uniform as a way to talk about the differences between what is expected and what is observed. Along the way, we will learn about how to annotate a figure, how to layer things on a Python plot (in `matplotlib`), and how to interpret a trend line as a 'regression' (and confidence intervals as representing the uncertainty about a trend line).

Finally, I look at a few ways in which we can discover expectations versus observations between two distributions (or with 'bivariate' data). I show means-comparisons tests (the *t-test* and the one-way *ANOVA*) and correlations (using *Pearson's r*).

0.4.4 Part IV. Social data science in practice: Four approaches

This is by far the longest part of the book. It covers four different approaches to computational social science: by language, by relationships, by time periods, and by geography, primarily through working with real data. In the bulk of these chapters I will use a single sustained example, but I will facet that data through specialised methods for each of these topics above.

Chapter 10 is on cleaning data. It is probably the most important of all of the chapters in this part. It starts with a discussion of how core aspects of social life can be encoded as data. I start with an example of a simple email message. From here we can learn about language, relationships, time, and space. Then, I introduce a freely available data export of a widely popular online platform, Stack Exchange. I show how we can clean this data and consider many of the same features as the example email. We convert the original data (which the program treats almost exclusively as strings) into meaningful types, such as a `datetime`, integer, or list. I am not using this data because I expect us to find really obvious statistical patterns or because it was the subject of a top-tier paper. Rather I have some more practical goals. I wanted data that was relatively neutral but relatable, so a look at the `movies` stack exchange seemed to fit the bill. And I also wanted a publicly available dataset that has lots of features that we see in a variety of *other* contexts. A surprising amount of what we need to demonstrate for natural language processing (NLP), networks, and time-series analysis can draw upon a single Stack Exchange export.

The next four chapters concern each of these key forms of measurement of social life as data. For each chapter I show how to create some analytical objects in Python and then ask some rudimentary questions about them. These chapters each represent an introduction to a specialised field: NLP, network science, time-series analysis, and geographic information systems. The geography chapter does not directly use the Stack Exchange data, as the geographic information in there is quite thin and hard to shape into something exemplary. But since space (and maps) are such a popular aspect of representing data, it would be remiss of me to exclude it, so I make use of some highly granular data on Covid-19 rates which allows us to see things mapped at the sub-country level.

 What about statistics?

Data science involves statistics by nature. If we have many data points, we have a distribution of them. Some data points will be larger and others small. But how much larger or how much smaller? Statistics can help us answer that. Classic statistics (i.e. the 'frequentist' approach) can help us say whether something is 'significantly' smaller or larger. More recent statistics (i.e. the 'Bayesian' approach) an help us say whether knowing something about social system can help us make better guesses about what happens in that system.

For many, this is immediately going to put them off programming. Many times I've heard students say they won't like programming as they aren't good at maths.[1] And if they aren't good at maths, then forget stats! Hopefully this book can help ease any anxieties about maths and stats. That's not because the book is free of maths and stats. This book definitely will have some statistics. But the stats is relatively basic and we will make only the barest assumptions about prior statistics knowledge. We might think of our usage of statistics in this book as that of a learning practitioner. Similarly, I try to keep the number of formulae in the book to a minimum. Instead, get ready for a lot of analogies, examples, figures, and practice data.

That being said, if you want to advance in data science, especially towards the hotly emerging fields of machine learning and artificial intelligence, you will inevitably encounter some pretty advanced maths (especially in linear algebra) and stats (particularly Bayesian statistics, not often taught in social science). I point to some resources for these topics in the relevant chapters (such as the linear algebra resources at the end of Chapter 3).

Data science is a set of practices that allow people to make sense of data, typically (but not necessarily) large volumes of data that make simple calculations difficult. Because of the scale of data produced, a lot of data science is rolled into a closely related field: machine learning. These are, however, two distinct fields. Machine learning refers to a set of practices that use patterns and inference to perform tasks on data. Machine learning algorithms are often very hungry for data. Training neural networks to come up with speech patterns or average faces might require huge sets of data (up to millions or billions words or photos; Bender et al., 2021). Thus, getting that data and making sure it is the right kind of data are very much tasks suited to data science as a precursor to machine learning.

Yet, not all data science leads to machine learning. Much of it can lead to visualisations, more traditional statistics, network analysis, and just descriptive tables with clear summaries. As I'll lay out in Chapter 1 and reinforce in Chapter 9 on visualisations, our goal is insight and wisdom from data, not just a data analysis for its own sake.

Writing and coding considerations

Before we begin, I wanted to outline some considerations of writing style in the book. You will first notice that I use I, you, *and* we pronouns in here. When I say I, this refers to me the author. So it might be about decisions I have made or things I have written. However, when referring to the code, I often talk about what *we* would do because I see the code as something that both you and I can run. So *we* would run the code below:

```
print("Hello again, world!")

Hello again, world!
```

---

[1] For this book, I have opted to adhere to standard British (as my current home) as much as possible, despite growing up in Canada. Thus, you will find us 'analysing maths' rather than 'analyzing math'.

Then I would use 'you' when I am speaking directly to you, the reader. You will notice above that the code and the results appear in different styles than the main text. The top line (starting with `print`) is a code block that can be run. The bottom line is the output from that code. I hope that you will run all the code as we go through the book.

When it comes to code I have a few conventions and quirks, as does anyone comfortable with a programming language. In general, I try to follow the Python style guide (outlined in PEP-8, https://www.python.org/dev/peps/pep-0008/). However, I take a few liberties here since I am trying to keep code succinct while maintaining readability.

When you see a block of text that is in a monospaced font `like this`, it refers to code. Usually this is code you would explicitly run or type into Python. However, sometimes I refer to a generic variable inside angle brackets (`<var_1>`) that I want you to replace with a real variable. For example, I might say `<DataFrame>.copy()` to mean any generic `DataFrame`. You would then use your own variable (such as `stack_df`) in there, like `stack_df.copy()`. I tend to try for short, descriptive variable names with underscores separating the words. I also like to have the type of variable as a suffix (`reddit_dict` or `example_list`), though this is purely optional.

I use comments sparingly. So when you see comments in the code, they really are meant to be read along with the code. Sometime we might even go a page without text *except* in the comments. That's rare, but possible.

The code for each chapter should be self-contained, but not the code for each code block *in* a chapter. This means I assume you will run every cell, especially the `import` statements, in order, so that the code later on works. I tend to keep import statements in their own cell. In working code you should place your import statements at the top of the code or notebook; however, here I tend to import them above just when I introduce them since I want to highlight *how* I import a specific library when I introduce that library.

0.6.1 My final tip before we go

Before we get fully into the book I wanted to offer one final reminder: *tinker!* Because this book contains code that can be run, it means you should run it for yourself and feel confident that it works. It also means you have the freedom to play with the code and make it work differently. I try to make the code very lean and straightforward in the hope that you will read every line. It will be much better if you slowly but carefully read every line of code than if you just read the text, skim the code, run it blindly, and hope for the best.

I recommend keeping a 'fresh' copy of every chapter available while using a different one to tinker. That way you should feel comfortable messing with the code while including your own additional cells, notes, and trials. Personally, I think this book reads best typeset as a book, but it is the most fun when you run it as code.

To help you out, there are extra resources:

* At the end of almost every chapter is an 'Extensions and reflections' section. Here I ask some questions that might help provide a direction for tinkering with the code or putting it into a small project.
* In many of the chapters I have a 'Further reading' section as well. This includes examples of books, articles, and sometimes online resources, that can build on what I have introduced in that chapter.

- On the book's GitHub page are activities for each chapter. These might be as simple as practice exercises or more involved project ideas that can be done with the code in the book. These are often mentioned in the 'Extensions and reflections' section.

These online resources are in addition to a huge and expanding ensemble of blogs, videos, and other books on data science. But they are only as good as your willingness to tinker and make the code your own. I can help guide you part of the way on your journey, but your curiosity is what will help you get from here to your research goals, wherever they may be. I hope this book helps inspire that curiosity and gets you on your way.

PART I

THINKING PROGRAMMATICALLY

1
INTRODUCTION: THINKING OF LIFE AT SCALE

=== **Learning goals** ===

- Understand and critique the notion of DIKW as a framework for data
- Think of online data beyond how it is displayed towards distributions
- Consider how to create workable code that is modular and practical
- Use FREE to determine how extensively you want to develop your code
- Use pseudocode to plan your code before writing complete Python.

From social science to what?

Ask a dozen data scientists to define their field and you'll get at least 13 answers, 12 from the scientists themselves and one from the cheeky data scientist who classifies all those answers and comes up with a meta-answer. It's a new field and frankly, it is not clear whether it's a field in its own right or a transdisciplinary practice meant to inform existing fields. One thing is for sure, though: people produce a lot of data.

Unfortunately, defining social science is probably just as hard as defining data science. Clearly sociology and political science belong in there, but what about linguistics? Psychology? Perhaps social psychology? It turns out that articulating the boundaries around specific scientific practices is itself a recipe for contention. Personally, I like to say I'm generous with theories and stingy with claims. We can, and should, find our ideas from a variety of sources all around us, but our claims about the world should be much more cautious. Within this context, I see social science as any practice that makes claims about groups of individuals *that could be* testable or falsifiable under clearly defined conditions. This is not to say that these conditions will be met. In fact, sometimes, it is pretty impossible to meet those conditions in real life with humans. This is because humans are clever and reactive creatures, but also because researchers aspire to be ethical and understand that we are both, in the grand scheme of things, researchers and potential subjects.

So rather than define data science directly I plan on side stepping the question by focusing on a more modest goal here: to understand what to do with some distributions of data. A distribution is a collection of measurements with some describable boundary. Each measurement is some encoding of the world. We can take a distribution as an anchor that helps keep us from drifting out towards many of the other interesting but not as central aspects of programming.

I first introduce a classic framework for situating data: the data–information–knowledge–wisdom (DIKW) hierarchy. Then I shift to thinking about programming. The code examples in this chapter are not designed to show much in the way of new skills about Python. Instead, they are meant to get you thinking about how to program or choose how involved you want your code to be. In particular, I introduce the FREE mnemonic and discuss pseudocode to help. This is primarily meant to get us ready for the chapters that come, each one of which will introduce a new skill or approach to handling a distribution, thinking about its qualities, accessing it from the web, or analysing it for its potential information content.

(PO)DIKW: A potential theoretical framework for data science

To my knowledge, there are no specific core tenets of social data science. We have key think-ers and papers, though these also tend to come from existing domains drawing from soci-ology, economics, political science, etc. And if you look for the key papers in data science, these tend towards being really papers in statistics, machine learning, physics or information science. Yet, when we think of data science as a science, it seems that there must be a basis for this. So below is an attempt to consider data science, and particularly the notion of 'social data science', from a theoretical perspective.

Below I draw upon an existing framework from information visualisation called DIKW, the data–information–knowledge–wisdom hierarchy. Yet, I preface this with PO, standing for phenomena and operationalisation. This is because the world is not filled with data. It is filled with phenomena, which we convert to data through operationalisation. Then once operationalised through measurement or encoding, we can see how it first *becomes* data and then serves as the basis for information, knowledge, and ultimately, wisdom.

Technical fields often start with the data as is, but this is where social science can come into play. By interrogating the ways in which phenomena have been encoded as data through operationalisation, we can come to investigate sociologically meaningful issues such as power or identity: who gets to encode and how? I won't be discussing these in depth here (again reiterating this book's focus on skills), but they will be very important for helping us contex-tualise the data as well as answer meaningful questions about it (or appreciate the limits of our craft). Thus, by backing up from data rather than taking it as a given we can both appre-ciate some of what a compelling framework like DIKW provides, but also how to critique what is left out.

1.2.1 What is data?

It turns out that it is even pretty difficult to define data. Originally it meant that which is given or self-evident, from the Latin *datum*. Around the mid-twentieth century, it became used explicitly to refer to transmissible and recordable computer information. The concept of measurable information goes back much further. Earliest records of numbers are gener-ally numbers of specific things, whether it was bushels, cattle, or people. We have records of scientists, engineers, and urban planners using coordinate systems in ancient Egypt, and ledgers in ancient Rome. With increased technological progress and sophistication in creat-ing abstract representations (like Descartes' now widely used (X, Y) plane), measurements and their representation have become more multidimensional, abstract, and recently pro-grammatic (see the review by Friendly, 2008). As measurements have proliferated, so has an interest in how to represent them, assess their quality, and deploy skills that make the measurement task easier. In recent years, the proliferation of data, particularly social and transactional data via the Internet, has coincided with an interest in a relatively generalised set of skills we now start to associate with data science.

Data is a plural but is often written as a singular (which it is here). This is because data is seen as a *mass noun*, like information or rice. We would say the 'the rice is cooked', by which we almost never mean a single specific grain of rice. Similarly, 'the data is being processed' would not refer to a single measurement. While data is a mass noun, we can make it a particular by referring to it as a set. Thus we can say 'data is reliable' and 'datasets are reliable'. Thus, it would seem that data science is focused on this mass of measurements. This is where we take it in this book by thinking about measurements in *distributions*. These collections of measurements are what we need in order to make claims. Distributions are contained in sets of data, which I colloquially refer to as datasets. There are, however, rather specific terms that we will encounter for this, whether we are working with data in Python (where the `DataFrame` is an important tool), or thinking about storing data in a 'data warehouse' or 'data lake' as next steps in one's data analysis pipeline. But it is important not to get lost in the technicalities of the terms. A social data science is about the measurement of people and their behaviour. This means that what is most relevant is considering whether what we measure links to what we seek to measure.

Right from the start we are confronted with the first issue in data science, even before we get to data: how to operationalise? Some say the world is full of data. And yes, the world does contain a lot of data. However, the world *is not reducible to data*. Rather, everything we observe is *phenomena*. Everything just is. This perspective comes from William James's notion of radical empiricism, or the idea that everything is real (Heft, 2001). Dreams are real, myths are real, fantasies are real. If you can think of it, it is real for it has been a thought, even if it has been nothing else. On the other hand, the substance of things might not be what it seems. I am not saying a dragon in a dream is an actual winged scaled lizard. But it definitely is an impression created by the mind that the observing mind recognises as a dragon. James used the notion of a stick halfway in a pond to convey this point. At the surface of the water, the stick might appear bent. Is it? Yes and no – the stick as an impression in the mind's eye is indeed as bent as it is observed. But the material stick itself might be quite straight. The water makes it appear bent. The bend is not a falsehood; it is a perspective. If you were studying light diffraction in liquids, this particular bend may be of interest. If you were trying to select the straightest stick from a few stuck in the water, this might not be the best measurement.

What radical empiricism asks us to confront is the chasm between phenomenon and operationalisation. The world as given is filled with phenomena, a 'blooming, buzzing confusion' in James's eyes. Yet despite this multisensory and overwhelming world of phenomena, we impose distinctions and perceive (as well as produce order). Almost as soon as babies open their eyes, it seems they can identify faces, perceive differences spatially, have proprioception (i.e. know where their body is in space), and do simple reasoning with matching tasks (Streri et al., 2013).

James's point to see the world as phenomena can be made more forcefully as a consequence of the fact the we are *not* born a blank slate. Even the youngest child will already have some cognitive biases in place that intervene in the ability to see the world as it truly is (Kahneman, 2011; Kahneman and Tversky, 1979). We as humans have capacities, some of which appear innate and others learned, which enable us to encode the world. Our perceptions are given to us and then strengthened and learned as time goes on. Our perceptions might work for the world at one scale, but not at another (Martin, 2010). Trying to see the world as it is involves carefully translating phenomena into data rather than simply assuming the world *is* data. Thinking of phenomena and data as different is an essential skill for thinking critically about the world, and thus for doing research that will lead to new insights and challenge existing understandings.

The way that we get from phenomena to data is to *operationalise*. Operationalisation is an extremely delicate and important step in any data science effort. Actually, it is a pretty important part of any scientific research. However, for some disciplines what needs to be operationalised is already given, either because of the nature of the discipline or the nature of the phenomenon. Consider the challenges of operationalisation in psychology. We might ask, 'Do extroverts need as much sleep after a party as introverts?' We know that extroverts are more likely to enjoy the company of others than introverts. In fact, I have heard mention of extroverts as being 'solar powered' while introverts are like having 'rechargeable batteries'. But what is an extrovert (Jung, 1921)? Theoretically, Jung introduced extroversion as being a state of attending to those outside the self. In practice, it is someone who scores above a certain threshold on an extroversion scale. And why that scale? Because it is seen as reliable. But what about those just below the cut-off, are they extroverts? Maybe. It actually depends on how we choose to model extroversion, as a continuous measure or as a binary.

Now the question then actually becomes a little more tedious: 'Do those who score greater than one standard deviation above the mean on a standardised extroversion scale report needing significantly more sleep than those who score one standard deviations below the mean?' We do not say this not because it sounds tedious, but because we often take 'an extrovert' to mean 'someone who scores greater than one standard deviation above the mean on a standardised extroversion scale'. Is this how everyday people see extroverts? Not at all, but it is a way to provide a consistent measurement. It is an *operationalisation* of the concept.

A key concern with operationalisation is when people confuse data for phenomena. For example, gender is the social manifestation of sex dimorphism, but when we take gender to mean sex we forget about all the biological edge cases associated with intersex persons, the cultural interest in challenging gender norms and binaries, the journeys of those with dysphoria to receive gender confirming treatment, the realm of fantasy, queer and drag performances, etc. We may simplify people based on demographics into generally male, female, and non-binary in our analysis as we believe it will explain variation. But that does not mean we can forget all the instances of gender variation, only that we have made a classification in order to help explain other data. We cannot forget that operationalisation tends to be about a *reduction in complexity of phenomena*, not about providing the most granular account of data. Thus, when we simplify we often end up excluding some cases on the margins. On the other hand, if we take every single instance of life as its own unique case, it becomes hard to accumulate knowledge and thus impossible to accumulate wisdom for what might come next. Thus, in research we tend to treat operationalisation as a necessary but delicate aspect of this research and we should always be mindful of whether we are being overly coarse as well as overly granular. Healy addresses this well in an article rejecting an adherence to excessive nuance (2017).

It is often hard to operationalise concepts from social life. What makes someone a 'friend' or 'a regular conversation partner'? What makes for a community online? If we think of a friend or a community as a social fact, understood by people, then we will have lots to debate. However, if we flip this on its head and say a friend *is* a declared friendship on Facebook or a community *is* a subreddit or Telegram channel, then we can start to measure and compare these things more easily. The only problem is that it is not necessarily true in a meaningful sense. This is in a way the opposite challenge to operationalisation, which we can call 'performativity' (Healy, 2015), where we take some agreed social process or convention and treat it as if it were a fact or given. This concept has a varied history starting in linguistics where Austin (1975) articulates how some social activities are considered as made real through words, like vows and contracts, thus suggesting speech can be *performative*. Since then, the concept has expanded, notably through feminist studies, where Butler (1989) refers to the performative element of *doing* gender rather than merely *having* one. More recent work in science and technology studies and sociology has expanded the concept to consider how social practices can *produce* relationships of a particular kind rather than merely manifest them. This was first via Callon in considering markets as performative (MacKenzie et al., 2008) as we seek to create the conditions for market relations rather than treat markets as some inevitable practice. Whether markets are indeed performative is contentious (Brisset, 2016). However, it cannot be seen as contentious for the web.

These days social networks are not mere analytical tools, but performative ones. Facebook, Twitter, and their ilk structure relationships to fit a social network (Hogan and Wellman, 2014). They make assumptions such as one account, one user; friendships can be defined and then they simply accumulate rather than fade; and a single feed to account for information from all these friends is a suitable way to learn about the world. Social life is not merely manifested on social media, but shaped by it. Thus, we can ask meaningful questions not just with the data but about what the data represents, and how users of this data react and adapt to knowing about this data. The way that a social media platform operationalises friends as accounts-to-follow might be very different than what is a socially meaningful friend.

Ultimately, we want our work to help facilitate *insight* or wisdom about phenomena through understanding. That is, we want it to explain how certain features or concepts that we measure (twitter interactions) can explain other measured or unmeasured concepts or behaviours (friendships or in-groups). And thus, this insight might draw on explanatory power (via statistical controls and estimates, clear presentations of data), predictive power (via metrics that evaluate and consider classification or models fitness), or from critique (where we question the provenance, fairness, or consequences of the collection and deployment of that data).

1.2.2 From data to wisdom

If data refers to measurements about the world, insight could either be knowledge about the contexts that gave rise to the data, or wisdom about how to use such knowledge in different contexts. An often repeated framework in information visualisation is that there is a hierarchy from data to wisdom in this manner (Rowley, 2007):

- *Data* refers to that which was measured and encoded in some manner.
- *Information* refers to a presentation of that data that signals differences we would understand.
- *Knowledge* is being able to understand the interrelatedness of the information (i.e. signals). If we can convey information in a graphic to another person, we can share knowledge (however limited).
- *Wisdom* is challenging to define. I like Cairo's definition with respect to DIKW: Wisdom is 'deep understanding of acquired knowledge, when we not only "get it," but when new information blends with prior experience so completely that it makes us better at knowing what to do in other situations, even if they are only loosely related to the information from which our original knowledge came. Just as not all the information we absorb leads to knowledge, not all of the knowledge we acquire leads to wisdom' (Cairo, 2011, p. 17).

We are trying to turn data into knowledge by identifying information (statistically or otherwise) that we can convey to an audience. We make the researchers wise as they understand how this knowledge relates to their existing frame of reference and possible future phenomena. Thus, knowledge requires us not only to confirm things in a quantitative or statistical sense, but also to link our specific findings to domain-specific or contextual knowledge.

Beyond the interface

At the risk of being terribly reductive, social sciences tend to focus on individuals as thinking persons with *agency*, and aggregations of persons, culture, and the built environment as *structure* (Archer, 2003). Humans express agency by interacting with these structures, reproducing, altering, or reconceptualising them (Emirbayer and Mische, 1998). It might be how individuals alter their behaviours in markets, how political movements form and position themselves (Margetts et al., 2015), or how policy-makers consider the use of behavioural nudges versus deliberation (John et al., 2009). Structure might refer to a variety of things in the social world, but we especially can understand structure as a force that constrains behaviour in some way. It might be that space constrains us to one small part of the world or that time limits what we can do or when we can do it. These structures need not be physical. They can be cognitive habits that reinforce certain power relationships or institutions (Zerubavel, 1998). Software (and thus almost all digitally mediated) interfaces structure behaviour in overt ways by providing clear guides on what behaviours are possible and expected (Gaver, 1991). These are typically *affordances* that feature or reveal data in ways that facilitate action. This could be a notification alert to show there's a new message, a popup that highlights the number of friends in common, or the arrows that signal to up- or downvote content. Affordances structure and represent data from a platform, but they are not the data on that platform.

This book primarily looks to retrieval of data from the web and social platform data in particular. To create compelling research questions in this space, we can think 'beyond the interface'. Facebook is not merely the page with the long newsfeed and the blue banner at the top. It is also a *data controller* (that's the legal term). It hosts data, presents it in a particularly curated way, regulates who gets to see what data and who does not. But as a user of Facebook's products, one might be inclined to think Facebook *is* the newsfeed. Yet, the newsfeed is just a representation of the data being held by Facebook. It's a form of algorithmic curation (Hogan, 2010). And that curation is based on decisions, ideas, and tests which may not be obvious to users (Eslami et al., 2016). It is also historically contingent – it did not have to be that way. It is but one view to the lived experience that is captured in these posts, replies, photos, and videos. To think beyond the interface is to think about how the data we see and record can be represented in a *different* format, a format that can help us answer questions about the world.

The way people often think beyond the interface is to translate data from one representation to another. We might start with a list of friends. That's a single, unordered, column of data: Ali, Barb, Cam, and Dot. Now, imagine linking more data about these friends to this single column. It could be birthdays, it could be their profile summary, it could be their friendships with each other or where they live. In each case, by combining the people and the additional meaningful data you can represent different features of your own friendship circle. We could see that Ali and Barb live in the same city or that Cam and Dot are friends with each other. We might discover that they all have birthdays in the spring or that you message these friends most in the summer and the winter but not the spring or autumn. Answers to these questions are available with the data already on Facebook, but not in the form that Facebook provides. With some systematic measurements, however, you might be able to both detect these signals and gain some knowledge through them.

By thinking beyond the interface we can learn not just about people's experiences but about aggregate patterns that inform or are influenced by these experiences. Sometimes we will see patterns, sometimes we will not. Some of those patterns will be coincidences, but some will point to an interesting feature about the data which is worth probing further. To do this often involves applying some programming skills to the data at hand as well as deploying some statistics.

In many senses, then, social data science is the *science of operationalisation of social life*. It is the science of taking data that is often objective but partial and using it to answer questions that enable us to talk about the world in scales beyond standard human experience. When we classify, we are operationalising concepts as soon as we decide what to train on and how to split the sample. We when are doing network analysis, text mining, regressions, or just descriptive analysis, a large amount of our time will be spent articulating what it is that our data represents and what we think it represents in a model. Reconciling measurement and phenomena is not exclusive to social data science, but it is central to papers in this field.

In this sense DIKW falls a little short. It is a useful starting point for thinking about how to represent data, but it fails to critique who gets to measure, how power intervenes in this process, and how the very act of measuring itself can change the object of inquiry. These sorts of concerns are a bit indirect for a practical book on data science skills, but they can be essential for asking interesting data science questions. What if Facebook discover some feature about social life that keeps people on the platform, but keep it secret? What if algorithms decide who is a suitable job candidate by measuring facial expressions or the sentiment of text? How do the logistics of international supply chains lead to exploitation, even for digital goods? For this, we can pivot from work in information visualisation to work in critical data studies. In this domain, we are seeing a tidal wave of incredible books on the topic. These might not help you do the data analysis more easily but they can certainly help motivate such an analysis.

I have placed a couple of great starting points for critiquing data science and operationalisation in the further reading section below. In particular, I want to raise the flag here for *Data Feminism* by D'Ignazio and Klein (2020). They not only talk about how data enacts and shifts power, but also remind us that if this is the case, then counter-data, or measurements of the experiences of those normally left out or marginalised, can be a powerful antidote to the notion that data is just 'there for the analysing'. Data is *not* the new oil. It is more like the new farm. It is not a pre-existing resource, but a part of the structured way we continually shape social life through measurement and feedback. And I say 'we' a little loosely here, as not everyone's voice is heard equally. This then leads to another crucial book I note below, O'Neil's *Weapons of Math Destruction* (2016). In this book she describes vividly the challenges and consequences of operationalisation as a concept and practice.

Up to this point I have spoken primarily of research design and how to interpret data, which seems pretty far from code. But for the rest of this chapter (and indeed the rest of Parts I and II of this book) we will be dealing with the nuts and bolts of programming. I want to suggest that the programming parts are not actually too far from this discussion since programming strategies are often about how we try to simplify and automate some tasks. By doing so we similarly might make compromises (like not making the code as robust or generic as possible). We do not just operationalise our analytic concepts. We also have to determine how complex or complicated to make the code that will collect, clean, and analyse our data. Thus, for the remainder of the chapter I will warm us up to programming with some points about how to think about and simplify a programming task.

Fixed, variable, and marginal costs: Why not to build a barn

I don't know where I first heard this joke, but I like it and I've been known to tell it in my programming classes. Why don't you ask a computer scientist for a glass of milk? Because they will build you a barn and fill it with cows just to make the second glass that much easier to get.

The idea behind the joke is that computer scientists will *by default* venture into a level of abstraction that is not really necessary. Get a jug of milk or a carton from the shop, you might say. It is quicker, simpler, and definitely cheaper than building a barn. But then why would anyone go through all the trouble to build a barn? The barn is not necessarily for the second glass of milk but about the *n*th glass. That is, all glasses after the first one. Drafting the program to get the first glass would be the *fixed cost* in this case. The *marginal costs* are the costs per iteration. In this mooving example, the marginal cost is the cost of getting any given glass once the system is set up. The joke works (with the right audiences at least) because we perceive the fixed cost to be somehow ridiculous. That is, starting your own farm just to simplify the act of getting a glass of milk seems excessive. In that sense, coding the way a computer scientist does might not be ideal for a data scientist. Code for the data scientist is meant to help deal with repetition and abstraction, but it is also code that is written for limited uses.

This is not to promote code that is overly linear, messy, or fragile. Rather, it is to suggest that in such work there are always trade-offs between doing the one big thing for all code and the many repetitive things instead of code. Below I give a sense of how to navigate these trade-offs as you continue your learning journey.

1.4.1 From economics to data science

One central part of microeconomic theory is the identification of fixed and marginal costs of production (Viner, 1932). It's a very useful set of concepts for programming as well. However, where microeconomics often (but not necessarily) speaks in terms of the value of money or capital, here we can think in terms of human effort or time.

The reason why we work with computers is often to facilitate work that can happen at shorter time scales. Processors can do the same repetitive task much more quickly and accurately than a human. That time saving allows us to see the aggregated results from many calculations. This is exciting because it allows us to get a characterisation of things at scales that we otherwise would be unlikely to perceive or do without great effort. For example, we now have weather stations that can make forecast models on demand for different parts of a country. Instead of one meteorologist per city, we have a system in place of readings that get synced. Public access to these readings means that third-party apps can use them to calculate a weather report for anywhere that is near enough to the readings.

In this case, the weather sensors are the fixed cost. These days that fixed cost includes sending up a weather satellite, which is very costly indeed. But the marginal costs can be pretty low. Historically, if you needed a weather reading for a farm halfway between London and Birmingham, you needed a meteorologist. However, nowadays if you have a series of readings across the country and an algorithm for predicting weather based on it, you simply feed in the readings and out comes the forecast. Is it as good as a meteorologist? Well, not always, but it does tend to be very reliable and it can scale to the weather for anywhere that the sensors record data.

I've heard before that computer scientists only know how to count three numbers: 0, 1, and n. The idea here is that if you have to do it twice, you really have to do it n times, and we should be able to specify some algorithm that allows us to do it n times. In reality there are still lots of issues with efficiency. But indeed, this is a foundational lesson in programming: *where possible shift marginal costs to fixed costs, but not if it will add overall costs.*

The overall costs should consider the cost in time; either time spent writing repetitive code or time spent running that code. I see this a lot when people first learn loops and functions. Below I show code without and then with a loop.

```
# Attempt 1. High marginal costs, low fixed costs
email1 = "user.example@mail.com"
email_parts = email1.split("@")
name1 = email_parts[0]

email2 = "generic.student@oii.ox.ac.uk"
email_parts = email2.split("@")
name2 = email_parts[0]

print(name1, name2)

user.example generic.student

# Attempt 2. Low marginal costs
email_list = ["user.example@mail.com",
              "generic.student@oii.ox.ac.uk",
              "dr.professor@oii.ox.ac.uk"]

print([x.split("@")[0] for x in email_list])

['user.example', 'generic.student', 'dr.professor']
```

Notice not only that the second attempt is shorter, but also that it includes a third email address. It takes the operations from the first section, puts them inside a `for` loop and prints the result as a list. If we were to add a new email to the first attempt, we would have to copy and paste or write new code from scratch. In the second example, we can simply add a new email to the list structure and the rest of the code will work as intended with no extra tweaking. In the first example, we would have to add more programming code such as `.split("@")` every time we add a new email. In that sense, the first one adds more *overall* costs because we have to write more code, with higher marginal costs, higher risk of bugs when copying and pasting, and just overall less readability. The second one requires a slightly higher fixed cost (by writing a list comprehension and `for` loop) but this upfront work pays off quickly.

In computer science terms we might say that the second example has code that is more abstract, modular, and reusable. These are all things we want out of our code. But what we really want is to make our analyses as complete and efficient as possible. And recall that what we want to minimise is not simply length of code, but time taken in the analysis. So that's where the joke comes in: building a barn represents an attempt at making the `get_milk()` routine more reusable, but in such an over-the-top way that it seems like the emphasis on fixed costs has gone too far.

1.4.2 The challenges of maximising fixed costs

Rarely in a computer science text will you hear about the virtues of code that is a one-off, or just hacked together. I do not want to change that. However, I do know that I have seen code that is often far more overwrought and abstract than it needs to be. We don't want to spend too much time planning and building that barn, but neither do we want to spend much time doing the same task repetitively. To balance the two goals, here are a set of pointers that have helped me:

1   *Pseudocode sections of your analysis before writing full Python.* I discuss pseudocode in Section 1.6. Generally, it allows you to think about the overall structure of your code rather than worrying about how to program everything right away. This way you can discover data you might need or methods that you can treat as black boxes.

2   *Refactor your code during your analysis, not after.* Refactoring is a way of taking repetitive or messy code and writing it in a way that makes it more elegant and ideally more robust. It is okay to spend an afternoon on your code midway through or late in your analysis and just redo the code. Sometimes you only know how to do certain things after having finished doing them, or you only know what is repetitive once you start on them and discover all the commonalities. If you have budgeted time to refactor, it will definitely pay off when you have to come back to the code, extend it, or share it with others.

3   *If you can do it by hand in a few minutes, do it, but document it.* Accept that sometimes it is just easier to recode a few variables by hand than to try to find a regular expression or other mechanism for automating this or discovering a more abstract way. When I say 'by hand' I do not mean literally reaching into the computer. But imagine you have one row where someone writes 'Egnland'. You might download a spellchecker and then do some automated analysis to sanitise the data. Or if it is a single exception you can just write `<data>.replace("Egnland", "England")` and move on. One thing I strongly recommend is not to edit raw data and then pretend that is the raw data. It's okay to have these sorts of small adjustments as long as they are documented. It's not okay to edit raw data. What happens if you receive an updated dataset? If you edited the raw data you'll be in trouble, but with a one-off line in the code, it will still work.

4   *Do not treat your analysis as the basis of a huge project for others.* Time and again, I have seen people slowed down by the sense that they need to create a code base that will not just be used for their analysis but for others in the field. The intention is admirable but

the realisation often gets in the way of doing a quality analysis. The best way to get your work reused is to have a paper published that others can cite. Thus, in all cases, I strongly recommend doing one-off analyses for yourself or your group and accepting that this code is not going to go very far. It should still be readable, serviceable, and well commented – for you and your team. But you should get some projects under your belt first and ideally contribute to other people's projects to get a sense of what it means to get your software used by others. You will discover a whole host of things you might not have considered (and admittedly that I cannot cover in this book).

Beyond these pointers, we can use the notion of FREE coding as a guide for our code to help us understand what to prioritise and what will be most effective in helping us accomplish our goals. This is covered in the next section.

 ## Code should be FREE

Below is an explanation of the idea that code must be FREE. It is a bit of a pun in the coding world, since there is a major movement in most technical arenas to make code free and open source. While it is important to familiarise yourself with the notion of free and open-source coding (Benkler, 2002; Lessig, 2000), this is a different matter. Here FREE is a mnemonic to help you understand how to focus your coding efforts:

- Functioning
- Robust
- Elegant
- Efficient

Think of your code as aspiring to meet these goals. Perhaps like a *hierarchy of code needs* starting with code that is 'functioning'.

1.5.1 Functioning code

Functioning code is code that gives the expected result.

In the case of functions and methods, this does not mean that you are meeting all eventualities. It means that if you give the program the expected kind of input, you will get the specific kind of result you expect as output. Each module (whether it is a script, a class file, or a program in its own right) has a notion of what is the correct input. For example, if you give me an integer and I say I will square it, then I should be able to do so for every integer.

```
def square(number):
    squarednumber = number * number
    return squarednumber


print(square(3))
```

Treated as a 'black box', we can say that if you give this function a number then it will return the correct, squared value. As a small note on language, when I say 'functioning' here, I mean code that runs as expected. There is also a notion of 'functional programming', which is a style of programming such as found in the languages Lisp, Haskell, and, to a certain extent, JavaScript. Regardless of the style of programming, our first need is to get the expected result with the code we write.

1.5.2 Robust code

Code that is functioning with the desired kind of inputs might not be functioning in other circumstances. What if the user sends in a string (which we know cannot be squared)? What if a user sends in a really long integer, longer than you would normally expect, but still an integer? This is where we need to think about how to ensure that our code is not simply functioning, but *robust*.

Python has a number of neat approaches to help ensure your code is robust. There are many in the Python documentation for handling errors (https://docs.python.org/3/tutorial/errors. html). Here are some key approaches:

* try/except statements. These allow you to catch an error and suggest an alternate course of action. There are many interesting features of these statements, including the use of else and finally.
* assert statements. This will throw an error if whatever you assert is false.
* raise statements. At any point you can simply use a raise statement to throw an error.

Generally speaking, if the code throws errors and stops it is robust, but not really functioning. Catching errors and notifying the user (such as printing a warning or to a log) is preferable to stopping the program. However, it is preferable to stop a program rather than repeatedly requesting bad data from a server. So different forms of robustness will be relevant in different circumstances.

One common strategy for handling robustness is to think in terms of either *inclusion* or *exclusion criteria*. When thinking of inclusion criteria we can pre-emptively test for just what we want to include. In this case we want to only include numbers. Since there are many kinds of numbers in Python, one additional way to be robust is to look for a general number. It turns out there is a number library for just such an occasion. Focusing instead on exclusion criteria, we could just try our code and if an error happens then provide a 'plan B' as an exception. This is a common programming strategy called 'duck typing', meaning if it walks like a duck and quacks like a duck, it's a duck. Here are two different approaches to handling bad input (pre-emptive and duck typing).

```
import numbers

def square(number):
    # pre-emptively checking for inclusion
    if isinstance(number, numbers.Number):
        squarednumber = number * number
        return squarednumber
```

```
    else:
        return float("NaN")

print(square("b"),square(2))

nan 4

def square(number):
    # duck typing to handle exclusion
    try:
        squarednumber = number * number
        return squarednumber
    except:
        return float("NaN")

print(square("b"),square(2))

nan 4
```

Beyond this are a great deal of strategies like `unittest`, which is a framework for methodically checking how different parts of a code interact, 'type hinting', which signals what kinds of data your code should expect, and commenting. Although commenting does not make your code more robust in a literal sense, it can make it a lot easier to read, meaning that when working on the code you will be more likely to know what to expect and how to anticipate it.

1.5.3 Elegant code

Code that is elegant is code that does not waste space or add unnecessary layers of complexity. It is not strictly necessary for the code to run, but it is often a crucial part of ensuring that all the code runs together well.

If we have to do some data processing and we do type out the same task repeatedly our code is not very elegant. It is often said that reusable code is good code. This might mean reused by someone else, but it often means reused within the same program. In the example above, our code is somewhat elegant in that it uses a function to perform some action and that function can be reused.

One way to make the code more elegant might be to remove the unnecessary `squarednumber` variable. We might also want to reconsider whether we should create a more generic `to_exponent` function instead of just one to square variables. In reality, our functions would do more than just square a number. However, we do not want to put *everything* in a single function. So learning how to keep functions modular enough to be reused but not so modular to be overcomplicated is an art.

```
def square(number):
    if isinstance(number, numbers.Number):
        return number * number
    return float("NaN")
```

```
print(square("b"),
      square(2))
```

```
nan 4
```

```
def to_exponent(number, power = 2):
    if isinstance(number, numbers.Number):
        return number ** power
    return float("NaN")
```

```
print(to_exponent("b"),
      to_exponent(2),
      to_exponent(3,3))
```

```
nan 4 27
```

Refactoring is the most useful way to ensure your code is elegant. Refactoring is where you go back through your code and look for commonalities or repetition. You investigate a way to do the repetitive thing only once (often in a function) and then rewrite the code to call this one function. It might also involve renaming variables or providing clearer reporting of data.

Elegant code should also be very readable code. Python can break over a line after a comma or by using a \ at the end of a line. In this book (and in my code) I try to keep my code to 80 characters width or less. Not only does that ensure it can be printed without breaking across the line, but it also forces me to be more careful with how I structure each line.

1.5.4 Efficient code

All else equal, we want our code to be as efficient as possible. However, that's assuming the first three needs are taken care of. Overall, efficient code tends to make use of low-level Python features. For example, 'broadcasting' (which can check for all equivalent calculations, do it once, and send the result to all cases) is more efficient than going through a `for` loop one element at a time. You will see this approach in my code later where I usually avoid `for` loops when working with a `Series` or a `DataFrame`. These sorts of tricks tend to come up when they are needed.

Checking for bottlenecks is a generally useful skill. One way to do this in Jupyter is to employ the `%%time` and `%timeit` magic commands. These are *magic commands* in that they are not in Python per se, but only in Jupyter (or more specifically only in iPython upon which Jupyter is based). The first `%%time` will print the time it takes to run that cell. The second, `%timeit`, will run a single line of code many times and report the average. The specific number of times it runs is set by default, but you can change that with the `-n` flag, so that `%timeit -n 1000: some_function()` will run that function 1000 times and take the average time.

```
%%time
```

```
newlist = []
```

```
for i in range(1000): newlist.append(i)
```

```
CPU times: user 639 ms, sys: 785 ms, total: 1.42 s
Wall time: 1.71 s

newlist = []

%timeit -n 1000 for i in range(500): newlist.append(i)

%timeit -n 1000 newlist = [i for i in range(500)]

%timeit -n 1000 newlist = list(range(500))

31.4 µs ± 3.15 µs per loop (mean ± std. dev. of 7 runs, 1,000 loops each)
14.9 µs ± 162 ns per loop (mean ± std. dev. of 7 runs, 1,000 loops each)
5.61 µs ± 38.7 ns per loop (mean ± std. dev. of 7 runs, 1,000 loops each)
```

There are more examples of how to profile and speed up code in Chapter 7 of VanderPlas (2016b) on 'profiling'. Beyond this there are many strategies for making code more efficient. For example, there is the use of cython, which compiles generally slow Python code to faster code in the C programming language. You can also compare different libraries, check options for specific packages, sample data rather than use all of it, and consider moving your notebook to the cloud.

 Pseudocode (and pseudo-pseudocode)

Pseudocode is a means by which we articulate what we want to do with code without being too careful syntactically. It's about clearing away the specifics or abstracting them from the code. When planning what you would like to do in your analysis it can be really helpful to write out pseudocode to get a sense of what steps you need to take *before* worrying about the specific Python syntax for those steps. The more detailed your pseudocode, often the easier it is to translate it directly into working code.

Although there is no real language called pseudo-pseudocode, pseudocode itself can vary from something really vague to something that looks like a formula or almost working code. More formal pseudocode uses specific mathematical symbols or follows the general syntax of a specific language. More informal pseudocode is simply a set of instructions, written in an inconsistent or conversational style like a homemade recipe. This is not a bad thing. The function of pseudocode is to help you organise your thoughts. Thus, if you write pseudocode in a certain way and it helps, then do not fret over its formality. However, when you go to share an algorithm with someone else, the more formally you describe it, the less likely that there will be ambiguity or misunderstanding about what you meant.

Have a look at the following four examples referring to the arithmetic mean (the classic measure of the 'average'). They are all pseudocode but vary in detail and formality.

1.6.1 Attempt 1. Pseudocode as written word

Add all of the elements together and divide by the number of elements.

1.6.2 Attempt 2. Pseudocode as mathematical formula

$$\bar{x} = \frac{1}{n} \sum_{i=1}^{n} x_i$$

Note that here, someone familiar with the formula could probably detect what is happening. However, if you do not read maths, then it can be a challenge, so I will provide a translation. This in itself might be seen as attempt 2a. The big E-like character means sum all the elements. The x refers to any element and $\bar{x}$ symbolises the average (or arithmetic mean) of these elements. So if you have n values, represented by $x_1, x_2, ..., x_n$, then the subscript x_i stands in for each one of these elements. i is the iterator and it goes from 1 to n (meaning all of the observations of x). So literally we are saying sum all the elements and then divide by the number of them.

1.6.3 Attempt 3. Pseudocode as written code

```
get a collection of elements
get count of elements
set total at zero

for each element:
    add value to total

result equals total divided by number of elements
```

1.6.4 Attempt 4. Slightly more formal pseudocode (in a Python style)

```
def average(elements):
    count = length(elements)
    total = 0
    for element in elements:
        total += element
    return (total/count)
```

This last one is how I might write it if I was not sure of the right words in Python but I had a sense of what I wanted to do. In this case it is almost like real Python except that I would need to replace word `length` with `len`. I might use more elegant Python in my code like a list comprehension or include more robustness features like type checking, but the final pseudocode as written would run as actual code with little fuss.

 Summary

I begin this chapter with a classic if imperfect framework for understanding how to situate data from the information visualisation field: DIKW, standing for data, information, knowledge, and wisdom. I admit that wisdom sounds a bit lofty, but I like the idea that there are some kinds of knowledge that can help us predict things in different contexts. It seems like a positive goal of learning and a good starting point for how to think of what we are doing with data. From here I remind us to think of the sorts of measurements we can take, how these affect what becomes data in the first place, and how these measurements exist *beyond the interface* when thinking about online data. Sometimes, instead of focusing on *how* we measure or detect a signal, we can investigate the important questions of *what* gets measured, who gets to measure it, and what is left out. For this I assert that we can lean on critical data studies and interrogate how we operationalise a concept.

From there I shift towards considering some matters with code. These are programming considerations that help us think of how to organise a program. The first was to be mindful of how programming can shift your workflow from marginal to fixed costs. So instead of, for example, transcribing every comment in a blog post, you can parse the post instead. If it takes 15 minutes to do the copy and pasting, it might be just as easy to do that yourself. But it would be fragile and begin to limit your imagination to the volume of data you can copy and paste in a sitting. Thus, code that takes a couple hours to put together at first might not seem worth it, but you can reapply it in larger contexts, over longer time periods, and repeat it in case you made an error the first time around. In this way, I want you to see programming not merely as automating, but as being able to see measurements at a different scale.

Then I share a few strategies to consider a hierarchy of coding needs. First the program has to be functioning with the right inputs, then be able to handle alternate inputs (robustness), then in a modular or reusable way (elegance), and finally, as efficiently as possible. Where production-level code might emphasise robustness and continuous uptime, code for research tends to emphasise being readable, easy to explore, and reproducible. It is often run only a few times, but the logic of why certain decisions were made in aggregating or filtering data have to be grounded and clear. To that end, I conclude by reminding about the benefits of pseudocode. It is often really useful to make step-by-step instructions of a workflow first and then fill it in with working code piece by piece.

 Further reading

For the programming part of this chapter, there is probably not enough there to recommend further reading. It's a bit of a leap to go from a simple mnemonic to recommending books on code architecture. So I will wait to recommend more technical books until the subsequent chapters. Below I wanted to mention some really compelling books in critical data studies that help to motivate research questions in data science.

- *Weapons of Math Destruction* (O'Neil, 2016). This is one of those books that just keeps showing up on every colleague's bookshelf. O'Neil does an amazing job of articulating how algorithms are involved in everyday decision-making in ways that make the world more calculable. She highlights how the very act of forcing measurement can itself undermine the goals of the system. It is a direct challenge to the notion that operationalisation is either easy or fair.
- *Data Feminism* (D'Ignazio and Klein, 2020). The authors make the case that feminism as a theory provides effective lenses for understanding how power is used to marginalise

and subjugate even as it can be used for productive ends. They talk about different ways in which data speak to (and from) power and turn the notion of 'we manage what we measure' on its head.

- *The Information* (Gleick, 2011). This book is more history of science than critical data studies. But it provides a really vivid picture of how the measurement of information came to be. It turns out the formula for information (Shannon entropy) is partially a product of history as well as necessity. By learning about how this fundamental property came to be we can also learn about what it means to encode anything as data in the first place. For an alternative take on this which is more vivid and philosophical, I highly recommend Hayles's *How We Became Posthuman* (1999).

Extensions and reflections

- Consider (PO)DIKW examples with data from social media. For example, what might we say about posting frequency (how often people make posts on any given platform, such as Facebook or Twitter)? Think, first, what is the phenomenon to be measured, then how you can make a distribution of such measurements. Then ask what information is apparent, what might that information tell us about the context, and what might it tell us more generally. Do we want our measure to be just the number of posts? The posts per day? Should this be bounded by a specific time window? Will it let us speak to issues with personality? What about as a marker of social connectedness? Is it a sufficient marker or are other measurements required?
- Reflect on any past code or practice code you have already written. Go back and try to rewrite it. Do you write it the same way twice, or do you make new decisions to 'tune up' the code? What are those decisions?
- If you had to apply the FREE principles to any coding you have done, how would you change it? Would you time certain operations to check their efficiency? Would you include catching more errors or different kinds of input? Perhaps make the logic more clear through refactoring?

2
THE SERIES: TAMING THE DISTRIBUTION

━━━━━━━━━ **Learning goals** ━━━━━━━━━

- Understand the Series as a data structure that allows indexing by both key and position
- Be able to change the index and values of a Series
- Perform operations on the Series that summarise it, like value_counts() and unique()
- Recode values in a Series using map and lambda.

 Introducing the Series: Python's way to store a distribution

Our first real social data science skill with Python starts here. As stated previously, we want to look not just at a single measurement, but at a distribution of them. These distributions have to be stored in some way.

The two core ways that are taught in an introductory Python course are to use the built-in data structures, list and dict. The former is a way of storing data *by position*. With a list we first add an element. It gets the index 0. Then when we store a second element it gets the index 1. We can repeat this continually and get a very long list. However, we can only access the elements in this list by position.

By contrast, in a dictionary in Python, we might have some data which we can link using some identifier or 'key', so instead of position we want to ask for the value by asking for the key first, as in user_count["France"]. This should work whether France is in the 1st, 6th, or 170th place in the set of countries for whatever measurement we are storing.

In most cases, data tends to come to us in one of these two forms: as an ordered list of elements or as a set of keys and values. To make life a little easier, we can use the Series, which handles both kinds of data. Further, if your Series happens to be full of numbers, the Series can report on a variety of statistical measurements such as the average (i.e. the mean()) of the data.

The Series is like a list, but the index can be labelled and you can give the Series a name. A Series is a class of object in Python within the pandas library. Therefore, you can import and then create an empty Series in two ways:

```
from pandas import Series
ser1 = Series()
```

or

```
import pandas as pd
ser1 = pd.Series()
```

The first way is preferable when the Series is the only thing you want to import from pandas. However, in most cases we want to import the Series, the DataFrame, and maybe some helper methods, so in my code I tend to use the second approach. In case you haven't seen this before, as is a way to give a library a different, typically shorter name. Here are some common examples: import pandas as pd, import numpy as np, and import networkx as nx.

When you first initialise a Series, if it is empty then it is not very useful. Instead create a Series with some data. Let's start with the days of the week as a list and convert it to a Series.

```
import pandas as pd
lweekdays = ["Monday","Tuesday","Wednesday","Thursday",
             "Friday","Saturday","Sunday"]
```

To turn this into a Series we could write:

```
sweekdays = pd.Series(lweekdays,name="Weekdays")

display(sweekdays)

0        Monday
1       Tuesday
2     Wednesday
3      Thursday
4        Friday
5      Saturday
6        Sunday
Name: Weekdays, dtype: object
```

This will transform the list into a Series with the name (Weekdays) and the default index (in this case 0 to 6, since we have seven elements). Notice that the name of the Series is an attribute of the Series-as-data. This is different from the name of the variable that contains the Series (sweekdays). We could reassign the variable to a different name (e.g., weekday_measures) and yet the Series would still have the name Weekdays when displayed.

Imagine that instead of simply listing the days of the week by themselves, we want a list where we have some *measurements*, based on days. We could count something per day, like the hours of sleep that night. So we could use a dictionary with the days as keys and the number of hours slept that night as the values. We can also create a Series from that dictionary, much in the way we did with a list. Except this time, instead of using 0 to 6 for the index, the keys of the dictionary will be the index. Consequently, I will give it a different name. I will call it SleepHours instead of Weekdays, since now the data that we are interested in is not a list of weekdays. The data here represents the hours of sleep per night. Observe:

```
dsleephours = {"Sunday":8.5,
               "Monday":7,
               "Tuesday":5,
               "Wednesday":6.5,
               "Thursday":7.5,
               "Friday":9,
               "Saturday":8}
```

```
sleephours = pd.Series(dsleephours, name="SleepHours")

display(sleephours)

print(f"The length of the Series is {len(sleephours)}.")
```

```
Sunday       8.5
Monday       7.0
Tuesday      5.0
Wednesday    6.5
Thursday     7.5
Friday       9.0
Saturday     8.0
Name: SleepHours, dtype: float64
```

```
The length of the Series is 7.
```

This is now a *distribution* of data in a Series. This Series is like the storage facility for data. To explore some patterns or meanings we have to take this data out of storage. We might not take all of the data at one time. Further, we might need to process the data in some manner before we can fully appreciate it. The first way to do this is to use len(<SERIES>) in order to get the length of the Series. In this case len(sleephours) was 7 for the seven days of the week.

There are three ways in which we tend to extract data from a Series: by *index*, by *value*, and as a *distribution*. See a description of each below.

2.1.1 Working from index

Working from index means that we will start with an index and get a value. For example, we might want to know if we got 8 hours of sleep on Tuesday. To work from index means we get data by querying the Series based on the index. Observe:

```
display(sleephours["Tuesday"])

# OR

display(sleephours[2])
```

```
5.0
5.0
```

This is very similar to a dictionary or list. We have an object, sleephours, and we have a way to index it, sleephours[<some_value>]. If we select either an integer representing position, from 0 up to the length of the Series, it will return the value in that row, much like a list. Further, since indices can themselves have a label, like "Tuesday", we can use the indices to extract a specific value regardless of its position. In this case, we queried for "Tuesday" and it returned the value there.

It seems that Tuesday night was a rough night, as the data shows only 5 hours of sleep. Did you notice that it printed `5.0` and not 5? We entered the number 5 as an integer into the dictionary above, but the column included some floats, so the whole column was converted. This sort of conversion happens in `pandas` with differing number types in the same column. It also happens when you have integers and missing values, since the missing value `np.nan` is itself considered float like `7.5` or `1.333333333`.

```
sleephours.dtype
```

```
dtype('float64')
```

The `Series` has a type, which is usually either a numeric class (`float64`), Boolean `True` or `False` values (`bool`), or generic (`object`), which includes strings.

```
X = pd.Series([True, False])
print(x.dtype)
```

```
y = pd.Series(["Left", "Right", "Up", "Down"])
print(y.dtype)
```

```
bool
object
```

Speaking of data types, notice that the index is now a string (e.g. `"Monday"`)? What happens if you use mixed types, so that you have both integers and strings in your index? The answer is that the program can behave in unexpected ways.

A numerical index (as integers) from 0 to *n* is not really ideal. It might be functioning, but it is not robust. If you sort again, the values will be out of order. The only advantage is that it is easy to come up with a new index: you should be able to use `len(<SERIES>)` since the default is that the first index is 0. In reality, if you care about the relationship between the index and the data, you'll use something more specific than an integer. But if the index does not matter for your work, then it's not a problem to stick with the default numeric integer index.

As a rule, try to avoid using integer numbers as indices unless they are sequential and start from 0. If you absolutely must use a number, try using a string version. `"0"` is a string, whereas `0` is a number. This way you can avoid accidents where you are trying to reference a row that is labelled 2 but in the third or *n*th place. Below I illustrate how accidents can happen with an integer index. This `Series` has the number 4 where it previously had `"Sunday"`. But notice that while it is the number 4, it is in the first position. So what happens when we query for `sleephours[4]`?

```
# Turn 4 into a string to see what sleephours[4] returns then.
sleephours = pd.Series({4:8.5,
                "Monday":7, "Tuesday":5, "Wednesday":6.5,
                "Thursday":7.5, "Friday":9, "Saturday":8})
```

```
display(sleephours[4])
display(sleephours["Thursday"])
```

```
8.5
7.5
```

Below I show how to reset the index using the `RangeIndex` object. This is the preferred approach over saying `ser1.index = range(len(ser1))`.

```
ser1 = pd.Series(["a","b","c","d","e"])
print(ser1)
```

```
0    a
1    b
2    c
3    d
4    e
dtype: object
```

```
del ser1[2]
print(ser1) # Notice that the index is now 0,1,3,4
```

```
0    a
1    b
3    d
4    e
dtype: object
```

```
ser1.index = pd.RangeIndex(len(ser1))
print(ser1) # Now the index should be back to 0,1,2,3
```

```
0    a
1    b
2    d
3    e
dtype: object
```

2.1.2 Working from values (and masking)

Working from values means that we will start with a value or set of values and discover the related indices. This is typically how we slice and filter data. To slice means we take a range of values, whereas to filter means we select values based on some truth condition. For example, we might want to filter a `Series` of Twitter accounts down to those which have been reported as bots. In this case, we would have a `Series` with the Twitter account name as the index and the value of `True` or `False` for `is_bot` as the values of the `Series`.

In our case, we have a `Series` with hours of sleep as the values. We could then ask which night entailed less than 7 hours of sleep. By using a Boolean operator (which evaluates to

True or False) we then get a new Series. It has the same indices but the values are now
True or False for whether the value is less than 7.

```
sleephours = pd.Series({"Sunday":8.5,
                        "Monday":7,
                        "Tuesday":5,
                        "Wednesday":6.5,
                        "Thursday":8,
                        "Friday":9.5,
                        "Saturday":8})
```

```
display(sleephours < 7)
```

```
Sunday        False
Monday        False
Tuesday        True
Wednesday      True
Thursday      False
Friday        False
Saturday      False
dtype: bool
```

This Series shows that on Tuesday and Wednesday we observed less than 7 hours of sleep.
Remember that sleephours < 7 returns a new Series. We can then label that new
Series and consider it a *mask*. A mask lets us see a partial amount of data. In this case, with
our mask we will only see data from Tuesday and Wednesday since they were the days that
returned True.

How do we apply a mask? We query for the data just like before. But instead of querying sleephours["Thursday"], we can query sleephours[<mask>] or, in this case,
sleephours[sleephours < 7].

```
sleepmask = sleephours < 7
```

```
display(sleephours[sleepmask])
```

```
Tuesday       5.0
Wednesday     6.5
dtype: float64
```

Building up this chain further, we can ask how many days are in this new Series with len()
(it's short for length). So if we want to know what proportion of days we observed the subject
having less than 7 hours of sleep, it could look like this:

```
days_sleep = len(sleephours[sleepmask])
total_days = len(sleephours)
avg_per_day = days_sleep/total_days
```

```
print(avg_per_day)

# Or in a more tidy format, where we treat the output as a float
# and ask for only two significant digits.
# This is an 'f-insertion'. I will be using a lot of these.
print(f"{avg_per_day:.2f}")
```

```
0.2857142857142857
0.29
```

Multiple masks at the same time

It common to want to filter using more than one condition, either using an 'and' condition (&) or an 'or' condition (|). For example, what if you want the extremes, like whether sleep hours is less than 7 or greater than 9? Done wrong, it is common to get the error "The truth value of a Series is ambiguous." followed by some details. First I will show that and then show how we can get the right data.

```
sleephours[sleephours < 7 or sleephours > 9] # Run this to get an error
```

```
sleephours[sleephours < 7 | sleephours > 9] # Run this to get a long error
```

There are two important issues to consider here. The first is that for a Series, we use the pipe operator, |, not the word or, even if the word or is used elsewhere in Python. The second is that we should remember the 'order of operations'. In the second case we used the right operator, but the order was off. It was evaluating first the Series sleephours < 7, then asking if that or sleephours is greater than 9. But 9 is a number not a Series, so the program gets confused. To avoid this we use parentheses:

```
sleephours[(sleephours < 7) | (sleephours > 9)] # This should run fine.
```

```
Tuesday      5.0
Wednesday    6.5
Friday       9.5
dtype: float64
```

2.1.3 Working from distributions

Working from distributions means that we will try to summarise the values in some way. A key distinction here is in the type of data, and in particular, whether the data is numerical or not. If the data in the Series is numerical, we can produce numerous statistical summaries of the data, such as the mean, median, mode, and skewness. If the data is non-numerical, we cannot do much more with a distribution than get the maximum, minimum (usually by sort order of bytes or strings), mode, and use a command to create a table of values.

Value counts

A common task is to summarise the counts of the different values in a `Series`. In other programs this might be called tabulating or getting a frequency count. In `pandas` it is the command `<ser>.value_counts()`. It is very useful and it is worth getting comfortable with it. It literally means: return a table that *counts* how many of each *value*. The results that come back are themselves a new `Series`. For the old `Series`, the unique values comprise the index, and the number of appearances comprise the values. By default, it sorts the data so the most common values are at the top.

```
display(sleephours.value_counts())
```

```
8.0    2
8.5    1
7.0    1
5.0    1
6.5    1
9.5    1
dtype: int64
```

In many cases, the values themselves might have an order. In this case, the values do have an order from least sleep to most. If you want to present the data sorted, you can sort by index (`<ser>.sort_index()`). If you want to sort by values, you can use `<ser>.sort_values()`. But we started sorted by values, so let's see the data sorted by index before proceeding (notice the `ascending=False` argument):

```
display(sleephours.value_counts().sort_index(ascending=False))
```

```
9.5    1
8.5    1
8.0    2
7.0    1
6.5    1
5.0    1
dtype: int64
```

So there were two nights with 8 hours' sleep and five nights with a unique value. It can get a little more interesting when we do something like coarsen the data or otherwise find a way to summarise it. One simple example here is to summarise a `Series` of true and false statements. In this case let's use 7 as a cut-off point as we are interested in days per week where people get more than 7 hours' sleep.

```
(sleephours > 7).value_counts()
```

```
True     4
False    3
dtype: int64
```

So the `value_counts()` command here counted the `True` values and the `False` values in the `Series` that gets returned from the Boolean `sleephours > 7`. We also used the parentheses to ensure the correct order of operations. Otherwise we would be asking if `sleephours` is greater than `7.value_counts()`, which wouldn't make sense.

When thinking about a distribution of real numbers, we might want to think less about sufficient sleep *per night*, but *average* time spent sleeping or some other way to express some ideal type or expected value. To that end, we can consider a variety of other measures directly included with a `Series`. Some obvious measures include the mean, standard deviation, median, max, and minimum. Other more statistically involved measures might include the kurtosis or the skew.

One tricky aspect of this is that there are at least two ways to summarise a distribution: using `Series`-specific methods and using built-in methods for any generic collection. A `Series`-specific method is one that looks like this: `<ser>.<method()>`. One for built-in collections (which could also apply to lists and dictionaries) looks like this: `<method>(<ser>)`. Here are a few built-in methods: `max()`, `min()`, `sum()`. On the other hand, the average (or the 'mean') is not a built-in method for collections. It is a method that comes with a `Series`. Thus `sleephours.mean()` will work, but `mean(sleephours)` will not. As example:

```
display(sleephours.max())
```

```
display(max(sleephours))
```

```
9.5
```

```
9.5
```

```
display(sleephours.mean())
```

```
try:
    display(mean(sleephours))
except:
    print("This did not work as planned.")
```

```
7.5
```

```
This did not work as planned.
```

2.1.4 Adding data to a `Series`

Sometimes we have a collection that we turn into a `Series`, as we did above. Sometimes we have a `Series` already and then want to add more data to it. Doing this relies on managing the indices. That is, you cannot simply add a value to a `Series`. You need to add an index and a value. First, I want to show this for adding a single element to a `Series`. Then I will show how to add multiple elements.

Adding a single element to a `Series`

Adding an element to a `Series` works very similarly to a dictionary. To recall, with a dictionary, you add a value using a key. So if you have a dictionary called `ex_dict`, then you can add a value by mapping it to a key like so: `ex_dict["dinner"] = "Pizza"`. If there is already a value there for `"dinner"`, then it will be erased and replaced with `"Pizza"`. If there is no value there, then it will be a new key–value pair.

Similarly with a `Series` called `ex_ser`, saying `ex_ser["dinner"] = "Pizza"` will either create a new row with the item `"Pizza"` or it will replace whatever was in that row. If you have a sequential index that starts from 0 (which is the default), then you can append data to the end with `ex_ser[len(ex_ser)] = "Pizza"`. So if you start with a `Series` with four items, they will have the index 0, 1, 2, and 3. So `"Pizza"` will then have the index 4. Be careful with this approach: if the index is out of order or not strictly sequential you might accidentally overwrite data. You can check whether an index already exists with the in operator: `if not 4 in ex_ser: ex_ser[4] = "Pizza"`.

```
ex_ser = pd.Series(["Toast","Salad","Pastry"])
ex_ser[len(ex_ser)] = "Pizza"
display(ex_ser)
```

```
0      Toast
1      Salad
2      Pastry
3      Pizza
dtype: object
```

```
if 2 not in ex_ser:
    ex_ser[2] = "Hamburgers"
```

```
if 4 not in ex_ser:
    ex_ser[4] = "Cookies"
```

```
display(ex_ser)
```

```
0       Toast
1       Salad
2       Pastry
3       Pizza
4     Cookies
dtype: object
```

So above there *was* a value for index 2, so we did not replace it with `"Hamburgers"`. There was not a value at index 4 so a new row was created and it included `"Cookies"`.

Adding multiple data to a `Series`

If you have more than one element that you want to add to a `Series`, then you have to com-bine them in some way. In past versions of `pandas`, you could use the `append` command, and you might still see it online. Unfortunately, it seemed to just confuse people as well as create inefficient code. So we will ignore that approach here and work with the preferred approach using `concat`. We will return to this in Chapter 5 where we show a more advanced approach using `merge`.

When you concatenate two collections you are attaching one to the other. It is like stacking them on top of each other. In order to do this, you first have to put the multiple `Series` objects that you want to concatenate in a collection (such as a list, a tuple, or a set). Then you pass that collection to `pd.concat(<collection of Series objects>)`. This method will return a new single `Series` with all of the values now combined into single object. The good news is that it does not matter if you try to concatenate two `Series` or 20. If they are all in that collection, then they will be in the resulting `Series`.

```
ser_m = pd.Series(["Kermit", "Piggy", "Gonzo"],name="Muppets")
ser_s = pd.Series(["Oscar", "Ernie", "Big Bird"],name="Sesame Street")
ser_f = pd.Series(["Mokey","Red","Boober"],name="Fraggles")

new_ser = pd.concat([ser_m,ser_s,ser_f])
display(new_ser)
```

```
0        Kermit
1         Piggy
2         Gonzo
0         Oscar
1         Ernie
2      Big Bird
0         Mokey
1           Red
2        Boober
dtype: object
```

Notice that the new `Series` kept the indices from the old `Series`. This might be the behav-iour you want, but in our case it is not. Also notice that it did not pass the `name` on to the new `Series` (which name would it choose?). The index can give us some headaches if it is not unique. Observe what happens when we ask for `new_ser[1]`. It will return all three values with that index:

```
new_ser[1]
```

```
1     Piggy
1     Ernie
1       Red
dtype: object
```

To avoid this, we can either create a new index (perhaps like we did above using `RangeIndex`). Or we can use an argument in the `concat` statement saying `ignore_index=True`.

```
new_ser = pd.concat([ser_m,ser_s,ser_f],ignore_index=True)
new_ser.name = "Muppets"
display(new_ser)
```

```
0        Kermit
1         Piggy
2         Gonzo
3         Oscar
4         Ernie
5      Big Bird
6         Mokey
7           Red
8        Boober
Name: Muppets, dtype: object
```

2.1.5 Deleting data from a `Series`

Just as we can add data either for a single row (like a dictionary) or multiple rows (using `concat`), there are ways to delete either a single row or multiple rows.

Deleting a single element

To delete a single element, this is the rare case where we do not use parentheses in Python. The command `del <ser>[<index>]` will remove that row from the `Series`. Observe:

```
sdemo = pd.Series(["Kermit","Piggy","Fozzie"],name="Before")
display(sdemo)
```

```
del sdemo[1]
sdemo.name = "After"
display(sdemo)
```

```
0       Kermit
1        Piggy
2       Fozzie
Name: Before, dtype: object
0       Kermit
2       Fozzie
Name: After, dtype: object
```

Deleting multiple data in a `Series`

It is not as obvious how to delete multiple data from a `Series`. Generally we do this by 'selecting in' the data we want. You will have seen this above as a mask. So if we have a

`Series` with numeric values, we can filter using a mask. Then we no longer have the data we did not want.

```
ser_old = pd.Series([3,5,7,9,11,14])
ser_new = ser_old[ser_old >= 5]
ser_new
```

```
1     5
2     7
3     9
4    11
5    14
dtype: int64
```

2.1.6 Working with missing data in a `Series`

A `Series` can have missing data. Typically this data is signified by NaN. This term is an IEEE standardised phrase for 'not a number' across computer languages. In Python, it is often employed by using `float("nan")`, by `np.nan` which is numpy's NaN object (and often printed by Python as `NaN` or `nan` depending on context), or by `pd.NA` which is the pandas missing-data object (which is often printed by Python as `<NA>`). It is less important to distinguish between different kinds of NaN values than it is to recognise NaN values in data and handle them meaningfully. Herein I generally use NaN to represent the concept (which also stands in for 'missing values') and to use `np.nan` when I am referring to specific Python objects.

As an example, we can create a `Series` with an index of 0, 1, 2, 3, 4, and no data. Then each of the columns will start off with `np.nan` values.

```
smuppet = pd.Series(index=[0,1,2,3],dtype=object)
smuppet[0] = "Kermit"
smuppet[3] = "Fozzie"
display(smuppet)
```

```
0    Kermit
1       NaN
2       NaN
3    Fozzie
dtype: object
```

There are three things we tend to want to do when dealing with missing data. These work whether you are seeing NaN or `<NA>`.

1   *Get rid of missing values*: use `<Series>.dropna()`. This will return a new `Series` without the entries that had NaN values.
2   *Replace missing values*: use `<Series>.fillna()`. This is for instances where we might have missing data and simply want to insert some value in their place. For example, if we

have a count of number of laughs a specific Muppet received in an episode, we might end up with missing data if the Muppet did not appear. In this case, `<Series>.fillna(0)` will fill all the missing values with 0. Note that this becomes a research decision.

3   *Filter in or out by missing values.* Rather than drop the missing values we often want to mask them for a single operation. Here we can use `<Series>.notna()` inside a mask.

Observe all three of these below:

```
# Filling the NaN values
display(smuppet.fillna("extra"))
```

```
0     Kermit
1      extra
2      extra
3     Fozzie
dtype: object
```

```
# Dropping the NaN values
display(smuppet.dropna())
```

```
0 Kermit
3 Fozzie
dtype: object
```

```
# Masking the NaN values
display(smuppet[smuppet.notna()])
```

```
0 Kermit
3 Fozzie
dtype: object
```

Sometimes we have to remove cases because of missing data. But sometimes the data is only missing for some variables and we should keep the case. Deciding when to keep data or drop it is a research challenge. There is no right answer, only a few wrong answers. For example, if a Muppet did not appear in an episode, their value for 'laughs in that episode' is *structurally* a zero, which is to say it was necessarily zero. Is counting that zero a sensible approach? If we include a bunch of zeros we might reduce the average laughs per episode per Muppet. If we do not include such zeros, we might reduce the number of Muppets we can discuss. The most important part of this exercise is to be clear with the reader about why you made one decision over the other.

2.1.7 Getting unique values in a `Series`

Depending on the data, you might want to know whether any values or how many values are unique. Some examples:

1   Reading log traffic data - how many of the IP addresses are unique?
2   Getting a stream of tweets - how many of the accounts are unique?
3   Checking that an index has entirely unique values.

The Series.unique() command will return a new Series with only one entry for each unique value. Note, however, that this is returned as an array, which is very similar to a list. The only challenge here is that it does not include the indices, which makes sense in a way – if you have two "Kermit" values, which index should it choose, the first? The last? So it decides here to choose none. If you want to turn the unique values back into a Series from an array, that's simple: just recast it as a Series. Here is an example:

```
ser1 = pd.Series(["Kermit", "Fozzie", "Kermit", "Piggy", "Fozzie"])
display(ser1.unique())

ser2 = pd.Series(ser1.unique())  # to transform back to a Series
display(ser2)

array(['Kermit', 'Fozzie', 'Piggy'], dtype=object)

0    Kermit
1    Fozzie
2     Piggy
dtype: object
```

2.2 Changing a Series

There are many ways to transform a Series. Below we focus on some of the key ones. First we look at how to change the *order* of the data. Then I show how to change the *type* of the data. Finally, we look at three ways to change the values of the data.

2.2.1 Changing the order of items in the Series

A Series can be sorted by the values (Series.sort_values()) or by the index (Series. sort_index()). The sort will be ascending by default, but you can change it with the argument ascending=False. This is one of many methods for the Series or DataFrame that require the inplace=True argument. Otherwise, it will return a new, sorted, Series and leave the old one in place.

```
ser1 = pd.Series( {"Kermit": "Frog",
                   "Piggy": "Pig",
                   "Fozzie": "Bear",
                   "Robin": "Frog"} )

ser1.sort_values(ascending=True, inplace=True)
display(ser1)

Fozzie    Bear
```

```
Kermit      Frog
Robin       Frog
Piggy        Pig
dtype: object
```

```
ser2 = ser1.sort_index(ascending=False)
display(ser2)
```

```
Robin       Frog
Piggy        Pig
Kermit      Frog
Fozzie      Bear
dtype: object
```

2.2.2 Changing the type of the `Series`

A `Series` has a type by default (referred to as the `dtype`, or 'data type', for the `Series`). The generic `Series` type is `object`. This could contain any value in Python as all values can be considered an object of some type. Sometimes, however, your `Series` can have a more specific data type, such as Boolean or `datetime`. Then you can do some useful things for that specific data type.

The way to alter the type of an object is to 'cast' it, and that goes for either a single object or a `Series`. To cast an object you encase it in the type you want. So if I want an object to be represented as a string variable I would say `str(x)`. If *x* cannot be converted into the string type, then the program will throw an error.

Similarly, if you have a string `"3"` and you want to make it a number you can simply type:

```
numval = "3"
strval = int(numval)
```

However, this approach is very fragile. With `"3"` it works fine, but with `"three"` or `"drei"` the program will throw an error. It knows that digits can be numbers but not the semantics of characters as words representing those numbers. More sophisticated methods exist for this challenge. One example is how pandas can automatically detect and convert dates as diverse as 'Thursday the 3rd of February' and '9:30pm 12/30/21' using the `to_datetime()` method. These will be introduced later in Chapter 10 on cleaning data.

In general, if you want to recast a data type for a `Series` you can use the `astype` method. Let's see how it works first, and then I will introduce a number of caveats.

```
sdemo = pd.Series([1,3,4,5])
display(sdemo)
```

```
0    1
1    3
2    4
3    5
dtype: int64
```

```
display(sdemo.astype(float) + 2)
display(sdemo.astype(str) + "2")
```

```
0    3.0
1    5.0
2    6.0
3    7.0
dtype: float64
```

```
0    12
1    32
2    42
3    52
dtype: object
```

Sometimes recasting does not work because the data cannot be converted into that form directly. Normally this will raise an error. So if you enter int("three"), Python will raise a ValueError. However, when using .astype you can set the optional errors flag to avoid this. The only problem here is that it will quietly return the original data. So notice that when I try to convert to a float below, it does not return the numbers as floats and leave the strings. Instead it returns the original Series.

```
sdemo = pd.Series([1,"three",4,"five point five"])
display(sdemo.astype(float,errors="ignore"))
display(sdemo.astype(str) + "2")
```

```
0                    1
1                three
2                    4
3      five point five
dtype: object
```

```
0                   12
1               three2
2                   42
3     five point five2
dtype: object
```

If you are just trying to convert strings to numbers, you can use the more specialised pd.to_numeric() method, which has an errors="coerce" argument. This will then turn what it can into a number and make the rest missing.

```
display(pd.to_numeric(sdemo, errors="coerce"))
```

```
0    1.0
1    NaN
```

```
2    4.0
3    NaN
dtype: float64
```

2.2.3 Changing `Series` values I: Arithmetic operators

You might have noticed in the section above that I added the number 2 to the `Series` in order to show how it works differently with a `Series` of numbers and a `Series` of strings. With a `Series` you can change the values using the standard arithmetic operators. These operators treat the `Series` like a collection of values and will do something to each value in turn. For example, if you say `Series + 1` it will add one to each value in the `Series`. If the `Series` is not just numbers (and valid) it will throw an error. `Series + "A"` will append A to each value in the `Series` if they are characters and throw an error otherwise.

```python
import numpy as np

ser1 = pd.Series([1,np.nan,7])
display(ser1)
```

```
0    1.0
1    NaN
2    7.0
dtype: float64
```

```python
display(ser1*2)
```

```
0     4.0
1     NaN
2    28.0
dtype: float64
```

```python
display(ser1-4)
```

```
0    -2.0
1     NaN
2    10.0
dtype: float64
```

```python
ser2 = pd.Series(["Kermit", "Piggy", "Fozzie"])
display(ser2 + " the Muppet")
```

```
0    Kermit the Muppet
1     Piggy the Muppet
2    Fozzie the Muppet
dtype: object
```

2.2.4 Changing `Series` Values II: Recoding values using `map`

A really common task in social statistics is to recode values. For example, you might have a list of text values (such as Strongly Agree, Agree, Disagree, etc.) that you want to turn into numbers. You might have a text entry form that you want to recode into more manageable categories. To recode these you can create a dictionary of values and then `map` those values on to your `Series`. So you would use the syntax `<Series>.map(dict_of_values)`.

A scenario that I encountered in a data cleaning exercise had to do just this. We asked people to label the gender of persons behind Twitter accounts. They were all politicians seeking election to be a Member of Parliament in the UK, so there was no need to create a not a person flag. At the time none of the candidates self-identified as non-binary. Even so, the coders gave six different ways of writing what was essentially male and female. In the original data we had over 2000 labels. But I have shortened them to 14 rows to show this example.

```
gender_series = pd.Series(['Male', 'Man', 'Male (sex)', 'Woman', 'Female',
                'Female ', 'Female ', 'Male', 'Male', 'Woman',
                'Female', 'Man', 'Male', 'Woman'])

print(len(gender_series))
print(gender_series.unique())
```

```
14
['Male' 'Man' 'Male (sex)' 'Woman' 'Female' 'Female ']
```

To recode the data, I first did a `unique()`, and then typed by hand the dictionary using those unique values. You can see that dictionary below. One thing that tripped us up was that someone had used `"Female "` with that trailing space. Notice that I did *not* go into the existing data and remove the space. I include that in my mapping so that if I have to do it again from raw data I won't skip over that case. Here's the resulting dictionary:

```
gender_recode_dict = {"Male":"M",
                # "Man":"M", # I'm leaving this out to show what happens
                "Male (sex)": "M",
                "Woman":"F",
                "Female":"F",
                "Female ":"F" }
```

Then to recode the values in the `Series`, we can now use `map` to replace the values in the old `Series` with the desired values in the new `Series`. Note that if the map does not contain a value in the old `Series`, then those values will not be included in the new `Series`. So above where I commented out `"Man"` this means that wherever we saw `"Man"` in the original `Series`, we now have NaN values. Uncomment that line and compare your results to the results below.

```
gender_recode = gender_series.map(gender_recode_dict)
gender_recode.value_counts(dropna = False)
```

```
F      7
M      5
NaN    2
dtype: int64
```

2.2.5 Changing `Series` values III: Defining your own mapping

In the above example, map() took in a dictionary and then mapped the keys found in the
Series to the values found in the dictionary. But what if you do not know the values? Or
rather, you want to calculate the values on the fly using the elements in the Series? This is
where lambda comes in.

As a trivial example, we might want to take every element in a Series of characters and
transform them into lower case. Using a dictionary would get really tedious. Here's a truncated example:

```
schars = pd.Series(["A","B","C"])
schars_lower = schars.map({"A":"a","B":"b","C":"c"})
display(schars_lower)
```

```
0    a
1    b
2    c
dtype: object
```

It would be really unpleasant to have to write *all* of the letters just to map them. In a string
we can use the <s>.lower() method:

```
"A".lower()
```

```
'a'
```

We can do this in a Series too using lambda. A lambda function (or an 'anonymous function') in programming is a function without a name. In Python, where a function takes in
any number of parameters and begins with def <function_name>():, lambda can take
parameters. So you can say lambda <var>: <var>.lower(). Inserting that code inside a
map method and then <var> will refer to every row one after the other:

```
schars = pd.Series(["A","B","C"])
schars.map(lambda x: x.lower())
```

```
0    a
1    b
2    c
dtype: object
```

You might be wondering why we do this complicated stuff when we have a for loop. Can
we not just loop over all the rows? We can, but it is slower and not recommended if you can

avoid it. It also makes the syntax really complicated as we have to get each value from the Series, change the value, then insert that back in the Series. Further, mapping benefits from efficiencies in how pandas calculates values for the entire Series.

Using functions inside `lambda`

Sometimes you want to do more than a single operation. Then you can define those details in a named function. Then use map() to call that named function. If your function only takes one argument (the value that map passes to the function), then the syntax looks like this:

```
def transformWord(word):
    return word[0].lower()

schars = pd.Series(["Alpha","Bravo","Charlie"])
new_series = schars.map(transformWord)
display(new_series)


0    a
1    b
2    c
dtype: object
```

In the example above, transformWord only had a single parameter (word). In this case, whatever map passed on from the Series would be sent to transformWord() as the word argument. So thus we could just say <Series>.map(transformWord). However, if we want to pass in multiple arguments, we can use lambda. Observe below how we use lambda to indicate which argument was the value passed from map() and which were other values that we pass on to the function. In this case, there's a wholeWord parameter. The default argument is False. But we can send wholeWord=True as well as each word from our Series inside a map() statement:

```
def transformWord(word,wholeWord=False):
    if wholeWord:
        return word.lower()
    else:
        return word[0].lower()

new_series = schars.map(lambda x: transformWord(x, wholeWord=True))
display(new_series)

0        alpha
1        bravo
2      charlie
dtype: object
```

 **Summary**

The Series is a very powerful tool for manipulating data. Like a list, it has ordered values. Like a dictionary, the values can be accessed by key (or in this case, by 'index'). I first showed how to create a Series using a list and a dictionary. I then demonstrated how to add and delete values. I demonstrated unique(), value_counts(), and map() as powerful tools for manipulating a Series.

In the next chapter, we will look at DataFrame objects. These are tables of data with rows and columns. Each column is treated like a Series. Thus, you will discover that many of the operations that we have learned for the Series directly apply to the DataFrame. We will wait until the DataFrame to recommend some further reading on this topic.

 Extensions and reflections

It is really important to practise the operations on Series. If you go to the page for this book on GitHub you will see some example exercises. To get you started here are some things you might want to practise:

- Adding data to a Series. Write a list of names of your three closest friends. Then write a second list of the names of three friends you have not seen in a while. Use the Series to combine these two lists.
- Do the above, but instead of a list, use a dictionary with name and days since you last spoke to that person. So the names of your friends become the index of the Series and the value is a guesstimate of the number of days since you last spoke. Combine the two Series (closest_friends and not_seen_friends) into one and get the average number of days.
- Try to define a function that you can use in a lambda statement. Here's a contrived example: Write a Series of your favourite foods. Then write a function that takes a string and returns only vowels. Use that inside the lambda to get a new Series of only the vowels for these words. Use this as the ridiculous new way to pronounce your food. Scare your friends and confuse your family at dinner!

3
THE DATAFRAME: PYTHON'S TABULAR FORMAT

Learning goals

- Use a `DataFrame` to store data in a row and column format
- Get data into a `DataFrame` from a list, dictionary, or `Series`
- Get data from a `DataFrame` as a column, row, or single cell
- Change a `DataFrame` by adding a column of data
- Understand how to use `map`, `apply`, and `applymap` to calculate things per column, across columns, and for the entire `DataFrame`
- See how `numpy` stores data in an array
- Distinguish between an array of numbers and a `DataFrame`.

 ## From the `Series` to the `DataFrame`

A `Series` is a flexible tool for managing a single distribution with an index. The index can be either the default sequence of numbers starting from 0, or it can be a list of labels. If we have two `Series`, each with the same index, we can combine them together. This will create a `DataFrame`. Depending on the nature of the research, we will either be building a `DataFrame` by merging together `Series` one by one or we will import a `DataFrame` from another context, be it a text file, a webpage, or some other format. In this section, we will be building small `DataFrame` objects from scratch in order to demonstrate their features and highlight the similarities and differences to these operations when done on a `Series`. Later we will show how to create a `DataFrame` from existing file formats.

For the uninitiated, you might wonder what is the advantage of using `DataFrame` objects over merely typing data into Excel or a similar spreadsheet program. It should become evident through working with data that while spreadsheets have a very low fixed cost (since you just load them up and start typing in data), they have a very high marginal cost, since every operation and new data point can involve lots of clicking, saving, and typing. We want to avoid marginal costs (where each new row or line of data takes up our time) so that we can more effectively scale from three or four rows up to three or four thousand (or million) rows. Beyond efficiency is a concern about robustness. Sometimes in Excel it is tempting to just change a column or a value with the keyboard and mouse. Here we want to caution against that. Everything you do from the raw data should be documented and replicable. This is much easier when all changes to the raw data are made in code.

A `DataFrame` with one column of data looks very similar to a `Series`. However, the `DataFrame` comes with some extra features. Not the least of which is that when you `display()` a `DataFrame`, you get a nice-looking HTML-formatted table. Observe the difference below:

```
import pandas as pd

smuppet = pd.Series({"Kermit":"frog",
                     "Fozzie":"bear",
                     "Miss Piggy":"pig"})
display(smuppet)
```

```
Kermit          frog
Fozzie          bear
Miss Piggy       pig
dtype: object
```

```
muppet_df = pd.DataFrame(smuppet)
```

```
display(muppet_df)
```

	0
Kermit	frog
Fozzie	bear
Miss Piggy	pig

In the output directly in Jupyter, the second display command had the words 'Kermit', 'Fozzie', and 'Miss Piggy' in bold with some text shading. This is a feature of Jupyter that means we can view a `DataFrame` as a rich table much like what you would see in Microsoft Excel with a regular body text font. Viewing such tables in monospaced text (as what happens when we display a `Series`) makes them harder to read. For this book I have exported these tables to LaTeX. They look similar to running `print(<DataFrame>.style.to_latex(hrules=True))` instead of `display(<DataFrame>)` with some additional typesetting.

You might also notice that above `"frog"` in the table is the number 0. This is just the index of that column since we did not name the column. In our case we have two options. We can name the `Series`, which will propagate the name to the `DataFrame`, or we can just name the columns in the `DataFrame`. Observe the same code, but this time we will name the `Series` first. Then below that we will change the name of the `DataFrame` column to something else:

```
smuppet = pd.Series({"Kermit":"frog",
                     "Fozzie":"bear",
                     "Miss Piggy":"pig"},
                    name="MuppetType")
```

```
muppet_df = pd.DataFrame(smuppet)
```

```
display(muppet_df)
```

	MuppetType
Kermit	frog
Fozzie	bear
Miss Piggy	pig

```
muppet_df.columns = ["ExampleNameChange"]
```

```
display(muppet_df)
```

	ExampleNameChange
Kermit	frog
Fozzie	bear
Miss Piggy	pig

A `DataFrame` has columns and an index. These you can query and treat as objects in their own right. So `muppet_df.columns` can be treated like a `list`. As such we can send it a new list to replace the names as long as the length is the same. We can do the same for the index, much as how we were able to replace the index with a `Series`. Remember you can access it simply through `<df>.index` (there's no `()` at the end, since we are just requesting an object that represents the `DataFrame`, not running a method *on* the `DataFrame`).

A `DataFrame` with multiple columns

Up to this point we have only seen `DataFrame` objects that look like nicely formatted `Series`. However, it is important for us to be able to compare multiple columns of data. To get these multiple columns of data, here are a few approaches:

1   From a list of lists (or equivalently, an array)
2   From a dictionary where the keys are indices (or column names) and the values are lists of data
3   By adding a new `Series` to an existing `DataFrame`.

These different ways of building a `DataFrame` will form the basis of a great deal of your work in data science. As you will see later, data comes in a variety of formats, but we need to transform it into a consistent and workable format for analysis. Thus, getting this data into a `DataFrame` will be of central importance. Although there are many possible ways to create a `DataFrame`, they essentially are variants on these three: from a list of lists, from an existing `DataFrame` or `Series`, and from a dictionary. `pandas` has a variety of built-in methods to help simplify the importation of data in other formats such as Excel, but in the end it tends to be an abstraction built atop these basics. These are covered in the next chapter on file types.

To create a multi-column `DataFrame` we will continue to use information about some of the Muppets we have already mentioned. This time, in addition to the 'type of Muppet', we will add a column about their first appearance as well as well as their gender.

3.2.1 From a list of lists

The way to create this data depends largely on how the data was initially formatted. For example, in a list of lists, it might look something like this:

```
muppet_list = [["Kermit", "frog", 1955, "male"],
               ["Miss Piggy", "pig", 1974, "female"],
               ["Fozzie", "bear", 1976, "male"]]
muppet_df = pd.DataFrame(muppet_list)
display(muppet_df)
```

THE DATAFRAME 51

	0	1	2	3
0	Kermit	frog	1955	male
1	Miss Piggy	pig	1974	female
2	Fozzie	bear	1976	male

```
muppet_df.columns = ['Name','Species','FirstAppearance','Gender']
display(muppet_df)
```

	Name	Species	FirstAppearance	Gender
0	Kermit	frog	1955	male
1	Miss Piggy	pig	1974	female
2	Fozzie	bear	1976	male

The column names were not in the original list so we added those above. But what about setting the first row (the Muppet name) as the index? There are a number of ways to do this. Here I use DataFrame.set_index() to make one of the existing columns the index. Observe:

```
muppet_df.set_index("Name", inplace=True)
display(muppet_df)
```

	Species	FirstAppearance	Gender
Name			
Kermit	frog	1955	male
Miss Piggy	pig	1974	female
Fozzie	bear	1976	male

Notice that Name above Kermit is now on a different line? That's because the index itself can have a name. In this case the column was named Name so that's now our index name. Index names can be useful if you have complex nested data. Later when we use DateTime as the index, we can have a Year index and a Month index within each year.

3.2.2 From a dictionary

To create a DataFrame from a dictionary object we can use the from_dict() method rather than just pd.DataFrame(dict). This has a few additional options that are relevant and enable us to determine whether the dictionary keys go in the rows as indices or in the columns as variable names.

```
muppet_df = pd.DataFrame.from_dict({"Kermit":"frog",
                                    "Fozzie":"bear",
                                    "Janice":"hippy"},
                                   orient="index")
```

```
display(muppet_df)
```

	0
Kermit	frog
Fozzie	bear
Janice	hippy

That was using only one column. If you have a collection for each row, then you can load it using the following syntax. Notice how it automatically turns the key into the index.

```
muppet_dict = {"Kermit": ["frog",1955,"Male"],
               "Miss Piggy":["pig", 1974, "Female"],
               "Gonzo": ["unknown", 1970, "Male"]}
```

```
muppet_df = pd.DataFrame.from_dict(muppet_dict,
                                   orient="index",
                                   columns=["species",
                                            "firstappearance",
                                            "gender"])
```

```
display(muppet_df)
```

	species	firstappearance	gender
Kermit	frog	1955	Male
Miss Piggy	pig	1974	Female
Gonzo	unknown	1970	Male

One new argument here is `orient="index"`. This means that the keys of the dictionary will be the indices for the rows. Otherwise, the dictionary would be treated in the other direction. Notice how below we use the `orient="columns"` argument and this makes the `DataFrame` along the other axis.

```
muppet_df_cols = pd.DataFrame.from_dict(muppet_dict,
                                        orient="columns")
```

```
display(muppet_df_cols)
```

	Kermit	Miss Piggy	Gonzo
0	frog	pig	unknown
1	1955	1974	1970
2	Male	Female	Male

With `orient="columns"` it makes `Kermit`, `Piggy`, and `Gonzo` the columns. Sometimes this is the behaviour we want, but not here. Remember, generally speaking, *cases in rows and variables in columns*. In the next chapter we will focus on a variety of data types that you can convert into a `DataFrame`: these include JSON, XML, CSV, and Excel data.

 ## Getting data from a `DataFrame`: Querying, masking, and slicing

3.3.1 Getting data about the `DataFrame` itself

To begin learning about a `DataFrame`, you will probably be interested in how many rows or columns it has. The most lightweight way to do this is probably `len(df)`, which will report the number of rows (or cases). The second simplest way might be to use `df.shape` which will report the number of cases and the number of variables. A more involved way is to use `df.info()` to get a report on the columns as variables, including their type and number of missing values. Finally, if you are interested in some at-a-glance descriptive statistics about the numerical variables in the `DataFrame`, you can use `df.describe()`.

```
print( f"The number of cases in the DataFrame is {len(muppet_df)}")
print( f"The shape of the DataFrame is {muppet_df.shape}",end="\n\n")
print(muppet_df.info(),end="\n\n")
print(muppet_df.describe())
```

```
The number of cases In the DataFrame is 3
The shape of the DataFrame is (3, 3)

<class 'pandas.core.frame.DataFrame'>
Index: 3 entries, Kermit to Gonzo
Data columns (total 3 columns):
 #   Column           Non-Null Count   Dtype
---  ------           --------------   -----
 0   species          3 non-null       object
 1   firstappearance  3 non-null       int64
 2   gender           3 non-null       object
dtypes: int64(1), object(2)
memory usage: 96.0+ bytes
None


       firstappearance
count         3.000000
mean       1966.333333
std          10.016653
min        1955.000000
25%        1962.500000
50%        1970.000000
75%        1972.000000
max        1974.000000
```

3.3.2 Returning a single row or column

To return an entire DataFrame you simply call it by name. In our example, muppet_df will return the entire DataFrame. To get a column in the data, it is like querying a list or a dictionary: you use the square brackets [and]. So if your DataFrame has a column called species, then the syntax muppet_df["species"] will return the respective column as a Series.

It turns out that the reason this works is because querying by column is the default *indexer* for a DataFrame. When you use <DataFrame>[*] you are using an indexer, as opposed to using <DataFrame>(*), which is a method.

There are different kinds of indexers for a DataFrame to accomplish different goals. Two in particular are worth considering here. These are the indexers that will return a row instead of a column. Recall that each row will have both a label and a position from the initial (zeroth) row to the last. Accordingly, one of the indexers will index by row label and the other by row position.

- **df[<col_label> or <col_indexpos>]** returns a column based on either the number of the column or the label of the column. **muppet_df["species"]** would then return the column for species. In this example, so would **muppet_df[0]**. So it certainly pays not to mix strings and integer numbers for column labels or indices.
- **df.loc[<row_label>]** returns a row based on the label of the row in the index. By default, the index is simply a list of sequential numbers, but that is merely the default. It could be anything. In our example it is the name of the Muppet. Thus, **muppet_df.loc["Gonzo"]** should return the row labelled **Gonzo** in the index.
- **df.iloc[<row_indexpos>]** returns a row based on the position of the row in the sequence of rows in the **DataFrame**. Since **Gonzo** is in position 2 (as Python indexes from 0), **muppet_df.iloc[2]** should return the **Gonzo** row.
- *Tip*: The indexer starts with **l** in **loc** for label and starts with **i** in **iloc** for index position.

```
display(muppet_df["species"])

Kermit              frog
Miss Piggy           pig
Gonzo            unknown
Name: species, dtype: object

display(muppet_df.loc["Kermit"])

species            frog
firstappearance    1955
gender             Male
Name: Kermit, dtype: object

display(muppet_df.iloc[2])

species         unknown
firstappearance    1970
gender             Male
Name: Gonzo, dtype: object
```

Use this opportunity to practise retrieving a row or a column. Try selecting different rows or columns with both numbers and labels.

3.3.3 Returning multiple columns

You can return multiple columns at once. This is handy when you want to filter and merge data. As a motivating example, imagine that you download data from Reddit and insert it into a table. It will have a ton of extraneous columns. The data you want to study might be a small subset of what is available. Asking for the columns you want and building your dataset from there is a prudent way to keep focused on a research question.

To ask for multiple columns, you must ask for them as a collection *inside* the indexer. This means it typically looks like square brackets inside square brackets. For example, asking for `firstappearance` and `species` in the same query would be as `muppet_df[["firstappearance","species"]]`. Whatever order you ask for them is the order they will be in the resulting `DataFrame`.

```
display(muppet_df[["firstappearance","species"]])
```

	firstappearance	species
Kermit	1955	frog
Miss Piggy	1974	pig
Gonzo	1970	unknown

3.3.4 Returning a single element

Getting a single element of a `DataFrame` is an extension of what we just did. Now that we have a `Series` (the row), we can then query for one element of that row.

Notice that when we queried for `.loc["Gonzo"]`, it returned a `Series` corresponding to Gonzo's row in the `DataFrame`. Since this `Series` has labelled indices (corresponding to column labels in the table) we can then use these labels to get one element from Gonzo's row. We can also use position in the `Series`, which I will show afterwards.

To get the year of Gonzo's first appearance, we can chain together `muppet_df.loc["Gonzo"]` with `["firstappearance"]`. This will then look like `muppet_df.loc["Gonzo"]["firstappearance"]`. Luckily, `pandas` provides a little syntactic sugar, so that you can put row then column in the same indexer: `muppet_df.loc["Gonzo","firstappearance"]`. Since `Gonzo` was in index position 2 and `firstappearance` is in column position 1, we could also write `muppet_df.iloc[2,1]`. Note that we write `iloc` and not simply `loc` since we are using index position.

You might be wondering now about whether you can use `muppet_df["firstappearance"]` first to get the entire column and then find `Gonzo` in that column. You sure can; however, it is worth pointing out that this is considered bad form. Generally speaking, go rows first. It is for this reason that while you can indeed query `muppet_df["firstappearance"]["Gonzo"]`, you can neither use the syntactic sugar of `muppet_df["firstappearance","Gonzo"]` nor `muppet_df[1,2]`. It is here that we are reminded that a `DataFrame` is not considered a completely symmetric data structure. Rather, rows are for cases and columns are for variables, and much of the logic of how to query the DataFrame falls from this distinction. Observe below how querying it in three different ways leads to considerably different speeds. The way with the syntactic sugar is also the most efficient.

```
# Let's get Piggy's year of first appearance:
%timeit x = muppet_df.loc["Miss Piggy","firstappearance"]
%timeit x = muppet_df.loc["Miss Piggy"]["firstappearance"]
%timeit x = muppet_df.iloc[1][1]
```

```
5.75 µs ± 71.5 ns per loop (mean ± std. dev. of 7 runs, 100,000 loops each)
45.2 µs ± 1.15 µs per loop (mean ± std. dev. of 7 runs, 10,000 loops each)
39.1 µs ± 622 ns per loop (mean ± std. dev. of 7 runs, 10,000 loops each)
```

3.3.5 Returning a slice of data

The last way of returning data that we should cover is a mask or slice. Slices and masks are incredibly useful for answering questions about data. They allow us powerful ways to filter the data in a DataFrame.

Slicing by position

You can use the colon (:) to indicate a range of elements. For example, muppet_df.iloc[2:] will get all the rows from position 2 onward. Putting a number after the column would be the position up to, but not including. So muppet_df.iloc[:2] will get all the rows up to but not including Gonzo in position 2.

```
display(muppet_df.iloc[:2])
```

	species	firstappearance	gender
Kermit	frog	1955	Male
Miss Piggy	pig	1974	Female

Boolean slicing (mask)

Recall in Chapter 2 we could filter a Series using a Boolean indexer. A DataFrame works the same way. You can evaluate against a column of data and it will return the rows that fit the criteria. So, in our table we could ask for Muppets that are male or Muppets that first appeared after 1967. This means we first focus on a column and ask whether that column meets some criteria. This becomes a Series of true or false statements. If the row corresponds to a true statement, it is kept. Observe:

```
display(muppet_df["firstappearance"] > 1967)
```

```
Kermit          False
Miss Piggy      True
Gonzo           True
```

```
Name: firstappearance, dtype: bool
```

And here we take the Boolean `Series` and use it as an indexer:

```
display(muppet_df[muppet_df["firstappearance"] > 1967])
```

	species	firstappearance	gender
Miss Piggy	pig	1974	Female
Gonzo	unknown	1970	Male

The Boolean query itself just returned a `Series` of `True`/`False` objects with an index that corresponds to the `DataFrame`. We then pipe this into an indexer and out come only the rows that were true: Miss Piggy, who first appeared in 1974, and Gonzo, who first appeared in 1970.

 ## Changing data at different scales

3.4.1 Adding data to an existing `DataFrame`

It is very common to attach new data to a `DataFrame`. You might be recoding a variable, doing some calculation, or just parsing the text that is already there. For example, since we have the year of the Muppet's first appearance, we could create a new column for 'decade of first appearance' by doing some calculation on that year value. If we want to link two `DataFrame` objects together, this is slightly more tricky and will be covered later in Chapter 5 on merging.

By column

It is pretty easy to add a single column to an existing `DataFrame`. To illustrate this, we will start with the simple `DataFrame` that has the Muppet name as the index and the type of character as a single column. Then we will add the year of first appearance as an example of how we can add a `Series`. Using `firstappearance`, we will calculate and insert into the `DataFrame` as `firstdecade` using data from an existing column.

```
muppet_df = pd.DataFrame.from_dict({"Kermit":"frog",
                                     "Miss Piggy":"pig",
                                     "Gonzo":"unknown"},
                                    orient="index",
                                    columns=["species"])

muppet_year = pd.Series({"Gonzo":1970,
                         "Kermit":1955,
                         "Miss Piggy":1974})

muppet_df["firstappearance"] = muppet_year
muppet_df["firstdecade"] = (muppet_df["firstappearance"] // 10) * 10

display(muppet_df)
```

	species	firstappearance	firstdecade
Kermit	frog	1955	1950
Miss Piggy	pig	1974	1970
Gonzo	unknown	1970	1970

One of the nice things about ensuring that cases are in the rows and variables in the columns is that it makes it easy to add new variables. Also, pandas can be pretty clever about linking the data. Notice above that the muppet_year dictionary had Gonzo first, but the DataFrame had Kermit first? Since Gonzo was in the *index* for both the existing DataFrame and the new Series, when they were merged the program was able to link the data together. In this case we can think of Gonzo's name as the *key* that links the data.

Did you also notice that we converted the dictionary to a Series first? Go back and try just adding the dictionary directly; it does not work correctly. Instead, it just adds the keys as a list and they are in the wrong order:

```
muppet_df_bad = pd.DataFrame.from_dict({"Kermit":"frog",
                                        "Miss Piggy":"pig",
                                        "Gonzo":"unknown"},
                                        orient="index",
                                        columns=["species"])

muppet_df_bad["firstappearance"] = {"Gonzo":1970,
                                    "Kermit":1955,
                                    "Miss Piggy":1974}

display(muppet_df_bad)
```

	species	firstappearance
Kermit	frog	Gonzo
Miss Piggy	pig	Kermit
Gonzo	unknown	Miss Piggy

Series and dictionaries have keys, but lists do not. You can actually add a list to a DataFrame, but it will be inserted in the order in the list. Observe:

```
muppet_gender = ["male","female","male"]

muppet_df["gender"] = muppet_gender

display(muppet_df)
```

	species	firstappearance	firstdecade	gender
Kermit	frog	1955	1950	male
Miss Piggy	pig	1974	1970	female
Gonzo	unknown	1970	1970	male

By row

Adding data by row is a little trickier than adding it by column, since pandas is set up to add data in columns by default. To add a row of data you need to use a slightly different syntax than for adding a column.

Generally, we do not want to continually add data as rows in pandas. One reason is that it creates and allocates memory to the computer every time we do this. So if you are using a loop to add rows to a DataFrame, you're actually creating a DataFrame of length $n + 1$ every time you iterate through – this will really slow down your code!

If you want to add a single row, you can do this using a label index (.loc). Just as you could create a column with df[<col>], you can create a row with df.loc[<indexlabel>].

```
muppet_df = pd.DataFrame.from_dict({"Kermit": "frog",
                                    "Miss Piggy": "pig",
                                    "Gonzo": "unknown"},
                                    orient="index",
                                    columns=["species"])

muppet_df.loc["Scooter"] = ["muppet"]

display(muppet_df)
```

	species
Kermit	frog
Miss Piggy	pig
Gonzo	unknown
Scooter	muppet

You cannot do this using a positional index, however, as this will throw an IndexError. While this might seem arbitrary, it's actually pretty consistent with how we add data to lists and dictionaries. When we add data to lists we append it, and then it has a position. You can have a list ll = ["a","b","c"]. If you try to add an element by running ll[3] = "d", Python will throw an error. However, if you go ll.append("d"), then you can access it via ll[3].

By contrast, if you have a dictionary dd = {"a":1, "b":2} and then if you say dd["c"] = 3 it will assign a value of 3 to the key of "c". It's the same with adding an entry to a DataFrame. See some examples of how this works below:

```
try:
    muppet_df.iloc[4] = ["Generic Muppet"]
    display(muppet_df)
except IndexError:
    print("You needed to have this index already in the DataFrame.")
```

```
You needed to have this index already in the DataFrame.
```

```
try:
    muppet_df.iloc[2] = ["whatever"]
    display(muppet_df)
except IndexError:
    print("You needed to have this index already in the DataFrame.")
```

	species
Kermit	frog
Miss Piggy	pig
Gonzo	whatever
Scooter	muppet

So `<df>.iloc` works like a list and you cannot create a new row by its position. As you may have guessed, `<df>.loc` works like a dictionary and you *can* create a new row by its index (like a key).

```
muppet_df.loc["Fozzie"] = ["bear"]
display(muppet_df)
```

	species
Kermit	frog
Miss Piggy	pig
Gonzo	whatever
Scooter	muppet
Fozzie	bear

Notice in these cases we said `muppet_df.loc["Fozzie"]` = `["bear"]` and not `muppet_df.loc["Fozzie"]` = `"bear"`. The first column contains strings but the row itself is a list of values. We just happen to only have one column in this example, so our row is `["bear"]`.

3.4.2 Adding one `DataFrame` to another

Every time you add a new index to a `DataFrame`, you are actually creating a new `DataFrame` with a length $n + 1$. For simple one-off changes this might not be an issue. However, in the case of building large data structures, namely when processing large volumes of data, you really want to instantiate `DataFrame` objects as rarely as possible.

pandas steers us towards this behaviour in the same way it does for the `Series`. In earlier versions of pandas (and perhaps online), you might see people use `<df>.append(<sec-ond_df>)`. This turns out to be very inefficient and so they are getting rid of this approach. Instead, just like with a `Series`, you can create a collection of `DataFrame` objects, such as a list, and call `pd.concat([<list_of_dfs>])`. Observe how we concatenate below.

```
df1 = pd.DataFrame({"col1":[0,1],"col2":["A","C"]})
display(df1)
```

	col1	col2
0	0	A
1	1	C

```
df2 = pd.DataFrame({"col1":[2,5],"col2":["A","B"]})
display(df2)
```

	col1	col2
0	2	A
1	5	B

```
new_df = pd.concat([df1,df2])
display(new_df)
```

	col1	col2
0	0	A
1	1	C
0	2	A
1	5	B

This small example hides a lot of complexity that we will want to tame to be proficient at wrangling data, which itself is a core skill for computational social science. For example, notice that the concatenated data did not update its index. Concatenation is featured more at the beginning of Chapter 5.

3.4.3 Changing a column or the entire `DataFrame`: `apply`, `map`, and `applymap`

We have already seen how to transform data in a series using `map()`. This command does something to every element in the `Series`. Now we can do this for the entire `DataFrame` as well, either on a per row or per column basis, or for literally every element in the `DataFrame`. Let's have a look below at some imaginary ratings for imaginary movies. We will use these to calculate some numbers either by row, by column, or for the entire table at once.

In the code below, I used a little shortcut. Instead of parsing the data, which is represented as CSV, I simply tell the program to treat a string *as if* it is coming from a file using a method called `StringIO`. Later, when we are reading from files, this will not be necessary. There we will use `pd.read_csv(<path_to_file>)` instead. In our example below, every moviegoer saw and rated the same four movies. This is an unrealistic expectation, but it's for illustration purposes.

```
import pandas as pd
from io import StringIO

movies = '''user,Ghosts of Hidden Valley,The Perspex Event,Stinker\'s Bad
Day,These Girls
user1,4,5,2,2.5
user2,3,3.5,4.5,1
user3,2,4,3,4
user4,4,4.5,2,4'''

movie_df = pd.read_csv(StringIO(movies),index_col=0)

display(movie_df)
```

	Ghosts of Hidden Valley	The Perspex Event	Stinker's Bad Day	These Girls
user				
user1	4	5.000000	2.000000	2.500000
user2	3	3.500000	4.500000	1.000000
user3	2	4.000000	3.000000	4.000000
user4	4	4.500000	2.000000	4.000000

Using `map()`

We have already seen in Section 2.2.4 how to use `map` on a `Series`. This returns a new value for each element in a `Series`. When using this on a `DataFrame`, we normally will select a specific `Series` from that `DataFrame` and then use `map` to do something with the values of that `Series`. So where before we saw `<Series>.map(...)`, seeing `<DataFrame>[<Series>].map(...)` is essentially the same thing. This includes the use of `lambda`, which we will see again regularly throughout this book. Below I show how to take a column of ratings and then make them out of 100 instead of out of 5.

```
movie_df["These Girls"].map(lambda x: x/5*100)
```

```
user
user1    50.0
user2    20.0
user3    80.0
user4    80.0
Name: These Girls, dtype: float64
```

Using `apply()`

The movie rating scale is 1 to 5, but let's say we want get a summary for each of the movies or each of the users. For this we can use `apply` which returns one element per `Series`. Below I show how to get the minimum value for each column.

```
movie_df.apply(min)
```

```
Ghosts of Hidden Valley    2.0
The Perspex Event          3.5
Stinker's Bad Day          2.0
These Girls                1.0
dtype: float64
```

```
# movie_df.apply(mean) # This will fail, recall discussion last chapter
print(movie_df.apply(lambda score: score.mean())) # This will succeed.
```

```
Ghosts of Hidden Valley    3.250
The Perspex Event          4.250
Stinker's Bad Day          2.875
These Girls                2.875
dtype: float64
```

Whereas `map` would take a `Series` and pass one row at a time into `lambda`, `apply` takes a `DataFrame` and passes one `Series` at a time to `lambda`. By default `apply` will pass each column as a `Series` one by one. To use rows instead, include the parameter `axis=1`. The default is `axis=0` to go columnwise. For example, with our example `DataFrame`, instead of asking for an aggregate score by movie (as we did above), we can ask for an aggregate score by user, such as the users' highest and lowest ratings.

```
movie_df.apply(lambda x: (x.min(), x.max()),axis=1)
```

```
user
user1    (2.0, 5.0)
user2    (1.0, 4.5)
user3    (2.0, 4.0)
user4    (2.0, 4.5)
dtype: object
```

Using `applymap()`

Imagine you want to do something to every element of the `DataFrame` rather than every column. This is where we combine the every-element-of-a-`Series` of `map` with the every-`Series`-of-a-`DataFrame` from `apply`. Combined they make `applymap`. Imagine we want to compare these ratings to the scores from popular rating service MetaCritic, which produces scores out of 100. To rescale each score so that it goes from 0 to 100, we can divide it by 0.05

(or divide it by 5 and multiply it by 100). Note that this assumes the score out of 5 could be 0 as well as 1 or 2.

```
display(movie_df.applymap(lambda x: int(x/0.05)))
```

	Ghosts of Hidden Valley	The Perspex Event	Stinker's Bad Day	These Girls
user				
user1	80	100	40	50
user2	60	70	90	20
user3	40	80	60	80
user4	80	90	40	80

Now you can chain these approaches together with other methods such as the slicing that we saw earlier.

If we slice using `iloc`, that can get us a range of users, such as the first two using `[:2]`. Then when we get the averages we will only get the averages calculated using the first two users.

```
movie_df.iloc[0:2].apply(lambda x: x.mean())
```

```
Ghosts of Hidden Valley    3.50
The Perspex Event          4.25
Stinker's Bad Day          3.25
These Girls                1.75
dtype: float64
```

Since `apply` works column-by-column by default, when we use `axis=1` we will get the average *user* score for the first two users rather than the average *movie* score for the first two users.

```
movie_df.iloc[0:2].apply(lambda x: x.mean(), axis=1)
```

```
user
user1    3.375
user2    3.000
dtype: float64
```

There are a huge number of ways to slice, summarise, and transform the data of a `DataFrame`. I find I continually return to this topic since it is not always intuitive. It is for this reason that I wrote it out in such detail. I hope that some repeat readings and practice exercises can help you become increasingly fluent in how to wrangle data with `DataFrame` objects.

Summarising `map()`, `apply()`, and `applymap()`

- **`map()`:** for a `Series`, either by itself or returned from a `DataFrame`, such as `df["var"]`. It will use each row as input and pass the value of that row to whatever is in the `map()` statement. The result returned is a `Series` as output.

- **apply()**: for a DataFrame. It will use each Series as input and pass the Series to the apply() statement. It will return a Series as output, with one element for each column (or row, with axis=1) in the DataFrame.
- **applymap()**: for a DataFrame. It will use each element in the DataFrame as input and return a DataFrame of equivalent dimension, with each element transformed according to whatever is in the applymap() statement.

Summarising lambda versus a named function

- *Function*: this is a standalone way of expressing how to take an input and perform some calculation on it, usually returning some output. It has a def <name>(args): return structure.
- *lambda*: an anonymous function. It doesn't have a name and will simply return whatever is performed after the colon. The only parameter is the variable after lambda commonly denoted as x. It has a lambda x: <do something to x> structure.
- *Implicit arguments*: for inside a map, apply, or applymap statement. If you want to use a function and it only takes one required argument, you don't need to use (lambda x: func(x)) inside the statement, you can just say (func).

3.4.4 Deep versus shallow copies

When we ask for data from Python, sometimes it will give us a 'view' of the original data. For example, when we create a mask for a DataFrame we are creating a view of the original data – this is called a 'shallow copy'. By contrast, sometimes Python will copy the data to a new location and then return that newly copied data – this is a 'deep copy'. Understanding when this happens can help address two issues we will encounter when we have to manage larger datasets:

1 Deep copies need their own memory space in the computer since they are now completely different DataFrame objects.
2 Altering or deleting data can lead to mishaps whereby changing data on a subset or copy of the data actually changes the original data.
3 Altering can also lead to accidents or warnings when you try to change the original data but actually end up working on a copy.

See what happens in the following code when we try to change the value of Gonzo's species from whatever to weirdo. Note that his actual species is contentious as per his entry on the Muppet Wiki (https://muppet.fandom.com/wiki/Gonzo).

```
# Reinitialise the data
muppet_dict = {"Kermit": ["frog",1955, "Male"],
               "Miss Piggy":["pig", 1974, "Female"],
               "Gonzo": ["unknown", 1970, "Male"]}

muppet_df = pd.DataFrame.from_dict(muppet_dict,
                                   orient="index")

muppet_df.columns=["species","firstappearance","gender"]
display(muppet_df)
```

	species	firstappearance	gender
Kermit	frog	1955	Male
Miss Piggy	pig	1974	Female
Gonzo	unknown	1970	Male

```
# Attempt 1 (which will fail)
muppet_df.loc["Gonzo"]["species"] = "whatever"
```

```
display(muppet_df)
```

```
/var/folders/bh/…/ipykernel_69156/3562961563.py:2
: SettingWithCopyWarning:
A value is trying to be set on a copy of a slice from a DataFrame
```

```
muppet_df.loc["Gonzo"]["species"] = "whatever"
```

	species	firstappearance	gender
Kermit	frog	1955	Male
Miss Piggy	pig	1974	Female
Gonzo	unknown	1970	Male

The error above (A value is trying to be set on a copy of a slice from a DataFrame) is very common. This is because we treated a shallow copy as if it were deep copy. Since pandas is worried that acting on the shallow copy will inadvertently change other data, it does not make the change and instead presents this warning. In this case, the shallow copy was the result of muppet_df.loc["Gonzo"], which is a Series, in which we *then* change the data for "species" to "whatever". If we do this as a single statement, we do not get an error.

```
# Attempt 2 (which will succeed)
muppet_df.loc["Gonzo","species"] = "whatever"
```

```
display(muppet_df)
```

	species	firstappearance	gender
Kermit	frog	1955	Male
Miss Piggy	pig	1974	Female
Gonzo	whatever	1970	Male

The original query failed because we created a deep copy by accident. We can see this error work the other way as well, which happens when we give the DataFrame a new label but we are actually still referring to the original DataFrame. That can be especially dangerous because it won't raise a warning, it will just change the data. Observe:

```
newmuppet_df = muppet_df

newmuppet_df.loc["Kermit","species"] = "lizard" #change in newmuppet_df

display(muppet_df.loc["Kermit","species"]) #it appears in original muppet_df

'lizard'
```

What happened above is we just renamed the original dataframe. One way to ensure that a newly assigned dataframe is a copy is to use the `copy()` method directly, as in `newmuppet_df = muppet_df.copy()`.

 ## Advanced topics: numpy and numpy arrays

Depending on how far you go in your data science journey, the `Series` and the `DataFrame`, while powerful, simply won't cut it. This is more the case for the use of advanced statistics. As I mentioned earlier, this book is not especially heavy on statistics. But at the same time, statistics is not something to be avoided at all costs. You can think of this book as being more about helping us to see what is *actually there* at different scales. In that sense, most of the exercises are relatively descriptive. The statistics element of data science helps us to understand how what we are seeing is more, less, or different than what we would *expect*, given some prior information.

Since a lot of statistics involves estimation and calculation, often making thousands or even millions of calculations to get a sense of an expected value, the tools for doing statistical work in Python need to be heavily optimised. One of the ways in which we optimise our tools is by stripping away all of the unnecessary overhead and just focusing on the data at hand. A `DataFrame` is nice because it has so much flexibility, but sometimes you just want to work with a lean calculating machine. That's where `numpy` comes in.

As a precursor to both `scipy` (or Scientific Python) and `pandas`, `numpy` is a tool for numerical Python calculations. It mainly concerns the generation and manipulation of the `array` data structure. Now an array is pretty much like a list, but it is multidimensional. I guess you could say it is a 'list of lists', but even then we are not quite there. A 'list of lists' looks very similar to a `numpy` array with a range of the first 12 numbers reshaped into a 3 × 4 array. But notice some slight differences.

```
import numpy as np

# Single vector
npa = np.arange(12)
print(npa,end="\n\n")

# Matrix reshaping
npbox = npa.reshape(3,4)
print(type(npbox), npbox, sep="\n", end="\n\n")
```

```
# List that looks like a matrix
lbox = [[  0,  1,  2,  3],
        [  4,  5,  6,  7],
        [  8,  9, 10, 11]]

print(type(lbox), lbox, sep="\n", end="\n\n")

[ 0  1  2  3  4  5  6  7  8  9 10 11]

<class 'numpy.ndarray'>
[[ 0  1  2  3]
 [ 4  5  6  7]
 [ 8  9 10 11]]

<class 'list'>
[[0, 1, 2, 3], [4, 5, 6, 7], [8, 9, 10, 11]]
```

So the structure of the code suggests that the numpy array looks pretty similar to a list of lists. However, the differences are more than aesthetic. See below what happens when we try to compare an array to a list, versus comparing the list to another list.

```
lbox2 = [[ 1,  1,  2,  3],
         [ 4,  5,  6,  7]]

print(lbox == npbox, end="\n\n")

print(lbox == lbox2)

[[ True   True   True   True]
 [ True   True   True   True]
 [ True   True   True   True]]

False
```

The first comparison, using the array, did an elementwise comparison. The second comparison (between two lists) just compared the whole data structure, which is somewhat trickier. If the list does not have the same dimensions as an array, it gives a warning (and in future will throw an error).

```
print(lbox2 == npbox, end="\n\n")

False

/var/folders/bh/.../4079372021.py:1
: DeprecationWarning: elementwise comparison failed; this will raise an error
in the future.
```

3.5.1 Reshaping in numpy

One of numpy's advantages is how extensively you can reshape arrays. Sometimes programs want data of the form [1,2,3] as if it were three columns, and sometimes it wants it in the form [[1],[2],[3]] as if it were three rows of one column each. Below see an example of how we might reshape 12 digits into three squares of four numbers.

```
np.arange(12).reshape(3,2,2)

array([[[ 0,  1],
        [ 2,  3]],

       [[ 4,  5],
        [ 6,  7]],

       [[ 8,  9],
        [10, 11]]])
```

numpy matrices are different from pandas DataFrame objects. In a DataFrame one often wants to alter the table in some way, such as adding a column, aggregating by group, or asking for a specific value at a specific index. numpy is less ideal for those tasks that involve selecting and filtering data. Instead, it really shines when it comes to calculations, particularly linear algebra calculations. Learning how to create and manipulate arrays in numpy will be especially important if you want to continue after this book in topics related to linear algebra (such as machine learning) or in big data analytics (with tools like cython for using Python with the speed of C, or using massive online databases such as via BigQuery).

One common use for numpy is to generate some random numbers. numpy has built-in ways to create distributions of numbers according to a variety of statistical formulae. Below I generate some random numbers and then look at generating a distribution of them, specifically a *normal* distribution, which means numbers are more common near the middle and become increasingly unlikely as you depart from the middle.

If we want to generate a single random number, sometimes we can simply use Python's random library.

```
import random

random.randint(0,10)

6
```

randint uses a uniform distribution, meaning that every number in the range should be equally likely. So if we wanted a uniform *distribution*, we might just use a for loop and call randint *n* times. However, a more direct way to get a distribution is to use a random number generator in numpy. For a uniform distribution (which we will see again in Chapter 9) we can use np.random.uniform(). First, however, I demonstrate the use of a normal distribution generator via np.random.normal(). This distribution should look like a bell curve if we plot it. The first argument here is the expected average value. The second value is the standard deviation (indicating how spread out the distribution will be). The third value is optional. Without it the method will return a single random number. By setting it to 20 we will generate an array with 20 numbers that should have an average of 0.

```
one_val = np.random.normal(0,10)
one_val
```

```
-9.391805503912419
```

```
dist1 = np.random.normal(0,10,20)
dist1
```

```
array([  7.57876718,  -4.20000049,   4.37429081,  -4.25482904,
       -11.22300565,  -1.68352881,  -1.16614186,   5.36379891,
       -21.18950199,   9.66849986,   6.51985317,   6.62690415,
       -22.36776092,  -8.48234805, -15.59005815,  12.77001212,
       -27.70267959,  -4.71790706,   1.73594751, -12.48957836])
```

Notice that even if it printed them five per line, the lack of square brackets shows us that this is really just one single long unidimensional array.

Different random number generators will have different parameters, such as the minimum and maximum value. You can check these parameters in Jupyter by placing your cursor inside the parentheses of a method and pressing Shift+Tab.

Arrays have a shape that can be expressed by a tuple, such as 3 long, 4 wide (3,4), or 10 subarrays of 2 long, 5 wide (10,2,5). You can paste this right in the generator to get numbers in this way. Look at what happens when we take the above method, use (2,3,4), and then print the resulting array and its shape:

```
dist2 = np.random.normal(0,10,(2,3,4))
```

```
print(dist2,dist2.shape, sep="\n\n")
```

```
[[[-10.59510118. -6.24292177  19.14292855   2.20196056]
  [ 21.66500485  -1.07352303  12.43986267   2.63942094]
  [ -2.5015364   -0.65590339  10.17590517  13.22182744]]

 [[ -8.63870312  -2.59635016  16.26923863  -0.04404013]
  [  8.19683335   4.50389897   8.87707632 -11.85240956]
  [ -2.1780215   -7.18873478  -2.33624153 -19.46997386]]]
```

```
(2, 2, 4)
```

```
print(dist2[0][1],dist2[0][1].shape, sep="\n\n")
```

```
[-2.5015364   -0.65590339 10.17590517 13.22182744]
```

```
(4,)
```

Let's show that random number generator on a plot (Figure 3.1). Recall that it is a `normal` number generator so the distribution of numbers should fall roughly along a bell curve.

```
import seaborn as sns # A plotting package (See more details in Chapter 9)
import matplotlib.pyplot as plt
%config InlineBackend.figure_format = 'svg' # Makes output crisper

dist = np.random.normal(0,1,(1000))
sns.histplot(dist)

plt.show()
```

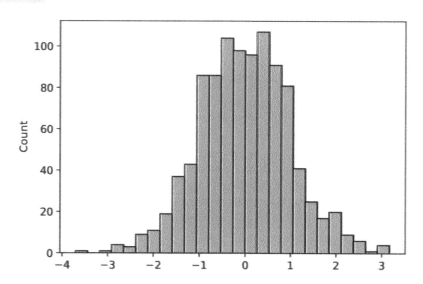

Figure 3.1 Histogram of normal distribution (*n* = 1000)

```
print(f"Array mean: {dist.mean():.2f},\nArray stddev: {dist.std():.2f}")
```

```
Array mean: -0.04,
Array stddev: 0.99
```

3.5.2 Linear algebra and numpy

To really get the most out of numpy will require some training in linear algebra. If you plan on advancing from the basics in social data science towards machine learning, being able to feel confident with the fundamentals of linear algebra will be essential. numpy is designed to accommodate linear algebra and so learning these two together is likely to be a powerful combination for data science.

Linear algebra is the branch of mathematics concerned with solving linear equations. Which on the face of it sounds a little tautological. It's like saying horse algebra is concerned solving horse equations. The emphasis here is on linear – the fact that we have a line or ordered sequence of numbers. So we are not trying to solve some equation for just one value, but a whole table of them. This allows us to come up with things like the line of best fit through all these numbers.

From a very reductive algebraic perspective it means taking formulae like $3x + z = 5$ and $6x + z = 4$ and then figuring out what x and z could be. But these formulae can represent all kinds of things. In the social media space, we might have a formula such as `tweetfriends = tweetscount*factor1 + accountlength*factor2 + error`. `factor1` and `factor2` are in there because the influence of the number of tweets might be different than the influence of the number of days since the account was opened. What is often interesting from a social science perspective is the *explanatory factors* for a given model. So knowing that `factor1` is large or small and accurate or unreliable is really useful. In that case it would be useful to know if tweeting leads to more Twitter 'friends'. Thankfully due to the magic of computers we do not need to compute these factors ourselves, but if we did, we would use linear algebra.

If the computer will do it, then why should we bother with linear algebra and not just leap-frog over it into some interesting measurements and stats? Because the deeper we get into this, the less the actual process of doing these calculations will be a mystery hidden behind some specialist library or method. For example, in Chapter 11 I introduce an important met-ric for getting useful information from text called TF-IDF (Jones, 1972). We will just use some matrix operations to calculate this, but out will come some clear numerical weightings for the most descriptive or interesting words in a text. It's also the case that most networks can be represented as an ensemble of 'adjacency matrices' which are specific kinds of matrices useful in network contexts (Borgatti et al., 2013). Finally, in later work you might engage in machine learning, where there is a real art to wielding `numpy` matrices effectively. Many machine learning approaches such as support vector machines, convex optimisation, and neural networks require you not only to have your data in a `numpy` matrix, but also to have the ranges in the matrix between 0 and 1. So rescaling your matrix will be important. We do not cover machine learning directly in the book, but we will show some rescaling in Chapter 9.

 Summary

The `DataFrame` is a staple of data science and thus of social data science. A surprising amount of what is done in data science can be described as getting the right data into a `DataFrame` from another shape, and aligning that data with other data that we might want to use. The `DataFrame` allows us to filter, make comparisons, and produce visualisations, both static charts and interactive diagrams.

 Further reading

It is hard to mention work specifically on `DataFrame` objects, when they are but a tool. However, there are some great resources out there for teaching data science in Python as well as some excellent resources on linear algebra.

• *Python Data Science Handbook* (VanderPlas, 2016b). An excellent book that covers similar ground to some of the technical sections in this book. It similarly has Jupyter notebooks available online on the book's GitHub page (https://github.com/jakevdp/PythonDataScienceHandbook).

- *Python for Data Analysis* (McKinney, 2012). This is often seen as the go-to book for learning about Python and pandas. It covers a lot of interesting aspects of pandas in clear detail. It's written by the author of pandas after all. It is particularly inspiring to see the variety of ways to wield a DataFrame. I have found that some of the sections might be a bit fast or slow depending on where you are in your learning, and its links to social science are pretty distant, but it is still a great reference.
- *Deep Learning* (Goodfellow et al., 2016). This is one of the seminal texts on machine learning. It gets very technical very fast. But it is also really clear and rewarding for the patient. I mention it this early because Chapter 2 of this book is a very effective summary of the key elements of linear algebra needed for starting on machine learning. The chapters are available from their book page in printer-friendly HTML (https://www.deeplearningbook.org).
- *Essence of Linear Algebra* (Sanderson, 2016). Admittedly, this is a YouTube series (https://www.3blue1brown.com/topics/linear-algebra) and not a book, but it is magnificent. Sanderson has many series on various mathematical elements of data science and machine learning. The *Essence of Linear Algebra* series was just revelatory compared to how I had considered the topic before.

 ## Extensions and reflections

The most important thing to do with a DataFrame is to practise using it. There are many resources online for showing you how to get data into and out of a DataFrame. The next chapter also deals with this. But for now I guarantee that taking some time to practise will really help.

- The muppet_df frame was created manually with three Muppets in there. Create a dictionary with a fourth Muppet and then add that to the DataFrame. Display it to check your results.
- Create a new column in the DataFrame with some more details about these four Muppets. If you want to recover data from the web, you can use that, or make something up. Now explore the ways to add that column to the DataFrame. Will it be a list or a dictionary? If it is a list, have you put the data in the right order? If it is a dictionary, have you used the right keys? Adding a row or a column is really worth getting right before moving on.
- Practise using map and lambda together. Try some simple exercises: create a new Series that is just the first letter of one of the other columns; write a new function and call it from inside the lambda.
- For numpy arrays it is really neat to think that an image is really just an array of RGB values. While we do not go into computer vision in this book, there are a few things you can get on really quickly and they also help learn more about numpy. The scipy website has a nice tutorial on manipulating images and using numpy (https://scipy-lectures.org/advanced/image_processing/). You can also find tutorials on the main package for computer vision in Python called opencv, which relies on numpy arrays to store the images for things like facial detection. One I like is by Tiwari (2020). He has also written an entire book, *Python for Scientists and Engineers* (Tiwari, 2021). It is available online and considerably more thorough than the blog post.
- The online GitHub repository for this book has some self-directed exercises for practising using a DataFrame.

PART II

ACCESSING AND CONVERTING DATA

4
FILE TYPES: GETTING DATA IN

================== Learning goals ==================

- Import tabular data such as CSV and Excel
- Understand how some data can arrive as nested rather than tabular
- Use `json_normalize` to take lists from nested structures and turn them into a `DataFrame`
- Understand how XML and HTML use tags and attributes to encode data
- Understand how Beautiful Soup (`bs4`) can be used to extract tags from XML and HTML data
- Use `xmltodict` where appropriate to sidestep XML parsing issues and treat XML as a dictionary
- Appreciate why serialisation (i.e. pickling) can be useful for storing data temporarily.

 Importing data to a `DataFrame`

Previously we introduced the `DataFrame` as a highly flexible table data format for Python. Now we have to get the data *into* that `DataFrame`. In a way, it is a tad unconventional to have a chapter on data formats this early. People often push that a bit later. However, in my experience, one of the first major challenges faced by students and researchers is that they have access to data in one format and need it in another. Data on the web typically does not come in a format amenable to analysis. Rather, it comes in a format that is based on the assumptions and ideologies of those who control the data.

It's impossible to cover all file formats or even a fraction of the possible shapes or types. Yet, below are a pretty standard ensemble of file formats. Hopefully, as you become increasingly confident in data wrangling, you will see how you can manage other kinds of data having been inspired here.

We begin with the CSV as it is the most directly reminiscent of a `DataFrame`. It has rows and columns (and often headers). Then we look briefly at Excel, which is incredibly common in industry. It might surprise you to know that Python can pretty competently read and write Excel, even multi-sheet documents with macros and formatting!

Then we shift tracks from *tabular* data to *nested* data (such as a tweet object that has details of the user alongside details of hashtags and locations all nested inside the same object). Data that is nested is often trickier to transform into a `DataFrame`, but there are a number of strategies and even some nice built-in methods to help out. Nested data is really common. You might have seen it already as an HTML page. But in addition to HTML, we will look at two very common formats for receiving data from the web: JSON and XML.

Before concluding we will introduce a kind of file format that is less common for reading other people's data but useful for writing your own: serialisation (or as it's called in Python, 'pickling').

Although these formats will get you much of the way, there is still one important format that is missing from this chapter: SQL. This is because much of what we want to do with SQL involves merging and grouping across tables. So we will see some SQL syntax instead at the end of Chapter 5 on merging and grouping.

4.1.1 A important note on file organisation

Starting with this chapter, I will be making use of existing data. This data is available on the webpage for this book, even if it is drawn from publicly available sources. You should store this data in a folder adjacent to the folder where you store your Jupyter notebooks, not in the same folder as the notebooks. This keeps your files and your data much more organised. I have opted to do that with the code below. So if this file is in a folder called chapters under a folder called book, then you should also have a folder called data under book, like so:

```
book
 |- chapters
 |- data
 |- exercises
 |- etc.
```

To access that folder we can use a *relative* path. I presently use the wonderful pathlib library in Python, which simplifies a lot of file operations and navigation that were previously scattered across a few libraries. With this library, every path is its own special path object. If you print it then it will look like a standard path (such as C:\Program Files\Anaconda or /users/ada/documents/book/). However, the path object is more flexible and allows for a nice tidy syntax. Below, I will create a path to the data_dir. Then I will check if that path exists, and if it does not, the program will create it. In there you should place your data. A path object is created using Path(). You can place a path inside the parentheses or you can use another approach. Here I use Path.cwd() to get the current working directory (which should be the directory with your Jupyter notebooks). .parent means the directory above. Then we can use the directory separator (/) to indicate that we want to see a folder in the directory above.

```python
from pathlib import Path

data_dir = Path.cwd().parent / "data"

try:
    if not data_dir.exists(): data_dir.mkdir()
except:
    print(f"There was an issue creating the directory at {data_dir}")
else:
    print(f"The data directory can be found at: {data_dir}.")
```

```
The data directory can be found at: /Users/accountname/Documents/GitHub/
fsstds/book/data.
```

4.1.2 Example data

This chapter uses example data from places online where the data is freely available for secondary use. These are available in the GitHub repository for this book. The path for the data folder is https://github.com/berniehogan/fsstds/tree/main/data. From here you can download the example files one by one. If you 'clone' the entire repository and you have a copy of GitHub desktop (or know how to use GitHub from the command line), you can then copy the entire repository, which will include the data as well as all the notebooks with the paths in the correct place. To remind you, these notebooks primarily contain the code.

 Rectangular data: CSV

To begin importing data into a DataFrame, we start with the humble CSV format, which stands for 'comma-separated values'. We start here because this format most closely resembles the DataFrame. A DataFrame has rows and columns, and similarly CSV data is organised according to rows and columns.

Reading in a CSV file should be pretty reliable. However, since CSV is not a strict format but more like a loose set of conventions, there are a few subtle considerations. For example, does the file have headers and indices? What character (usually a comma, of course) separates the values? What character indicates a complete blob of text (i.e. a string) that might include a comma?

For CSV we can use a variety of approaches in Python, including the csv library itself. That library does not work directly with pandas. Instead, it imports data into dictionaries or lists. Let's briefly see how it works in an example.

4.2.1 Using the csv library

csv.reader() will take in a CSV file and return a data structure that you can use, typically by looping over it. What it returns is a parsed line.

```
import csv

with open(data_dir / "MuppetsTable_simple.csv") as filein:
    file_reader = csv.reader(filein, delimiter=',', quotechar='"')
    for row in file_reader:
        print(row)
```

```
['Name', 'Gender', 'Species', 'Appearance']
['Fozzie', 'Male', 'Bear', '1976']
['Kermit', 'Male', 'Frog', '1955']
['Piggy', 'Female', 'Pig', '1974']
['Gonzo', 'Male', '', '1970']
['Rowlf', 'Male', 'Dog', '1962']
['Beaker', '', 'Muppet', '1977']
['Janice', 'Female', 'Muppet', '1975']
['Hilda', 'Female', 'Muppet', '1976']
```

CSV and quote characters

The CSV format uses a delimiter character to separate out the data, typically a comma
(,). But what if your CSV has a string which itself has a comma inside? Imagine having
a location column that includes a city and a country, such as in the string "Gander,
CAN". We can avoid tripping up the parser by using a quote character, such as double
quotes. That way the parser will not stop at the comma inside the quotes but consider it
all one string. But there is a small gotcha that is worth mentioning: different programs
(and different languages) use different quote characters! For example, Microsoft Word
has a tendency to replace the symmetric double quote (") with asymmetric open and
closing quotes (" and "). Then if you copy and paste these auto-completed quotes into
your data it will not parse in the right place. We can observe this (and fix it) in the
MuppetsTable_broken.csv file.

```
with open(data_dir / "MuppetsTable_broken.csv") as filein:
    file_reader = csv.reader(filein)
    for row in file_reader:
        print(len(row),row)
```

```
5 ['Name', 'Gender', 'Species', 'Appearance', 'Notable Phrase']
5 ['Fozzie', 'Male', 'Bear', '1976', 'Wocka, Wocka!']
5 ['Kermit', 'Male', 'Frog', '1955', "It's not easy being green."]
6 ['Piggy', 'Female', 'Pig', '1974', '"I don't care what you think of me',
' unless you think I'm awesome. In which case you are right."']
5 ['Gonzo', 'Male', '', '1970', 'Weirdos have more fun.']
6 ['Rowlf', 'Male', 'Dog', '1962', '"Boy', ' is this piano outta tune! I
love outta tune pianos."']
5 ['Beaker', '', 'Muppet', '1977', 'Meep']
5 ['Janice', 'Female', 'Muppet', '1975', 'Groovy, man']
5 ['Hilda', 'Female', 'Muppet', '1976', "Gonzo, aren't you a little old
to carry around a teddy bear?"]
```

See how the two rows had six items. These rows had the " " characters, which broke the
parser, instead of the expected " characters. This helps remind us that the data that comes in
has to be consistent. It also reminds us that sometimes we actually have to clean a little of it
ourselves. In general, any change we make to data really ought to be embedded in code. So,
I will do that myself below:

```
with open(data_dir / "MuppetsTable_broken.csv") as filein:
    new_table = filein.read().replace('"','"').replace('"','"')

    fileout = open(data_dir / "MuppetsTable_fixed.csv",'w')
    fileout.write(new_table)
    fileout.close()
```

We can cross-check our work.

```
with open(data_dir / "MuppetsTable_fixed.csv") as filein:
    file_reader = csv.reader(filein)
    for row in file_reader:
        print(len(row), row)
```

```
5 ['Name', 'Gender', 'Species', 'Appearance', 'Notable Phrase']
5 ['Fozzie', 'Male', 'Bear', '1976', 'Wocka, Wocka!']
5 ['Kermit', 'Male', 'Frog', '1955', "It's not easy being green."]
5 ['Piggy', 'Female', 'Pig', '1974', 'I don't care what you think of me,
unless you think I'm awesome. In which case you are right.']
5 ['Gonzo', 'Male', '', '1970', 'Weirdos have more fun.']
5 ['Rowlf', 'Male', 'Dog', '1962', 'Boy, is this piano outta tune! I love
outta tune pianos.']
5 ['Beaker', '', 'Muppet', '1977', 'Meep']
5 ['Janice', 'Female', 'Muppet', '1975', 'Groovy, man']
5 ['Hilda', 'Female', 'Muppet', '1976', "Gonzo, aren't you a little old
to carry around a teddy bear?"]
```

This time we can see that each row as five items, making it a nice rectangular dataset.

Before going to pandas, I want to highlight one other nice thing about csv: the use of the DictReader. This returns a dictionary with the header as the key and the values in that row as the value. If there's no header line, you can specify a list to be the keys using the field-names argument, such as fieldnames = ["Name","Location","User"].

```
with open(data_dir / "MuppetsTable_fixed.csv") as filein:
    reader = csv.DictReader(filein)
    for row in reader:
        print(row['Name'], row['Appearance'])
```

```
Fozzie 1976
Kermit 1955
Piggy 1974
Gonzo 1970
Rowlf 1962
Beaker 1977
Janice 1975
Hilda 1976
```

4.2.2 Using the **pandas** CSV reader: `read_csv()`

To import into a DataFrame directly using pandas, you can use the pd.read_csv() method as below:

```
import pandas as pd
```

```
df = pd.read_csv(data_dir / "MuppetsTable_fixed.csv")
display(df.iloc[:,:4]) # Using iloc to get first four columns.
```

	Name	Gender	Species	Appearance
0	Fozzie	Male	Bear	1976
1	Kermit	Male	Frog	1955
2	Piggy	Female	Pig	1974
3	Gonzo	Male	NaN	1970
4	Rowlf	Male	Dog	1962
5	Beaker	NaN	Muppet	1977
6	Janice	Female	Muppet	1975
7	Hilda	Female	Muppet	1976

Just like the `csv.reader()`, the pandas `pd.read_csv()` method has many arguments to help handle the variety of scenarios that you will encounter in the way data is formatted. A few parameters worth mentioning here:

- `sep` or `delimiter` (default = `','`). Although the data is often separated by commas, `csv` actually stands in for a variety of textual tabular data. Sometimes for example, you'll see a tab-separated file, which may be `data.csv`, `data.tsv`, `data.txt`, or just simply `data`. In that case you can set `sep` to be `'\t'`. You can set the separator for a variety of circumstances. Watch how sometimes people use # or ‖ to separate columns.
- `header` (default = `"infer"`). pandas is pretty clever at inferring whether the file has a header or not. Yet, it is still useful to set it to either `True` or `False` as the case may be.
- `quotechar` (default = `'"'`). So above we assumed that the quote character was ". This way, we could have something like `"Wocka, Wocka!"`, which has a comma in it, and still have it treated as a single cell of data. Sometimes people use a single quote, and sometimes people forget to use a quote at all which can make wrangling the data really, really unpleasant.

 ## Rectangular rich data: Excel

Excel is the popular spreadsheet program from Microsoft. Files can be stored as either `.xls` or `.xlsx`. The original `.xls` is a proprietary file format, but the details can still be reasonably handled by `pandas`. The second one (`xlsx`) was published as an open standard and is in fact a wrapper over a specific format of XML.

In general, we simply want to import a sheet with `<sheet>` = `pd.read_excel(<file_path>)`.

If you are looking for tabular data from the web, it is not rare to see it in an Excel sheet rather than CSV. Here we can see an example sheet downloaded from the World Bank's Databank (https://databank.worldbank.org/). I took a few popular indicators (Population, Internet diffusion, carbon dioxide emissions, and gross national income (GNI)) and exported them to Excel using their online portal. There are a few other ways to collect this data, but this way shows an Excel sheet. There are some advantages to Excel when viewed in the software application itself, including formatting and multiple tabs. One issue with Excel, however, is that a spreadsheet *sheet* is not really a `DataFrame`. The sheet can have all kinds of writing and formatting that do not really work with the notion of cases in rows and variables in columns. This data is available on the book GitHub repository, but you can also find an equivalent export from the World Bank pretty easily and it is worth seeing what datasets they have available.

```
wb_df = pd.read_excel(data_dir / "World Bank Indicators 2012-2021.xlsx")

display(wb_df.info())

<class 'pandas.core.frame.DataFrame'>
RangeIndex: 1069 entries, 0 to 1068
Data columns (total 14 columns):
 #   Column           Non-Null Count   Dtype
---  ------           --------------   -----
 0   Country Name     1066 non-null    object
 1   Country Code     1064 non-null    object
 2   Series Name      1064 non-null    object
 3   Series Code      1064 non-null    object
 4   2011 [YR2011]    1064 non-null    object
 5   2012 [YR2012]    1064 non-null    object
 6   2013 [YR2013]    1064 non-null    object
 7   2014 [YR2014]    1064 non-null    object
 8   2015 [YR2015]    1064 non-null    object
 9   2016 [YR2016]    1064 non-null    object
 10  2017 [YR2017]    1064 non-null    object
 11  2018 [YR2018]    1064 non-null    object
 12  2019 [YR2019]    1064 non-null    object
 13  2020 [YR2020]    1064 non-null    object
dtypes: object(14)
memory usage: 117.0+ KB

None

display(wb_df.iloc[:,:3])
```

	Country Name	Country Code	Series Name
0	Afghanistan	AFG	Population, total
1	Afghanistan	AFG	Total greenhouse gas emissions (kt of CO2 equivalent)
2	Afghanistan	AFG	GNI, Atlas method (current US$)
3	Afghanistan	AFG	Individuals using the Internet (% of population)
4	Albania	ALB	Population, total
...	...	...	...
1064	NaN	NaN	NaN
1065	NaN	NaN	NaN
1066	NaN	NaN	NaN
1067	Data from database: World Development Indicators	NaN	NaN
1068	Last Updated: 04/08/2022	NaN	NaN

At the bottom of the display it says the data is 1741 rows and 3 columns (since we only asked for the first three). Notice that it doesn't display all the rows. Instead these are truncated. After the fifth row (most likely) you'll see a row that looks like this:

```
. . .      . . .      . . .      . . .      . . .      . . .
```

This is to indicate that there's data unseen. Similarly if there are too many columns (something `pandas` works out itself) then it will also truncate the columns, but in this case we only asked for the first three columns, so noting is truncated. You should also notice that at the bottom we have not data, but a bunch of NaN cells. This is because `pandas` is trying to include all the text on the first sheet in its `DataFrame`, including that little bit at the bottom where it says:

```
Data from database: World Development Indicators
Last Updated: 04/08/2022
```

There are a number of strategies to clean this up. You might be inclined at first to just open the file in Excel, delete the junk data and start again. Please don't! Remember from the above section on CSV where we programmatically changed the quote character – anytime you change the data, I strongly recommend you *do it with reproducible code*. So just like above where we had to create a cleaned CSV with the correct quote characters, here, we will create a cleaned `DataFrame`. But how?

I'm not going to shy away from using a spreadsheet program to view the data and get an intuition. It is fine to use Excel to read the data. And realistically a lot of temporary work can be done in Excel if you don't need to save or store your data. However, in the case of academic work, it is very bad practice to make lasting changes by hand rather than in a reproducible and documented way.

When I open the data in a spreadsheet, I discover that only the bottom five lines appear to have missing data. We can check by using `df.tail()`. Recall that both `head()` and `tail()` take an argument for the number of lines. So let's cross-check that:

```
wb_df.iloc[:,:4].tail(7)
```

	Country Name	Country Code	Series Name
1062	World	WLD	GNI, Atlas method (current US$)
1063	World	WLD	Individuals using the Internet (% of population)
1064	NaN	NaN	NaN
1065	NaN	NaN	NaN
1066	NaN	NaN	NaN
1067	Data from database: World Development Indicators	NaN	NaN
1068	Last Updated: 04/08/2022	NaN	NaN

Sure enough. This suggests we should be able to slice the data. I want to ensure that I don't have to do this every time, but I still want to document this change. Therefore, I will actually write this `DataFrame` back to Excel rather than merely delete it in the original.

Note that the first `xlsx` file actually had two sheets: the one with the data and a second sheet called `Series-- Metadata` with some important facts about how the data was collected. Here I am just writing the `DataFrame` from the first sheet to a new Excel sheet.

```
# Remember the [:-5] is what slices off the last five rows
wb_df.iloc[:-5].to_excel(data_dir / "Cleaned_Popular_Indicators.xlsx",
                         index=False)
```

Feel free to reimport this file or view it in a spreadsheet program to see the difference. One thing you'll notice is that above I did not write the index to the data. That's because the index carried no specific meaning here. However, whether you want to keep the index or not will depend on the type of data you have and whether the index represents meaningful data (such as an ID number or timestamp).

In addition to the built-in `pandas` reader, Python has extensive packages for reading and writing to Excel, as well as adding formatting. Perhaps the most widely used of these is XLSXWriter (https://xlsxwriter.readthedocs.io/), but there are many more, as compiled by Python for Excel (https://www.excelpython.org/).

 Nested data: JSON

Data are measurements about the world. `DataFrame` objects are analytical devices for making comparisons and examining the data at varying levels of scale. But the `DataFrame`'s row-by-column arrangement doesn't always reflect the way that data about the world is organised.

An important concept to consider when wrangling data is *nesting*. That is to say, data structures can be nested inside other data structures. Twitter is a useful case here. If you collect raw tweet data (something we will be doing later in the book), you'll see that it looks kind of like a dictionary structure. But it is not simply a list of key–value pairs. This is a list of key–value pairs:

```
tweet = {"tweet":"This is the tweet",
         "likes":123,
         "retweets":141,
         "time":"Saturday, March 14, 2015."
         ...}
```

Compared to this, a tweet object would have dictionaries nested inside other dictionaries. For example, one dictionary will include details about the account that sent the tweet. So it might look a little more like:

```
{
  "created_at": "Thu Apr 06 15:24:15 +0000 2017",
  "id_str": "850006245121695744",
```

```
    "text": "1\/ Today we\u2019re sharing our vision for the future of the Twitte
        r API platform!\nhttps:\/\/t.co\/XweGngmxlP",
    "user": {
        "id": 2244994945,
        "name": "Twitter Dev",
        "screen_name": "TwitterDev",
        "location": "Internet",
        "url": "https:\/\/dev.twitter.com\/",
        "description": "Your official source for Twitter Platform news, updates & e
                        vents. Need technical help? Visit https:\/\/twittercommunit
                        y.com\/ \u2328\ufe0f #TapIntoTwitter"
    },
    "place": {
    },
    "entities": {
        "hashtags": [
        ],
        "urls": [
            {
                "url": "https:\/\/t.co\/XweGngmxlP",
                "unwound": {
                    "url": "https:\/\/cards.twitter.com\/cards\/18ce53wgo4h\/3xo1c",
                    "title": "Building the Future of the Twitter API Platform"
                }
            }
        ],
        "user_mentions": [
        ]
    }
}
```

As we can see here, it is an unruly combination of dictionaries and lists nested within each other. Fortunately, Python has no trouble with objects nested inside other objects. The data above is termed JSON or JavaScript object notation. It is a combination of lists and dictionaries as they would be formatted for JavaScript (which means there are tiny differences compared to Python, but it is basically the same).

4.4.1 Loading JSON

To load JSON into Python directly you can use the `json` library. It provides a means to load data into memory (`json.loads(<THE_DATA>)`) and a means to take a data structure and transform it into valid JSON for writing to disk (`json.dumps(<THE_DATA>)`).

The data shown above is in a JSON structure that a Twitter data parser can understand. That said, this is Twitter data from their prior v1.1 API. Twitter have recently released a new v2 API which focuses on data minimisation so you would get much less data by default but it might show a similar nesting. We will encounter that API in Chapter 7. In the tweet above, we can see a hierarchy, which I sketch part of below:

```
object
 --created_at
 . . .
 --user
   --id
   --name
   --screen_name
 --entities
   --hashtags
 --place
 . . .
```

Below, we will work with a simpler data structure just to demonstrate JSON.

The file omdb_Muppet_search_page_1.json is data that I downloaded from the site Open Movie Database (https://omdbapi.com/). To collect machine-readable data it is common to use an application programming interface (API). When dealing with data from the web, this term usually means that a server has a series of web addresses that you request data from, but instead of an HTML page, you would get some data that you would have to parse.

The OMDB has a simple API (i.e. a pipeline for requesting specific data) which I used to search for movies or shows that include the word 'Muppet' in the title. By requesting data using the right address, my program received some JSON. As you will see below, the JSON referred to the first 10 entries of movies with the word 'Muppet' in the title. Any subsequent entries would have to be collected using a supplementary call.

```
import json

mdata = json.loads(open(data_dir / "omdb_Muppet_search_page_1.json").read())
type(mdata)

dict
```

Below I will print the first 500 characters of the JSON as text. However, you will see that I use the parameter indent with the argument 2. This means that it will indent each line two spaces for each level of nesting. Every time the data has an open { or [it would imply another deeper level of nesting. Printing in this manner is referred to as 'pretty printing'. Printed without the indent it would look much harder to comprehend. Remove indent=2 to see for yourself. Also try removing [:300] to print *all* the data (it's just 10 entries).

```
print(json.dumps(mdata, indent=2)[:300])

{
  "Search": [
    {
      "Title": "The Muppet Christmas Carol",
      "Year": "1992",
      "imdbID": "tt0104940",
      "Type": "movie"
    },
```

```
{
   "Title": "The Muppet Movie",
   "Year": "1979",
   "imdbID": "tt0079588",
   "Type": "movie"
},
{
   "Title": "The Muppet
```

Since the top level of the JSON is a dictionary, we can explore the data structure by asking for the keys and then observing the values. In general, it is preferable to have some guide or schema for how the data is structured, but in my experience it is very common to need to explore it yourself to understand the structure.

```
mdata.keys()
```

```
dict_keys(['Search', 'totalResults', 'Response'])
```

In this case, as in many, the top-level keys segment out the JSON into a part that contains rows of data and a part that helps with managing the flow of data. In this case, `Search` is a list of the results. We will focus on the value for `Search` later. `totalResults` gives us the number of total rows (of which `mdata` contains the first 10) and `Response`, which is a Boolean `True` or `False` for whether the response contains data or an error.

There is nesting here because `Search` is a list of the first 10 responses. Each response itself is also a dictionary: a dictionary in a list in a dictionary.

```
print(mdata['totalResults'],
      mdata['Response'])
```

```
62 True
```

```
print(mdata['Search'][0])
```

```
{'Title': 'The Muppet Christmas Carol', 'Year': '1992', 'imdbID':
'tt0104940', 'Type': 'movie'}
```

Although `json.dumps` is for writing JSON data to disk, it is also useful as a way to nicely print a dictionary, just to help us examine its structure.

```
print(json.dumps(mdata['Search'][0], indent=2))
```

```
{
  "Title": "The Muppet Christmas Carol",
  "Year": "1992",
  "imdbID": "tt0104940",
  "Type": "movie"
}
```

While JSON is a nested structure, there is a convenience method in pandas to help in turning it into a DataFrame. The command json_normalize() takes a list of dictionary objects and then creates a table based on the keys, so that

```
results = { "Search":[
                {"Title":"Ghosts of Hidden Valley",
                "Year":2010},
                {"Title":"The Perspex Event",
                "Year":2018}]
        }
```

can use pd.json_normalize(results["Search"]) to transform into a table with a row for each element of the Search list.

```
pd.json_normalize(results["Search"])
```

	Title	Year
0	Ghosts of Hidden Valley	2010
1	The Perspex Event	2018

By doing this with the JSON search data we can load mdata in a similar manner.

```
mdf = pd.json_normalize(mdata["Search"])
display(mdf.iloc[:,:3])
```

	Title	Year	imdbID
0	The Muppet Christmas Carol	1992	tt0104940
1	The Muppet Movie	1979	tt0079588
2	The Muppet Show	1976-1981	tt0074028
3	Muppet Treasure Island	1996	tt0117110
4	The Great Muppet Caper	1981	tt0082474
5	Muppet Babies	1984-2020	tt0086764
6	It's a Very Merry Muppet Christmas Movie	2002	tt0329737
7	A Muppet Family Christmas	1987	tt0251282
8	Muppet*vision 3-D	1991	tt0102481
9	Muppet Classic Theater	1994	tt0213096

Notice above that we ran json_normalize(mdata["Search"]). Below I will show what happens when we do this on just mdata (the parent dictionary).

```
pd.json_normalize(mdata)
```

	Search	totalResults	Response
0	[{'Title': 'The Muppet Christmas Carol', 'Year" ...	62	True

This is not what we want. It shows that `json_normalize` takes each entry of the dictionary as a row. So if we used `mdata`, we had one entry with these three keys (`Search`, `totalResults`, `Response`). What we really wanted was 10 entries, each with the keys `"Title"`, `"Year"`, `"imdbID"`, `"Type"`, `"Poster"`. Thus, we pass `mdata['Search']` instead.

Nested markup languages: HTML and XML

4.5.1 HTML: Hypertext Markup Language

JSON is pretty similar to Python. You can recognise the dictionaries as having { and the lists as having [characters. Markup languages look a little different. They typically use tags to open and close levels of the hierarchy. Below I will show how to parse two of the more popular markup languages, HTML and XML.

A markup language is a formal syntax that appends characters to either side of data in order to give the enclosed data some meaning. For example, you can enclose the words **big deal** in asterisks like that to tell a program that it should be printed in bold. This book was written in a simple markup language called Markdown. This is a light syntax used to encase certain words. It does not carry many semantics. However, HTML and XML use tags that carry a lot of meaning. By encasing values in *tags*, such as `<title>Here is a title</title>`, we can arrange data in a nested way and determine what the data represents. In that case, `Here is a title` was nested in the title tags, but we can nest tags in tags, hence the hierarchy. We can also put other attributes in the tags themselves, like `<title font="Helvetica">Here is a title</title>` where `font` is an attribute of the `<title>` tag with a value of `"Helvetica"`. Notice that the ending tag is just the first tag with a / inside to denote that it is a closing tag. Some tags are self-closing, which is denoted `<tag />`. On its own a self-closing tag does not seem that interesting, but it often carries a lot of relevant data in the attributes.

HTML is the markup language used all over the web. Here is some really simple, but valid, HTML.

```
<html>
    <head>
        <title>
            This is the title!
        </title>
    </head>
    <body>
        This is a webpage! <p/>
        Learn more about the web through <a href="https://w3c.org">the W3C</a>
    </body>
</html>
```

If you were to copy that text, paste it into a plain text file with the extension `.html`, and open it in a browser, you will see a blank page with the title bar saying 'This is the title!' and a single line saying 'This is a webpage!' in the plain, default format. Underneath should be a line saying 'Learn more about the web through the W3C'.

The tags give meaning and thus structure. They are also sources of data. For example, we can extract the body text ('This is a ... W3C') which is a *value* encased in the <body> tags. We can also extract a link, https://w3c.org/, which is an HREF *attribute* of the <a> tag.

HTML data is pretty far from tabular data. It's nested and relies on files that exist alongside the HTML like a CSS (cascading style sheet) file, via some imported JavaScript. Many of the tags (like the many <div> tags that proliferate in modern HTML) are not semantic, but more to help with layout of the page and the layout of the code that renders the page. Nevertheless, HTML data is still data that can be used. There is lots of work to be done that involves parsing HTML. For example:

- Comments and other textual data have HTML in them.
- Sometimes there is no API, but the data is really consistent (like Craigslist ads).
- A page might have some tables on it.
- You're collecting data by crawling the web.
- You might want to extract the links on a page and do some analytics on them.

In Chapter 6 we will use HTML directly in order to collect web data using Python's requests library.

4.5.2 Wikipedia as a data source

In my courses and my research I lean a lot on data from Wikipedia. It is truly a marvel of the Internet age. The accuracy and quality of pages on Wikipedia are often high and the data that is available from the site is often staggering in its depth. In past work I have made use of Wikipedia pages, pages for authors, statistics for page views and edits, pages in different languages, and more. In research I like to suggest that Wikipedia is a great place to start but not a great place to end. This means an emphasis on critically engaging with the content as well as checking out the sources.

One of the nice things about Wikipedia is that, as a freely accessible encyclopedia, there's always content that can be used in teaching and research. In this chapter we will use a snapshot of a Wikipedia page that has been stored in the data folder. We will compare that snapshot as formatted HTML as well as unformatted XML with 'wikitext' (i.e. text that uses the wiki syntax behind the scenes; see https://en.wikipedia.org/wiki/Help:Wikitext).

4.5.3 Wikipedia as HTML

On the web, Wikipedia is formatted as HTML. It has links that go both within Wikipedia as well as links that go to other sites. The page will have a consistent format regardless of the Wikipedia entry. You can see the underlying text that we are working with by opening Canada_Wiki.html in a text editor, or see it formatted by opening it in a web browser. The page should look similar to https://en.wikipedia.org/wiki/Canada, although the live page will undoubtedly have had at least a few tweaks to the content between when the book was published and when you look at the page. In fact, while the page has likely been edited between when this book was written and when you are reading it, you should still be able to see the exact version of this page on the site. How? This page will have a revision number referring to the specific revision of the page.

Below we will open the page as well as do a little parsing.

```
with open(data_dir / "Canada - Wikipedia.html") as infile:
    wiki_HTML = infile.read()

print(len(wiki_HTML))
```

```
1091805
```

At this point `wiki_HTML` is just raw text. Printing the length shows it is a long series of characters, so it is probably the page as expected. We can preview the text by printing a range of characters such as `print(wiki_HTML[:200])` for the first 200 characters. This gets as far as showing that the title of the page is Canada. So far, so good.

```
print(wiki_HTML[:200])
```

```
<!DOCTYPE html>
<html class="client-nojs" lang="en" dir="1tr">
<head>
<meta charset="UTF-8"/>
<title>Canada - Wikipedia</title>
<script>document.documentElement.className="client-js";RLCONF={"wgBreakF
```

4.5.4 Using Beautiful Soup (bs4) for markup data

The Beautiful Soup library takes in a blob of markup text and parses it for use. When you use the library it is conventional to call the parsed text a *soup*. We use a soup to help us find text that could be anywhere on the page. Since XML and HTML documents are hierarchical, if we did not have this ability we would have to navigate through the hierarchy. In the above example of HTML, getting the text from the title hierarchically would be `soup.html.head.title.text`. However, the soup knows that title is a tag so you can just ask for `soup.title.text` and it will return `"This is the title!"`. This ability to just look for tags is especially useful for things like looking for links (which all start with the `<a>` tag, as in `<a href="https://www.duckduckgo.com/">Search with DuckDuckGo</a>`.

To see Beautiful Soup in practice, let's import it (`import bs4`) and then use it to process an HTML page and an XML data file both representing the same data. We will use Wikipedia in both cases since it renders on the web as HTML but is exported for analysis as XML, so conveniently we can compare the differences. To remind you, both `Canada - Wikipedia.html` and `Canada - Export.xml` should be in the data folder on the course webpage. See below how we first parse the page, print the title text, and look for links.

```
import bs4

soup = bs4.BeautifulSoup(wiki_HTML, 'html.parser')

print(soup.title.text)
```

```
# Query the soup for all 'a' tags (knowing that 'a' tags refer to links)
links = soup.find_all("a")
print(len(links))
```

```
Canada - Wikipedia
4381
```

This approach came up with 4381 unique links in the HTML page for Canada. This is a considerable number of links. Even for a single page on Wikipedia, we are already approaching a scale that would be hard for a single human coder to work with. What if all 200-plus countries in almost 100 Wikipedia languages each have their page? Getting the URLs on each one would be a huge task!

4.5.5 Data scepticism

It is healthy and useful to be sceptical of overly mechanistic approaches. This is especially important when copying other people's code or using 'black box' algorithms. Scepticism implies that we express some uncertainty about whether the data we have is the data we want. We can alleviate this scepticism through a number of approaches, though no single approach will be sufficient, as we shall see throughout this book. Some tactics for checking data:

- Plotting distributions: are there unexpected outliers?
- Spot-checking results: do they look like what you expected?
- 'Tops and tails': looking at the first and last results – are they appropriate?
- Tabulating results: does `value_counts()` give the sort of result you expected?

In this case, we will be spot-checking the results for now and tabulating later. These are often considered as 'preprocessing' tasks in a data pipeline, but that implies you know what to look for to clean up your data. Before we create a pipeline for many pages, it is useful to start with a single page and look for any errors that might end up being systematic errors.

```
import random

print("Head: ", links[0])
print("Tail: ", links[-1])

spot = random.choice(links)
print("Random: ", spot)
```

```
Head:   <a id="top"></a>
Tail:   <a href="https://www.mediawiki.org/"><img alt="Powered by MediaWiki"
height="31" loading="lazy"
src="/static/images/footer/poweredby_mediawiki_88x31.png"
srcset="/static/images/footer/poweredby_mediawiki_132x47.png 1.5x,
/static/images/footer/poweredby_mediawiki_176x62.png 2x" width="88"/></a>
Random:   <a href="/wiki/Toronto" title="Toronto">Toronto</a>
```

The first tag is clearly not a URL. We can determine this by looking in the tag attributes. Normally with an a tag there's a href attribute which points to the URL. An external URL would have a :// included, such as https://, sftp://, or http://. However, the top tag has id="top" inside, which is just for internal navigation.

To check the attributes of a tag you can call <tag>.attrs. They will be returned as a dictionary of key–value pairs. Observe:

```
links[-1].attrs
```

```
{'href': 'https://www.mediawiki.org/'}
```

The following code snippet uses the attrs feature to check if href is an attribute of the a tag.

```
href_links = [x for x in soup.find_all('a') if 'href' in x.attrs]

print(f"There are {len(href_links)} 'href' links in this file.")

print(f"The first 'href' link:\n{href_links[0]}")
```

```
There are 4377 'href' links in this file.
The first 'href' link:
<a href="/wiki/Wikipedia:Featured_articles" title="This is a featured article.
Click here for more information."><img alt="Featured article" data-file-
height="438" data-file-width="462" decoding="async" height="19"
src="//upload.wikimedia.org/wikipedia/en/thumb/e/e7/Cscr-featured.svg/20px-Cscr-
featured.svg.png" srcset="//upload.wikimedia.org/wikipedia /en/thumb/e/e7/Cscr-
featured.svg/30px-Cscr-featured.svg.png 1.5x,
//upload.wikimedia.org/wikipedia /en/thumb/e/e7/Cscr-
featured.svg/40px-Cscr-featured.svg.png 2x" width="20"/></a>
```

This particular link was internal to Wikipedia. This means that if you click on it you will go to another Wikipedia page. We can determine this since it starts with /wiki/ Wikipedia:Fea.... A simple way to check if it is an external link is to take all the links returned via href and check which ones include ://. We can use <tag>.get(<attr>), which will get the attribute value for whatever is the attribute key <attr>. For example, if we see <a href="https://www.eff.org">Electronic Frontier Foundation</a>. We can then use x.get('href') and it will return https://www.eff.org.

```
href_ext_links = [x for x in soup.find_all('a') if
                  'href' in x.attrs and # Do this if clause first
                  '://' in x.get('href')] # since this depends on first if

print(f"There are {len(href_ext_links)} 'href' & '://' links in this file.")
print(f"The first 'href' and '://' link:\n{href_ext_links[0].get('href')}")
```

```
There are 950 'href' & '://' links in this file.
```

The first 'href' and '://' link:
https://en.wikipedia.org/w/index.php?title=Canada&action=edit

```
href_int_links = [x for x in soup.find_all('a')
                  if 'href' in x.attrs and "://" not in x.get('href')]

print(f"There are {len(href_int_links)} 'href' internal links in this
file.")
print(f"The first 'href' internal link:\n{href_int_links[0].get('href')}")
```

There are 3427 'href' internal links in this file.
The first 'href' internal link:
/wiki/Wikipedia:Featured_articles

If you sum together 950 (the external href links), 3427 (the internal href links), and 4 (the <a> tags without an href attribute, then you get the total, 4381, so all links are accounted for.

We will do a little more with HTML in Chapter 10 where we clean the HTML out of some comments. At this point, however, I wanted to note some of the limitations of HTML. For example, what is the revision ID of this page? Below we will see how to get the revision from structured XML really easily. But here it is not so straightforward. It is indeed embedded in the HTML ... somewhere. A good exercise for you is to open the HTML in a browser, view the source, and look for 'wgRevisionId'. It will be a key buried inside some JavaScript. If you find it and the value associated with that key (it will be a 10-digit number), then you can find this exact version online at https://en.wikipedia.org/w/index.php?title= Canada&oldid=<wgRevisionId> by replacing <wgRevisionId> with the number.

4.5.6 XML

XML stands for 'Extensible Markup Language'. XML files can be generic or have a document type. For example, the popular GraphML format for social network analysis is really just XML with a specific schema that is used for network graph types.

Like HTML, XML is a markup language that uses *less than* (<) and *greater than* (>) symbols to encase the element tags.

```
<start>
    <middle>
        <end1>    Here is an element! </end1>
        <end2>    Here is an element! </end2>
    </middle>
</start>
```

Elements have an 'element tree'. Above, start is the root node, middle is a child node, and end1 is a child of middle. End1 and end2 are siblings. XML is a 'self-documenting' style, which means that you can insert details about the elements into the document itself. For example, at the beginning of the Canada-- Wikipedia Special Export.xml file is a tag that points to the specific XML schema used for Wikipedia data.

```
with open(data_dir / "Canada - Wikipedia Special Export.xml") as infile:
    wiki_XML = infile.read()

print(len(wiki_XML))
print(wiki_XML[:300])

277240
<mediawiki xmlns="http://www.mediawiki.org/xml/export-0.10/"
xmlns:xsi="http://www.w3.org/2001/XMLSchema-instance"
xsi:schemaLocation="http://www.mediawiki.org/xml/export-0.10/
http://www.mediawiki.org/xml/export-0.10.xsd" version="0.10" xml:lang="en">
  <siteinfo>
    <sitename>Wikipedia</sitename>
```

Most of the time, we will not be so concerned with the top of an XML document. Rather, we usually just want to navigate the element tree to get to the element(s) that are of concern to us. Sometimes, parsers will already be written which take the XML and load it into a data structure for us. This is the case with GraphML, the common format for social network data. We cover the use of GraphML in Chapter 13 on networks.

Getting data from a webpage or XML into a DataFrame is often trickier than using JSON. There are some approaches that can help, but they will depend on the kind of XML that is being wrangled. The Wikipedia XML we saw above has all the important data as text between tags. By contrast, the Stack Exchange data that we will be using as the extended example in Chapter 10 has all the data as attributes in self-closing XML tags.

XML and character encoding

Computers use data as a stream of bytes, but we read it as a stream of text. Bytes and text are very similar, but there are some slight differences that can throw off a program trying to read or parse one rather than the other. If you get an error below, it might be that depending on how you downloaded the file (such as using an older browser), you will get the XML as byte data rather than text and the program will throw an error. If that's the case, where it says bs4.BeautifulSoup(wikitext, "lxml"), you would first *decode* the text as in bs4. BeautifulSoup(wikitext.decode("utf8"), "lxml").

```
import bs4

wiki_XML = wiki_XML.replace('<text xml:space=','<wikitext xml:space=')

soup = bs4.BeautifulSoup(wiki_XML, 'lxml')

print(soup.mediawiki.page.revision.id.text )

1079679373
```

Since the XML data includes important information inside structured tags, it is a lot easier to get the revisionID here simply by querying .revision.id.text rather than searching for it through JavaScript nested inside an HTML document.

Navigating XML

Navigating XML involves moving up and down or sideways along an *element tree*, which is the term for how we think of the tags as being nested inside or adjacent to each other. In the case above it was clear that I know where to go for the text I wanted (`mediawiki.page.revision.id`). In general, however, navigating to the right element is a bit tedious. Some people prefer the use of Python's built-in `ElementTree` package. In either case, what you will be doing with your code is navigating a tree structure. Trees tend to use the following nomenclature that borrows from both the natural tree but also the notion of a family tree:

- *Root.* The base or primary node is called the root node.
- *Parent and child.* A parent is a node that has nodes nested within, like `ID` nested within `revision` above. In that case, `revision` is the parent node and `ID` is the child node.
- *Sibling.* Two child nodes with the same parent are siblings. For example, `sitename` and `dbname` are both children of `siteinfo`.
- *Leaf:* a term sometimes used to indicate a child node with no children of its own.

Below I use Beautiful Soup to navigate through the tags so that I can get to the data I want. I also use the recent Python 'walrus' operator `:=` below. This does a comparison and assigns the comparison to a variable. I check if the tag has a name, in which case I print it.

```python
# for i in soup.children: print(i.name)
# for i in soup.html.children: print(i.name)
# for i in soup.html.body.children: print(i.name)
# for i in soup.html.body.mediawiki.children: print(i.name)
# for i in soup.html.body.mediawiki.page: print(i.name)
for i in soup.html.body.mediawiki.page.revision:
    if name := i.name: print(name)
```

```
id
parentid
timestamp
contributor
minor
comment
model
format
text
sha1
```

```python
print(soup.html.body.mediawiki.page.revision.id)
# Notice how we can shorten it (and get the text directly):
print(soup.revision.id.text)
```

```
<id>1079679373</id>
1079679373
```

Beautiful Soup allowed us to shorten the text to `soup.revision.id`. What if we tried `soup.id`?

```
print(soup.id, soup.id.parent.name, sep="\n")
```

```
<id>5042916</id>
page
```

It's a different number since there are multiple id tags and this selected the first one (which was `page.id`) as we can discover through `soup.id.parent`. On the other hand, `revision.id` would uniquely indicate which revision.

Using **xmltodict**

One clever approach to sidestepping XML is to turn the entirety of the XML document into a JSON file, so then you can work with it like a dictionary. This is using the external `xmltodict` library that you will have to download yourself. I know a lot of students have preferred this method to navigating XML in the past. The only thing to note (which tripped me up), is that in the resulting `dict` object, if a key has @ at the beginning (e.g. `@href`), that means it was an attribute of a tag, whereas a key without @ at the beginning (e.g. `revision`) is the tag itself with the value being whatever was encased in between the `<>` `</>` tags.

The advantage of Beautiful Soup is that you get to query by the tags directly and you can avoid some of the issues with a nesting structure (e.g. by iterating through all the `<a>` tags). The advantage of `xmltodict` is that you can then use `json_normalize` (there's no equivalent `xml_noramlize` to my knowledge) or `pd.from_dict()` to pipe the XML data into a `DataFrame`. This works well when the XML is an export of many similar entries, such as many revisions of a page or many rows of data. The ideal approach will depend on the structure of the data. I have used both Beautiful Soup and `xmltodict` in recent times for different tasks.

```
# You may need to install xmltodict.
# This code is extra careful to check for the right version of Python for
# installation. In fairness, 'pip install <library>' usually works fine.

try:
    import xmltodict
except ModuleNotFoundError:
    import sys
    !{sys.executable} -m pip install xmltodict
    import xmltodict

with open(data_dir / "Canada - Wikipedia Special Export.xml") as infile:
    doc = xmltodict.parse(infile.read())

print(doc.keys())
print(doc['mediawiki'].keys())
print(doc['mediawiki']['@xmlns'])
```

```
odict_keys(['mediawiki'])
odict_keys(['@xmlns', '@xmlns:xsi', '@xsi:schemaLocation', '@version',
'@xml:lang', 'siteinfo', 'page'])
http://www.mediawiki.org/xml/export-0.10/
```

Finding the revision of the page through this approach is very tedious since we don't have any shortcuts like `revision.id.text`. Instead, we must navigate through the whole nested dictionary. This does not seem particularly useful here, but in Chapter 10 we will see how it is easy to transform an entire XML export into JSON data and then upload it into a `DataFrame`.

```
print(doc['mediawiki']['page']['revision']['id'])
```

```
1079679373
```

Now you can navigate to https://en.wikipedia.org/w/index.php?title=Canada&oldid= 1079679373 and see exactly the version of this page that we used for parsing.

 Serialisation

Sometimes, you want to close a program and pick up right where you left off. This might mean ensuring that all the objects are in the state that you want them to be with no further processing. This process of creating a file that will represent the state of some values is called *serialisation*. In Python this process is called 'pickling'.

One useful approach with pickling is when you are processing text on a server, you can pickle your current state of each object. Then if the program goes sour (e.g. it loses connection to an external server), the program can pickle all the variables marking your progress when it shuts down so you can pick up where you left off after addressing any issues with data collection. You can only serialise one object at a time, but that object can be a collection of other objects.

Since these files are meant for the computer, they will be written and read as *bytestreams*. In this case, we have to let Python know we are reading bytes with the rb and wb arguments in our `open()` command, instead of the classic r for read, and w for write.

```
import pickle

data_example = {'RevisionID':1079679373, 'PageID':5042916}
data_for_pickle = [data_example,'Other Data',3.1415]

pickle.dump(data_for_pickle,
            open(data_dir / 'temp.pkl','wb'))

# Check to see if the data comes back as we expected
data_from_pkl = pickle.load(open(data_dir / 'temp.pkl','rb'))
print(data_from_pkl)
```

```
[{'RevisionID': 1079679373, 'PageID': 5042916}, 'Other Data', 3.1415]
```

4.6.1 Long-term storage: Pickles and `feather`

Because pickles are so tightly coupled to the specific version of Python (and even the libraries installed), they are really handy for short-term storage but too fragile for long-term storage. Instead, one should use one of the file formats discussed above, such as CSV, XML, JSON, or even Excel, which has extensive support and care with backwards compatibility.

If you find yourself with really demanding storage needs, you will probably want to seek out extra resources on this. One possibility would be to look into the `feather` package. It was co-written by the creator of `pandas`, Wes McKinney, and is very fast, compact, and scalable to very large data.

With the information you have here, implementing work in `feather` shouldn't be a challenge, especially with numerous online tutorials. Regardless of the file type you choose, remember to check both writing the file to disk and rereading it before you put it away for a while.

 Summary

File formats might not be the most exciting topic and are certainly one that is often considered far away from traditional social science, or so one might think. In practice, I certainly remember as a postgraduate the trials of getting data for SPSS and having to convert it to Stata or SAS. Prior to the massive rise in the use of Python and R, quantitative data in social science was almost exclusively accomplished using programs that were for pay, syntactically unorthodox, and often incompatible with each other. By contrast, what we see here is that Python is free, that the file formats are not software-specific, and that it is assumed that Python should be able to open the data. This is great news not just for data science, but for science. In general, we want science to be as open as possible. Obviously, some data must be restricted for reasons of privacy, but the norm now is towards being less locked into a single product or version.

Social science often dreams of that perfect world in a potentially dangerous way. An emphasis on survey research and qualitative coding of transcripts implies that claims are made with data of a specific shape and size. We might be inclined to call this the 'independent case model'. It has each row as a case and columns to represent variables. It looks a lot like a `DataFrame`, and for good reason. The tabulation of cases allows for all kinds of statistical routines that otherwise are not as accessible or tractable.

What I am suggesting here is that the process of transforming social life into this table does not have to happen as a part of data collection. The data can be collected from a variety of sources, in a variety of ways. Granted, independent random sample data collection is still an excellent way to make a generalisable claim. However, an emphasis on generalisability to a population bounded by national borders sometimes unduly restricts our ability to make claims about a specific population or group that spans borders or exists primarily online. Having all of the comments from a message board or all of the pictures posted in a forum means we can make very extensive claims about that board as a social system. Stated differently, we do not start by looking for places where life imitates the `DataFrame` and try to come up with questions to ask. Instead, we start with the data in the shape we can get it and then work on transforming it into a `DataFrame`.

As we step outside of what we can do with survey research we will find that there are all kinds of ways of creating and managing data for the purposes of making claims. In the next chapter we begin to embark on this process of reshaping data so that it can meet our needs.

 Extensions and reflections

- Did you know that you can get JSON from a Reddit site simply by replacing `www.reddit.com` with `api.reddit.com`? Go to a particular subreddit and make that change, save the data and get it into a `DataFrame`. Try some early exploration such as learning what are the columns, how to filter to data that has been upvoted, or even just cross-check the data in the `DataFrame` with what you would see through the interface. For example, there are a lot of columns. How will you navigate them? Will you export to Excel and view in a spreadsheet? Print columns? Scroll through Jupyter? There are many approaches to data reduction here. One example might be to first check if a column has all missing values and remove it.
- You can extract multiple Wikipedia pages at the same time from Wikipedia's special export. They will come down as XML. Here is a command to get the first thousand edits to the article 'Data' from the terminal (not within a Jupyter Lab notebook) 'using `curl`'. This is a commonly used application to collect data from the web:

```
curl -d "" 'https://en.wikipedia.org/w/index.php?
           title=Special:Export&pages=Data&offset=1&action=submit'
           -o "wiki_data_batch1.xml"
```

- If you run that from the Terminal (or on Windows PowerShell replacing `curl` with `invoke-RestMethod`), you will get a relatively large XML file (around 12 MB) with the first thousand revisions of the article for 'data' on Wikipedia. If you can wrangle that data using XML and get it into a `DataFrame`, you can start to look at how the page changes over time. For example, when did DIKW appear? Was it always there? The skills for assessing the change over time will partially depend on some of the techniques in Chapter 12, but at least being able to ask `df["text"].map(lambda x: "DIKW" in x)` should already start to give you some ideas. Try using `xmltodict` and `pd.json_normalize` to start your exploration. Some example code related to this is available on the book's GitHub page.

5
MERGING AND GROUPING DATA

================= Learning goals =========

- Understand how to add new data to a `DataFrame` in either columns or rows
- Add new data using `pd.concat` (as a 'one-to-one' merge)
- Use a 'one-to-many' merge as a way to link data at different scales
- Employ different joins to exclude or include data
- Group data so that you get an aggregate per-group statistic
- Understand how to group mean and grand mean centre a variable
- Use these operations in SQL (via `sqlite`) as well as in Python.

 ## Combining data across tables

Data that we want often exists in multiple places. We might want data from conversations online, from tables about the users who take part in those conversations, aggregates about the site, or data from the country of origin of different users. Combining all these data takes a variety of skills for different circumstances. In this chapter I cover three common and important circumstances for combining data:

- *Concatenation.* When you have two or more datasets that have the same columns. The resulting `DataFrame` is like simply attaching one `DataFrame` to another.
- *Merging.* When you have data from two datasets that have different columns or are on different scales. You need a key that links data from one table and data from another table. For example, with country-level statistics about a user, you would use the country code as a key.
- *Grouping.* When you have data that you want to aggregate and get group-level statistics, such as the number of users in a group, average score per group, and maximum score. Grouping produces a second table with one row per group rather than one row per case.

Before concluding the chapter, I also introduce SQL as a means for merging and grouping tabular data outside of Python.

 ## A review of adding data to a `DataFrame` using `concat`

The simplest case of combining data is just adding more data to a `DataFrame`. This is often referred to as *concatenation* since we are attaching data rather than changing its shape. Thus if we have one row in one table and concatenate it to a second table with 10 rows, we have a new `DataFrame` with 11 rows. The same can be said if we concatenate by column (though for columns the syntax is sometimes a little easier if we are only adding a single `Series`).

5.2.1 Adding rows

When adding data where we have the same columns, it is typically because we have new cases. This happens when we are processing data and want to add rows one at a time as the data comes in. Imagine you have a stream of tweets and you add a new tweet to the existing DataFrame. Below we create three small data frames with different values. This way you can observe what happens to the values when we try to combine this data, particularly when the two tables are not in the same shape.

```
import pandas as pd
```

```
testList1 = [["a","b","c","d"],["g","h","j","k"]]
testFrame1 = pd.DataFrame(testList1)
display(testFrame1)
```

```
testList2 = [["m","n","o","p"],["s","t","u","v"]]
testFrame2 = pd.DataFrame(testList2)
display(testFrame2)
```

```
testList3 = [["x","y","z","aa","bb","cc"],["e","f","q","w","ww","www"]]
testFrame3 = pd.DataFrame(testList3)
display(testFrame3)
```

	0	1	2	3
0	a	b	c	d
1	g	h	j	k

	0	1	2	3
0	m	n	o	p
1	s	t	u	v

	0	1	2	3	4	5
0	x	y	z	aa	bb	cc
1	e	f	q	w	ww	www

Attempt 1: Adding the frames together

For string variables the word 'concatenate' refers to the + symbol. Thus we concatenate like so:

```
print("mile" + "stone")
```

```
milestone
```

Thus, if we use the + operator with two DataFrame objects will it also concatenate them? Not really. Observe:

```
list1and2 = testList1 + testList2
display(list1and2)
```

```
[['a', 'b', 'c', 'd'],
 ['g', 'h', 'j', 'k'],
 ['m', 'n', 'o', 'p'],
 ['s', 't', 'u', 'v']]
```

```
frame1and2 = testFrame1 + testFrame2
display(frame1and2)
```

```
frame1and3 = testFrame1 + testFrame3
display(frame1and3)
```

	0	1	2	3
0	am	bn	co	dp
1	gs	ht	ju	kv

	0	1	2	3	4	5
0	ax	by	cz	daa	NaN	NaN
1	ge	hf	jq	kw	NaN	NaN

The plus symbol (+) was employed to mean 'concatenate' for a list, but for a DataFrame it was a sort of cell-by-cell addition (or 'Hadamard addition'), where cell A1 from the first table is literally concatenated/added to cell A1 from the second table. Then it created some missing data in the third attempt (frame1and3) since it concatenated the columns 4 and 5 with nothing (i.e. NaN).

Attempt 2: Concatenating frames

To concatenate the DataFrame objects you can use a pd.concat() statement instead of frame1 + frame2. By default, concat adds data by row, so the second element in the list of things to be concatenated goes *below* the first element. Observe:

```
display(testFrame4) = pd.concat([testFrame1, testFrame2, testFrame3])
display(testFrame4)
```

	0	1	2	3	4	5
0	a	b	c	d	NaN	NaN
1	g	h	j	k	NaN	NaN
0	m	n	o	p	NaN	NaN
1	s	t	u	v	NaN	NaN
0	x	y	z	aa	bb	cc
1	e	f	q	w	ww	www

This is the same as what we saw in Chapter 3, but now we can see what happens when we add data with a different dimension. It creates missing data for the rows or columns where no data already exists, but otherwise concatenates the data ensuring that the right data are in the right columns.

5.2.2 Adding columns

Single columns of data

For a single column of data, the syntax is typically df[<colname>] = <col>. Remember that it is not a number. We can look up columns by number using df.iloc[:,<col_num>] but we cannot create them this way.

There are two scenarios for successfully adding a single column to a DataFrame:

1   *Data in a list.* If the data is in a list, then you can add it to the DataFrame and it will assume the first item goes in the positionally first row. So be careful if you sort your data before you add a list.
2   *Data has an index.* If the data has an index (i.e. it is a Series), then it doesn't have to be the same length. The program will look for the index to match and include only those cases where the index matches. The program will not do this with a dictionary (i.e. matching dictionary keys to DataFrame indices). The program will treat the dictionary keys as a list and then expect them (like a list) to be ordered and the same length as the DataFrame.

```
df = pd.DataFrame(testList1)

display("The original data:", df)
```

```
The original data:
```

	0	1	2	3	4	5
0	a	b	c	d	66	33
1	g	h	j	k	77	44

```
dd = {0:"AA",1:"BB",2:"CC"}
lll = [33,44,55]
ll2 = [66,77]
ss = pd.Series(lll) # ,index=[2,1,0])

for col in [dd,lll,ll2,ss]:
    print(f"Data to try:\n{col}")
    try:
        df[len(df.columns)] = col
    except ValueError:
        print("Error: Please add cols of the correct length or use a Series.")
    else:
        print("Data successfully added")
    print()
```

```
Data to try:
{0: 'AA', 1: 'BB', 2: 'CC'}
Error: Please add cols of the correct length or use a Series.

Data to try:
[33, 44, 55]
Error: Please add cols of the correct length or use a Series.

Data to try:
[66, 77]
Data successfully added

Data to try:
0    33
1    44
2    55
dtype: int64
Data successfully added

display(df)
```

	0	1	2	3	4	5
0	a	b	c	d	66	33
1	g	h	j	k	77	44

Notice how the list with two elements [66,77] did not throw an error. That's because it was in the same dimension as the Series. However, the list with three elements [33,44,55] threw an error before we converted that list into a Series.

Why did it work for a Series? Because the Series had an index with the numbers 0 and 1, just like the DataFrame, so it mapped the value for 0 onto the first row and the value for 1 onto the second row. Uncomment the index=[2,1,0]) above and try again. Doing so, the last column will have numbers in a different order. That's because the concatenation used the index and the index was different between the two objects.

Multiple rows or columns of data

If you want to add multiple rows or columns, then you first need to turn this data into a DataFrame of its own. Then you can run the pd.concat commands as above. For adding columns you would want the optional argument axis=1.

```
testFrame4 = pd.concat([testFrame1, testFrame2],axis=1)
testFrame4.index = ['top-row', 'bottom-row']
display(testFrame4)
```

	0	1	2	3	0	1	2	3
top-row	a	b	c	d	m	n	o	p
bottom-row	g	h	j	k	s	t	u	v

The issue with not using unique indices is that you can unintentionally edit the wrong cell. In the frame above we see that there are two columns named 0, so that when you want to change data for one column but not the other, you run into trouble. See below:

```
testFrame4.loc["top-row",0] = "test"
```

```
display(testFrame4)
```

	0	1	2	3	0	1	2	3
top-row	test	b	c	d	test	n	o	p
bottom-row	g	h	j	k	s	t	u	v

We can circumvent this issue in two ways. The first is to use `ignore_index=True` as a parameter for our `concat` statement. This will create a new set of columns numbered from 0 to n. But if we want to preserve these indices but also create a way for the columns to be uniquely referenced, we can use a multi-level index.

5.2.3 Multi-level indexed data

Multi-level indices allow for sub-indexing for the `DataFrame`. Imagine you want to look at some work by city in the USA and you have some people in Springfield. Which one? There are 34 states with a township or population named 'Springfield'. So we could then use a second index with the state. In this duller example, we can just use some bland labels of `left` and `right`, which will be the top-level columns and then the existing numbers 0, 1, 2, 3 as the sub-columns.

```
testFrame4 = pd.concat([testFrame1, testFrame2],axis=1,
                    keys=["left-side-vars","right-side-vars"])
```

```
testFrame4.index = ['top', 'bottom']
display(testFrame4)
```

	left-side-vars				right-side-vars			
	0	1	2	3	0	1	2	3
top	a	b	c	d	m	n	o	p
bottom	g	h	j	k	s	t	u	v

Now we can uniquely access a column or element. To do that you place both indices starting with the top one inside of an indexer. Since we have two levels for the column names, we can access data like so:

```
print("Query a Series from multi-indexed data:")
print(testFrame4["left-side-vars",3])
```

```
Query a Series from multi-indexed data:
top        d
bottom     k
Name: (left-side-vars, 3), dtype: object
```

```
print("Query a single item for multi-indexed data:")
print(testFrame4["left-side-vars",2]["top"])
```

```
Query a single item for multi-indexed data:
c
```

5.2.4 Transposing a `DataFrame`

To transpose data is to swap the columns and the rows. It is like flipping the `DataFrame` on its side. To transpose a `DataFrame`, simply append `.T` and it will return a transposed `DataFrame`.

```
display(testFrame4.T)
```

		top	bottom
left-side-vars	0	a	g
	1	b	h
	2	c	j
	3	d	k
right-side-vars	0	m	s
	1	n	t
	2	o	u
	3	p	v

Notice now that this is done that we have a multi-level index rather than multi-level columns.

 The 'key' to merging

When you merge two tables, you need to link the data somehow. Maybe you have people and their current country of residence in one table and you want to bring in more country-level statistics. You can use the country name as the *key* that links the data. Imagine we have a user named Pedro in a user database for a news media site called `users_df`. Imagine there is a column in the data called `country`. And in Pedro's row the value is `ES`, the two-character ISO code for Spain. We then have a second `DataFrame` with details about country-level values, such as overall readership, population, and literacy rates. If the country data has a column with the two-character country code `ES`, then we can link the data. If the key is not the same, then the data will not merge. For example, imagine we download data from the World Bank and it has the three-character country code (`ESP`) instead. We would first have to merge in a separate file that converts the three-character codes to the two-character codes.

5.3.1 One-to-many versus one-to-one relationships

With concatenation above we used a one-to-one relationship. That is, the data that was present once in the first table is present once in the merged table, and the only thing that might change is the columns or indices. That makes sense when we add rows or add columns. But we might want to add data where one measurement applies to multiple cases in our data. In this case, we might have many users from Spain, so for each user we would want the same measurement concerning Spain in the column for each user. That is, we have *one* measurement in one table that links to *many* rows in the other table.

Since we are describing a one-to-many merge, that means that one of the tables should have only unique entries. Imagine if our table of country-level statistics had two countries with the `ES` code. Then it could not be useful as a key. In the country-level data there should be only one row with `ES`. We would call this a 'unique key'. If this key is the one that is meant to uniquely identify this case or this row by design, it is often called a 'primary key'. Some database programs enforce this strictly so that every row necessarily has a primary key. If you try to create a duplicate entry in that column, it will throw an error.

The users in this example did not need a unique key because they all want the same data about Spain. However, there might be times when you want to uniquely identify a user. For example, in this data it is likely, depending on circumstances, that we could have more than one Pedro in our data. In the Stack Exchange data used in Chapter 10 there is a second unused table called `users.xml`. If you wrangle that table, you will discover that there is a column called `DisplayName`. We should not use that for merging since there are multiple users with the same `DisplayName` (there are dozens of users with the `DisplayName` 'Chris' for example). However, each user has a unique `Id`. This would be an appropriate key.

As the name suggests, a one-to-many mapping means that data from one row in one table gets mapped on to (potentially) many rows in the other table. In this case, we had a table of country-level statistics with one row for Spain. Then the values in this table get mapped by the merge onto every row with a user from Spain. Fortunately, we do not have to do this for every country one at a time. Instead, the merge will match the data so that the table with one value gets mapped onto the many rows in the second table linked by a key.

To show this in action, below I use some of the countries and territories of the United Kingdom in a `country_df` table. Then we map the single score per country on to the multiple people from that country in our `users_df` table. In the examples, I want you to notice that while both tables contain the four countries of the UK ('England', 'Wales', 'Scotland', and 'Northern Ireland'), `country_df` will also contain Jersey, while `users_df` will contain a user from the

Isle of Man. Notice that by default these two places are removed when we merge because the keys are not in both tables.

```
d = {"England":53,"Jersey":.1,"Northern Ireland":2,"Scotland":5,"Wales":3}

country_df = pd.DataFrame(pd.Series(d),
                          columns=["Population"])
display(country_df)
```

	Population
England	53.000000
Jersey	0.100000
Northern Ireland	2.000000
Scotland	5.000000
Wales	3.000000

```
people = [["Ali",32,"Wales"],
          ["Barb",35,"Northern Ireland"],
          ["Cam",21,"England"],
          ["Dot",45,"Northern Ireland"],
          ["Ellen",21,"Scotland"],
          ["Farah",50,"England"],
          ["Grant",28,"Scotland"],
          ["Hannah",36,"England"],
          ["Idris",40,"Isle of Man"]]

people_df = pd.DataFrame(people,
                         columns=["Name","Age","Country"])
display(people_df)
```

	Name	Age	Country
0	Ali	32	Wales
1	Barb	35	Northern Ireland
2	Cam	21	England
3	Dot	45	Northern Ireland
4	Ellen	21	Scotland
5	Farah	50	England
6	Grant	28	Scotland
7	Hannah	36	England
8	Idris	40	Isle of Man

In `country_df` I used the country names as the index. In `people_df` our index was just sequential numbers. This is not a problem. In `pandas` you get to say whether your key is the index or is a variable in the `DataFrame` itself.

In the merge statement we refer to one DataFrame as the 'left' DataFrame and one as the 'right' DataFrame. You can merge two tables in either order but it will lead to slight differences in the resulting output (which are mainly aesthetic and will be shown later). How to know which DataFrame is on the left and the right? The first DataFrame reading left-to-right is the 'left' and the second one is the 'right'. I've printed a generic version of the statement below. You will notice that you need to stipulate both the names of the tables (as <Left_DataFrame> and <Right_DataFrame>, respectively). Then you can refer to either the column, which is going to be the key, or use the index as the key. You can do this differently for the left DataFrame and the right DataFrame.

```
new_df = <Left_DataFrame>.merge(<Right_DataFrame>,
                    left_on=<left_keys> {or left_index=True},
                    right_on=<right_keys> {or right_index=True})
```

```
# Here we use the 'country' column for the key for the left DataFrame.
# We use the index for the key in the right DataFrame.
merge_df = people_df.merge(country_df,
                    left_on="Country",
                    right_index=True)
display(merge_df)
```

	Name	Age	Country	Population
0	Ali	32	Wales	3.000000
1	Barb	35	Northern Ireland	2.000000
3	Dot	45	Northern Ireland	2.000000
2	Cam	21	England	53.000000
5	Farah	50	England	53.000000
7	Hannah	36	England	53.000000
4	Ellen	21	Scotland	5.000000
6	Grant	28	Scotland	5.000000

Let's see that again, except I will switch the left and right tables.

```
merge_df = country_df.merge(people_df,
                    left_index=True,
                    right_on="Country")
display(merge_df)
```

	Population	Name	Age	Country
2	53.000000	Cam	21	England
5	53.000000	Farah	50	England
7	53.000000	Hannah	36	England
1	2.000000	Barb	35	Northern Ireland
3	2.000000	Dot	45	Northern Ireland
4	5.000000	Ellen	21	Scotland
6	5.000000	Grant	28	Scotland
0	3.000000	Ali	32	Wales

Notice that when we first merged with `people_df` on the left, the columns from that `DataFrame` showed up on the left-hand side in the new table. Similarly, when we used `country_df` on the left-hand side, the columns from that `DataFrame` (which here is simply 'Population') appear on the left-hand side. The rows in the new table appear in order of the left-hand side table. So in the first one with `people_df` on the left it went `Ali`, `Barb`, etc., and the second one with `country_df` on the left had the rows in order of `England`, `Northern Ireland`, etc.

 Understanding joins

Regardless of whether we merge `people_df` into `country_df` or the other way around, in both cases it seems that we lose `Jersey` and `Idris` from the `Isle of Man` in the process. What happened? By default, when you merge in pandas it does a kind of join called an *inner join*. An inner join means only return rows where the key is in both tables. There are other joins to consider. Personally, I found it somewhat hard to recall which was which until I made the connection between keys and sets. Below I will explain what sets are (both in Python and loosely speaking in maths as well) and then connect them to merges.

5.4.1 A join as a kind of set logic

A `set` is a data structure that contains only unique values. So if you have a list like `ex1 = ["Spain","France","Spain","Italy","Italy"]` and you convert it to a set `set(ex1)`, it will only be the following: `{"Spain","France","Italy"}`.

```
s1 = [1,2,2,3,4,5,5,5,5,5,6]
print("As a list:\t",s1)
print("As a set:\t",set(s1))
print("As an array:\t",pd.Series(s1).unique())
```

```
As a list:      [1, 2, 2, 3, 4, 5, 5, 5, 5, 5, 6]
As a set:       {1, 2, 3, 4, 5, 6}
As an array:    [1 2 3 4 5 6]
```

Since sets contain at most one copy of any object, we can ask whether an object is in the set or in multiple sets. This is like the keys in a merge. In an inner join, if the key is in both tables then we keep the row with that key. Similarly, with set logic there is an operation called *intersection* which means the elements that are common in both sets.

There are other set operations worth considering as well. For example, another important operation is called *union*, which means include all the items from either set. Remember, if the sets are `{1,2,3}` and `{1,3,5}` then the union does not mean `{1,2,3,3,5}` since sets only contain unique elements. The union would be `{1,2,3,5}`. Below I show these two operations and a couple of others that will be relevant for joins.

```
setCount = set([1,2,3,4,5]) # the first five numbers
setOdd = set([1,3,5,7,9]) # the first five odd numbers

print(f"setCount:\t{setCount}")
print(f"setOdd:  \t{setOdd}")
print()

print("Union (all of the elements from both):\t\t", setOdd.union(setCount))
print("Intersection (all elements in common):\t\t",
    setOdd.intersection(setCount))

print("Set subtraction (setCount minus setOdd):\t", setCount - setOdd)
print("Set subtraction (setOdd minus setCount):\t", setOdd - setCount)
```

```
setCount:      {1, 2, 3, 4, 5}
setOdd:        {1, 3, 5, 7, 9}

Union (all of the elements from both):        {1, 2, 3, 4, 5, 7, 9}
Intersection (all elements in common):        {1, 3, 5}
Set subtraction (setCount minus setOdd):      {2, 4}
Set subtraction (setOdd minus setCount):      {9, 7}
```

Did you happen to notice that it printed the sets with { } like dictionaries and not [] like lists? This is because dictionary keys also work like sets. In a dictionary you can have {'a':'apple', 'b':'banana'} but you cannot have {'a':'apple', 'a':'asparagus'}, since keys would be duplicated.

To translate these operations to merging, we can think of set operations as the way we do joins between DataFrame objects. Here are the joins available with merge:

- *Outer join.* The *union* of both DataFrame objects. So if there is a key in either the left_keys or the right_keys, the new table will have a row corresponding to that key.
- *Inner join.* The *intersection* of both DataFrame objects. So if there is a key that exists in both the left_keys **and** the right_keys, then the new table will include a row with that key.
- *Left join.* All the rows corresponding to the left_keys are kept regardless of whether there is a match in the right_keys. So if we have a row in the left table that doesn't have a match in the right table, it will have missing data for the columns we merge in from the right table. If we have a key in the right_keys that is not in the left table, that is discarded. This is often useful when our variable of interest is the one we want to keep at all times, such as respondents to a survey. We don't care if there are country values for other countries, but we do care if we discard respondents to the survey.
- *Right join.* Same as a left join, except we keep all the keys from the right-hand-side DataFrame.

Below I will use some synthetic data to illustrate each of these.

5.4.2 Inner join

An inner join is the equivalent to a set intersection. We get rid of the keys and the corresponding rows where there is no match in the other table. From the `people_df` we lose `Idris` from `Isle of Man` and from `country_df` we lose `Jersey`. This is the default behaviour when merging.

```
merge_df = people_df.merge(country_df,
                           left_on="Country", right_index=True,
                           how='inner')
display(merge_df)
```

	Name	Age	Country	Population
0	Ali	32	Wales	3.000000
1	Barb	35	Northern Ireland	2.000000
3	Dot	45	Northern Ireland	2.000000
2	Cam	21	England	53.000000
5	Farah	50	England	53.000000
7	Hannah	36	England	53.000000
4	Ellen	21	Scotland	5.000000
6	Grant	28	Scotland	5.000000

5.4.3 Outer join

The outer join is equivalent to the union of two sets of keys. Whereas the inner join removed both `Isle of Man` and `Jersey` from their tables, an outer join will keep both of these keys and the corresponding rows, but mark the missing data as `np.nan`. Also notice below that the index is now pretty messed up. This is because the index isn't reset. If you uncomment the line below to reset the index, it fixes this and numbers all of the elements sequentially.

```
merge_df = people_df.merge(country_df,
                           left_on="Country",
                           right_index=True,
                           how='outer')

# merge_df.reset_index(inplace=True, drop=True)
display(merge_df)
```

	Name	Age	Country	Population
0.000000	Ali	32.000000	Wales	3.000000
1.000000	Barb	35.000000	Northern Ireland	2.000000
3.000000	Dot	45.000000	Northern Ireland	2.000000

2.000000	Cam	21.000000	England	53.000000
5.000000	Farah	50.000000	England	53.000000
7.000000	Hannah	36.000000	England	53.000000
4.000000	Ellen	21.000000	Scotland	5.000000
6.000000	Grant	28.000000	Scotland	5.000000
8.000000	Idris	40.000000	Isle of Man	NaN
NaN	NaN	NaN	Jersey	0.100000

5.4.4 Left join

Below we will merge with how='left'. The left table is people_df since it appears to the left of merge_df. This way we keep all of the people, regardless of whether their country has data in country_df.

```
merge_df = people_df.merge(country_df,
                           left_on="Country", right_index=True,
                           how='left')
display(merge_df)
```

	Name	Age	Country	Population
0	Ali	32	Wales	3.000000
1	Barb	35	Northern Ireland	2.000000
2	Cam	21	England	53.000000
3	Dot	45	Northern Ireland	2.000000
4	Ellen	21	Scotland	5.000000
5	Farah	50	England	53.000000
6	Grant	28	Scotland	5.000000
7	Hannah	36	England	53.000000
8	Idris	40	Isle of Man	NaN

Notice how this time the index was the same as in the original left table.

5.4.5 Right join

This is pretty much the same as the left join, except it is merging on the right instead of the left. Compare the indices in the following to the indices above. Why are they different?

```
merge_df = people_df.merge(country_df,
                           left_on="Country", right_index=True,
                           how='right')
display(merge_df)
```

	Name	Age	Country	Population
2.000000	Cam	21.000000	England	53.000000
5.000000	Farah	50.000000	England	53.000000
7.000000	Hannah	36.000000	England	53.000000
NaN	NaN	NaN	Jersey	0.100000
1.000000	Barb	35.000000	Northern Ireland	2.000000
3.000000	Dot	45.000000	Northern Ireland	2.000000
4.000000	Ellen	21.000000	Scotland	5.000000
6.000000	Grant	28.000000	Scotland	5.000000
0.000000	Ali	32.000000	Wales	3.000000

They are different because Python treats NaN as a floating-point number. This means that once you place a NaN in the index it convert the entire index to `float` rather than `int`. You really should never have a NaN for an index.

 ## 5.5 Grouping and aggregating data

To recap, a one-to-many merge takes the one element and 'broadcasts' it to all the many rows that have the same key. In effect, you are creating copies of the one row for each of the many rows that match. But what about doing that in the other direction, that is, taking many rows and reducing them to a single row? That is *aggregating* data.

Most objects in Python, whether they are strings, numbers, dates, or even more complex objects, can be sorted somehow. If you can sort a collection, then you can find the maximum, minimum, and most common values. Thus, for any `Series`, you can use `count`, `max`, `min`, `mode`, and `len` to aggregate the `Series` into a single object. For numerical data we can further get some statistical measures such as the `mean`, `median`, `dispersion`, and `skew`. You might say that any approach that involves taking a `Series` or a collection and returning a single object or value is an aggregation.

Aggregating over subsets of the data rather than the whole `Series` is not merely a technical skill. It is an essential part of how we perform an analysis in many social scientific domains. We can look not only at the population of a country, but also at the population by some subcategory such as region, gender, political affiliation, or Internet user. We might want the average value per region, or by ethnic group. For personal network analysis, we would aggregate on a per-respondent basis, for example getting the count of the number of supportive persons nominated by the respondent. Often the cutpoints for the groups are ambiguous, and even discovering which data belongs in which group can be a meaningful scientific contribution. This applies whether we are classifying animals, movie genres, or sports. Here we are going to assume that the categories for grouping the data are already given to us from the data. Trying to infer categories within which to group the data is a type of 'classification task' suitable for machine learning. We are not doing much of that in this book, but you can see some examples of approaches that lead up to such classification in Chapter 13, where we classify nodes in a network using *community detection*, and Chapter 11, where we classify text in documents using a *naïve Bayes classifier*.

To aggregate across some distinct set of categories, we will first *split* the data into distinct groups, such as country in the above example. Then we can *apply* some aggregation function to the groups and it will return a Series with one value for each group. You have already seen this in action as this is what happens during a value_counts() method. The data is first split into groups, one group for each collection of objects with the same value, then the method applies the count operation to each group individually, then these count results are *combined* into a Series, which is normally printed for reading. This approach is generally referred to as the 'split–apply–combine' method from the approach by McKinney (2012) and Wickham (2011).

In the example below, if we want to get the average age by country we can similarly use split–apply–combine. Note, for example, that we have two people from Northern Ireland, Barb who is 35 and Dot who is 45. Their average age would be 40. To do this programmatically (i.e. for all users across all countries), we would first want to group the data by country (df.groupby('Country')). Then within each group we apply an aggregation (in this case the average or .mean()). Then we want to combine all the results so we have a new Series with countries as indices and the average age as the values. In the example below, notice that we will have two columns that are numeric, Age and Tweets. The split–apply–combine method will return a new DataFrame with the average age and the average number of tweets. Below it is just one statement: people_df.groupby('Country').mean(), which I then assign to group_df.

You will notice that when I print group_df I also include .style.format("{:0.1f}"). This is because when you take the average sometimes the numbers can be really long (like 4.333333333333). So the .style.format() says apply this style for all columns. Then the {:0.1f} is a bit complicated to unpack but it effectively means turn this floating-point number (hence the f) into one with one decimal place .1. Change that number to a 2 for two decimal places, etc.

```
people_df = pd.DataFrame([["Ali",32,"Wales",3200],
              ["Barb",35,"Northern Ireland",202],
              ["Cam",21,"England",657],
              ["Dot",45,"Northern Ireland",24],
              ["Ellen",21,"Scotland",81],
              ["Farah",50,"England",9723],
              ["Grant",28,"Scotland",664],
              ["Hannah",36,"England",200],
              ["Idris",40,"Isle of Man",1]],columns=["Name","Age","Country","Tweets"])

group_df = people_df.groupby('Country').mean()

display(group_df.style.format("{:.1f}"))
```

	Age	Tweets
Country		
England	35.7	3526.7
Isle of Man	40.0	1.0
Northern Ireland	40.0	113.0
Scotland	24.5	372.5
Wales	32.0	3200.0

We can do more than one form of aggregation at a time. Observe below how we use multiple forms of aggregation with the .agg(<list_of_aggregation_methods>) method.

```
display(people_df[['Country','Age','Tweets']]
            .groupby('Country')
            .agg(["sum","mean"])
            .style.format("{:.1f}"))
```

	Age		Tweets	
	sum	mean	sum	mean
Country				
England	107.0	35.7	10580.0	3526.7
Isle of Man	40.0	40.0	1.0	1.0
Northern Ireland	80.0	40.0	226.0	113.0
Scotland	49.0	24.5	745.0	372.5
Wales	32.0	32.0	3200.0	3200.0

5.5.1 Mean centring

One example of a use for the split–apply–combine method is what's called *mean centring*. It's a way of transforming the data so that the midpoint of the distribution is zero, instead of whatever the mean is. For example, imagine you have a dataset of holidays per year across industries. Centring on the average of the whole dataset would be 'grand' mean centring. So we take the average of the entire dataset, subtract everyone's value (each employee and their holidays) and this becomes the new score. Centring on a subgroup, such as the values per sector or per country, would be 'group' mean centring. Then, a case gets a zero if it has the average for its group, not for the whole dataset. Group mean centring makes use of both aggregation and merging in the same operation. Thus, it is a *grouping* operation.

Grand mean centring and group mean centring are forms of *normalisation*, but certainly not the only ones. They are ways we can normalise scores to make their ranges consistent across distributions, and thereby allow for comparisons across them. For example, imagine you are examining differences in activity in a Facebook group. You have a distribution of posts, each one with a countable number of replies. Grand mean centring means your new variable is 0 if a post gets the average number of replies. Group mean centring, such as grouping by person, means that a post would get a score of 0 if it had *that person's* average number of replies per post.

Programmatically, grand mean centring isn't that much of a challenge:

1   Calculate the aggregated value for the Series: var_mean = df[<Column>].mean().
2   Create a new column with the old value minus the mean: df[<NewColumn>] =
     df[<Column>] - var_mean.
3   Formatting. This last one is optional but I really appreciate seeing nicely formatted numbers
     like 36.7 rather than 36.6666666667 which are often produced when calculating means:
     df.style.format('{:.1f}').

For group mean centring, it is more of a challenge because we are first doing an aggregation to get the scores per group, but then we have to merge the *one* score per group to the *many* rows included in that group. Then we can do the subtraction of the value from the mean to centre it.

1   Use split-apply-combine to get a `Series` for the averages per group: `mean_df = df.groupby(<Column>).mean()`.

2   Merge in the values so that each row gets the mean scores for that row's group: `df.merge(mean_df, left_on=<Column>, right_index=True, suffixes=['','_mean'])`. Note the use of the `suffixes` parameter, which is used to distinguish an old variable from a merged in variable with the same name. The argument `['','_mean']` says append `''` to the left-hand column names and `'_mean'` to the right-hand column names.

3   Create a new variable which is the original value minus the mean: `df[<Column_gc>] = df[<Column>] - df[<Column_mean>]`.

4   Don't forget formatting! If you cannot format the entire table, then you can use a dictionary to specify the formatting for each variable: for example, `df.style.format({'var_mean':{:.1f}, 'count_data':{:.0f}})`.

Below I use our existing data to get group-mean-centred variables by country.

```
group_df = people_df.groupby('Country').mean()

# Try to omit suffixes parameter and observe
gmc_df = people_df.merge(group_df,
                         left_on="Country", right_index=True,
                         suffixes=["","-mean"])

# I use _gc suffix for group-centred
for i in group_df.columns:
    gmc_df[i + "-gc"] = gmc_df[i] - gmc_df[i + "-mean"]

# We only want *_gc and *_mean columns to be formatted.
# The others are count data.
format_dict = {}
for i in group_df.columns:
    format_dict[i + "-gc"] = '{0:.1f}'
    format_dict[i + "-mean"] = '{0:.1f}'

display(gmc_df.style.format(format_dict).hide(axis='index'))
```

Name	Age	Country	Tweets	Age-mean	Tweets-mean	Age-gc	Tweets-gc
Ali	32	Wales	3200	32.0	3200.0	0.0	0.0
Barb	35	Northern Ireland	202	40.0	113.0	-5.0	89.0

(Continued)

Dot	45	Northern Ireland	24	40.0	113.0	5.0	-89.0
Cam	21	England	657	35.7	3526.7	-14.7	-2869.7
Farah	50	England	9723	35.7	3526.7	14.3	6196.3
Hannah	36	England	200	35.7	3526.7	0.3	-3326.7
Ellen	21	Scotland	81	24.5	372.5	-3.5	-291.5
Grant	28	Scotland	664	24.5	372.5	3.5	291.5
Idris	40	Isle of Man	1	40.0	1.0	0.0	0.0

5.6 Long versus wide data

Depending on how your data is structured, you are likely to have either long or wide data of interest. Wide data is like a survey where you have one row per person and then each person has a cell that lists off their favourite music genres. Long data instead has one row per person per genre, so you will have multiple rows with the same person. This is really common in network studies, so let's use that as a synthetic example.

Imagine we have a class of five people (Ali, Barb, Cam, Dot, Ellen) and we ask each of them to nominate their friends in the class. We can store this as a dictionary. When we put it in a DataFrame it can look like this:

```
nominate_dict = {
    "Ali": "Dot,Ellen",
    "Barb": "Cam",
    "Cam": "Ali,Barb",
    "Dot": "Ali,Barb,Cam,Ellen",
    "Ellen": "Dot"}


nom_df = pd.DataFrame.from_dict(nominate_dict,
                                orient="index",
                                columns = ["Nominations"])

# Transform each string into a list
nom_df["Nominations"] = nom_df["Nominations"].map(lambda x: x.split(","))

display(nom_df)
```

	Nominations
Ali	[Dot, Ellen]
Barb	[Cam]
Cam	[Ali, Barb]
Dot	[Ali, Barb, Cam, Ellen]
Ellen	[Dot]

This is wide data. One challenge with wide data is that we often don't know how wide it is, that is to say, if we were to split Nominations into n1,n2,n3,n4 will that be enough or too many? Sometimes it is easier not to worry about creating more columns. Instead, we *reshape* the data so that it is long instead. It will have more redundancy, but it can handle someone making 1, 4, or 400 nominations without the whole DataFrame getting wider.

To reshape a column so that it is long, first we have to ensure that we have a collection, not a string, in the column we want to reshape. If Nominations is a string (e.g. 'Dot,Ellen') then it should be split so that it is a list (e.g. ['Dot','Ellen']). Then we can use df.explode() to transform that one column to a long format.

```
long_df = pd.DataFrame(nom_df["Nominations"].explode())

display(long_df)
```

	Nominations
Ali	Dot
Ali	Ellen
Barb	Cam
Cam	Ali
Cam	Barb
Dot	Ali
Dot	Barb
Dot	Cam
Dot	Ellen
Ellen	Dot

5.6.1 Advanced reshaping

In addition to explode are a number of ways to reshape data. Two topics in particular stand out as interesting extensions of what we have seen here:

1   df.melt() - this is like using df.explode() except instead of taking a single column with a list inside it takes multiple columns.
2   df.pivot_table() - this is like a melt, groupby, and aggregate all in one. It is pretty tricky at first, but depending on how you are exploring your data it can be a really powerful and fast way to notice differences across groups.

 Using SQL databases

This is another relatively lengthy chapter, but it would not be complete without discussing SQL. While all the merging and grouping we saw above was done in Python, a truly vast amount of merging and grouping is done in SQL. SQL stands for 'Structured Query

Language', which is a syntax for interacting with tables in databases. Many of the operations you would do in SQL we have already covered conceptually in Python. Yet, you will often need to bring data into Python from an SQL database.

There are a variety of 'flavours' of SQL that include some slight differences in syntax and power. These typically correspond to different types of databases, such as *PostGRES*, *MySQL*, *Oracle*, and *Microsoft SQL Server*. Most of these are databases that run on servers, often away from one's personal computer. Yet one kind of database, `sqlite`, is common on personal computers. It is like a database in a flat file with no need to run a server to interact with it. As you may guess, we will be working with `sqlite` databases in this chapter.

Earlier, when discussing JSON and XML in Chapter 4, I mentioned I would wait to show SQL until we got to merging and grouping. The reason is that most of what you will be expected to do in SQL is to select, merge, and group data that you can then work on further in Python. You can do more complex work in SQL, but that would require another book with the many details of SQL. And while SQL runs really deep it is not very flexible for many data science tasks. Here we just want you to get familiar enough that you can go out and start interacting with databases yourself and then doing your analyses in Python.

5.7.1 SQL basics

Data accessed using SQL is stored in a *database*. A database is a collection of tables that you can work with together in a single SQL session. In order to get data from a database you need to make a *connection* to it. Then you send queries via the connection and the database returns a result.

Depending on how you make your connection to the database you will get a *cursor* or the entire result. Why a cursor? The idea behind databases is that they tend to store more data than you will need. So the cursor allows you to page through the data rather than get all of it at once. The cursor also allows you to set up a number of queries and then run them all on the SQL database in one go. Below we will create a table in a database and then add some data to the table. You can see how the cursor and the connection interact to send and receive data from the database.

```python
import sqlite3 as lite
from pathlib import Path

data_dir = Path.cwd().parent / 'data'

# This is the 'connection' to the database.
# If no .db file exists at that path one can be created.
con = lite.connect(data_dir / 'example.db')

# The cursor interacts with the contents of the database
cursor = con.cursor()

cursor.execute('''CREATE TABLE if not exists users(id INTEGER PRIMARY KEY,
                    name TEXT unique,
                    age INTEGER,
```

```
                        country TEXT,
                        tweets INTEGER)''')
con.commit()
```

What you saw above was mainly Python, but the following code *is* SQL:

```
CREATE TABLE if not exists users(id INTEGER PRIMARY KEY,
    name TEXT,
    age INTEGER,
    country TEXT,
    tweets INTEGER)
```

This is what you would run either from an SQL terminal prompt, in an app, or here via the `sqlite3` library for Python. In Python, this is done by constructing an `execute` statement. However, the cursor only interacts with the data once the execute statement is committed to the database by the connection. The reason for this distinction between connection and cursor is the fact that for many databases out on the web a large number of different connections are all trying to do things to the database at the same time. Imagine how active a shopping database is at Amazon! Using the connection and commit statements helps to keep things consistent in the database despite a potential flurry of reads and writes.

We can see that, unlike Python, SQL seems to want to cast (i.e. stipulate the type of) every variable. Indeed, SQL tends to strongly cast variables in order to estimate how much memory the database is going to need. During the casting we also observe some other things happening. Some flavours of SQL even want you to specify the character width for strings, so with MySQL you might see `VARCHAR(128)`, meaning a column of strings of a maximum 128 characters in length. Here we see `id` is cast as an `INTEGER` and also referred to as a `PRIMARY KEY`. This means `id` is an index that must remain unique and there will be one value for every row in the table. `sqlite3` will automatically manage that primary key for you. You can see that in action below. When we add rows to the table we don't add a value for `id`; `sqlite3` just increments the values for us. We also see that `email` is `unique`. This means that if you try to add a row with a duplicate email it will reject that and throw an error. Finally notice that while SQL commands are not typically case-sensitive they are often written in upper case.

Below, let's add some data to this table. We do this in SQLite by using a statement of the form `INSERT INTO <table>( <var_name1>...) VALUES <var_val1>,<var_val2>,..., <var_valn>`. Notice, however, that we create eight insert statements with the cursor (one for each row during our `for` loop), but we only use a single `con.commit()` statement at the end to make all the changes at once.

```
for i in range(len(people_df)):
    insert = f'''INSERT INTO users(name, age, country,tweets)
            VALUES("{people_df.Name[i]}",
                    {people_df.Age[i]},
                    "{people_df.Country[i]}",
                    {people_df.Tweets[i]})'''
    cursor.execute(insert)
con.commit()
```

When I'm working with SQLite tables, I like to cross-check them visually. There are a number of ways to browse an SQLite database, but one of the easier approaches is the open-source and cross-platform program, DB Browser for SQLlite (https://sqlitebrowser.org/). With this program you can browse the data and run the very same kinds of queries we show here. I use it as a lightweight way to check that my insert statement works.

5.7.2 Using SQL for aggregation and filtering

With our table in hand, we can now show briefly in SQL some of the same operations that we did in pandas. I cannot focus on all of them here, but to get you started I will show the split–apply–combine method in an SQL query. This involves learning about a couple of key operations in SQL:

- count(<column_name>). This is an aggregation method to count the instances of rows being selected: SELECT count(<column_name>) FROM users.
- GROUP BY. This is the way we get data into subgroups so that we can aggregate by group rather than for the entire table. Using GROUP BY with count is similar to value_ counts() in pandas.

We will call this query in such a way that the result will feed directly into a pandas table using the pd.read_sql(<QUERY>, <CONNECTION>) method. This method requires at least two arguments, one for the query and one for the connection to the database. For our first query, we start by calling all the data into pandas.

```
# First, let's just import the entire table as a DataFrame
pd.read_sql('SELECT * FROM users',con)
```

	id	name	age	country	tweets
0	1	Ali	32	Wales	3200
1	2	Barb	35	Northern Ireland	202
2	3	Cam	21	England	657
3	4	Dot	45	Northern Ireland	24
4	5	Ellen	21	Scotland	81
5	6	Farah	50	England	9723
6	7	Grant	28	Scotland	664
7	8	Hannah	36	England	200
8	9	Idris	40	Isle of Man	1

```
# This time lets report a grand aggregation by counting all rows
pd.read_sql('SELECT count(name) FROM users',con)
```

	count(name)
0	9

```
# Below we report a group aggregation by counting rows within country
pd.read_sql('SELECT count(name), country FROM users GROUP BY country',con)
```

	count(name)	country
0	3	England
1	1	Isle of Man
2	2	Northern Ireland
3	2	Scotland
4	1	Wales

```
# This time we add a new function (avg) to show how we can do more than
# simply count with our aggregations. But the column names are getting ugly.
pd.read_sql("SELECT count(name), avg(tweets), country FROM users GROUP
BY country",con)
```

	count(name)	avg(tweets)	country
0	3	3526.666667	England
1	1	1.000000	Isle of Man
2	2	113.000000	Northern Ireland
3	2	372.500000	Scotland
4	1	3200.000000	Wales

For this last query, I am going to use three ticks so that I can have the query break across the page, sort the variables using the ORDER BY parameter, tweak the styling by using df.style to hide the index, and rename the variables using SELECT <var> as <newname>. So lots of additions, but it produces a pretty legible table.

```
# A final query that shows the data in a well-formatted DataFrame
pd.read_sql('''SELECT count(name) as Count,
               avg(tweets) as AvgTweets,
               country FROM users GROUP BY country
               ORDER BY AvgTweets desc''',
            con).style.format({'AvgTweets':'{:.1f}'}).hide(axis='index')
```

Count	AvgTweets	country
3	3526.7	England
1	3200.0	Wales
2	372.5	Scotland
2	113.0	Northern Ireland
1	1.0	Isle of Man

Finally, let's have a brief look at merging in SQL. To merge we will need a second table. So the first thing to do is take our country_df table and transform it into a SQL table called country. I do this in a manner similar to the way I did `users_df`, which is to first execute a `CREATE` statement and then iteratively create `INSERT INTO` statements for each row in the table. Then we can see how merging the two tables allows SQL to return an entirely new merged table without needing pandas to do the merge.

```
cursor.execute('''CREATE TABLE if not exists
    country(id INTEGER PRIMARY KEY,
            name TEXT unique,
            population FLOAT) ''')

for i in range(len(country_df)):
    insert = f'''INSERT INTO country(name, population)
                VALUES ("{country_df.index[i]}",
                        {country_df.Population[i]})'''
    cursor.execute(insert)

con.commit()

display(pd.read_sql('''SELECT users.name, age, country, country.population
                FROM users INNER JOIN country
                on country.name = users.country''',con))
```

	name	age	country	population
0	Ali	32	Wales	3.000000
1	Barb	35	Northern Ireland	2.000000
2	Cam	21	England	53.000000
3	Dot	45	Northern Ireland	2.000000
4	Ellen	21	Scotland	5.000000
5	Farah	50	England	53.000000
6	Grant	28	Scotland	5.000000
7	Hannah	36	England	53.000000

What tripped me up in this merge is that *all* of the variable are listed in the `SELECT` statement from both tables. They are being selected from `users INNER JOIN country on country.name = users.country`, which returns a single result. Since both tables have a column called `name`, SQL wants you to use the table name to differentiate which `name` is the right one (e.g., when do we expect `users.name` and when `country.name`).

5.8 Summary

Merging is a big, complex, and technical topic that needs both a bit of computational theory and a lot of practice. However, it is a decidedly useful topic in the social sciences. We tend to believe in the social sciences that local effects are conditioned by macro forces. These macro forces do not exist in the same form everywhere. For example, in different states in the USA one may or may not have easy access to contraception. Thus, understanding life course events will need to take into account differences by state. The likelihood of starting a business will vary by country with differences in tax rates, investments, and corruption. The propensity to return a personal favour will depend on how large, diverse, and spread out one's network is. Finally, one's educational outcomes are defined both by the classroom and the school, not just one's personal talents and support. Thus, being able to merge and aggregate implicitly teaches us to consider the multiple scales of social life intersecting each other. In the absence of this we are left with just individual rows in cases, which is convenient for a table but not for explaining reality.

 Further reading

- *Tidy Data* by Wickham (2014). While there exist very formal and challenging books on 'database normalisation' in this paper, Wickham has been able to distil much of that down to some really straightforward ideas about why we keep data in some shapes and not others, how to minimise redundancy, and how to meaningfully link data. In the past 10 years, Wickham has not only been writing on these topics (including the aforementioned 'split-apply-combine' method) but also been producing packages in R to help with data science tasks. I admit that the one thing I long for in Python is more work like Wickham's (e.g., the `ggplot2`, `dplyr`, and `tidyverse` packages). If you want to go further in comparing R and Python, Wickham also has a textbook called *R for Data Science* (Wickham and Grolemund, 2017).
- There are many courses out there for specialising in specific databases and their skills. It is hard to suggest which might be the best, but I would consider investigating lessons freely available on YouTube if they have a linked GitHub repository. Courses for certification can be expensive and often unnecessary for the scope of research. These popularly include MySQL, Microsoft SQL Server, and Oracle. For a more general overview of how databases work, I like the long set of PowerPoint slides at http://www.esp.org/db-fund.pdf (strikingly from 1995) by Robbins which is very agnostic to the specific implementations of databases. Instead it provides a very visual version of some of the topics I have discussed here (Robbins, 1995).

 Extensions and reflections

- It can be tricky to start working with a third-party database. There are a vast number of online resources to help. Many of them focus on certifications, when really that is for more production-level code. Nevertheless, using online tutorials for other SQL tasks can help. Try searching for 'sql database practice'.
- Notice how easily we shifted from using `sqlite` to using the `pandas read_sql` method. Now try a GROUP BY statement in the `read_sql` and explore just how much of what we saw above you could do in SQL. Could you do all of the Python for group mean centring in SQL?
- `value_counts()` is an obvious form of split-apply-combine. What might be a less obvious approach that is still useful? Is it always about changing what we do in the 'apply' part?

- Instead of using the `DataFrame` that I gave above, create your own two `DataFrame` objects, with different data. If you're stuck for ideas, I often recommend food (just not too much). What about describing a dataset with a list of meals and their prices, then a second dataset with a set of customers and their food allergies. How you could you set up a merge so that you can identify which foods have allergies for which customers? Do you need a third table consisting of ingredients?
- In Chapter 10 I look at cleaning up a large dataset from Stack Exchange. Once you have worked through that chapter you will have a very big `DataFrame` with tens of thousands of rows. At the end of that chapter are some more exercises that use merging, since we can then use merging to do things like merge the names and locations of the users (from `Users.xml`) with the behaviour on the posts (from `Posts.XML`).

6

ACCESSING DATA ON THE WORLD WIDE WEB USING CODE

Learning goals

- Understand the different parts of a URL, including arguments and paths
- Make use of `requests.get()`, including setting a user agent using a `user-agent` string
- Understand how paging can be used with a URL in order to build a `DataFrame` of content on Reddit
- Consider data minimisation as a key ethical issue in the use of online data with specific considerations for volume, velocity, and variety.

Accessing data I: Remote access of webpages

Data is, unsurprisingly, a central part of the computational approach to social science. We need data, often a lot of data. Furthermore, with online social data, we generate huge amounts every day, much of which can be accessed by someone for some purpose.

The purposes we have for accessing data are often to make claims about the social world. These claims take place at a variety of scales, from the scale of the user (how users differ) or of groups or communities, to the scale of entire forums, or even entire platforms. Across all these scales are differing ways in which data can be collected and parsed for usage. Yet, there are some commonalities across the different contexts. Many of these commonalities are technical. In this chapter we are going to focus first on the technical skills for accessing data from the open web. I will mainly focus on some relatively easy sites for data access. But these are meant as examples to show how we collect data. Between the examples herein and the ones shown in the next chapter on authenticated APIs, I hope that this gives you a feeling for how to embark on data collection.

The purpose of focusing on the technical commonalities is that they tend to endure where platforms do not. Ten years ago, Facebook data was an exciting opportunity. Then, for reasons related to the platform's ambitions and concerns about privacy, Facebook made accessing data generally more difficult, and in some cases revoked virtually all access for outside researchers. While some Facebook data is hard to access, data on other platforms might be easily available. For example, at present, Telegram is becoming increasing relevant for understanding geopolitical conversations (with many Telegram channels sending updates of events and communities around the world). Meanwhile TikTok is capturing the youth and entertainment market and is bustling with activity. Thus, while the platforms change and what data can be accessed changes, there are some standards for data that persist. For example, text tends to be displayed in HTML, but sent in JSON or XML. The way text is received usually can be handled by the `requests` library in Python, but operating on a platform might require something more akin to a browser or browser-simulator. Data tends to come down in batches and servers have a few ways to indicate their tolerance for third parties collecting data.

Much like how the chapters on the `Series` and the `DataFrame` really work together, similarly the topics in this chapter and those in the next chapter also tend to work together. So, for example, in this chapter we will need to make use of some APIs, but we will not be drawing too much attention to that part of the task. Similarly, the ethical issues that are raised in this chapter also apply to work where you must authenticate in order to collect data.

To begin the discussion I will introduce some terms that you might already be familiar with, such as URL and IP address. I explore the `requests` package for sending and receiving data in Python. Then I discuss how one can use these programs to access webpages, extract some data, and 'crawl' the web. Finally, in the latter part of this chapter I pivot to questions about ethical care in one's methodology. How much data to get, how to manage the data, and how to present it are partially normative (and hence ethical) questions. But that does not mean they exist outside of the research and merely provide 'brakes' for our otherwise hungry data ambitions. Rather ethics allows us to consider ourselves as participants in the ways of knowing about the world. Who gets to know what, and how, are questions that touch on ethics but also on social science.

6.1.1 What is a URL?

We start with the URL. URL stands for 'uniform resource locator'. It is the means by which we seek out data on the web. Granted, not all data science or computational social science happens via the web, but an awful lot does. This is using the web either as a object of inquiry in its own right (looking at how webpages are linked, structured, or evolve), or as a the means to collect data concerning something else (such as collecting some statistics about a country via a web portal). When you enter a URL into a web browser it uses a domain name system (DNS) lookup service in order to find the machine-readable address (the Internet Protocol (IP) address) that will allow your request to find its way to the correct server (and similarly to send the response back to your computer). Let's have a look at some DNS lookups using some simple URLs of different kinds and their associated IP addresses.

```
import socket
import requests

#1. External server IP
print("IP for Google:", socket.gethostbyname("google.com"))

#2. Localhost IP
print("IP for localhost:", socket.gethostbyname("localhost"))

#3. Local network IP
local_ip = socket.gethostbyname(socket.gethostname())
print("My machine's IP Address on the local network:", local_ip)

#4. External computer IP: Actual IP commented for privacy
my_external_ip = requests.get('https://api.ipify.org').text
print("My machine's IP Address to others on the web:",
    my_external_ip.split('.')[0] + ".xxx.xxx.xxx")

IP for Google: 142.250.187.206
IP for localhost: 127.0.0.1
My machine's IP Address on the local network: 192.168.0.134
My machine's IP Address to others on the web: 51.xxx.xxx.xxx
```

In the above code I imported the `socket` and `requests` libraries. A socket is one point of a two-way link between two connected devices or 'endpoints'. The IP address then is how one endpoint finds the other one. We do not normally use `socket` directly because we normally are not trying to resolve IP addresses explicitly. Most of the time it is good enough to have the URL and use `requests` to receive the content. But these kinds of IP addresses are worth examining as they highlight different parts of the whole internet network.

1   *External server's IP.* The first IP address I received was for Google, or at least this specific instance of Google at this time. Note that IP addresses can and do change. This was done with `socket.gethostbyname(<URL>)`. Try entering that IP address directly into your browser – it should bring up the current Google search page.

2   *Localhost.* The second IP address is to be expected by convention. The term `'localhost'` refers to your computer. This is where you are probably running Jupyter Lab (unless you are running the code in Google Colab, Binder, or another an external service). Localhost is typically given the IP address 127.0.0.1 by default. You can check this if you are running Jupyter by replacing `localhost:8888` with `127.0.0.1:8888` and it should still work.

3   *Local network.* The third IP address refers to this computer's IP address on a local network. It is common for networks to have multiple devices under the same subnet. They typically precede with `192.168.XXX.YYY` where XXX is typically 0 and YYY would be any number between 0 and 255. In order to get the IP address on my local network, I first ask for the name of the host (my computer) on my local network. You can do this yourself simply by printing `socket.gethostname()`. Then I pipe that name rather than `localhost` or `google.com` into `socket.gethostbyname()`.

4   *My external IP.* Finally, this is my IP address on the web. Although I do not want to immortalise my IP address in this book, you can discover your own external IP by printing the `my_external_ip` variable. If you are connecting to a socket over the web, such as another server to request some data (i.e. a webpage or an image), this is the IP address they will see.

IP addresses and ethics

It is worth considering that in some jurisdictions external IP addresses are commonly (and in many places legally) considered a form of personal data on a par with email and names. It is considered personal data in the EU and UK General Data Protection Regulation (GDPR). So if you would not store and publish a list of survey respondents' names and emails, you should similarly take such care with IP addresses. They do not *necessarily* stay the same, but it is common. Further, that works two ways as well. People also have found creative ways to obscure IP addresses in order to collect more data, data on more sensitive topics, or data that is otherwise inaccessible. I do not recommend obscuring your IP address, but I understand there is still a place for it in some legitimate scientific research, much like there can be a place for deception (e.g. in audit studies and some carefully controlled experiments; Riach and Rich, 2004). But much like deception, the burden should be on the researcher to justify obfuscating IP addresses using standard ethical principles and regulatory guidelines rather than to assume it is fine by default.

In the work below and in the next chapter it will be assumed that you will be identifying yourself to the server, and this will be an important part of the research process.

6.1.2 URL parsing

The IP address is the connection to an external server. However, the URL can contain much more data that will be useful to a server. Being able to read and construct URL strings will allow a program (or a programmer) to make specific requests to a server and in doing so extract useful data. Let's have a look at a URL which contains much of what we are interested in:

```
[Transfer    [sub.Domain    [Subdirectory  [File    [Argument
protocol]    name]          path           type]    strings]
https://     api.reddit.com /r/learnpython .json    ?after=t3_a4r234
```

Some notes on the terminology seen here:

- *Transfer protocol.* How are we transferring the file? Some common protocols are HTTP, HTTPS, FTP, and SFTP. All of these tend to run on IP addresses.
- *Domain name.* The human-readable root page address such as bbc.co.uk. This is registered in a naming service so that when you look it up it returns the machine-relevant IP address.
- *Top-level domain.* The part after the last period in a domain name. For bbc.co.uk it is co.uk.
- *DNS servers.* Lookup tables for returning the IP address when given a name. There are several of these throughout the world and they are like the phonebooks of the internet. These help translate between the name that you submit for as the URL and the IP address.
- *Port.* Sometimes you see a port, like on localhost:8888, which is the where different servers will listen for different kinds of activities. For example, web traffic is typically on ports 80 (for clear text) and 443 (for encrypted text).
- *File extensions.* A webpage does not have to include a file extension, but it will then be assumed to be either text or HTML. Sometimes you'll see a page with a .php extension but yet it seems like HTML. That's because PHP stands for 'Pre-Hypertext Processor'. It's a language for generating HTML. On the back end it looks like code but to the browser it will look like HTML.
- *Argument strings.* After the end of a web address you can include arguments. These are formatted as key-value pairs. They are appended to the URL using a ? to denote when the URL ends and the arguments begin. Then multiple arguments are chained using &. In the above example, there is one parameter, after, with the argument t3_a4r234.

URLs have to be properly formatted to work. But by processing URLs programmatically, you can discover means to automate or scale a data collection task. To explore a request from a URL, let's examine the following URL: https://www.google.com/search?client=firefox-b-d&q=Why+are+red+M%26M's+%231%3F. This is the URL that appeared in my browser address bar when I typed 'Why are red M&M's #1?' into the search bar. Here we see that the URL contains two parameters: client and q. The first refers to the browser (I'm presently using Firefox on a desktop, hence the argument firefox-b-d). The second is the search query parameter, q. Notice that the argument does not look the same as what I typed. Instead it has + for spaces. It replaces the space character because that character also signifies the end of a URL. But the other characters # and & are also reserved characters in URLs, so they need to be escaped. For & the code is %26. A full reference and discussion of these escape codes can be found at the W3C (https://www.w3.org/International/questions/qa-escapes). Usually you do not need to do this by hand as code libraries (such as `requests`) can prepare your text for you.

Let's reproduce this URL. First I'll use a `PreparedRequest` model. That will prepare a request instead of sending it. (Normally it is just called in the background.) Then below we will discuss web requests generally and send this one off to the Internet.

```
URL = "https://www.google.com/search"
params = {"client":"firefox-b-d", "q":"Why are red M&M's #1?"}

req = requests.models.PreparedRequest()
req.prepare_url(URL, params)
print(req.url)

https://www.google.com/search?client=firefox-b-d&q=Why+are+red+M%26M%27
s+%231%3F
```

6.1.3 What is a web request?

Receiving data from the web typically requires that you make a 'request'. This is where you prepare some information to send to the web and then receive some information in return as a 'response'. There are a number of libraries in Python that can be used to interact with the web, such as `sockets`, `pycurl`, and `urllib`. That said, generally we can make use of the `requests` library as it combines a lot of the features of these, including help with preparing URLs and downloading content. To manage a request there are a number of parts to it that work together and are worth spelling out in detail.

1   *The request URL.* This we have seen above. You send the URL and you should be able to get back some content. When we used `requests.get("https://api.ipify.org")` we sent a GET request to `api.ipify.org`.
2   *The request header.* When we sent that request we did not just blindly ask for that data, but we also sent some data of our own with the request. That is our 'header' data. Part of that header data includes the 'name' of the requesting computer or 'user agent'. We can, and often should, customise the request header so that it includes a unique or at least descriptive user agent name. We will see that below.
3   *The request payload.* When we send a GET request all the information that the server expects should be in the actual URL and header. But what if we want to send confidential information like a password or upload some comments in a comment field? These do not go in the request URL or header. Instead they go in a separate 'payload' which `requests` can help you put together. Then instead of using `requests.get()`, you would use `requests.post()` to send a POST request that includes the URL and the payload, typically with the 'data' parameter.
4   *The response header.* Any content that comes back from the server will include a header. That header can be parsed as a dictionary with parameters and arguments. The most important parameter is probably the response status code. This code lets your program

know if the request was well formed and the response has been returned successfully (response: 200), whether the content is not found (response: 404) or any other number of issues such as a malformed request (response: 503). You can find a list of these codes at the W3C (https://www.w3.org/Protocols/HTTP/HTRESP.html). There are other useful details in the response header such as the type of content (e.g., json or html) and some details for managing your queries. For example, if you are querying Reddit or Twitter then the response header can let you know if you've sent too many queries too quickly.

5   *The response payload.* The response payload is typically the content that you want from the server. This forms part of the requests object. Usually you would collect this content by reading the request response. This response comes down encoded (meaning that it is written in a format amenable to computers). Thus, it is a 'bytestream'. It is for this reason that if you are downloading an image then you will have to write the response using open(<filename>, 'wb') and not simply 'w'.

```
req = requests.get(URL, params)

# The actual URL that is returned from the server based on what we sent.
print(req.request.url)

# The headers that we sent to the server
print(req.request.headers)

https://consent.google.com/ml?continue=https://www.google.com/
search%3Fclient%3Dfirefox-b-d%26q%3Dwhy%2Bare%2Bred%2BM%2526M%2527s%2B%
25231%253F&gl=GB&m=0&pc=srp&uxe=none&hl=en&src=1
{'User-Agent': 'python-requests/2.27.1', 'Accept-Encoding': 'gzip, deflate,
br', 'Accept': '*/*', 'Connection': 'keep-alive', 'Cookie':
'AEC=AakniGMPgRXDRNbctRjVcIym_dP2CbfYczlGZhhhVeqaiVPqq-4QtZAR_A; __Secure-
ENID=4.SE=JjQVyp3rW6FlxOxrozW7fKq3zEIF78umotqhMLHc4v2HbqiJZFce8m2wqpf
mCrXORG-UqcQB5GPWEur53QVVvMB1-C6DqT9XnHgsg6TmArBvzDRZ6jHyazsmBszXPx-
2M52oaJJY3Pp2uLx49y5VHTQ3RhGz4ZclcjqiqClFqoQ; CONSENT=PENDING+770'}
```

Examining req.request.url, we see that Google redirected the query through a different URL where we are asked about user consent. There are other ways to query Google using an API, but this helps to simulate the browser experience. It also shows some of the puzzles that must be considered if one is to extract data from the open web rather than from structured pipelines of data. I sent some accompanying data indicating that my user-agent was python-requests/2.27.1 and some other details including Cookie. Then we received some data in response. This data includes the response headers, which contains a host of details, and the response content, which is normally the data we want. This content is what is normally rendered in a browser window.

```
dict(req.headers).keys()

dict_keys(['Content-Type', 'Vary', 'Cache-Control', 'Pragma', 'Expires', 'Date',
'Cross-Origin-Resource-Policy', 'Permissions-Policy', 'Cross-Origin-Opener-
```

Policy', 'Content-Security-Policy', 'Report-To', 'Accept-CH', 'Content-
Encoding', 'Server', 'X-XSS-Protection', 'X-Frame-Options', 'X-Content-Type-
Options', 'Alt-Svc', 'Transfer-Encoding'])

Below I use .decode('utf8') to print the content in a more human-readable form. Try
removing that to see the bytestream (and notice the differences).

```
print(req.content[4000:4500].decode('utf8'))
```

/a> and data to:<ul><li>Deliver and maintain services, like tracking outages and
protecting against spam, fraud, and abuse</li><li>Measure audience engagement
and site statistics to understand how our services are used</li></ul>If you
agree, we'll also use cookies and data to:<ul><li>Improve the quality of our
services and develop new ones</li><li>Deliver and measure the effectiveness of
ads</li><li>Show personalized content, depending on your settings</li><li>Show
personalized or generic ads,

Most of the time you will simply be piping the content of the request into some other file
format. For example, if it is a webpage, you might just want the text content from which you
extract URLs. However, if you are collecting content with some regularity or simply need to
debug your program, it helps to be able to examine the request itself, including the status codes.

An example web collection task using paging

Web data collection tends to operate in two different flavours. The first one you might think
of is web crawling or spidering. That is where we will take a page or set of pages, download
them, parse their page for links, follow those links, and continue until we get some stopping
criterion. However, it is helpful to think of the web not just as HTML but as data that can be
transferred using URLs, including HTML. In that sense, we might be collecting data in JSON,
CSV, HTML, XML, or any other file type.

When the data we want comes from a database on the World Wide Web, it is common for
the data to be sent in batches. For example, we might have a list of search results and the
page only shows the first 10. We might want those 10, we might want *all* the results, or we
might have *practical limits* on the results we collect. Those practical limits might come from
the server (e.g., the way it limits the number of queries per hour or number of requests to a
specific database) or from the researcher (there is just way too much data to collect and manage, like all search results for the word 'data').

In these cases, there is typically a way to *page* through the data. In the example below, we
will do a partial crawl of Reddit. In doing so, we will create a DataFrame of Reddit posts that
come from more than one request to Reddit. Notably, each request contains within it some
guidance as to how to make the next request so you get all the data, ideally without gaps or
duplicates between the requests. The useful reason to go to Reddit is that it is easy to get the
data as JSON rather than HTML. HTML is what the browser expects, but we just want the
data, not the layouts, the banners, the ads, etc.

To get started we can look at the JSON that comes from a single subreddit. In this case, I'm choosing the Aww subreddit (r/aww) as it is well moderated and includes adorable photos of cute fluffy animals. We can look through the most recent 1000 posts on this subreddit, but the posts will only come in batches of 25. There will also be some eccentricities in the posts data that we should contend with (things like sticky posts which mean we sometimes will get a batch of 26 or 27 rather than 25).

To first collect data from Reddit we have to create a request. It is recommended that the request be identifiable to Reddit, so we will use a custom `user-agent` string. It is also recommended that you do not use the same `user-agent` string that I use, but create your own variation. `user-agent` strings can be used to manage traffic to a server. Thus, if we are both querying Reddit it will not try to slow one of us down if the other one is also trying to access data at the same time.

Note that because I am going to be making multiple requests to Reddit and I will want to identify myself the same way each time, I am using a `Session()` object. This means that instead of using `requests.get()`, I'll first create a session s and then use `s.get()`.

```python
import requests
import json

s = requests.Session()
s.headers.update({'user-agent': 'MacOS:redditapitester:v1 (by u/user)'})

req = s.get('https://api.reddit.com/r/aww/new')
sample = json.loads(req.content)

print(sample.keys(), sample['kind'], sample['data'].keys(),
      sep="\n")

dict_keys(['kind', 'data'])
Listing
dict_keys(['after', 'dist', 'modhash', 'geo_filter', 'children', 'before'])
```

Notice that I have already imported the data using the approach seen in Chapter 4. Thus, the JSON looks to us like a dictionary. We can navigate a dictionary of JSON then to learn about the data. The top level is just some admin (with `kind` and `data`) as keys. The value for `kind` is `Listing`, which is unremarkable. But under `data` we have more keys. You can print the value of each in turn if you want to play with the data yourself. To spoil the surprise, `after` is a value that allows us to page through the data. But what data? The value for the key `children` is a list of posts. These posts are the data we seek and `after` is how get the next set of such posts. First let's transform `children` into a `DataFrame`. Then we will see how to add new rows by paging. I use `sample['data']['children']` and not `sample` or `sample['data']` because the result of `sample['data']['children']` is a *list* and therefore each entry in the list will get its own row in the table.

```
import pandas as pd
```

```
red_df = pd.json_normalize(sample['data']['children'])
print(red_df.info())
print(red_df.columns[:20])
```

```
<class 'pandas.core.frame.DataFrame'>
RangeIndex: 20 entries, 0 to 19
Columns: 179 entries, kind to data.author_cakeday
dtypes: bool(31), float64(25), int64(12), object(111)
memory usage: 29.8+ KB
None
Index(['kind', 'data.approved_at_utc', 'data.subreddit', 'data.selftext',
       'data.author_fullname', 'data.saved', 'data.mod_reason_title',
       'data.gilded', 'data.clicked', 'data.title', 'data.link_flair_richtext',
       'data.subreddit_name_prefixed', 'data.hidden', 'data.pwls',
       'data.link_flair_css_class', 'data.downs', 'data.thumbnail_height',
       'data.top_awarded_type', 'data.hide_score', 'data.name'],
      dtype='object')
```

I did not print the DataFrame here for brevity in the book, but you can explore it with commands like red_df.head(10) to see the first 10 rows. Notice that I printed the first 20 columns and there are 203 in total. Not all of these will be relevant in your research. But let's keep them there for now since they come with the data by default.

Recall that a URL string can include arguments. These occur after a ? as we saw in the Google search query. By adding arguments to the URL string that the server must process we can customise the data that comes back. In this sense, we are now using an API. By using differences in the web address and the arguments, we are *interfacing* with a database for customised data. This means that we can now look for an API reference to help us navigate the right URL strings.

In this case, Reddit will expect us to include the after value from these results to get the next set in order. Other APIs might use a different key, such as results_page, result, or next. In this case, we take that after value and place it in the URL following the ? as a key–value pair. To keep the example lightweight, I will only collect the first 100 or so results. Notice the approach I use below and how it leans into concatenation (see Chapter 5 on merging). I just store the JSON results in a list. Later I will turn each one into its own DataFrame and then combine them all once. This can be contrasted with a slower approach of making the DataFrame first, and then adding each new set of results as they come in. With a max_count of 100, 25 results at a time, and a sleep interval of 2 seconds between requests, that means the code below will probably take about 10 seconds to run.

```
import time
```

```
after = "" # The first time is empty (and won't throw an error on Reddit)
results = [] # The list of result objects
count = 0  # Where we start
max_count = 100 # Note: Reddit might not give results for maxcount > 1000
```

```
while True:
    reddit_link = f"https://api.reddit.com/r/aww?after={after}"

    content = s.get(reddit_link)
    if not content:
        break

    result = json.loads(req.content)
    results.append(result["data"]["children"])
    count += len(result["data"]["children"])

    if count >= max_count:
        break
    else:
        after = result["data"]["after"]

    time.sleep(2)

print(f"We have received {len(results)} batches of data to be processed.")
```

We have received 4 batches of data to be processed.

Below I can combine them all now using concat and a list comprehension, so instead of four lists of dictionaries, each with details of a Reddit post, we will have four DataFrame objects. Then we concatenate them into a single long DataFrame. I also recommend resetting the index or else we will have four rows each with an index of 0, ..., 24. Finally, due to a quirk in the data (since the data we want is *actually* under result["data"]["children"][0]["data"] or result["data"]["children"][1]["data"], our headers ended up being data.title and data.author instead of merely title and author. Consequently I clean that out before continuing.

```
reddit_df = pd.concat([pd.json_normalize(i) for i in results],
                      ignore_index=True)

reddit_df.columns = [i.removeprefix("data.")
                     if i.startswith("data.") else i
                     for i in reddit_df.columns]

display(reddit_df.info())
```

```
<class 'pandas.core.frame.DataFrame'>
RangeIndex: 100 entries, 0 to 99
Columns: 179 entries, kind to author_cakeday
dtypes: bool(31), float64(25), int64(12), object(111)
memory usage: 118.8+ KB
```

None

And now we have a distribution of data that we can use to explore and consider. Below I plot that distribution. When I ran this code, my version of the data looks relatively skewed. We will see how to make nicer, more illustrative plots in Chapter 9.

```
import matplotlib.pyplot as plt
%config InlineBackend.figure_format = 'svg'

ax = reddit_df.ups.sort_values().plot(kind="hist");
ax.set_xlabel("Upvote score")

plt.show()
```

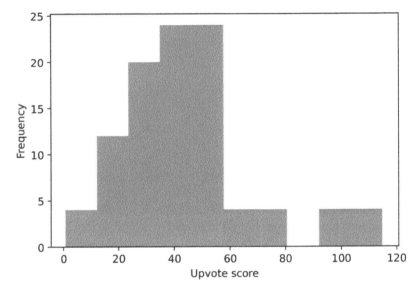

Figure 6.1 Histogram showing the distribution of upvotes among recent posts in Reddit's r/aww subreddit (*n* = 100)

Paging helps us iterate through results. That way we can accumulate results in a single table and then treat many results as a single distribution. The exact number you get will depend on the circumstances. Being able to articulate what is a sufficient sample is challenging and should generally be done on rational grounds (e.g., all posts a week before and after an event; all tweets with a specific hashtag) but can be done on practical grounds at a pinch (e.g., the maximum number of results allowed by the server; all the data we could store). This is a very different experience than seeking a representative survey. We normally would not want a 'random' sample of posts, nor would it often be helpful, since posts clustered by time tend to better encapsulate some event or period of activity. Determining *how* to sample randomly is also quite challenging. So we instead tend to seek out *coverage* and thus consider what are appropriate forms of inclusion or exclusion criteria for our data.

Other web-related issues to consider

6.3.1 When to use your own versus someone else's program

There are a variety of programs out there that automate some of the complexity of gathering data on the web. For example, YouTube-dl (https://youtube-dl.org/) is an open-source project that automates the collection of videos from YouTube. Would it be appropriate to use this rather than making your own? Usually. It is common to use these third-party programs. The issue is that sometimes they do not work as expected and it is still your responsibility to assert the quality of your sample. It is also the case that these programs come and go. I recall when I was working on a Facebook downloader, I was responsible for upkeep with every change and sometimes we could not get to it immediately while other people were using this program (NameGenWeb) for their Facebook research (e.g., McConnell et al., 2018).

If your sample has some skew or bias that is a result of one of the parameters of these programs, whether that is because the program only collects the first image from a Tumblr post, does not collect all comments on Reddit, etc., this is still your responsibility as a researcher. For this reason, I tend to prefer to find a simple but very methodical way to interact with sites themselves rather than rely on tools or preprocessed datasets. The one exception is a 'wrapper', as we will see in the next chapter. Wrappers make this process feel more like Python code and so that works *with* rather than *against* my interest in being specific and deliberate in data collection choices.

6.3.2 Are there ways to simulate a browser?

There are two excellent packages in Python that can help simulate a browser in some ways. These are often for complex tasks that involve navigating a server or page that does not have an API. The package `MechanicalSoup` runs a mini browser in your Python kernel that then allows you to interact with pages as if you were working with a browser. It is based on the very popular program written in Perl called `mechanize`. This led to the creation of `PyMechanize`, which does a similar job in Python, but development appears to have stalled. The other alternative is `selenium`, which is a program that *automates* browsers. So you could then interact with Chrome or Firefox programmatically. `selenium` is often used by web developers to automate testing of interactions on browser pages. Beyond these are third-party programs that can crawl the web for you, but these tend to come and go.

 Ethical issues to consider

6.4.1 What is public data and how public?

Much like setting up a camera in a town square and pointing it at everyone all day, collecting egregious amounts of web data for its own sake is not recommended. While individuals generally do not have the same expectation of privacy in public spaces as they do at home, there are still rules and limits to behaviour in public that targets specific people. To the same extent, we might think that there are some ethical principles for collecting and performing research on web data. Data is public in the sense that it is available without indicating one's specific identity or authentication. Thus, a lot of data that you may think is public, such as that which is available on one's own Facebook feed, is not really public, even if it is accessible to someone (Zimmer, 2010). The same applies to comments on bulletin boards where you need to be registered to view the content. Generally speaking, if you need to be authenticated to get data from a space you should connect with the data controller or a responsible party first. And even if the data is public but contains sensitive information it is still good practice to get in contact.

It is not advised to misrepresent yourself when collecting data online, either by spoofing multiple accounts, or creating false personae. This might seem like a good idea at the outset but should be done only under very carefully considered conditions. This is akin to audit study work offline, where people pose as prospective tenants, job applicants, or seeking a relationship in order to gauge the reactions or preferences of people (Pager, 2007; Riach and Rich, 2004; Sandvig et al., 2014). Depending on the research design, there are considerable ethical challenges that need to be considered. Below I will speak only to the broad strokes of ethical work with big data. For other work, it is worth seeking out professional guidelines. The Association of Internet Researchers has long maintained very considered guidelines on ethical work with online data (Franzke et al., 2019). Many universities have also begun to articulate their own specific best practices. For example, members of my department helped to draft Oxford's best practice guide which covers a number of nuances to ethical Internet research (https://researchsupport.admin.ox.ac.uk/files/bpg06internet-basedresearchpdf).

I return to this issue again in the next chapter, where I take a sort of flip-side approach after discussing APIs. There I ask what we should expect of platforms and whether the current provisions are good enough. But here, after the discussion of publicly accessible data, I think it is worth considering one key ethical issue: data minimisation.

6.4.2 Considering data minimisation as a basic ethical principle

There are certainly more ethical principles than one. We may take as a principle a right to be forgotten (Mayer-Schönberger, 2011), or a right to explainability in AI (Wachter et al., 2017). Principles do not mean laws, however, as Wachter et al. point out with respect to algorithmic fairness. For example, there is no explicit right to explainability in GDPR, even if many governments and policy-makers consider it an important principle (perhaps wrongly; Edwards and Veale, 2017).

There are a variety of ways of approaching ethics of data. For one approach that informs and applies the Association of Internet Researcher's guidance, see Lomborg (2013). There the author emphasises the perceived privacy of the individual and the 'distance principle' which allows us to reflect on how close individuals are to the data that we are analysing of them. For example, in-depth chat logs would be much closer to human subjects research even if it is non-reactive because of the depth of the characterisation of the person.

We can think of data minimisation as a general principle: take only what you need. Further, it is one that has been encoded in a number of laws (such as Article 5(1I) of the EU GDPR) and practices (such as the Twitter v2 API). However, it is often hard to know precisely ahead of time whether you'll need all the data you take. An era of big data has previously been defined as being about data of considerable volume, velocity, and variety. All three of these have their own relationship to data minimisation worth reflecting on before beginning data collection.

Volume

It is expected that the total volume of data you are asking for would be meaningful for your research. Holding on to large quantities of other people's data can open you up to risk, particularly if you are in an organisation that would be compelled to comply with a subject access request. This data may contain personal details of other people or otherwise simply be unwieldy. Also, it can be expensive for a server or otherwise unnecessary. If you want to do a complete crawl of a website or its data, consider whether the site has a data export policy or an IT administrator to speak to. For example, I was once given an entire site dump simply by asking the web administrator for it, saving considerable cleaning for me and bandwidth charges for them.

Sites like Wikipedia, Stack Exchange, and IMDB provide pretty extensive data dumps. Other sites such as Facebook and Twitter have specific avenues for researcher engagement. Finally, with respect to what data is available, sites often have a public guide to what they expect is available through automated means in the form of a `robots.txt` file under the main domain. Try it for yourself: see those for the BBC (https://www.bbc.co.uk/robots.txt), Google (https://www.google.com/robots.txt), and Wikipedia (https://en.wikipedia.org/robots.txt). These normally refer to specific crawlers like the Google search engine crawler, but can also refer to any automated means. Notice under the comments for the `robots.txt` on Wikipedia: 'Please note: There are a lot of pages on this site, and there are some misbehaved spiders out there that go *way* too fast. If you're irresponsible, your access to the site may be blocked.'

Velocity

Data is transferred at a specific speed. Big data normally means that vast quantities of data can be transferred around the world very quickly. But there are still limits. These limits may be by convention or by technical design. This is one area commonly encountered in web research through the notion of *rate limiting*. Above with both Reddit and Wikipedia, we used `time.sleep(<duration>)` in order to ensure that we were not making too many queries too quickly. Sometimes rate limiting is even a legal matter. Too much data too quickly can be considered a denial-of-service attack or a distributed denial of service.

Variety

While data about individuals can be public, there is also a sense that public observation is not meant to be targeted, at which point it could be considered stalking, voyeurism, or harassment, depending on the circumstances. While we rarely invoke those terms explicitly online, there have been many cases where data was accessible, but it was the triangulation of data across multiple sources that was the problem. This issue is not specific to the internet. For example, in 1970, the book *Tearoom Trade* (Humphries, 1970) was published as a covert ethnography of gay and bi men who sought illicit sex in public places. The author followed the men back to their cars and noted down the licence plates to determine whether these were out-of-state travellers or locals as well as liberal or politically conservative. He then interviewed these subjects under false pretences to discover how they felt about homosexuality. Indeed, all of the information about their licence plates was public, and their behaviour was ostensibly (and inappropriately) in a public place. Yet, the combination of these features was very threatening to the subjects, regardless of the nature of their conduct.

Linking data online is very common for commercial identity providers, but that does not make it right. From Sweeney's (2002) notion of *k*-anonymity (where most people are uniquely identifiable with only a smattering of signals) to Zimmer's (2010) contentions that triangulating Facebook data is not okay just because the data is public, there have been many examples of how variety of data can be an issue even if velocity and volume are taken care of. Twitter, for example, explicitly address triangulation and discourage it in their Developer Terms under 'off-Twitter matching' under restricted use cases (https://developer.twitter.com/en/developer-terms/more-on-restricted-use-cases).

 Summary

This chapter has introduced the web as a site of data access. This means understanding what goes into a URL and an IP address as well as how to build a request to get data from a URL. I showed how to collect data using URLs and provided an extended example using Reddit that allowed us to collect JSON data and page through some search results. I briefly discussed the request and response headers and highlighted how we can add data to a request header, specifically a 'user-agent' string. I used a `session` object so we could have headers that persisted between requests. I did not show how to store and manage cookies in Python, but this is available alongside a host of other features in the `requests` library. More involved work might require the use of a package like `selenium` or `MechanicalSoup`.

I concluded with some reflections on practices to ensure your work is considerate. Here they mainly concern minimising the Vs of big data: volume, velocity, and variety. In the next chapter we will look at how these are also governed by the policies of a platform. This means that we will be adhering to APIs but should also reflect critically on how this access might steer us to be able to answer some kinds of questions with data but not others.

 Further reading in ethics of data access and privacy

In the next chapter, after we discuss APIs, there are some readings about collecting more data from the web. Here I wanted to invite you to consider some interesting work concerning online data, ethics, and privacy.

- *Understanding Privacy* by Solove (2008). An excellent introduction to the world of data privacy and some key concepts and tensions therein. Often I see this work alongside Nissenbaum's engaging *Privacy in Context* (2009). There she makes the argument for privacy as a form of contextual integrity, an often discussed, considered, and challenged idea.

- There are many papers that engage with this issue, as it is an evolving one where new challenges and ideas emerge regularly. The journal *Research Ethics* regularly publishes work concerning social science and digital data, such as Sugiura et al. (2017) and Mason and Singh (2022) both on the challenges of the web as a public and private space.
- *Big Data* by Mayer-Schönberger and Cukier (2013) makes the case that the qualities of big data make for qualitative changes in how we understand it, including ethically. Not everyone agrees that the changes are qualitative; they may be more a matter of degree (cf. Zwitter, 2014). Do you?
- With respect to data ethics and social networks, there was recently an entire special issue of the journal of *Social Networks* dedicated to this (Tubaro et al., 2021). Many of the issues overlap concerning matters of triangulation and representation.

 ## Extensions and reflections

- In this chapter I introduced the `requests` library and showed how to collect data from the open web. We did not go as far as building a crawler, however. The paging algorithm is close, as it iterates through a set of pages. But why not try a crawler? Download a page from the web, extract the URLs, and then rinse and repeat. You will quickly discover that this task can get out of hand as you navigate extraneous trackers and JavaScript libraries. So, here is one activity I enjoy trying: build a crawler on Wikipedia. Parse one page and then get the links to other Wikipedia articles. For example, consider how this can be used to answer questions in navigation or culture. There is an activity on the book's GitHub page related to this where I build an 'egonet' around a Wikipedia page.
- Browse a social media page for an account you have on a web browser. Download and save the HTML for a social media page of interest, such as Facebook, Tumblr, or TikTok. Try to extract the meaningful data that you saw on the page. For example, where you have a photo, that photo is linked to a URL which represents the photo. Can you find out where it is in the HTML? Can you find some obvious text on either side of the photo that would allow Python to return the photo's URL? If you do that, then you can start to compare multiple profiles. You might want a little help here, and so think about returning to this task after reading Chapter 10 on cleaning data.

7
ACCESSING APIS, INCLUDING TWITTER AND REDDIT

========= Learning goals =========

- Understand what an API is and why they are useful
- Be able to get and use a token in order to get data from a server
- Appreciate how wrappers can often abstract away API details and treat data on the server like a Python object
- See how to create bespoke queries for Twitter using the v2 search API
- Critically appraise what features of an API are available for what purpose.

Accessing APIs: Abstracting from the web

While it is important to understand the web as a site for downloading data such as a webpage directly, it is also important to understand the web as a means for querying for specific objects using standard web protocols. We have already seen this in the previous chapter where we used changes in the URL string in order to change the data that we were collecting from Reddit. I referred to that specific instance as paging, but we were also implicitly working with the Reddit application programming interface.

APIs are a central part of the web from both technical and political points of view. They define the structure of accessible data as well as help to define who can access that data and under what circumstances (Lomborg and Bechmann, 2014). Collecting data from platforms, whether it is Facebook, Twitter, Reddit, Instagram, Telegram, WeChat, Amazon, Google, etc., will almost certainly entail working with APIs. Fortunately, there are some consistencies and standards to APIs. Thus, instead of spending many chapters, one on each API, I rather want to cover some of the key concepts that will permit you to access data from most APIs. We will work up in complexity from a single text line API to querying Twitter and Reddit's APIs directly and through API wrappers. Notably, I will not be spending considerable time *navigating* APIs. I will show some brief examples of how to get authenticated data from Twitter and Reddit, but I will not dedicate much time to the different features of the APIs themselves.

The chapter includes a short reflection on APIs and research designs. In so far as social science work tends to take place on scales of months or years, the researcher will need to consider the stability and accessibility of the API over this timespan. I will discuss some lessons learned and shared for project management. I will also reflect on the epistemological concerns this situation raises. In contrast to self-reported work, where we can confidently assume there will be people to give informed consent in the future, in computational social science work, the APIs and platforms we investigate might not be there by the time the paper is published. This can have knock-on effects for scientific practice which I introduce.

To begin, let's start by thinking about the ways in which we identify ourselves to servers, specifically through the use of keys and tokens. Typically, these credentials permit access to the data via APIs, so we usually need these before doing much with APIs directly.

7.1.1 Identifying yourself: Keys and tokens

Data controllers (platforms, servers, etc.) often permit others access to some data in some structured form. This literally needs to happen all the time when browsing the web. News sites pull in tweet data, Instagram photos, or YouTube videos. Sometimes data controllers will make very specific data easily available to anyone (e.g., in the previous chapter we were able to get the data from the Aww subreddit without any authentication. Admittedly, we altered our `user-agent` string, but that is more of a courtesy since some servers (including Reddit) will throttle requests made with default `user-agent` strings like `python-requests/2.27.1`. If we want more granular data at larger scales, we often have to register with a server and then make use of some credentials produced through registration.

The prevailing system for sharing data based on user authentication is called OAuth. OAuth is a set of protocols and conventions that allow users, projects, and servers to securely identify themselves to exchange data. There are differing levels of security, depending on the circumstances. As researchers we often have a different security model than someone who is building an app for the web, as we are typically requesting data for our own use rather than acting on behalf of another user. Sometimes platforms will have a simplified workflow for these instances. Other times we still have to authenticate *as if* we were a user, which can be more complicated, and then request data. In either case, we are likely to encounter both *keys* and *tokens*. Typically through sending a key, a token, or some combination of these and other credentials, we identify ourselves to a server, which will then permit access to some specific data.

The difference between a key and a token, generally, is that a key is *per project* and a token is *per user* or per instance. Since researchers are often the one user for a project, the difference does not matter that much. But these APIs are often structured for developers who are thinking about authenticating users, not just those who want to research a platform and download some data. We often encounter APIs where we need to create a token per session that combines the project's key with some credentials from a specific user to create a user-specific token. We will see examples of tokens below.

For our first API example, I want to recall an API we briefly saw in the previous chapter. It did not require any authentication at all. We sent a GET request to `ipify.org` and it returned our external IP address. It did not ask for any authentication.

```
import requests

my_external_ip = requests.get("https://api.ipify.org").text
print(my_external_ip.split(".")[0] + ".xxx.xxx.xxx")

51.xxx.xxx.xxx
```

The next API we saw was Reddit, where we similarly used GET requests, but we also modified our `user-agent` string. However, that did not authenticate us so we could identify ourselves using any user agent we wanted. Normally when we authenticate we have to send some credentials to the site and then receive some authorisation from the site. Because we did not ask for very much data from Reddit we did not really notice whether or not we were authenticated. But if we were to ask for more data, such as getting all the comments per post or getting more search results per request, we would want to be authenticated.

A site that currently offers free API keys and a simple interface is The Cat API. This service allows you to query for pictures of pets, not dissimilar to those found on r/aww. It will not likely be useful for much research, but its API is very simple and the documentation shows pretty clearly how to construct queries for data. Navigating to `https://www.thecatapi.`

`com/signup`, I was able to sign up simply by adding my email address and giving a reason for use. The API key was emailed to me. It looked something like `aa1111bb-2222-22cc-dd3e-e44ffff5a66b` (all tokens and IDs are substituted in text with similar-looking tokens). The email message said add this to the request header with the key `x-api-key`. In the previous chapter we saw how to add key–value pairs to the request header when we changed the `user-agent` string, which was also in the request headers. We can apply that below.

```python
import json

s = requests.Session()
s.headers.update({'x-api-key': 'aa1111bb-2222-22cc-dd3e-e44ffff5a66b'})

req = s.get("https://api.thecatapi.com/v1/breeds/search?q=Norwegian")
results = json.loads(req.content)

if len(results) > 0:
    print("Name:",results[0]['name'],
          "Description:",results[0]['description'], sep="\n")
```

```
Name:
Norwegian Forest Cat
Description:
The Norwegian Forest Cat is a sweet, loving cat. She appreciates praise and
loves to interact with her parent. She makes a loving companion and bonds with
her parents once she accepts them for her own. She is still a hunter at heart.
She loves to chase toys as if they are real. She is territorial and
patrols several times each day to make certain that all is fine.
```

7.1.2 Securely using credentials

Above I had to include my real API key from The Cat API and then remove it once I received the data, otherwise my personal key would be printed in this book and thus used by others. Depending on the API, sharing your personal key is not a problem. In fact, many forms of authentication depend on sharing public keys that are combined with private keys to decrypt a message or confirm a user's identity. Regardless of whether a site refers to these credentials as keys or tokens, we should consider a secure way to store them. Storage depends on whether we expect these credentials to persist between sessions. So normally a key does not change very often. You would want a place to keep that key written down. But for some cases, you will receive a new token every time you run your program, which means it only needs to be kept in memory.

Since we do not want to store these credentials in the code directly, where should they go? One prevailing practice is to consider credentials as *environment variables*. Your computer will have a series of these which you can access as key–value pairs via `os.environ`. They are read by the operating system. One such variable might be the path to Python (`os.environ["CONDA_PYTHON_EXE"]`).

```
import os
```

```
print(os.environ['CONDA_PYTHON_EXE'])
```

```
/Users/accountname/opt/anaconda3/bin/python
```

Environment variables are conventionally stored in a system file named simply `.env`. Thus, you should consider adding a `.env` file to the same directory as your code or in the root directory of your project. In that file you add credentials as key–value pairs. Below I write my key to a `.env` file for the root of this book, which is the directory above where I run these commands. So the folder structure would look like this:

```
[book]
- [chapters]
- [data]
- .env
```

Then we can use the `dotenv` package to add our credentials to the system's environment variables. This workflow helps keep our credentials out of the code folder. So if you want to pack up the code, you do not send your credentials. Also, the format of the `.env` file is pretty standard so it can be used to transfer your credentials to a cloud provider if want to transfer your work to a server. I also want to note below a change in syntax. Since `dotenv` currently does not use `pathlib`, I am using `".."` as a string instead of `Path.cwd().parent` as an object. And now since I want to write a program that will work on windows with \ folder separators and Mac/Unix / folder separators, I use the generic `os.sep` which will set the right folder separator. Hence, `..{os.sep}.env` should be the path to a `.env` file in the directory above where this code is run, regardless of operating system.

```
# pip install python-dotenv
import dotenv
```

```
ENV_PATH = f"..{os.sep}.env"
```

```
dotenv.set_key(ENV_PATH,
    "CAT_API_KEY", "aa1111bb-2222-22cc-dd3e-e44ffff5a66b")
```

```
dotenv.load_dotenv(ENV_PATH)
print(os.environ.get('CAT_API_KEY'))
```

```
aa1111bb-2222-22cc-dd3e-e44ffff5a66b
```

So now my code above can be modified to be more secure:

```
s = requests.Session()
s.headers.update({"x-api-key":os.environ['CAT_API_KEY']})
```

```
req = s.get("https://api.thecatapi.com/v1/breeds/search?q=Norwegian")
print(json.loads(req.content)[0]['temperament'])
```

```
Sweet, Active, Intelligent, Social, Playful, Lively, Curious
```

Now that we can securely store credentials, let's get some credentials for a widely popular platform for research, Twitter.

 ## Accessing Twitter data through the API

Twitter is a hugely useful platform for collecting data for computational social science research. It would take more than a entire volume to try and tame all the possibilities for how to collect data on Twitter alone. However, the reason why I am showing it now is that, despite its complexity, it is actually pretty easy to get started on the Twitter API and even the basic free access gives a considerable amount of data. To get started on this section, however, you will need a Twitter account. If you are then logged into Twitter, you can navigate to https://developers.twitter.com/. There you should be able to sign up for a developer account. Approval for a basic developer account should happen immediately so long as you provide credentials such a telephone number. That being said, both the process and the reliability of getting accounts has been somewhat inconsistent over the years.

Verifying your account will immediately lead you to receive three important credentials: an *API key*, an *API key secret*, and a *bearer token*. The bearer token is useful in a research context where you (or your lab) are the only ones with access to the code and can securely use a single token. However, since this token will represent you to Twitter they are very coy about it. Copy that bearer token to somewhere secure because Twitter only shows it once. If you lose it, you can generate a new one, and only one works at a time. We can use the bearer token to authenticate ourselves to Twitter similarly to how we used the CAT_API_KEY to authenticate ourselves to The Cat API.

```
# dotenv.set_key(ENV_PATH, "TWITTER_BEARER_TOKEN",
# "AAAAAAAAAAAAAAAAAAAAAAAAI4bbbCCCCCCCCCdEf%1GGggGgGgGgGGG222jk4155%5LmMMmm66Nnn
# 6oOoooPpPPp7qqqQ8rrrrr999r0SSSSSSSS00tTt")

dotenv.load_dotenv(ENV_PATH) # This will refresh the environment variables
print(len(os.environ.get('TWITTER_BEARER_TOKEN')))
```

114

Below we will make a request to Twitter using this bearer token. Notice how we simply add it to our headers and then we can receive JSON data back from Twitter. One thing to note below is that we are making a request to the *search* endpoint. So we need to give it a search string. Twitter has very formal and involved search query strings and people will share these in forums and GitHub repositories. For simplicity, I will show a relatively basic (and true to form) query for *The Muppet Show*, using the phrase "(muppet show)". Also, I will restrict it so that it does not include retweets, using "-is:retweet". You can see how to employ a variety of search parameters from Twitter's own query-building support page (https://developer.twitter.com/apitools/query).

Feel free to change the query below to enliven the results for your own interest. We are here just exploring *how* to get the data.

```
url = "https://api.twitter.com/2/tweets/search/recent"

BEARER = os.environ["TWITTER_BEARER_TOKEN"]
headers = {"Authorization": f"Bearer {BEARER}"}

QUERY = "(muppet show) -is:retweet"
MAX_RESULTS = 10

params={"query": QUERY,
        "max_results":MAX_RESULTS}

response = requests.get(url, headers=headers, params=params)

assert response.status_code == 200, \
    f"Code {response.status_code}. See error: {response.json()}"

tweets = response.json()
print(tweets.keys())


dict_keys(['data', 'meta'])
```

7.2.1 Troubleshooting requests

I hope that when you ran this you also received a response which had data and meta keys. If you did not receive a response of 200, the program threw an error (using the assert syntax here). This happens to me pretty often when just starting a project or playing with an API. It's useful to be familiar with how to troubleshoot these codes as they are standard across HTTP responses, so similar patterns might apply if you are troubleshooting the YouTube or Spotify APIs.

Here are a few common ones:

- *Code 401 (Unauthorised)*. This means Twitter does not know who you are. This is often because you have sent the wrong token or formatted it incorrectly. I once failed by sending "Authorization": "<token>" insted of "Authorization": "Bearer <token>" as it expected, so be patient with API-specific details.
- *Code 403 (Forbidden)*. Twitter recognises who you are but you are not permitted to access that specific endpoint. One reason for this is trying to access an endpoint for which your tier does not have permission. The basic Twitter developer account does not have access to the full historical archive so if you try to query "/2/tweets/search/all" instead of "/2/tweets/search/recent" you will receive this error.
- *Code 404 (Resource not found)*. Check your query to make sure it actually goes to the right endpoint. I got this query once by searching for "/2/tweets/count/recent" instead of "/2/tweets/counts/recent".

There are many other responses that might happen, for example if you reach your monthly download cap or make too many queries in too short a time span. Python wrappers can sometimes be helpful in that they abstract away the details and thus make it a little more difficult to send the wrong thing (like sending `<token>` rather than `"Bearer. <token>"`). They can often also help with rate limiting by knowing how long to wait rather than throwing errors or repeatedly querying for data while the program should wait. Nevertheless, it is also worth seeing how to collect this data directly by just building the right URL, adding the right credentials, and parsing a result.

In the case of the query above, hopefully we have `tweets` with the keys `['data', 'meta']`. If you explore `tweets['data']`, you will see that it should be a list of up to 10 tweets.

```
tweets['data'][0] # Actual content simulated for book
```

```
{'id': '10000000000000000001',
 'text': 'It\'s time to get things started with The Muppet Show'}
```

Note that in the interests of privacy, I have replaced all the actual tweet IDs, user IDs, and text with simulated data. This is also following conclusions from Williams et al. (2017), whose surveys suggest people do not mind being used in academic research generally, but would assume that they would be reported anonymously or contacted ahead of time for direct mentioning. Regardless, the *shape* of the data should look very similar to what you would receive if you were to do this yourself.

7.2.2 Access rights and Twitter

Twitter, like many sites, allow differential access to their API. The essential API tier is free. It permits access to 500,000 tweets per month, and only from a recent time window. Depending on your research, that might be plenty. However, for a lot of work, that might either be too few tweets or too restrictive a time period. For example, if you wanted to look into the early use of the #blm and #metoo tags you would need access to `2/tweets/search/all`.

The `essential` key will give you access to the `/2/tweets/search/recent` endpoint, whereas `elevated` and `academic` keys will give you access to `2/tweets/search/all`. Academic access is not automatic, so you should consider making use of essential first. In my classes, the experience of getting approval was somewhat opaque and variable. Some people received academic access almost immediately, others were granted it days later, and others were rejected. While there was no obvious pattern, those who had Twitter accounts registered with two-factor authentication or with academic email address, as well as those who wrote more clearer rationales, appeared more successful.

Twitter, like many sites, has not only a terms of use (which most people skim and accept), but also a terms for developer use. This actually can have some important implications for your work. For example, Twitter discourage you from sharing whole databases of tweets, but prefer if you share only the IDs to be 'rehydrated' by a third party. That way, if people delete their tweets in the meantime, the projects do not have to manage such deletion (since they are not sharing the now-deleted content). I strongly recommend reading the developer agreements. In particular the document on restricted use cases is often pertinent to research (https://developer.twitter.com/en/developer-terms/more-on-restricted-use-cases).

7.2.3 Strategies for navigating Twitter's API

If you were successful in getting a batch of tweets, you will have discovered that Twitter only returned the id and the text. This is not very much. We will want to take an interest in a variety of information related to the tweet. Twitter used to package up a very large and thorough tweet object in their v1 and v1.1 APIs (such as the example I present in Chapter 4). This, however, does not really work with our evolving sense of data protection. One common data protection principle (noted for example in Article 5(1) the EU's GDPR) is *data minimisation*. In this case, it is better for us to explicitly ask for specific data related to a tweet or its author than to try to collect as much as possible which will just need to be cleaned or managed later.

In contrast to Twitter, you may have noticed in the previous chapter that Reddit returned very full JSON, rather than something more austere like the recent Twitter API. This may change in the future. What is noteworthy is that the JSON led to us creating a very wide DataFrame with hundreds of columns that would inevitably need to be cleaned out before doing most analysis tasks. In this case, however, we have the opposite issue. It is sometimes difficult to know which data you are allowed to access, given that some of it is available to some people but not everyone. Checking the API documentation for Twitter is your best bet as these things do change over time.

The first place to look is the 'data dictionary' for the Twitter API (https://developer.twitter. com/en/docs/twitter-api/data-dictionary/). In the data dictionary you will see what objects are available (such as 'Tweets', 'Users', and 'Lists'). The keys for each object are the things you can ask for with the tweet. For example, I can add a tweet.fields key to my parameters and the tweets will now come down with keys for those fields. Below I add a few useful ones: author_id, conversation_id, created_at, and in_reply_to.

```
params={
    'query': QUERY,
    'max_results':10,
    'tweet.fields':"id,author_id,conversation_id,created_at,"+
                   "in_reply_to_user_id"}

response = requests.get(url, headers=headers, params=params)

assert response.status_code == 200, \
    f"Code {response.status_code}. See error: {response.json()}"

tweets = response.json()
print(tweets.keys())

dict_keys(['data', 'meta'])

tweets['data'][0]

{'id': '10000000000000000002',
 'conversation_id': '10000000000000000002',
```

```
'text': "These politicians are like a muppet show!!",
'author_id': '20000000000000000001',
'created_at': '2022-05-10T00:00:00.000Z'}
```

The JSON now has several more columns. Similarly to the previous chapter, we can now transform these tweets into a table using `json_normalize`. In this case, `pd.json_normalize(tweets['data'])` should give you a table with 10 results. The various data from the tweet should then be in its own column.

```
import pandas as pd
```

```
df = pd.json_normalize(tweets['data'])
df[["id","conversation_id","author_id","in_reply_to_user_id"]]
```

	id	conversation-id	author-id	in-reply-to-user-id
0	1523855408850300928	1523855408850300928	1057754786764775424	NaN
1	1523854149833555969	1523854149833555969	41180660	NaN
2	1523849183479750658	1523849183479750658	305566189	NaN
3	1523837792186298368	1523837792186298368	1057754786764775424	NaN
4	1523836664459583489	1523836664459583489	438897163	NaN
5	1523827155687329798	1523813426274910215	1242558135623180288	1255661817118031872
6	1523824207167119361	1523824207167119361	1043560965919449089	NaN
7	1523824121699659776	1523776961574670336	1466786065960759298	184216437
8	1523824059737423872	1523824059737423872	178123456	NaN
9	1523819874627506176	1523819874627506176	22859603	NaN

Before moving on, I wanted to show how Twitter allows you to 'expand' the Tweet object in the v2 API. An expansion used to be nested inside the tweet object. In the older API details about a user and geography would be nested inside each tweet object. This not only would undermine data minimisation, but also goes against the notion of tidy data (Wickham, 2014). If you were to ask for all tweets from a single user, then you would get a lot of redundant data with each tweet object. Here instead we use the `expansions` key. This will then request further data, in this case on the users who have made the tweets. I'm keeping the other parameters the same as before, just adding two `expansions` keys: data about users through `user.fields` and data about places in the tweets through `place.fields`. First let's run with these parameters, and then we can explore how the data came back.

```
params['expansions'] = "author_id,geo.place_id"
params['user.fields'] = "id,username,name,description,public_metrics"
params['place.fields'] = "id,country,country_code,full_name"

response = requests.get(url, headers=headers, params=params)
```

```
assert response.status_code == 200, \
    f"Code {response.status_code}. See error: {response.json()}"

tweets = response.json()
print(tweets.keys())


dict_keys(['data', 'includes', 'meta'])
```

Notice there is now an 'includes' key. This will be a separate list of expansions. We now include a 'users' table. We can look at the first user with tweets['includes']['users'][0]. Or transform the entire list into a table using pd.json_normalize(tweets['includes']['users']).

```
users_df = pd.json_normalize(tweets['includes']['users'])
users_df.iloc[0]


description
id                                      2000000000000000002
name                        It's not easy being rgb(0, 255, 0)
username                            kermitthedatascientist
public_metrics.followers_count                        31415
public_metrics.following_count                         1123
public_metrics.tweet_count                               42
public_metrics.listed_count                               0
Name: 0, dtype: object
```

Using tweet counts to manage requests

It helps to know how many tweets you are going to download before tying up system resources. This is especially true on the academic tier where you can get access to the full archive search. So in addition to querying the tweets directly, consider the use of the tweet counts endpoint 2/tweets/counts/recent in addition to the tweet search endpoint (recall that this is 2/tweets/search/recent). For example, just how many results would we get by querying for *The Muppet Show* if we collected all the tweets within the recent tweets time window (presently 7 days)?

```
params={'query': QUERY}
url = "https://api.twitter.com/2/tweets/counts/recent"

response = requests.get(url, headers=headers, params=params)

assert response.status_code == 200, \
    print("There was an error retrieving the results:", response)

count_data = response.json()

len(count_data["data"])
```

It appears that by default here the count endpoint will provide counts per hour for the last 7 days. You can see this by exploring `count_data["data"]`. It will have one count per hour and one for the part-hour interval since the last hour (24 × 7 + 1 = 169 as seen in the `len` above). This is the default granularity, but you can set the granularity to be more or less coarse and thereby ask for how many tweets per day or minute. `count_data["meta"]` should tell us the total in that window:

```
count_data["meta"]
```

```
{'total_tweet_count': 1113}
```

If you have access to the historical tweet archives through an academic developer key, simply combining the tweet count endpoint with some creative search queries and you can get some fascinating results about when and where some concepts, links, or hashtags spread.

Using an API wrapper to simplify data access

API wrappers will abstract away a lot of the details of what we have done before. This is both good and bad. The advantage is that some APIs make authenticating tricky or have very strange syntax for accessing specific objects or resources. API wrappers can often be more up to date than some documentation and already be able to manage errors and response codes. Sometimes, however, I feel there is a rush to go right to a wrapper without understanding the limits or potentials of the underlying API. And while it might be a matter of taste, I find that some wrappers are written in a way that just makes it more confusing to collect data. Hopefully the above discussion will help you consider APIs even if you cannot find a wrapper.

Many wrappers would be found on GitHub and registered with PyPi, meaning they can be installed with `pip`. Among those is `praw` or the Python Reddit API Wrapper. I think it is a good example of how a wrapper can simplify some aspects of data access. It is available through `pip install praw`.

```
import praw
print(praw.__version__)
```

```
7.5.0
```

7.3.1 Collecting Reddit data using praw

It is possible to use `praw` without authenticating to Reddit, but the documentation suggests that you will both experience rate limits and access limits. Therefore, we will get some credentials for Reddit first, add them to our `.env`, and use them to create a `praw.Reddit` object which we will use to query the site.

You will need the following credentials:

- *A Reddit account.* You can register a free account at https://www.reddit.com/.
- *A Reddit app.* This will give you a `client_id` and a `client_secret`. I discuss this in detail below.

* *A specific user agent.* This should follow the convention of `<platform>:<app ID>:<version string> (by u/<Reddit username>)`. For example, `MacOS:redditapitester:v1 (by u/berniehogan)`.

Once you have registered for a Reddit account, navigate to https://www.reddit.com/prefs/ apps. If you are already a Reddit user, there might be some apps already given permission shown there, such as a 'Reddit iOS'. At the bottom will be a button saying 'Are you a developer, create an app...'. Click on that button so we can create an app which will retrieve some credentials for use. Similarly to the Twitter example above, we are developing an app for ourselves to collect data and not for others. Thus, select the 'script' option and name your app. It will also ask for an *about URL* and a *redirect URL*. The about URL should probably be a personal page for this project or your own research. The redirect URL is used primarily for oAuth-based work, which is not so relevant here. Press 'create app' and you will see some credentials that you can use.

The `client_id` key will be listed near the top under the phrase 'personal use script'. Mine looks like 'AAA11bbbCCdEE2fGGh3ijK'. Then below you will be able to find the `client_secret` key. Click on 'edit' and the key should be revealed. Mine looks like 'aBc-De1FgGgHIJ2KlMnO3PQRs-TuvwX'. We should set these and our `reddit_username` in our `.env` file. For more complicated work you might want to investigate how `praw` recommends doing things using a similar `praw.ini` file. Below I show the code to set the keys in the `.env` file. However, it is commented, since you should only do this once and only with your keys. You can load the keys repeatedly.

```
# dotenv.set_key(ENV_PATH, 'REDDIT_CLIENT_ID','AAA11bbbCCdEE2fGGh3ijK')
# dotenv.set_key(ENV_PATH, 'REDDIT_CLIENT_SECRET',
#                 'aBcDe1FgGgHIJ2KlMnO3PQRs-TuvwX')
# dotenv.set_key(ENV_PATH, 'REDDIT_USER', 'berniehogan')

dotenv.load_dotenv(ENV_PATH);
```

Now we should be ready to create a `praw.Reddit` object and use it to access data programmatically rather than by specifying queries through `requests.get` statements.

```
user_agent = f"MacOS:redditapitester:v1 (by u/{os.environ['REDDIT_USER']})"

redd = praw.Reddit(user_agent = user_agent,
                   client_id = os.environ['REDDIT_CLIENT_ID'],
                   client_secret = os.environ['REDDIT_CLIENT_SECRET'])
example_post = next(redd.front.hot())

print("The hot post now is:", example_post.title)
print("Submitted by: u/", example_post.author.name)

The hot post now is: World Peace finally achieved through adorable pets
Submitted by: u/YetAnotherRedditorOnThisSite
```

Notice that we are no longer dealing with JSON directly. We have a Reddit object, redd, which can query for the front page (in this case sorted by the default 'what's hot' rating). You can query for data by subreddit, and sort that data in a variety of ways. The author of the post was itself an object, a 'user' object, for which we can query name and other details. Many of the details we can query might already be in large chunks of JSON that we have already requested. Sometimes praw might need to query for the data again. But fortunately all of this is abstracted from the user who simply needs to call the right method and let praw sort out the implementation.

7.3.2 Building a comment tree on Reddit

Comments on social media forums often take the form of a *tree*, like a folder structure or family tree. A post is usually the root and each comment starts a branch. Then people can either reply to an existing comment or start a new branch. So each comment will have a parent, which is either the post or the comment to which this one replies.

Below I will first capture the comments for a specific Reddit post. The API will not return all the comments upon the first request. You would need to manually check each comment thread to see if there are more comments that need to be included. But praw manages that. These comments will have an id for the comment, and also a parent id for whether they are linked to a previous comment or to the post itself. With these two pieces of data you can construct a comment reply network. I provide some tips on how to build networks in Chapter 13; for now I merely wanted to introduce a way to get these comments using a wrapper.

Again, keeping with the Muppets theme, I have selected a post where leading puppeteer Frank Oz does a Q&A (referred to as an AMA or 'ask me anything') with the Reddit community. It's id is 7o6bxv. To see the post live you can navigate to https://redd.it/7o6bxv. You might notice that this redirects you to https://www.reddit.com/r/iAmA/comments/7o6bxv/im_frank_oz_film_director_and_performer_ask_me/.

```
example_post = redd.submission("7o6bxv") # This will refresh the object.

print("Title:", example_post.title)
print("Before:",len(example_post.comments))

Title: I'm Frank Oz, film director and performer: Ask Me Anything
Before: 159
```

I am sure there are more than 159 comments in this post. To add them to our post, we can run ex_post.comments.replace_more(). However, this will only add upwards of 100 comments at a time. The documentation recommends doing this in a loop that might catch an exception. You can see more tips in the documentation on comments (https://praw.readthedocs.io/).

```
example_post.comments.replace_more(limit=None)
print("After:",len(example_post.comments))

After: 468
```

Instead of 159 we have more (this time 468, though in previous attempts I received more and less). When navigating to the page it says there are 1200 comments. Accessing all of these may require you to not only include the `client_id` and `client_secret` in your `praw.Reddit` object but also your username and password. This will then allow you to retrieve *authenticated* queries, which will allow you not only to query for things from your own Reddit feed but also to access considerably more data per request. Regardless, if you want to work with the comment objects you get, you can first transform them to a list and then continue from there either inserting into a `DataFrame` or perhaps building a network of comments. You can see an example of how I build a comment network from a Reddit thread in the exercises in the GitHub repository for this chapter.

```
comment_list = example_post.comments.list()

mentions = len([comment for comment in comment_list
                if "Frank" in comment.body])

print(f"Frank was mentioned in {mentions} comments",
      f"or {mentions/len(comment_list):0.1%} of the time")

Frank was mentioned in 182 comments or 17.2% of the time
```

 ## Considerations for a data collection pipeline

One comment thread or one post on Reddit is hardly enough. Typically you would want to get either a sufficient or a complete sample of a community or search query. Yet, 'complete' data might mean data that is too large for a laptop or too slow for your needs. Similarly, on Twitter, you might want to have something running for a while in order to collect a sufficient volume over a certain timeframe. These are considerations for a data collection pipeline. These pipelines can vary considerably, depending on the project and its scale. There are ways to run a script on a computer that continually check for new tweets. That computer does not need to be your personal laptop or desktop. In many cases, it is a server that you log into through a terminal. In some cases, it is an instance of what you primarily interface with online.

7.4.1 Version control systems and servers

Traditionally, to start a data collection pipeline you would have a folder for a project (e.g., for the code in this book) which has code that is synchronised or placed under version control. When you first start you might just want to keep it in a Dropbox, OneDrive, or Google Drive folder on your machine. But really, you ought to keep the files synchronised using a version control system like GitHub. I tend to prefer the GitHub Desktop app, but there are many ways to use GitHub, including through the browser, the terminal/PowerShell, through interesting third-party apps such as GitKraken, and even Jupyter Lab extensions.

With your data in a version control system like GitHub, you can then remotely log into another computer and clone the code to that location and run the code from there. There are third parties that provide server instances for you to code in free or cheaply (such as Heroku), but universities often have server support. You normally access them by logging in to a URL with your credentials. The prevailing approach is to use `ssh` or Secure Shell to turn your terminal command line into one that refers to a remote server. You might enter the following command in the terminal (not Python): `ssh <user>@<host>` with the username you would have been given or registered (like `bhogan002`) and the hostname being some other computer's address (often an IP address with a port specified like 192.168.0.1:1043). So the command might look like: `ssh bhogan002@192.168.0.1:1043`. It will prompt for a password, but there are ways to streamline this process if warranted.

If your credentials are successful, then the terminal screen will be replaced by a welcome message and a new prompt that represents the working directory for the server rather than your computer. From here you can type commands and they will run on the server. If you type `exit` you will return to the prompt. If the server is configured with a recent version of Python (ideally Python 3.9 or above) and the libraries that you require, you can run your code there. Most Python libraries will not require administrator access to install, but some might require you to install them using either `conda` or `brew` which may or may not be on the server.

While on a server you can use a program called `screen` to create a permanently running command. If you *attach* or *detach* the screen, that means you make it visible or invisible to you. This way you can log in, start up a screen and then within that screen run your commands. When you detach from that screen, it becomes invisible to you, but it does not stop the scripts. Then you can log out of the server without stopping a script. If you log back in, you will not see any progress until you type `screen -r` to reattach the screen. Then the program and any output (such as a counter or progress message) will be shown.

7.4.2 Storing data remotely

If you are working on data then you will probably want to store what you have collected. Accessing a server to run programs does not mean accessing large amounts of storage. These can be decoupled if the storage runs as a database on a server. You might then read and write from a database on the same server or via a remote IP address. Servers like Heroku offer add-ons for databases where you can store your data. If you just have storage space on your server, you might be inclined to save your data as text files. This can work and it can be very fast. But generally more scalable solutions would involve running a database and saving the data to that. If you do not want to think hard about your data but just want to dump it for now and process it later, MongoDB allows for easy storage of JSON data. So as your Reddit responses or tweets (or etc.) come in, you would write it to MongoDB via some connection provided. Many people also use Amazon Web Storage, which can provide a lot of storage that you would write to. Generally cloud storage makes it cheaper to write data than read it.

7.4.3 Jupyter in the browser as an alternative

Lately, cloud services have enabled more abstract options that mean you will not be directly interacting with a server through `ssh` and cloning projects through a terminal. Instead, you might run a Jupyter notebook you have written via an online platform and use that platform's storage and processors.

- *Google Colab* (https://colab.research.google.com/). An increasingly robust option is Google's online environment for running Jupyter notebooks. If you have a Google Drive, you can upload a Jupyter notebook to your Google Drive and then click on it. It will open in Colab much like a spreadsheet would open in Google Sheets. You can set Colab to connect to different processors or to keep running when you close your browser window. Google Colab looks very similar to Jupyter Lab, but there are a few subtle differences. One important one is how to check on sessions. Colab has fewer menu items, but one of them is 'runtime'. Under this menu item you can view sessions. Select the running notebook to see how things are going. You might want to ensure that you are not running too much in the cloud if you are paying for cycles. Sometimes this can get out of hand quickly if you are running something complicated for a long time. Also, as software in the cloud, it treats storage somewhat differently. There is a Colab notebook (https://colab.research.google.com/notebooks/io.ipynb) that demonstrates a number of approaches to input/output.
- *Binder* (https://mybinder.org/). A more public option than Colab is Binder. It is put together by the BinderHub federation, a consortium of non-governmental organisations, universities, and research institutes, such as GESIS in Germany and the Alan Turing Institute in the UK. From Binder you can launch a notebook located in a GitHub repository or URL and it will create a virtual machine for running the code. Currently, there is less flexibility in processor power than via Colab, but it does not require a Google account

APIs and epistemology: How data access can mean knowledge access

I wanted to end this chapter with a little bit of a more widescreen view about what data is available and how that shapes our research. In the next chapter, we start to think about research questions and how to make claims. But this implies access to the data to make the claims. Epistemology refers to the study of knowledge or the way of knowing. We might come to know something through sensory experience or through something more indirect. We come to know things about a social structure or community by measuring features of that community and aggregating or comparing them in some meaningful way.

To return to Reddit, you might notice that there are scores in the API for both upvotes (`data.ups`) and downvotes (`data.downs`), but the downvote data is empty and the upvotes data is equivalent to the score. Doesn't Reddit make use of downvotes? It does, but it was discovered several years ago that bots were also making use of the downvotes to game things on Reddit. Thus, Reddit removed access to the downvote scores but the JSON still retains that column (and theoretically for some with privileged access it might actually show the real downvote count). This indicates that while the data is available, our ability to know that data is compromised. Thus, research papers on whether downvotes are reliable signals or merely bullying will not be written.

This issue returned recently with a usability change on YouTube. In a similar fashion, in 2022 YouTube stopped showing users (and via the API) the 'dislike count' on their videos. They asserted that this was indeed to stop brigades of cyberbullies downvoting some video. However, it might also be that advertisers (or governments) do not like seeing downvotes. We might seek to critique why some can access this data and not others. Before we accept the cyberbullying case (which certainly has some validity in some circumstances), we might ask about different values. Should this be set by a user? It turns out that on home improvement videos, many hobbyists attend to the dislike count. Regardless of whether an electrician received a thousand or a million likes, anecdotally the dislike count still seems to help people assess safety. Can we research this now? Not if the API does not permit it. With privileged access, which may or may not even be possible, we might get access to the now-private dislike scores. But even then, what we learn about the private dislike score is different than what we learn from a world where that score is used and interpreted by users. Having it available through an API allows us to think beyond the interface, since we can potentially sort by dislikes or otherwise use it in ways other than what was available on the screen.

In the previous chapter I concluded with some considerations about ethics. These suggested that you, the researcher, ought to be ethically mindful of the way in which you are abiding by good research principles, including data protection principles such as data minimisation. This is absolutely still the case. However, framing adherence to rate limits or data minimisation as about an individual virtue can obscure the role that platforms play in influencing what data is available to whom and for what purpose. It may be unethical to scrape a site for something that does not have a public API, but what if it has an API that it shares with advertisers but not scientists? Who gets to know about the data and at what scale? And thus who gets to intervene at that scale gets tied closely to details that often get obscured via technical API discussions.

One place where this became quite real for academia was in the USA, where the Computer Fraud and Abuse Act asserted that it would be criminal (rather than merely potentially unethical) to violate a site's terms of service. In the previous chapter I noted that we ought to practice data minimisation, but that it is one of many ethical principles, including a principle of fairness. What happens if you cannot research a platform because they have asked you not to do that in the terms of service? This was tested in an American federal court, where *Sandvig v Barr* contested the notion that violating the terms of service should be criminal (Metaxa et al., 2021). Sandvig, supported by the American Civil Liberties Union, argued that research which sometimes required tester accounts, pseudonyms, and exploring APIs, which would do virtually no harm but violate a terms of service agreement should be protected from prosecution. The government ruled that the particular work in the case was free to proceed and that a precedent was set for other such academic work.

Generally speaking, these APIs are not primarily there for academic usage. We are not inherently entitled to access this data. We can find ways to access it through programs, even creatively using browser emulators like `selenium`, but we cannot guarantee that access will always be available (or available ethically). As in Sandvig's case, we can establish that much research, particularly research online examining fairness, algorithmic bias, and discrimination, should not be impeded by predatory and overreaching terms of service. Yet, we must also acknowledge that data controllers can and do often circumvent access, change APIs, and create disincentives to repurpose data for academic work (Hogan, 2018; Rieder et al., 2015). Projects that depend on sustained access to an API or work as services that repurpose data from an API tend to be fragile and will often cease to work after a short period of time. While I do not want to discourage creative work with third-party APIs, I do want to be a little more cynical about this aspect of data collection than is normally the case in these texts.

To drive this point home, you might consider looking at multiple editions of the really excellent book *Mining the Social Web* by Matthew Russell (see Russell and Klassen, 2019). Each edition features some cookbook recipes for getting interesting data from a variety of sources (such as Wikipedia, Facebook, and LinkedIn). But the APIs and even the sources of data have changed considerably over the years, with sources coming and going. I do worry about the longevity of the various libraries and wrappers I've featured in this book. Twitter has been a steady source of data and even made it easier for academics, and so I think it is a reasonable place to start. Others, such as LinkedIn and Facebook, have placed considerable restrictions on previously available data and thus make it challenging to do some forms of work on their platforms. This is especially the case with data on a social graph, like the set of one's contacts on LinkedIn or their friends on Facebook.

7 6 Summary

The web is not just a place where we download documents and parse them for data, but a regulated space that uses detailed endpoints, parameters, and credentials in order to determine who can access what data, how quickly, and in what form. We have accessed data in varying levels of authentication, from ipify's simple query to get an IP address and The Cat API's API key-based access, to accessing Twitter and Reddit with more involved approaches. I have shown how to safely manage tokens and keys using a `.env` file. One such token was the Twitter bearer token which allows us to query Twitter for details about tweets and users. I showed some examples of the extensive flexibility of Twitter's API but also some limitations. For example, the essential access tier does not permit access to the `/2/tweets/search/all` or full archive search option, but the academic tier does.

While Twitter has an extensive and flexible API that focuses on data minimisation, many other sites do not. Reddit's API, for example, returns large blobs of JSON, which we previously wrangled into a `DataFrame`. This meant we had to remove extraneous data if we wanted to retain a coherent and usable `DataFrame` for analysis. However, Reddit also has an API wrapper that allows us to query for specific things like `submission.author.name` without directly having to wrangle the data ahead of time.

In the last third of this chapter I focused on some practical considerations for research design. I began with concerns for the data collection pipeline, where I alluded to the use of `screen` on a remote terminal and the use of Google Colab for running Jupyter notebooks remotely. I then concluded with some reflections on what data is available and how that can affect not just the research we do, but the research we can do. This is therefore a good time to pause from specific technical skills and start to pivot to considerations for the research process where social science meets data science. I take this up in the next few chapters.

7 7 Further reading

For a discussion about APIs it is hard not to assert that you should read the documentation for the various APIs. But I admit that this does not feel very friendly and frankly a lot of documentation is not great. Twitter and Spotify have some really clear documentation, but not everyone does. When I was learning how to engage with APIs I found working through code snippets that others have created was very useful. Having these in Jupyter Lab can be especially helpful. The third edition of *Mining the Social Web* (Russell and Klassen, 2019) has some nice snippets in its GitHub repository (https://github.com/mikhailklassen/Mining-the-Social-Web-3rd-Edition).

On the topics of APIs and Internet policy there are a number of solid entry points. Gillespie does really extensive work in this domain, much of which is journal publications and essays, a personal favourite being 'The Politics of "Platforms"' (Gillespie, 2010). His recent book *Custodians of the Internet* (Gillespie, 2021) is adjacent to the issue of APIs by articulating how platforms moderate content. Also adjacent to this issue are concerns over algorithmic fairness and our ability to audit it. In addition to the example above of *Sandvig* v *Barr*, Noble's *Algorithms of Oppression* (2018) makes an incredibly strong case for reconsidering the neutrality of algorithms in the information society. She uses qualitative and systematic trace data to show how inequalities by race and gender remain entrenched in our search results, news-feeds, and advertisements. This again shows the importance and effectiveness of using trace data to make systematic comparisons to audit platforms.

 Extensions and reflections

- Construct your own Twitter data analysis pipeline on your computer. Start small and then think about what tools you'll need to expand. First consider the scope of your data collection, have a means for dealing with errors, ensure that you have a way to either periodically 'flush' the data to a file or a database, and think about strategies for what happens if you have uptime or connection issues. You can see one simple example of a streaming Twitter collector in the repository for this book. You can see that it uses Gmail's lightweight app tokens to have a simple way to send me an email message if there is an issue with the file.

- Explore an API directory. There are many directories out on the web that index and summarise APIs. One useful and regularly updated directory is from the GitHub account 'Public APIs' (https://github.com/public-apis/public-apis). This site categorises APIs as well as lists whether they require authentication and have a set of HTTPS endpoints. From this directory, find the link to the *arXiv* API. arXiv is a widely used repository of academic pre-prints. If you browse the documentation, you will see its API uses keys, REST queries, XML, user-agents, paging, and search terms as arguments, all techniques featured in these chapters. Try to get a distribution of articles using a search query (e.g., "cryptography" or "climate change") and then plot the years in which that query was most popular.

- There are packages for many platforms in Python. `spotipy`, the Python wrapper for Spotify, is generally quite thorough. It has some extensive documentation and a GitHub repository (https://github.com/plamere/spotipy/) with lots of little code snippet examples. Practise collecting data by trying to receive some information about what songs to play after your favourite song from the Spotify API. You will probably want to first find a way to get search results from the API, then select or check to confirm that you have the right result. Then check out the `show_related.py` snippet. Obviously getting your own data is not quite the same as doing wider research, but the goal is to first confirm you can access the *kind* of data you want, then develop a plan to get that data at the *scale* you want.

PART III

INTERPRETING DATA: EXPECTATIONS VERSUS OBSERVATIONS

8
RESEARCH QUESTIONS

- Understand how a research question is used to focus and motivate research
- Distinguish between prediction and explanation as separate but useful approaches
- Articulate how operationalisation is constraining in order make claims
- Consider how boundaries around distributions are a key way to make claims through comparison.

 ## Introduction

This chapter is a bit of an intermission in relation to the technical matters in the book. Here we will discuss the notion of research questions. A research question is a common device for structuring scientific research, especially social science research. As we shift towards more data science, research questions can become even more valuable, because it is so easy to get lost in the data. It is absolutely not the case that we can assume 'the end of theory'.

First I will define a research question, followed by a discussion of how it fits in the standard article model. Then we will discuss some approaches to focusing. We will conclude with some data-science-specific issues with research questions, mainly related to prediction versus explanation (and the related concepts of induction versus deduction).

8.1.1 What is a research question?

Simply stated, a research question is a focusing device. Practically speaking, a research question changes as research evolves. Research does not need a single research question. It can have several. But the more research questions you have, the harder it is to focus. So this is not the place to list every question you wish to ask of the data. Rather, it is where you translate your academic intuitions into a goal-directed exercise meant to be defensible before other academics.

A research question is not the same thing as a hypothesis. Whereas a research question is a focusing device, a hypothesis is a disconfirming device. A hypothesis is a testable, falsifiable claim. The hypothesis follows the hypothetico-deductive method formalised by Popper (Musgrave, 2011). The idea is that we pose a specific question which can be falsified with data as part of building a theory. A theory for Popper must be synthetic (as in not just facts), falsifiable, and corroborated. The emphasis on falsification in important in that within a hypothesis-driven framework we never prove something, only disprove or fail to disprove.

While the hypothesis is a central tool in the confirmation of scientific claims, it is not realistically the only route to scientific discovery. Popper himself had reacted with scepticism to theories that were asserted inductively or through mere intuition. In providing a staunch defence of deductive reasoning, he persuaded many people that this was as reasonable a route as one might find to objective knowledge. Admittedly, the hypothesis is an incredible intellectual device when the research design supports it. That said, there are many cases where the invocation of a hypothesis provides more of the veneer of science than the actual practice. As Haig notes, '[i]t is important to differentiate between the abductive generation of hypotheses, and their comparative appraisal in terms of inference to the best explanation' (Haig, 2015, p. 1).

Fortunately, research questions are a little more generous than hypotheses. Research questions tend to be more descriptive in nature. We describe the potential relationships between elements in our data or within our data generally. Embedded within a hypothesis is a claim that would be made with the data. With a research question we not so much trying to make claims as simply trying to make sense.

Notably, a research question might not even appear in a paper as a question, but rather as a statement that focuses the inquiry. For example, take a recent exemplary computational social science paper, 'The Geometry of Culture', that looks at the change in word association over time (Kozlowski et al., 2019). We do not look much at word embeddings directly in the book, but it will follow from the introductory work in Chapter 11 and is featured centrally in a complementary text on computational social science (McLevey, 2021).

Kozlowski et al. employed a huge number of texts across the twentieth century and examined whether similar associations persisted across time (such as *man + doctor* or *woman + nurse*). The authors were interested in whether these associations became less salient. In the paper you will not find a clear statement of what the research question is. Yet, the research question is quite apparent from the text in a couple places. First, early in the article they set up the question of cultural change and then assert: 'The precise ways these cultural dimensions of class relate to one another, however, and how these interrelations have evolved over time, remain open empirical questions' (Kozlowski et al., 2019, p. 906). They then list several considerations in this domain and note three possible relationships between class and cultural change. They then follow this up by saying: 'we propose formal text analysis as a promising avenue for recovering widely-shared understandings of class from historical populations no longer available for direct observation' (Kozlowski et al., 2019, p. 908). By the end of the paper, they have articulated how some cultural associations seem to have endured over time, while others have shifted.

 ## Inductive, deductive, and abductive research questions

The way that research questions appear in academic papers does not often reveal how the authors came to those specific research questions. For example, Kozlowski et al. (2019) use a consistently declarative style by asserting 'We apply X' or 'We argue Y'. However, somewhere along the way the authors were less certain of this approach and were looking either to make use of some corpus of data, apply some methodology, or explore some existing question. Yet the paper itself does not reveal this, as it exists as a finished product with a clear statement.

The process of arriving at a question is itself multifaceted and unpredictable, even in the case of something as presumably fixed as an experiment. For example, what is important: the variables that you are measuring or the concepts behind the variables? Are you testing differences in extroversion or differences in being talkative? We would take talkativeness as a signal of extroversion, but it is not a perfect signal. Extroversion, on the other hand, is itself an abstraction. Jung originally considered it in terms of an orientation to external states, but that itself was also partially an intuition (Jung, 1921). In the early 2010s a number of papers asked whether extroverts were more active on social media sites (Golbeck et al., 2011; Quercia et al., 2012). But extroversion itself was measured using self-reported studies, not behavioural work. This begs the question: is extroversion a subjective feeling, a cognition, or a set of behaviours? Does extroversion *cause* talkativeness or is extroversion *expressed* as talkativeness?

To help unpack this question we can consider the distinction between inductive and deductive research questions. And then for good measure we will include abductive questions as I consider these the most useful even if they are typically the least commonly mentioned.

Inductive research questions start from data, or rather from phenomena. We make claims by observing patterns in this data. We might observe that in one setting some kinds of speech are voted up and other kinds of speech are voted down. For example, if we take all the comments on a subreddit and rank them from highest to lowest score, then we count which words are in the highest- and lowest-scoring posts. This would be a pattern. Some subreddits might emphasise certain memes or phrases to signal their in-group behaviour, or to indicate people who have opinions that differ significantly from those common in the group. Our question is inductive partially because we do not express a prior expectation about the setting, we are just looking to let the data speak for itself.

Deductive research questions start from concepts and then seem to detect those concepts using observations from the world. This often involves translating the concept into a workable frame so that it can be detected and distinguished from other signals or biases. For example, if we believe that extroverts are more likely to have many friends on social media, we look for datasets that have both scores of extroversion and scores for the number of friends or posts. Or we can go out and ask people about their extroversion and correlate it with trace data. We then report the results and whether the difference was considered statistically significant. Such deductive questions often lead to a specific hypothesis, such as 'there is a positive relationship between number of friends and extroversion'.

8.2.1 Deductive research questions and the null hypothesis

In statistics textbooks, there is often a secondary hypothesis, *the null hypothesis*, that we see less often in published papers, but is important from a conceptual point of view. The null hypothesis is based on the assertion that we do not prove a hypothesis, only fail to disprove it. So we employ a null hypothesis that 'there is no relationship between the measurements of interest'. Then when we do find a relationship we have disproven the null hypothesis. It's a bit roundabout in a way, but the logic checks out, as an example of 'contrapositive logic'.

The reason why we go through this process is that we can almost never fully establish the causal relationship linking one measurement to the next. Doing so is theoretically very challenging (Pearl, 2009). However, we can get our ideas closer to the true explanation(s) for some event or measurement by eliminating the things that definitely do not relate and further specifying the things that do relate. By establishing a relationship between friends and extroversion, we do not say that extroversion *causes* many friends, but it is associated with it.

In the next chapter where I visualise distributions, we will be focusing on the null hypothesis as our *baseline* expectation. For example, I look at the average number of births per day in the UK. Since human sexuality is not strictly seasonal and can occur across the year, our *null hypothesis* is that the number of babies born per day follows a uniform distribution. But does it really? Are there not some reasons that you might intuitively know that would mean some days are particularly *unlikely* to be associated with births? But what if we don't have a specific theory about this already, just a hunch? Here is where we can enlist the third form of reasoning, *abductive reasoning*.

8.2.2 Abductive reasoning and the educated guess

Abductive research questions are strangely the least commonly discussed even though they are, in my opinion, the most common. Coming from the work of C. S. Peirce (father of pragmatism), abduction is about how we translate our intuitions into claims (Peirce, 1878). The reality is that we might not actually have started with the concept of extroversion or measures of talkativeness online. We are more likely to have started simply by perceiving a difference in our environment that we think can be explained. We might notice that there appears to be a patterned difference among our own friends and family on social media and then try to explain it. From abduction we can then reach towards either deduction by translating our intuitions into concepts and seeing where these concepts can be measured effectively. Or we might reach towards induction and simply amass data that we try to correlate with frequency of posting.

Abductive reasoning tends to concern the relationship between the researcher's intuition and an evaluation of what explanation is probably true (a.k.a. 'reasoning to the best explanation'). That is, it is less concerned with the isolation of specific factors done in deduction or the means of ensuring a coherent set of distinctions or classifications in inductive work. Instead, it is about what is most plausible. This is admittedly not a strong basis for making a theoretical claim. It is why we still tend to aspire to deductive work when possible. This is especially the case when you have competing theories and no clear way to determine which one would otherwise be the most plausible. However, abductive reasoning can fruitfully and ought to be applied to the generation of hypotheses even in cases where it might be a challenging to test such hypotheses directly. In fact, some assert that abduction should be rescued from this restrictive notion of reasoning to the best explanation as it divorces abduction from its strength in being creative as Pierce originally intended (McAuliffe, 2015).

I introduce these notions and especially abductive reasoning pretty early in the chapter because I want to walk alongside these ideas for the remainder of our consideration of research questions. In particular, I want to communicate that the way that we manage our biases is intelligible and a normal part of the scientific process. Eliminating our biases is not possible because we are situated in a society. We are already marked by class, wealth, gender identity, sexuality, ethnicity, language, physical appearance, religion, family history, social networks, and more. We should not deny these markers, for they make us who we are. Further, these markers are often sites of inequality or injustice that we wish to rectify (or at least demonstrate scientifically) through more research. Abductive reasoning gives us the opportunity, the licence, to think about how our own social position can be a meaningful site of intuitions.

8●3 Avoiding description: Expectation and systematic observation in science

To be so bold in trying to unify these three approaches to reasoning, I offer a more simplified framework here, that of *expectation* versus *observation*. Expectations are what we think we are going to find when we systematically engage with a subject. Observations are the measurements that we collect. Scientific claims are produced as we understand the potential differences between the measurements we collect systematically and the expectations we have for those measurements.

Why might we assert that that the observation has to be systematic? That is because we want each observation to be fairly representative of the subject at hand. Imagine we test this relationship with three people. The first we give a survey with an extroversion scale. For the second we download their message data and look at the number of different people they interact with weekly. For the third we film them and look at the number of people they talk to at an event. All three approaches (a survey approach, a trace data approach, and a naturalistic approach) are valid in their own way, but comparing across them means we might pick up on different things per observation, thus compromising the comparison. All three approaches can give us something to learn about the research question, but they are not sufficiently similar for us to make the same claim across three methods. To be systematic we would want to ensure that we can fix the approach so that we can thereafter understand the differences within that approach, as well as speculate on whether these differences occur because of the method or because of a real difference in the phenomenon being measured. For example, in health there is 'white coat syndrome', where blood pressure measurements are systematically elevated in the hospital since some people get nervous having their blood pressure taken there (Pioli et al., 2018).

Making the link between expectation and observation is also an excellent way for computational social science to elevate beyond descriptive work. It is a common criticism that computational social science work is relatively descriptive. For example, imagine we do not know how many people are tweeting vaccine misinformation, so we do a map of who forwards tweets from whom and then cluster it. So now we have a descriptive account that is systematic. This might be an excellent example of data journalism, but is it data science? By setting up expectations from analogous contexts, we can ask questions beyond 'what is there'. Is this map different from what we expected? Did we expect anti-vaxxers to talk mainly among themselves? Did we expect them to talk to others in a positive way or to behave atypically with respect to posting frequency, number of friends, initiation versus reply behaviour?

When we think that our work is really about oscillating between examining prior work to learn what to expect and systematically collecting data to compare with these expectations we can thus embed inductive, deductive, and abductive questions in our work.

- Abductive questions work when we have an intuition about a phenomenon and want to translate that into a systematic form. We might then choose a form that tests a specific hypothesis (deductive) or looks for patterns in the data (inductive).
- Inductive questions work when our expectations are vague but we have a systematic way to collect data that we expect will create patterns and distinctions.
- Deductive questions work when our expectations are specific and based on prior literature.

In all cases, we can do better than descriptive work by being frank about what we expect to find and why we expect to find it. This will also allow us to either embed our own personal experience in the research collection process or find ways to minimise our biases in this process, depending on the circumstance and the specificity of the question.

Prediction versus explanation

In everyday language we talk about what might happen in the future. We have a sense of what to expect and then when things do not go according to plan we often update our expectations for the next time. Below I offer an extended example with a circus to translate this sort of work into something more focused for research questions.

Let's consider the challenges in booking a circus. Perhaps hiring a small circus for a 10-person birthday party is overkill. Yet, if you were booking that circus for a town fair, then knowing how much demand there was for a show would suggest whether to have the circus for one show, two shows in a day, or shows across a range of dates. In everyday language, we might say that we have to *predict* demand. But what we really mean is *forecast* demand. What's the difference? Well, it is an important distinction that shows up in data science pretty regularly, even when we are not forecasting.

To predict with data is not to estimate the likelihood of a future event, but to give a best guess with available data. Thus, when we have a regression model, we are using it to make a prediction, not of the future but of all the data we have. In our circus example, we can use data about town sizes, wealth, prior circus attendance, etc. to build a model. If that model is a regression it will be a 'line of best fit' through the distribution of data points (past circuses in towns like this one). Then when we predict, we are making a generalised guess by considering all the relevant factors in our data-driven model. So, if our model says that attendance is about 5% of the town, then having a circus in a town of 10,000 will mean around 500 people will likely show up. But this fictitious model also says that attendance rises with income, so that having an average income in the town one standard deviation above the mean, more people will attend the circus. Then we look at the values for our town, find that it is about average in income for the country and so it's not going to add or take away any people from the earlier tally of 500. So that becomes our prediction.

What do we do with a prediction then depends in part on our epistemology (or, plainly spoken, our approach to knowledge). Are we trying to understand what makes a circus successful in general or how to plan a circus for our town in particular? The former is about explanation. The latter makes more sense for prediction.

- *For explanation.* We want to understand which variables make for a successful circus and to what extent. This is a common social science approach to the creation of knowledge. In this approach, we construct (or employ) measurements as *social facts* which we then use in our models (Durkheim, 1982). Knowing some of these measurements will help us explain an outcome and knowing others will not help. We have statistics to tell us how confident we are in whether a measurement will help us explain an outcome and to what extent. Typically, the individual measurements are of interest. So we would care whether population, income, weather on day, and ethnic composition of town make a difference to the attendance figures for the circus. We use past studies in similar or related contexts to give us a sense of the expected general direction and strength of association.

- *For prediction.* We are usually less concerned about the specific variables or measurements that help explain an outcome. Instead, we want to maximise the value of the outcome. So, a circus company might want to know which town to offer their show, or what route through the country might have the optimal cost-benefit ratio, knowing the issues with set-up times and transport for the circus.

It is not the case that prediction is less scientific than explanation, but rather the things that we are scientific about are perhaps slightly different, depending on the approach. When we are focusing on explanation, we are often using statistical significance to say that we are confident one thing helps *explain* another. We might further want to know whether one thing causes another, which is much more complicated. But whether or not we can say with confidence one thing causes another, we can still be confident that an association between the two sets of measurements can be detected. We can further say with some confidence whether that relationship persists when we account for other measurements.

We often talk about 'controlling for variables' in our models. I can give an example of this with our circus planning. Imagine that we have a year's worth of measurements of cities. Population and average income explains some variation in attendance, but not a lot. We have a theory that ethnicity makes a difference. We write a literature review suggesting why, we find the ethnic composition of the towns in a database and merge that in with our existing data, and then we discover that it helps explain the model. More specifically, we discover that towns with more Latin Americans have higher circus attendance. Now we would not say there is a necessary relationship between ethnicity and circus attendance, so surely there is some proximate variable that explains this relationship. Someone else (or the author) might build on this finding by locating the weather when the circus was in town, merge in that data and discover not only that is weather significantly related to the circus, but also that when you account for the fact that Latin Americans live in disproportionately more southern locales where the weather is warmer, it becomes apparent that our initial relationship could be considered spurious. That is, it is not that Latin Americans prefer the circus, but that they, like many people, prefer to go to a fair when the weather is nice. Our story then is about the relationship between the circus and human behaviour. We learn that humans prefer the circus in warm weather and that this is not specific to ethnicity.

When we predict we might not be as easily able to distinguish the various factors that make a difference in our models, but that might not be our goal. For example, when we are planning a route for our next circus tour across county fairs, we cannot control the weather, even if we know that it helps to explain variation. Even if we do have data on past year's weather for the potential cities, this can still only be a guess for what next year's weather will be like. We can feed that into a model that will give us a 'best guess' for the route that will work.

8.4.1 Prediction and resampling

While we cannot predict the future, we can predict within our data to see which measures help and to what extent. For prediction tasks this is often done with resampling. We take one part of the data and *train* on it, then another part of the data and *test* on it. For example, we could take half the cities and do a regression on them to get the best guess for attendance. Then we apply these values to the other half of the cities and see how we did. How accurately did the data from the training set help us predict the data in the test set? What would improve the training set so that it better predicts the test set? In this way, we tend to be focused on learning about how to maximise an outcome rather than explain what role a specific factor plays. For example, we might find that with the amount of data points we have, one model (such as a support vector machine) will predict the data better than another model (such as a logistic regression). When we resample, this also gives us a handle on outliers. If we train on 10 different chunks of data and then combine these (i.e. 'bootstrapping'), that can attenuate the effects of one outlier in one of the samples.

As an example, imagine there's a circus-obsessed town where even the houses are circus themed. If you have attendance figures from this particular town in your model, then every-thing else about that town will also strongly influence any predictions. So whether it scores lower on deprivation index or has more people of a given ethnicity, these will all be associ-ated with high circus attendance, even if they are not directly related since they just come with being a crazy-circus town. Since it might be one of 1000 towns that held a circus, if you train on 900 and test on the other 100, you have a 10% chance of not training on crazy town. Seems like bad odds, but you don't do this once, you do this calculation lots of times, each time getting an estimate of how good your prediction was. In the end, you get a distribution of prediction scores. The effect of one town then is limited on the resulting distribution.

Linking hypotheses to approaches

Loosely speaking, we can now see a relationship between inductive and deductive research questions and prediction versus explanation. Deductive research questions are theory-driven. This is to suggest they are driven by a sense of prior expectations and specific measurable relationships between phenomena. When we use traditional inferential statistics to explain phenomena we are aligning our method with a deductive, theory-driven approach. We often have reasons for considering how the specific explanatory variables relate to a response vari-able. If we do not explain all of the variation in a response variable, it doesn't matter. Life is complicated and it's hard to explain it with simple models. What matters for our analyses is whether the measurements we have relate reliably to some response, not whether it fully explains the response. We know we can measure distance to nearest metropolis and so we can place that in our circus attendance model. So we first determine whether it is worth col-lecting this data and producing this measurement (we often have different choices for how to collect some data). Then we often first do a bivariate test of association, such as a correlation or a chi-squared test. If that shows there's some relationship, we start exploring multivariate models that can account for this relationship. But overall, our focus remains on the original relationship and how it holds up to these tests.

For inductive hypotheses we have less interest in the meaning of any given relationship so long as it explains the outcome. Whether it is distance to a metropolis, ethnic composition, wealth, past circus attendance, or number of popular singers from the county, we are less interested in a theory about any one of them, than a theory about high circus attendance. So this aligns well with predictive approaches – we are looking for the best model fit. As a pretty simple example, we can think of a correlation table. We look to find the strongest correlations and pay attention to those relationships. But we might have more sophisticated approaches such as stepwise regression that takes variables in or out of the model depending on whether they help explain the response as a sort of survival of the fittest for the best model. More complex still are approaches like LASSO regression, which find ways to select an ensemble of variables that collectively help explain the most variance with the least information. Even more complex are neural network and transformer-based models. For these approaches we can use pre-trained models that help us predict our case. This is where the circus metaphor breaks down, since we simply don't have that many circuses to consider in this way. For approaches based on neural networks we might need thousands or millions of data points. Some models, for example, train on all text written on Wikipedia or every picture of a flower on Flickr. So then when it sees your text it might be able to 'fill in the blanks' or classify a flower it hasn't seen.

Where does abduction reside in this prediction versus explanation distinction then? Well, I would assert that abduction is what we actually do in the construction of claims in practice. It's the reality of scientific practice, particularly with data. We tweak our prediction models based on hunches, or we use models to explain, but we go in search of new variables as old ones reveal partial answers. In the example of weather being a better explanatory variable than ethnicity it was implied that we had weather data accessible. This is not a given. Actually getting this data, merging in the weather charts based on the region that is the most appropriate, takes finesse. But we might discover it's not 'weather data', but we do some variable selection technique to determine it's actually sunshine. So even if it's cold but sunny, people go to the circus. This is like embedding some inductive prediction task (what's the best measurement of weather?) inside a deductive explanatory task (does controlling for weather make spurious the relationship between circus attendance and ethnicity?). So really we tend to oscillate between these different tasks as we search for new knowledge of the world around us and use abduction to motivate our direction.

Operationalisation

Perhaps the most important topic in social data science is operationalisation. This is the practice of taking a concept and translating it into something that can be measured. It is a classic matter in science generally, but it takes on a newfound urgency in social data science. This is because as we draw upon vast amounts of data, there is a temptation to translate the patterns we see in data into concepts that we discuss in everyday life. But the things we see in data do not always match those concepts perfectly, meaning that we will have to make some sort of compromise in the act of making a concept operational.

As an example of the challenges in operationalisation, take the notion of a 'strong tie' from social network analysis. In a seminal paper, Granovetter (1973) asked if 'weak ties' (like acquaintances) are more useful than strong ties (like immediate family) for job information. It was a simple enough question. But yet, to actually test that theory, one had to define weak and strong ties. In the paper, he identified several features that he thought would make a strong tie, and then applied these to survey research. They were elements like 'supportive', 'personally meaningful', and 'in regular contact'.

In more recent work on social networks, data has come not from self-reported surveys, but from trace data. We could collect networks of email, Twitter followers, school classes, and even proximity without the need for self-reported answers. But if strong ties have this supportive and affective dimension, it is now somewhat lost in trace data. We might have the number of emails between people, but not the content of those emails, and certainly not the self-reports of how all the senders feel about all the receivers. So then how has a tie been operationalised? In an early classic study of email networks, Tyler et al. (2003) created a tie between people if they shared 30 messages and sent at least five each. The issue is that simply sending one email made it too noisy. But was 30 right? Would it be right in different contexts or for people who have just arrived? Every time we exclude messages or people (e.g., they excluded mail sent outside the organisation), we are shaping and refining our perspective but also creating an analytical object that is just a little further from the phenomena under study.

This is but the tip of the iceberg. Researchers working on Twitter networks, Facebook friends, and all manner of comments between people online need to make some inference about what constitutes a meaningful relationship between two people or two user accounts. That is, they have to *operationalise* this concept. Gilbert and Karahalios (2009) explore this by comparing the self-reported strength of relationship between Facebook friends and computational features of Facebook data such as numbers of friends. At the time, they asserted that a little over half of the variation in friendship strength could be predicted using trace data from Facebook. More recent work from Rajkumar et al. (2022) has explored this issue with massive data from LinkedIn.

If we measure strong ties as 'many emails', we are then really making claims about people who email each other a lot, not people who necessary care a lot about each other. These may correlate but not perfectly. And the way they correlate might make a big difference to how we interpret the model. As an example, I have only sent my parents a fraction of the email messages I have sent my colleagues. Yet, I am much more likely to go out of my way to support my parents than the people I know from work (even if I do like my colleagues or contact them regularly).

The good news is that because operationalisation is not always perfect and must necessarily be different in different contexts, there are often many ways in which we can explore the same general concept. For example, what a strong tie means on Twitter versus email is not simply a matter of data cleaning, but will likely lead to different theories about how relationships are maintained. Thus, as technology evolves, so must our concepts and our understanding of how to measure them.

 Boundedness and research questions

Research questions are typically bounded in some way. These boundaries are often implicit or underspecified. For example, we are all necessarily bounded by time. We cannot see into the future, and often much of the past is lost to us and needs to be reconstructed. But we are also bounded by culture and our historical frame. There was in the last few decades a concern about psychology and behavioural economics as these two disciplines tend to use a lot of experimental designs. And the people that they include in these experiments tend to be 'WEIRD', that is, 'Western, educated, industrialised, rich, and democratic' (Henrich et al., 2010). From the outside looking in, this might seem completely normal (hence the cheekiness of the acronym WEIRD for something many people would see as normal). But WEIRD people might act in ways that are more self-interested and rational, ways that make assumptions about their own relation to authority, and to what constitutes justice, fairness, and order, all of which may depart from other cultures.

We ought to consider these boundaries rather carefully when we make claims that extend beyond our data. Usually we want claims that extend beyond our data. Sunshine leading to people attending a fair was a claim we wanted to extend beyond our data, for example. However, the extent to which we extend these claims should really be filtered through an understanding that the data we collected was local in some way. We visit boundedness again in Chapter 13 on networks, where I note near the end how networks have long wrestled with what's been called the 'boundary specification problem' (Laumann et al.,1989).

This interest in locality is also the basis of interest in algorithmic bias. This is currently a hot topic in machine learning, data science, and the social science of technology. Bias means that the data we train on is in some way representative more of some local domain than the more general domain where we reapply the data. A now classic example is Buolamwini and Gebru's examination of facial detection algorithms (2018). By coding a number of faces signifying different racial identities then testing their accuracy in commercial models, the authors were able to demonstrate how prevailing facial detection algorithms were far better at detecting white male faces than black female faces. They then reasonably asserted that the original detection algorithms were biased in their training data. This bias is not a problem for science, strictly speaking, as we should expect this work to be provisional and always in need of updating. The data was trained in a local way and so the performance metrics behaved accordingly. The problem was that these systems were treated *as if* they were not trained on a restricted or local dataset but on 'faces' generally, thereby erasing key important and consequential intersectional differences. If such systems were deployed with the claim that they were able to treat everyone fairly, this would not be accurate and would create unfair consequences. Thus, at the intersection of these boundary issues come new insights not just about the world, but also how we choose to look at it, and correct for our own biases.

Being able to account for the locality of the data therefore can open up opportunities, particularly when you can compare two or more different localities. This might be word associations between two different forums, or the same forum over time. It might be data on purchasing behaviour from two different towns or commenting behaviour based on different political agendas. Some can turn this into a research opportunity in its own right, as Hale did when exploring the 'bridge blogging' of people who blog in multiple languages (Hale, 2012).

 Summary

Research questions are focusing devices to help us transform a collection of data into a means for making and interrogating claims. They may be more focused on predicting some outcome or explaining some factor in that outcome. In order to do that we normally have to assert how we are letting some measurement stand in for some concept. In classification work in data science, especially in machine learning, this might come from large-scale efforts to label data. Often our questions emerge by articulating some comparison group that we suspect might lead to different observations than we would expect. When we think of distributions not just as sets of data, but as *bounded* sets of data, we can start to appreciate how comparing different sets of data can reveal information to help us address our research questions and our broader research intuitions.

In the next chapter I return to more practical efforts by focusing on the relationship between visualisation and statistics. We have conceptually asked about the difference between what we observe and what we might expect. In the following chapter we show that difference visually and test whether it is worth considering statistically. We do this first by comparing some observed data to an ideal-type distribution. Later in the chapter we look at two or more distributions in conjunction.

 Further reading

- *Bit by Bit* by Salganik (2019). This book brings together ideas from the field of computational social science like no book has done so clearly and succinctly before. It shows a variety of examples of research designs to consider.
- *The Practice of Social Research* by Babbie (2020). This is an excellent book from cover to cover. It is in its fifteenth edition as of this writing, but I would think that the quality changes only slightly between editions. It addresses many issues with research design from a standard social science frame. The resources on trace and computational social science data are limited, but the logic regarding how to ask about social data is very sound.

 Extensions and reflections

Here are a few engaging and influential papers in computational social science. I have reproduced below what each one asserts. Seek out each paper and derive a research question that the authors could have had at the beginning of the research process and how it likely changed by the time they completed their work.

- In 'Measuring Influence in Twitter: The Million Follower Fallacy' Cha et al. (2010, p. 10) say: 'Using a large amount of data gathered from Twitter, we compare three different measures of influence: indegree, retweets, and mentions. Focusing on different topics, we examine how the three types of influential users performed in spreading popular news topics.' In the paper they note that the different metrics for measuring influence have a differential effect depending on whether the topic has some personal or political relevance.
- In 'Gender Shades: Intersectional Accuracy Disparities in Commercial Gender Classification', Buolamwini and Gebru (2018, p. 1) state: 'we present an approach to evaluate bias present in automated facial analysis algorithms ... we evaluate 3 commercial gender classification systems using our dataset and show that darker-skinned females are the most misclassified group'.
- By contrast, in the paper 'You Can't Stay Here: The Efficacy of Reddit's 2015 Ban Examined through Hate Speech', Chandrasekharan et al. (2017) provide very explicit and detailed research questions, such as 'RQ1: What effect did Reddit's ban have on the contributors to banned subreddits?' and 'What effect did the ban have on subreddits that saw an influx of

banned subreddit users?'. These questions are set up in a relatively exploratory way (and concerning real hate speech, so be mindful of this when reading). Similarly, what sort of abductive hunches do you think led to the research being set up in this way?

Students often start with research questions that reflect their own experience. For example, think about a time online when you read or saw something that made you feel good. Ask how you could go about detecting a signal that such content would make someone feel good. Would you use a sentimental analysis or perhaps extract some keywords associated with positive ideas? Use different research questions to ask about different facets of this relationship between a person and the content they like.

Consider how Kramer et al. (2014) conducted an experiment on this very topic by prioritising newsfeed content on Facebook based on positive or negative sentiment to see if it affected the user's own sentiment. This paper has generated considerable discussion for its ethical challenges. I highly recommend reading both this paper and some of the work that has contextualised it, such as Hallinan et al. (2020). How would you have designed the experiment differently?

9
VISUALISING EXPECTATIONS: COMPARING STATISTICAL TESTS AND PLOTS

━━━━━━━━━━━ Learning goals ━━━━━━━━━━━

- Produce a distribution using a random number generator
- Plot a distribution using `matplotlib` and `seaborn`
- Understand how a trend line (as a regression line) can be calculated
- Annotate a figure with interesting details based on expected values and confidence intervals
- Use simple statistical tests to compare two groups (*t*-test and ANOVA) and two distributions from the same group (correlations, regressions)
- Distinguish between a linear and logarithmic scale for extremely skewed distributions.

The purpose of visualization is insight, not pictures.

Ben Shneiderman (Card et al., 1999, p. 6)

 Introduction: Why show data?

Plotting (or the visual display of data) is a means of expressing your data in a form that makes it more intelligible to the viewer (regardless of whether that viewer is you or another person). Visualisation is a regular part of data science, and used far more heavily in the lab than in scientific reports. That is to say, if you've only read research but not been a part of it, you might be underestimating how much visualisation is used. Making insightful charts is only partially about having the right data. It also involves having the right skills and knowing how to apply them. Information visualisation is now a maturing field with its own conferences, journals, and key questions. We can borrow liberally from the InfoVis community to help us understand not just how to present data, but to understand that data itself.

Generally speaking, we are looking for charts that convey 'a difference that makes a difference' (Bateson, 2000). That is, if a chart shows us some pattern, relationship, or insight we might not have otherwise seen, then it makes a difference in our interpretation of the data. Sometimes that difference simply isn't there to show. But often that difference is just waiting to be represented once you know what you're looking for and how to show it.

When we convey differences visually, we run the risk of over- or underestimating the significance of a relationship depending on how we frame the image. Things like cropping a distribution to show bars that start at 75% to convey a 'big difference' between 78% and 81% might be a distortion of the significance of the difference. On the other hand, if everyone gets a score between 75 and 85, then perhaps cropping to that window might be effective and reasonable. The point is to convey the data at a scale that not only shows a difference but also helps communicate the significance and ideally the substantive interest of that difference.

In this chapter, I work from the prior discussion on expectation versus observation to think about visualisation as one of several tools for revealing something from quantitative information. To that end, the other key tool we can use is statistics. In this chapter I will be introducing and discussing some elementary statistical approaches. The discussion will not be especially mathematical. Rather, instead I will be putting these statistics in dialogue with visualisations to show how both work to reveal patterns in data and thus help us make claims about the world. In some cases, the visualisation might suggest some claim but the claim is too noisy to be robust, which the statistics can reveal. Other times, the pattern in the data might be obvious when visualised and that suggests new ways of testing or characterising the data statistically.

This approach draws from a beguiling example by Anscombe (1973). This is a set of four distributions, each with very similar descriptive statistics, but which when plotted show that they are very different patterns. Ascombe's quartet is available as demo data from a visualisation library that comes pre-installed with Anaconda called `seaborn`. It can also be installed through `pip`. To get started, let's visualise that data.

```python
import numpy as np
import matplotlib.pyplot as plt
import seaborn as sns
%config InlineBackend.figure_format = 'svg'

df = sns.load_dataset("anscombe")

# LM plot adds a regression trend line to a scatter plot
sns.lmplot(x="x", y="y",
           col="dataset", hue="dataset", data=df,
           ci=None, height=2, col_wrap=2,
           palette="muted",
           scatter_kws={"s": 20})

plt.show()
```

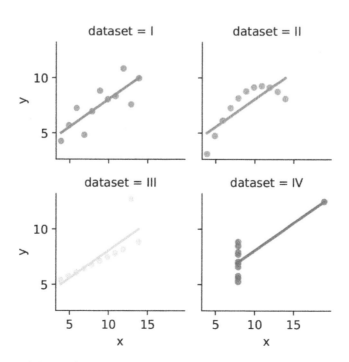

Figure 9.1 Four plots showing the distribution and trend lines of Anscombe's quartet

The first graph in Figure 9.1 is a single line with points distributed loosely around it. The second is a curved line, the third has an outlier on the y-axis, but it is otherwise evenly distributed on the x-axis, and the fourth has an outlier both on the y- and x-axes. Below I show some descriptive statistics about all four. This is also an opportunity to see a groupby operation in practice.

```
display(df.groupby('dataset')
        .agg(["mean","count","std","median"])
        .style.format("{:.2f}"))
```

	x				y			
	mean	count	std	median	mean	count	std	median
dataset								
I	9.00	11.00	3.32	9.00	7.50	11.00	2.03	7.58
II	9.00	11.00	3.32	9.00	7.50	11.00	2.03	8.14
III	9.00	11.00	3.32	9.00	7.50	11.00	2.03	7.11
IV	9.00	11.00	3.32	8.00	7.50	11.00	2.03	7.04

The table indicates that the measures are not all exactly the same, but they are very similar. In particular, the median Y values are slightly different. Honestly, if I did not look at a plot of the data, I almost certainly would not be able to tell a big difference just looking at the tabular results.

 ## Visualising distributions

Distributions are the cornerstone of data science. They represent a collection of measurements. We tend to be interested in whether there exists a pattern in a distribution, whether a distribution can be categorised, or whether one distribution helps us explain another. Normally our distributions would come from measurements, such as a distribution of the number of tweets sent per account with the hashtag #BLM. Much of the challenge in presenting this data aesthetically and effectively comes down to revealing features of a distribution or multiple distributions together.

As you will recall from other chapters, I tend to use real data where possible. However, there is some merit in using synthetic data to illustrate points. Synthetic distributions can serve as a baseline of expectations. So when we say something is or is not normally distributed, we are comparing it to an ideal-type distribution that looks like a bell curve. While the comparison should be done statistically (e.g., by using a test of normality or skewness), the difference can be presented visually to illustrate the claim and give us some intuitions about the data.

Below I show three ideal-type distributions: uniform, normal, and exponential. These tend to represent differing dynamics in a dataset. Not all distributions will look like these, but all distributions have a shape. That shape can hold information about the underlying phenomena we measured. So first let's explore 'ideal type' shapes and then examine how some real-world cases stack up. To visualise these I will be using a combination of `seaborn` and `matplotlib`. `seaborn` is a library that extends `matplotlib` and as such there are lots of places where the two packages interweave.

To get started, know that when we invoke some plot we create a `matplotlib.pyplot` object (or a `plt` object for short). This object is first imported and then refreshed every time we run a new plot such as `pd.Series().plot()`, `sns.histplot(<array>)`, or `plt.plot(<array>)`. The default output format for these plots is PNG, which is not very crisp, so I use the iPython magic command `%config InlineBackend.figure_format = 'svg'` in order to ensure the plots herein are vector format (note that you only have to set this config option once per notebook). Vector formats like SVG (scalable vector graphics) are sharp at any resolution. Then I set the size of the figure.

For the three distributions, I create three subplots `plt.subplots(1,3)`, which are labelled `ax1, ax2, ax3`. These will be three columns (or three pictures next to each other). If I put `(3,1)` instead, it would be three rows (or three pictures stacked on top of each other).

The three example distributions are generated as follows:

* `np.random.uniform(size=1000)`,
* `np.random.normal(size=1000)`,
* `np.random.exponential(size=1000)`.

I tweaked the `ylabel` and the `xlabel` to make the charts readable. To finish up I used `plt.tight_layout()` to help the arrangement of the three figures. The plot will show at the end of the cell, but you can also use `plt.show()` to display it. Calling `plt.show()` (or ending the cell with a `;`) can often avoid Python printing extraneous text in the results.

```
fig, (ax1,ax2,ax3) = plt.subplots(1,3,figsize=(6,3))

plt1 = sns.histplot(np.random.uniform(size=1000),ax=ax1)
plt1.set_xlabel("Uniform Distribution")

plt2 = sns.histplot(np.random.normal(size=1000),ax=ax2)
plt2.set_xlabel("Normal Distribution")
plt2.set_ylabel("")

plt3 = sns.histplot(np.random.exponential(size=1000),ax=ax3)
plt3.set_xlabel("Exponential Distribution")
plt3.set_ylabel("")

plt.tight_layout()

plt.show()
```

The output is shown in Figure 9.2.

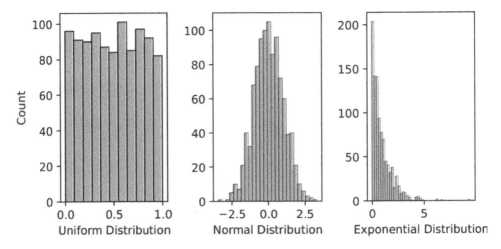

Figure 9.2 Plots of three example distributions (*n* = 1000 per distribution)

9.2.1 Uniform distribution with histogram

A uniform distribution implies that every number is equally probable. In social sciences we might think of this as a sort of 'equality of opportunity' situation. A histogram plots counts of data over some range. It counts the frequency of observations within a range that it calls a bin. The number of bins can vary and we can set it. So if we have a uniform distribution from 0 to 15 that means that we should see a relatively flat line across the bins on the *y*-axis. We will do 8000 random draws, or np.random.randint(0,16,8000).

With a range of 16 we should observe approximately 500 (or 8000/16) draws of each number. Because it is random, the count of the draws won't be perfectly 500 in each bin. That said, the more observations we have, the more likely it will approximate

$$draws_n = \frac{observations}{range},$$

assuming the numbers truly are generated at random.

Below I will plot a distribution of these numbers as a histogram. The histogram will create bins. In theory there should be equal number of draws in each bin. We create 16 bins for 16 numbers. You can create uneven bin sizes but they will make for artificially noisy-looking data. Try to change the bins parameter to 5, 10, and 13 and see how it changes the shape of the distribution.

```
# Seed means that I should see the same random number sequence every time
# I use this random number generator. Different seed, different sequence.

rng = np.random.default_rng(seed=123456)
distribution = rng.integers(low=0, high=16, size=8000)

# Printing the distribution as a table first:
import pandas as pd

dist_table = pd.Series(distribution).value_counts()
print(dist_table.sort_index())
```

```
0      507
1      516
2      482
3      511
4      524
5      508
6      462
7      488
8      520
9      506
10     514
11     489
12     480
13     500
14     494
15     499
dtype: int64
```

```
fig, ax = plt.subplots()

ax.axhline(500,
           linestyle=":", color='black',
           label="Expected value")

sns.histplot(distribution, bins=16,
             label="Uniform distribution")

ax.legend()

plt.show()
```

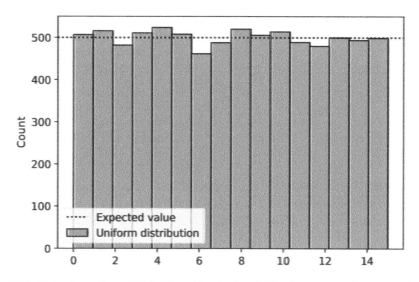

Figure 9.3 Plots of a uniform distribution with a horizontal line to compare the expected and observed values (*bins* = 16, *n* = 8000)

Figure 9.3 shows that all the numbers were selected approximately 500 times as expected. We show the expected value using a horizontal line that was drawn with `ax.axhline()`. Notice that in both figures I included `label="<some name>"`. These then become what is displayed in the legend when we call `ax.legend()`.

While the line in Figure 9.3 looks visually like it is very close to all the points, suggesting it is indeed a uniform distribution, we can also test this statistically in a number of ways. Two important ways are a chi-squared test of independence and an ordinary least squares regression.

9.3   Testing a uniform distribution using a chi-squared test

Roughly speaking, the chi-squared test asks, if you have some table with a distribution, and you expect every cell to have a proportionally equal chance, how likely it is that you would see results like this.

Thus, we use it as a 'test of independence' since we are looking to see if the groups have an equal chance. With four groups you would expect a quarter of the data in each group. So you run a chi-squared test and it gives you a number that you convert into a *p-value*. The *p*-value is the probability that you would see such a distribution even if the data were random. So if the *p*-value was 0.63, that means that 63 times out of 100 you could expect to see a distribution this noisy with random data. We tend to think that if you only see a distribution this extreme one time in 20 (or 5% of the time) then that's notable. In fact, for this cut-off we would say that the result is statistically significant, though it's worth nothing that this cut-off is not an absolute rule, just a guide. We see this in a lot of research where people report on a relationship or some observed value if the *p*-value is less than 0.05.

In the case of our distribution, we can run a chi-squared test on the tabular version of the distribution. Recall we had 16 numbers so we have a 16 × 1 table. We run a chi-squared test on it below using the `scipy.stats` package, one of several useful stats packages in Python.

```
import scipy

chisq,pval = scipy.stats.chisquare(dist_table)

print(f"This time the distribution has a p-value of {pval:0.3f}")
print("The expected value is", dist_table.mean())

This time the distribution has a p-value of 0.910
The expected value is 500.0
```

A *p*-value of 0.91 suggests that 91% of the time we could see results that extreme (i.e. that far away from `500, 500, 500, ...`) and still consider it random. Thus, we cannot detect any statistical significance. Or stated more carefully, learning about this distribution cannot help us discern any statistically significant deviation from an expected value. Thus, we could have just asked for the average value (`dist_table.mean()`) for the whole distribution, and it would have done as good a job as knowing how many per `0, 1, 2, ..., 16`.

```
dist_table.mean()
```

```
500.0
```

That was too easy. But imagine if our algorithm had a thing for the number 7 and disliked the number 13. So let's take 90 from 13 and give it to 7. The total number of draws will still be 8000, but 7 will be an outlier of around 590 and 13 will be an outlier around 410 (see Figure 9.4). The average should still be 500. But now the chi-squared test will detect that there are cells with values far outside the expected value.

```
dist_2 = dist_table.copy()
```

```
dist_2.loc[7] += 90
dist_2.loc[13] -= 90
```

```
fig, ax = plt.subplots()
```

```
ax.axhline(500,
           linestyle=":", color='black',
           label="Expected value")
```

```
sns.scatterplot(x=dist_2.index, y=dist_2.values,
                label="Uniform distribution with two outliers")
```

```
ax.legend()
```

```
plt.show()
```

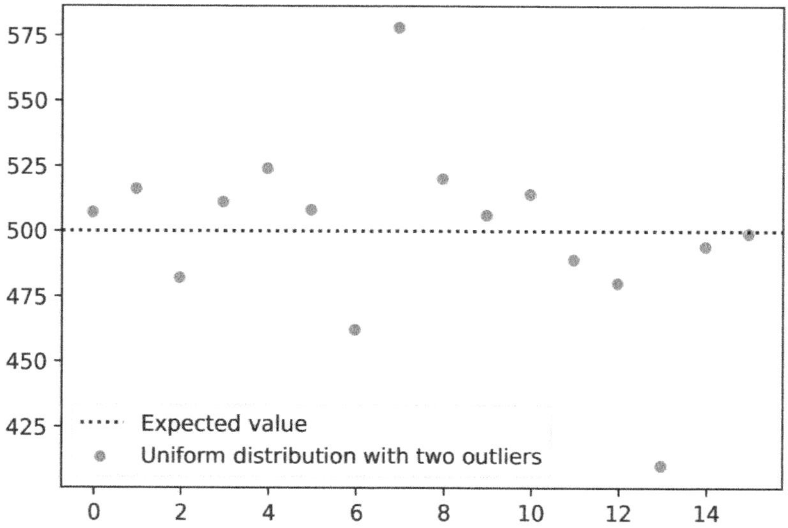

Figure 9.4 Scatter plot showing distribution of counts from a random uniform draw (*bins* = 16, *n* = 8000)

```
chisq,pval = scipy.stats.chisquare(dist_2)

print(f"This time the distribution has a p-value of {pval:0.3f}")
print("The expected value of the distribution is still", dist_table.mean())

This time the distribution has a p-value of 0.002
The expected value of the distribution is still 500.0
```

So in the second case, the *p*-value suggests that there is a statistically significant difference detected in the data. That means we have at least one cell that should not show a value that extreme by random chance. The chi-squared test did not say *which* cells had significant greater or lesser observations than was expected, only that it detected some. For more granular details you will need other tests as shown below.

Testing a uniform distribution using regression

The thing about the chi-squared test is that it treats every cell as independent. So it doesn't matter if the order is 0, 1, 2, 3 or 0, 3, 7, 1. You can do a chi-squared test on a set of categories or a set of orderable groups such as counts per week. It just asks whether there are a difference between the observed count in each cell and the expected count in each cell. If the cells are orderable in some way, then it seems like we should be able to test whether there is a *trend* rather than merely some outlier.

Let's return to our uniform distribution. This time, in addition to the horizontal line at 500 which is the *expected* value, let's draw a trend line through the numbers. As above, I am plotting the range of outcomes on the *x*-axis and number of observations of each outcome on the *y*-axis.

```
fig, ax = plt.subplots()

ax = sns.regplot(x = dist_table.index, y = dist_table.values,
                 line_kws={"label":"Trend line"},
                 label="Observed counts")

ax.axhline(500, linestyle=":", label="Expected trend")

ax.legend()

plt.xticks(range(0,16))

plt.show()
```

The trend line (see Figure 9.5) is an interesting feature of this visualisation. It shows the line going down relatively steeply. But also notice the shaded area in behind the trend line. This area is the 'confidence interval'. The thing is, while the trend line here might suggest that the relationship is negative, we are not *certain* that this is the case. The confidence interval

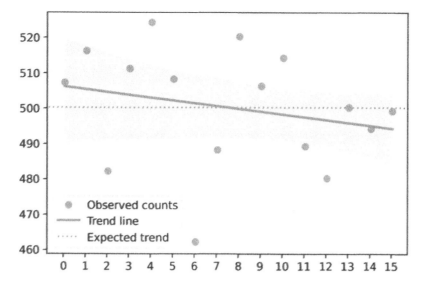

Figure 9.5 Regression plot showing trend line (with shaded confidence intervals) across distribution of counts from a random uniform draw ($bins = 16, n = 8000$)

gives us a range for our relationship. If within that range we can draw a line that goes up and a line that goes down, we cannot be certain that the true relationship is one where the trend typically goes up or typically goes down. This is like the null hypothesis I mentioned in the previous chapter.

In this case, we *expect* that the random number generator will create a distribution that has an even number of draws across the range of numbers. But since each number is drawn independently from that distribution, we similarly should not expect that the generator will produce bins with exactly the same number of draws. From the visualisation we *observe* a trend line that does not fit our expectations. It looks like the trend is going downwards, implying that larger numbers are less common than smaller numbers. But the confidence interval suggests that we are not totally confident in this trendline. To go a bit further here we must first appreciate some of the basics of a regression (trend) line.

A regression line is characterised by the formula

$$\hat{y} = a + bX.$$

The observed value for y is what we have already seen. It is anywhere between 410 and 590, with most values around exactly 500. But the predicted value ($\hat{y}$) is what we get from a regression. An ordinary least squares (OLS) regression uses calculus to locate the line. This line then can be characterised by the values of a and b. a tells us where the line is at 0, and then b tells us how much the line is going to trend upwards or downwards for some value of X.

We can run an OLS regression using `statsmodels`. I will not go deeply into how we build a model in `statsmodels`, but the documentation is helpful. The important thing is that our OLS model is built using some value for Y (`dist_table.values`), some value for X (`dist_table.index`) and we get an estimate (`est`) for the trendline that uses X to predict Y. To fill in the numbers we need for a and b, we get these from `est.params`.

The first parameter, est.params[0], is the constant or *a* from our formula above (and that's always the case). params[1] through params[<n>] refer to each variable we use to explain our distribution. In this case, we are only using one variable, dist_table.index, which is just the number sequence from 0 to 15. So we calculate some fitted values one-by-one with pred = [a + (b1*i) for i in X] (or we can do it the easy way with est.fittedvalues() which should give the same result as pred). Below I use those specific values to plot dotted lines from where the data was observed to where it was predicted. These dotted lines represent 'residuals', that is, they are the unexplained variation (or I guess 'residue', but no one calls it that) left over from our line of best fit.

```
import statsmodels.api as sm

fig, ax = plt.subplots()

X = [int(x) for x in dist_table.index]
y = dist_table.values

ax = sns.regplot(x=X, y=y,
                 line_kws={"label":"Expected trend line"},
                 label="Observed data")

# New part: The regression model explicitly
X2 = sm.add_constant(X)
est = sm.OLS(y, X2).fit()

a = est.params[0]
b1 = est.params[1]
pred = [a + (b1*i) for i in X]

# We use the predicted values from the regression to draw
# vertical lines from predicted Y (along the line) to observed Y.
ax.vlines(X, y, pred,
          linestyle=":", color="grey",
          label="Distance between observed and expected")

ax.legend()

plt.xticks(range(0,16))

plt.show()
```

If the residuals are really far from the line that means the trend line can be 'the best guess' but still not do a good job. Our trend line in Figure 9.6 appears to always be far away from some of the numbers. This is how we assess statistical significance. It is statistically significant generally when the predicted values closely match the observed values.

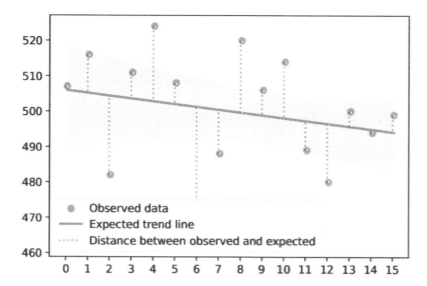

Figure 9.6 Regression plot showing trend line across distribution of counts from a random uniform draw (*bins* = 16, *n* = 8000). Plot also includes vertical lines highlighting distance between predictions on the trend line and observations (as dots)

We can do this in two ways from our model. The first is asking whether the 95% range of the coefficient stays above or below zero. If the upper and lower range of the coefficient is positive, then we are confident that the trend line will go up. If the upper and lower range of the coefficient is negative, then we are confident the trend line will go down. Here, the coefficient is negative, but what about the *confidence intervals*?

```
conf_ints = est.conf_int()

print(f"When X = 0, Y is predicted to be {est.params[0]:0.1f}.")
print("When X is 0, 95% of the time Y is predicted to be between "
      f"{conf_ints[0][0]:0.1f} and {conf_ints[0][1]:0.1f}.",end="\n\n")

print("When X increases by 1 unit, Y is predicted to increase by",
      f"{est.params[1]:0.1f}")
print("When X increases by 1 unit, 95% of the time Y is predicted to",
      f"increase by somewhere between {conf_ints[1][0]:0.1f} and "
      f"{conf_ints[1][1]:0.1f}.")
```

```
When X = 0, Y is predicted to be 505.9.
When X is 0, 95% of the time Y is predicted to be between 488.7 and 523.1.

When X increases by 1 unit, Y is predicted to increase by -0.8
When X increases by 1 unit, 95% of the time Y is predicted to increase by
somewhere between -2.7 and 1.2.
```

When we got the confidence intervals for a (i.e. the intercept at $X = 0$) the model was very confident that the value was around 500. It was positive 95% of the time and around that value. On the other hand, b_1, the slope of the trend line, is between –2.7 and 1.2 95% of the time, which means we cannot be confident that it will go up or down. Normally this might be an issue if we expect the independent variable to trend upwards or downwards. But in this case, we expect that as the numbers increase from zero there will be no significant trend upwards or downwards in how frequently the numbers are randomly drawn using our random number generator.

I mentioned there are two ways to do this, but I only showed the confidence intervals. Briefly, the other way is to check the p-values for the coefficients. As with chi-squared above, p-values let you know how likely it is to see this value if there was no relationship. Again, as with chi-squared, if the value is below 0.05 we would say that observing a relationship this uncommon if the two variables were completely independent.

```
est.pvalues

print(f"The pvalue for the constant 'a' is {est.pvalues[0]:0.3f}")
print(f"The pvalue for the coefficient 'b1' is {est.pvalues[1]:0.3f}")

The pvalue for the constant 'a' is 0.000
The pvalue for the coefficient 'b1' is 0.400
```

The p-value at the intercept indicates that our constant is very likely to be around 500 (with $p_a < 0.001$). The p-value for the coefficient (our numbers going from 0 to 15) is considerably above 0.05, meaning that if the two variables were independent (that is, the count 0, 1, 2, … and the values 507, 516, 482, …) we could still likely see a distribution like this. Hence the visual trend line is a fluke. It showed a linear downward trend, but not a *statistically significant* downward trend.

Admittedly, using a random number generator to test a null hypothesis is not that interesting. But it does help provide a contrast to Anscome's quartet. With the quartet, we observed statistical summaries like the mean and median that were generally similar, but plots that indicated that the four sets of data are qualitatively different. In the random number example, we showed that while a trend line existed, it was not actually statistically significant. Next, let's show an example where the trend line *is* significant.

9.4.1 Testing against a uniform distribution: Births in the UK

A real-world application for considering uniform distributions comes from the Office of National Statistics in the UK. They have made publicly available a table of the number of births per day in the UK from 1995 to 2014. This is again a single distribution. In theory it should be uniform as babies are born throughout the year. Is it really? Not quite. Using both visualisations and statistics, we can reveal both *trends* and *outliers*. It is available in the book's GitHub data folder but also from https://www.ons.gov.uk/visualisations/nesscontent/dvc307/line_chart/data.csv.

Since `read_csv` reads this table in handily and gives it an integer index from 0 to 365 for each day of the (leap) year, no real further processing is necessary. Later in Chapter 12 we will be a little more sophisticated with time ranges and dates in pandas.

```
from pathlib import Path

birth_df = pd.read_csv(Path.cwd().parent / "data" / "average_birth_data.csv")

print("The average number of births per day was",
    f"{birth_df.average.mean():0.0f}\n")

The average number of births per day was 1813

display(birth_df.head())
```

	date	average
0	01-Jan	1573.500000
1	02-Jan	1712.450000
2	03-Jan	1795.250000
3	04-Jan	1834.350000
4	05-Jan	1824.350000

First I will merely plot the distribution and give it a trend line (see Figure 9.7). From here we should be able to see some artefacts that will be worth inquiring about later.

```
fig, ax = plt.subplots()

sns.regplot(x=birth_df.index, y=birth_df.average,
            scatter_kws={"color":"red", "alpha":0.3})

ax.axhline(birth_df.average.mean(), linestyle=":")

plt.show()
```

Much as before, we are interested in:

1   Whether the trend line is increasing or decreasing
2   Whether the expected value crosses through the confidence interval
3   Whether there are any notable outliers.

We did a `regplot` on this birth data much like we did with the randomly generated numbers. We didn't even have to transform the data. We just used the index for 0 through 365 for the *x* values and then the `average` column for the *y* values. This time it appears that there are both

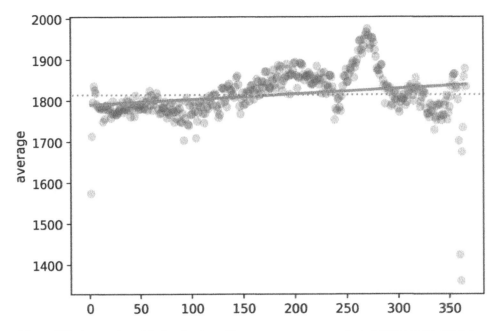

Figure 9.7 Regression plot showing trend line across average number of births in the UK for 1995-2014 (one marker per day)

outliers and a trend line that departs from horizontal (even when considering the confidence interval). This suggests a few things that we might want to test statistically.

Using a chi-squared test, we can be confident that some of the 365 days are significantly different from what is expected, but the test cannot say more than that. For more we will need to either report some tabular data or annotate the figure.

Below I will first report an OLS model. Then I will present an annotated figure that shows not only the distribution, but also some additional features of matplotlib. Instead of extracting all the numbers from the model using est.params and est.pvalues, I will use a nice external package for Python (based on code in R) called stargazer that renders regression results in a format that is near ready for publication. It is different from the default output from Python. It is less verbose, but still has everything we are looking for.

```
x = birth_df.index
Y = birth_df["average"]
X2 = sm.add_constant(X)

est = sm.OLS(Y, X2).fit()
# print(est.summary()) # <- For the default Python output.
# pip install stargazer

from stargazer.stargazer import Stargazer
from iPython.core.display import HTML
```

```
stargazer = Stargazer([est])
stargazer.show_model_numbers(False)
stargazer.show_confidence_intervals(True)
stargazer.significant_digits(2)
HTML(stargazer.render_html())  # Book features stargazer.render_latex()
```

	Dependent variable:
Const	1788.94***
	(1777.20, 1800.69)
x1	0.13***
	(0.08 , 0.19)
Observations	366
R^2	0.06
Adjusted R^2	0.05
Residual Std. Error	57.26(df = 364)
F Statistic	22.01*** (df = 1.0; 364.0)
Note:	* $p < 0.1$; ** $p < 0.05$; *** $p < 0.01$

This time both the intercept and the independent variable ('days since New Year's') were significant. Now since this is days of the year and it is cyclical, we certainly cannot use this to forecast. It's more a test of whether the data is balanced throughout the year or unbalanced in some way. A proper extension of this would be to look at time-series models, such as an autoregressive integrated moving average (ARIMA) model, which can detect seasonality in data. Looking at the figure again, we can start to see why the outliers and trends appear the way they do. Much of it might have to do with the romantic wintertime holidays in the UK, including Christmas/New Year and, to a lesser extent, Valentine's Day.

Let's return to the figure, but this time we will annotate it with some extra details for these days.

9.4.2 Annotating a figure

While Figure 9.7 shows us an interesting set of trends, it also helps to guide the reader explicitly to what you are looking to say. In this case, I want to suggest that the holiday season including Christmas and New Year have two pretty significant effects on the birth rate. First, we can highlight the period of 9 months after the Christmas holidays to show the holidays' effects on conception. We can look to the lowest point on the graph (which is 26 December) to highlight the effect the holidays have on births. We can also give the figure some labels for X and Y as well as tick marks that are clearer than 0, 50, ...

So in Figure 9.8 you will see the following new features:

- A grid to help with reading the figure, using `ax.grid(True)`
- X and Y labels, using `ax.set(xlabel=<TEXT>, ylabel=<TEXT>)`

- *X* ticks that look like months rather than numbers (see code)
- A `vspan` that covers a 40-day range approximately 9 months after the winter holidays, using `ax.axvspan(Xstart,Xend,<STYLES>)`
- A `vline` that highlights precisely 268 days after 25 December
- An example of how to annotate a single point (with offset) using `plt.text(x,y,<TEXT>)`
- A way to save the figure as a crisp PDF rather than blurry JPG (`plt.savefig(<PATH.EXTENSION>)`)
- And a legend that illustrates relevant features of the plot, which we convey to Python by adding `label="<LABEL TEXT>"` to the plot elements.

Among the many additional options I have not used is the ability to set the title of the plot. I generally do not recommend doing that in Python. The reason is that when you place a figure in a research paper, the title (e.g., 'Figure 1. The results of the study') is not *in* the image, but is a part of the document and written in the text above the figure. Thus, if you print it in the plot image it will look out of place in the academic document or may have to be cropped. For APA (American Psychological Association) style (which is common in social sciences), clear detailing of figures can be found on their website (https://apastyle.apa.org/style-grammar-guidelines/tables-figures/figures).

```python
import numpy as np
import matplotlib.pyplot as plt
import matplotlib.dates as mdates

# I create ax here first so we can layer some elements behind the plot
fig,ax = plt.subplots()

# Set the ticks to be on the months, format the months using the DateFormatter
ax.xaxis.set_major_locator(mdates.MonthLocator())
ax.xaxis.set_major_formatter(mdates.DateFormatter('%b'))

# Add a vspan on the x-axis to 95% of births a full term after December 25
# Parameters for estimating births comes from Jukic et al.,
# https://www.ncbi.nlm.nih.gov/pmc/articles/PMC3777570/
# They estimated among their sample a mean 268 days (sd 10).
xmas = 359
mnbaby = 268
sdbaby = 10
yr = 366

ninemoslater = (xmas + mnbaby - yr)

# 2 Standard deviations above and below gets us 95% of births
# So 20 days before and after will display 95% of impact of a
# particular day. In this case, Christmas Day.
bottomrange = ninemoslater-sdbaby*2
toprange = ninemoslater+sdbaby*2
```

```
ax.axvspan(bottomrange, toprange,
          color='grey',alpha=0.5, label="95% range")

ax.axvline(ninemoslater, linestyle=":",
          color='black', label="9 months after Dec 25")

ax=sns.regplot(x=birth_df.index, y=birth_df.average,
               data=birth_df, robust=True,
               marker="+", ci=None,
               scatter_kws={"color":"red", "alpha":0.5,},
               label="Avg. per day")

# Get the x,y coords of minimum (Boxing Day)
minday = birth_df[birth_df.average==min(birth_df.average)]

# Offset x by 40 and y by 10 so the label fits nicely in frame.
# For the text I used a newline and some formatting for a round number
plt.text(x=minday.index[0]-40,
         y=minday.average.values[0]+10,
         s=f"{minday.date.values[0]}\n({minday.average.values[0]:.0f})")

ax.set(xlabel='Day of the year', ylabel='Average number of births')

ax.legend()

plt.show()
```

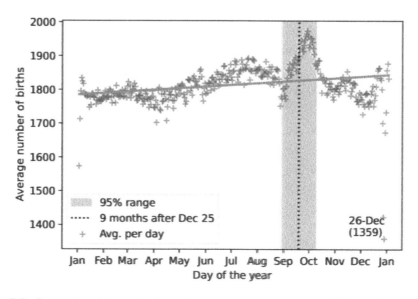

Figure 9.8 Regression plot showing trend line across average number of births in the UK for 1995-2014 (one marker per day with annotations for Christmas and 9 months thereafter)

That code was much more involved, but I hope you can see where the detailing went into helping to tell (but not prove) a story. In terms of the data, we can see that there is some clear seasonality in births in the UK. It is generally uniform, but somewhere around the day 260 mark we see a peak. Since babies take approximately 9 months from conception to birth, this means that the winter holidays appear to be a rather cosy time for couples interested in making babies. On the other hand, the very same winter holidays are explicitly not a preferred time for delivering babies. A pregnant person has some capacity to delay the delivery of a baby, especially when that delivery is surgical (i.e. Caesarean). As such, 25 and 26 December are clear *outliers* as people often hold off delivering babies on those days.

9.4.3 Normal versus skewed distributions as being interesting

In addition to the plain uniform distribution, there are a variety of distribution generators that model features we might see in everyday life. Two really relevant ones are the Gaussian distribution, which is often called the 'normal' distribution or the bell curve, and the power curve, which is an extremely skewed distribution that is often seen when measuring features online.

A normal distribution is one where the average value is also the most common, and values far away from the average are increasingly rare. That means that if we have a mean of 100 and a standard deviation of 10 we won't often see a value of 120 or 80 (but it could happen roughly once every 95 chances or so). We are even less likely to see a value of 130 or 70. Getting a value of 180 or 10 would be as rare as winning the lottery. Thus, a normal distribution tends to imply that we have a relatively stable expected value and differences from this expected value become increasingly unlikely. We also assume that it is symmetric, so a difference from the mean is as unlikely whether it is a difference above or below the mean. The classic example is height. Men's and women's height both tend to have relatively normal distributions (Tanner, 1981), although regional events and circumstances can skew this (A'Hearn et al., 2009). These distributions overlap so that it is not surprising to see women who are taller than the average man, but it is not as common as seeing men who are taller than the average woman.

When we view data on opinions we often see roughly normally distributed data. Seeing a plot of attitudes that looks like a bell curve would suggest most people feel roughly the same way about a topic but a few would strongly agree and a few would strongly disagree. We sometimes see data that is different from normal in two interesting ways. The first is when the data is somehow skewed left or right. The second is data that is not unimodal (typically it is bimodal), that is, is when the data has two or more peaks. These peaks could represent either polarisation, where most people really either feel strongly for or against something, or two underlying distributions merged together, like how human height has two peaks, one representing the average height for women and one representing the average height for men.

 Comparing two distributions versus two groups

As interesting as univariate distributions are, I think that there is much more to be learned from comparing two distributions jointly, or comparing how multiple distributions can help inform the shape of some outcome. In a way, this is the basis of modern applied statistical approaches to social sciences: we look for ways to measure phenomena and theorise about how these measurements can help predict other measurements or predict phenomena that are harder to measure directly. For example, Sandy et al. (2013) examined the predictive power of both demographic and psychographic (e.g., personality) variables on a variety of preferences. They discovered heterogeneity in which ones would help explain preferences for a variety of consumer goods, with demographics explaining more variation in some and personality more in others. But neither substantially explained preferences, leading perhaps to the rush to employ behavioural data online to predict preferences.

This section on bivariate relationships, then, is an opportunity to complain about the phrase 'correlation does not equal causation'. This phrase, which you may have already encountered, is important. It means that because we see a relationship between two variables, that does not mean that one variable caused the other. It's an important point, so what is there to complain about? In reality, establishing causality is difficult and even getting the motivation to look for it might require significant effort. You would not make that effort unless you likely thought there would be something worth looking for. Further, while one variable you have measured might not have caused the other variable to have its distribution, *something* caused that distribution. An exploration of causality is beyond the scope of this book. Causal analysis is an emerging subfield of statistics and philosophy that involves specialised statistical tools such as counterfactual analysis and difference-in-difference regressions. Thus, I might prefer to replace 'correlation does not equal causation' with 'prediction does not equal forecasting'.

Below, I explore the bivariate relationships. We will not make assertions about one variable causing the other. But that should not deprive you of the imagination to do so. When learning about data, I want you to explore correlations rather than shy away from them and to generously posit with an open mind possible explanations for these relationships (including 'luck', i.e. a 'spurious' relationship). Combined with a thorough search of literature, you may have some very robust expectations for your data. Then with the right models and data you may be able not only to predict some interesting relationships, but also to make assertions about how these associations came to be. Notably, below I will not be using social or social media data. To keep it lightweight, I will be using a dataset on flowers that comes with the `seaborn` visualisation library. This has the advantage of us not using causal language since this is by no means a book about flowers, but it will still allow us to reveal some compelling relationships in the data.

9.5.1 Constraining our work based on the properties of data

Recall from above that we should consider the plot as a communicative act. It is seeking to convey a point to a reader. This bears repeating when we visualise multiple distributions since it is possible to layer a lot of data on a single figure, but more data doesn't always mean more insight. It can sometimes just mean more confusion or more opportunities to misinterpret a relationship. Instead of thinking about what can be *shown in* the figure, consider what can be *read from* the figure. In that sense, the sort of visualisations we use will depend on the nature of the underlying relationship to be represented. For example, are we comparing a single continuous measurement across two groups, or two continuous measurements for a single group?

For bivariate work, one of the key distinctions is whether the data is continuous or discrete.

- *Two continuous distributions.* Distribution 1 has a range and distribution 2 has a range. Thus, we use a plane and project all the values along both axes within or around this range. You can see this in a scatter plot. Scatter plots work but sometimes many points overlap on top of each other, making it hard to tell which area of the plot is denser than others. Below I show an alternative to a scatter plot which does this as a 'heatmap'.
- *One continuous and one categorical distribution.* In many cases we have either binary (e.g., yes/no) or multinomial data (*n* discrete cases, e.g., $treatment_1$, $treatment_2$, *control*). We often want to examine the shape of some distribution (e.g., time to task completion) by a categorical variable (people who drank coffee, tea, or water). So we will show two (or more) plots side by side, or sometime in the same figure.
- *Two categorical distributions.* For two categorical distributions it really depends on the *cardinality* of the data. Cardinality of a categorical distribution refers to the number of unique entries in it. For the question 'did you brush your teeth this morning?' you might have a cardinality of 3 for 'true', 'false', 'can't remember'. A second column with brands of toothpaste might have many different kinds, let's say 10. Then you would need to visualise 3×10 counts. This normally is best done in a table, though the table can often have additional helpful features like a heatmap to highlight especially popular cells, or recoding so that all the rare brands of toothpaste simply get coded as 'other', and instead of 30 cells, we might have two big brands and 'other', so now the cardinality is 3×3.

To complicate the matter, there are more kinds of data conceptually than continuous and categorical distributions. In social sciences you often still hear about measurements according to a classic typology from Stevens (1946). This includes the following:

- *Interval* data where there is some measurable and even interval between the numbers but no true zero. Examples include credit scores, room temperatures, timestamps, and SAT scores.
- *Ratio* data where there is some clear notion of zero. Examples include the duration of an activity, numbers of messages sent, and scores on a video game.
- *Ordinal* data where there is an ordered rank between categories but no absolute distance between the ranks. Examples include Likert scales (such as 1 for *strongly disagree* and 5 for *strongly agree*).
- *Categorical* data where we can distinguish different sets as categories but not meaningfully rank them. Examples include favourite colours, religious affiliations, and content tags.

These are often used in determining how to measure data in social sciences. That being said, they do have their detractors, including prominent statisticians Guttman and Tukey. This is due to the fact that these measurements, while useful from a research design perspective, might not be adequate from a statistical analysis perspective. The effective discussion by Velleman and Wilkinson (1993) reminds us that ultimately we are constrained by how much information we can recover from the data, not by these sorts of presentational distinctions.

In statistical work, you are more likely to hear about two distinct classes of distributions: *parametric* and *nonparametric*. For a parametric distribution or analysis, the values in the distribution matter (like 40 versus 500 apples). For a nonparametric distribution or analysis, it's merely the rank order that matters (e.g., strongly agree is greater than agree is greater than neutral, regardless of whether one interval is greater than the other interval). Also in statistical work you are likely to be concerned conceptually (and computationally) with whether the data is count data, which is not divisible, (such as number of coin flips) or measurement data, which is divisible (such as a time duration).

9.5.2 Two continuous distributions

Below I create two synthetic distributions. *dist₁* will be normally distributed, so its peak will be in the middle and it should be roughly symmetric around the peak. *dist₂* will be log-normally distributed. That means it will look like a bell curve when represented on a log scale, but like a really skewed bell curve on a linear scale. I then use a `seaborn` plot called `jointplot`. It works like a scatter plot, but it also shows a histogram of values on the top and the side, to help understand how *dist₁* and *dist₂* both inform the pattern in the frame. I include the `hex` argument for the `kind` parameter. This means that each hexagon will represent the number of points that fall inside it (Figure 9.9). This gives us a sense of the density of the distribution in a way that scatter plots can sometimes make difficult. Try to run this without the `kind="hex"` parameter (which will just layer dots on top of each other) and see the difference.

```
SIZE = 2000
np.random.seed(13)
dist1 = np.random.lognormal(0,.5,SIZE)
dist2 = np.random.normal(0,2,SIZE)

# sns.scatterplot(x = dist1, y=dist2)
sns.jointplot(x = dist1, y=dist2, height=3, kind="hex",)

plt.show()
```

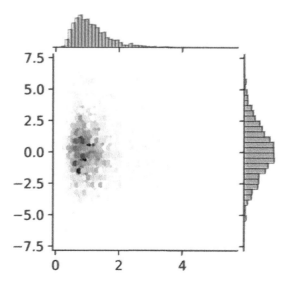

Figure 9.9 A joint plot showing two distributions as histograms and a joint distribution as a hexagonal heatmap

In Figure 9.9 most of the points are in the middle near the left-hand side. This is because they are in the middle of one distribution (recall that with a normal distribution, most points fall near the mean). And for the other slightly skewed distribution plotted along the *x*-axis most of the points fall near 1, even if there is a heavy tail. The joint distributions look like a cluster in the centre but that does not give us much new information. We might now ask, will knowing the location of a case in one of these distributions allow us to accurately predict that case's value in the other distribution? The visualisation shows a blob in the centre but it shows neither a trend (when one goes up the other goes up or down) nor a set of clusters (where there might be multiple distinct and dense 'blobs' in the chart). Again, this is where we can jointly use statistics and visualisations to both gather and test intuitions.

Because we have two continuous variables we can use a *correlation* (or, more strictly, a Pearson product moment correlation). This measure works when you have many pairs of observations. It calculates whether the distance between the pairs is smaller than the average distance between any two numbers. It is reported as *r* and varies from −1 (perfectly anti-correlated) through 0 (not correlated) to 1 (perfectly correlated). There are many guides for what constitutes a good *r* value depending on your expectation. Depending on the domain and the number of observations, however, you might have different expectations. Engineers working with how much force it takes for steel to buckle might want observations that are extremely precise, with $r > 0.99$. Sometimes massive studies (like the small experiments that Google or Facebook might do with user interfaces; Kramer et al., 2014) will get tiny *r* values, but they will be very confident about these values since they have so many observations to work with.

When dealing with statistical relationships, we tend to include both the *strength* of the relationship (e.g., how steep a trend line) but also the *significance* of that relationship (how likely are we to see such a steep trend by chance). Below, I use `pearsonr` from `scipy`. It's very simple and reports two numbers, the first being the strength and the second being the significance.

```
from scipy import stats

stats.pearsonr(dist1, dist2)

(0.00590821749715962, 0.7917331952877843)
```

Before getting into the details of those numbers, notice that this library comes from `scipy`. I used this one because it reports both *r* (the first number) and the *p*-value (the second number). The *p*-value tends to be low when the correlation is high (that's good), but it can depend on the number of observations. The *p*-value will always increase in a correlation with more observations, and thus for some big data work you will surely get 'significant' correlations (i.e. $p < 0.05$) even if the substantive relationship is really mild or explains very little of the overall variation in the distribution. Thus we do not use the *p*-value to assert the *strength* of the relationship, only the *significance* (meaning again the odds that we would see a relationship this extreme if the underlying distribution was random). So low odds of seeing such a relationship by chance (i.e. low *p*-value) means that the relationship is likely real, but how much *x* predicts *y* is still a matter for the *strength* of the relationship. So in this case, the correlation is approximately 0.006, which is really small and likely just random. This is reinforced by the really high *p*-value ($p = 0.792$), which suggests that the odds of observing a relationship at least this strong if the data is random is really high.

9.5.3 PRE scores

A PRE score is any statistical method that will illustrate the *proportional reduction in error* from using some data to predict some other data. This is a useful concept as it means we can assess how much error in one distribution can be reduced by knowing the measurements from another distribution. Pearson's *r* is not a PRE, but it is close. In the regressions above, I noted but did not draw attention to the R^2 value. That value *is* a PRE score. It means that by knowing our explanatory variables we can reduce the amount of error in guessing the response variable by R^2 per cent.

Real-world bivariate data that shows correlations and clusters

In contrast to the above two independent random distributions, the distributions in the following real-world dataset are very correlated. They represent measurements of flowers. The iris dataset is one of several that comes with seaborn so there's no need to download it separately. It includes measurements on three kinds of iris flowers: *versicolor* ('blue flag'), *setosa*, and *virginica*. These have striking blue/purple petals but are considered different species of flowers. Below we will see measures of the length and width of the petals as well as the length and width of the sepals (the green leaf-like bit just below and encasing the flower).

```
df = sns.load_dataset('iris')
df.columns = [x.replace("_","-") for x in df.columns]

display(df.sample(6,random_state=13))
```

	sepal-length	sepal-width	petal-length	petal-width	species
55	5.7	2.8	4.5	1.3	versicolor
64	5.6	2.9	3.6	1.3	versicolor
21	5.1	3.7	1.5	0.4	setosa
101	5.8	2.7	5.1	1.9	virginica
112	6.8	3.0	5.5	2.1	virginica
33	5.5	4.2	1.4	0.2	setosa

For each one of the measurements, we could look at the overall distribution, or facet (i.e. subgroup) that distribution by the different kinds of flowers. Here I use the hue parameter to define the different groups, each getting assigned its own colour.

```
sns.kdeplot(df["sepal-width"], hue=df["species"])

plt.show()
```

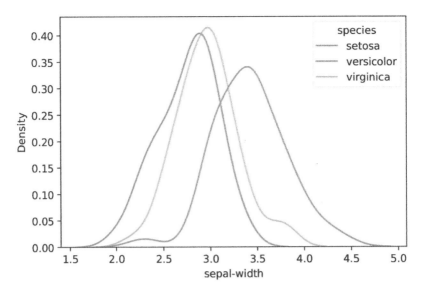

Figure 9.10 Kernel density estimate plot showing distribution of sepal widths, highlighting differences between three species of flower

In Figure 9.10 I combine this faceting by flower type (as colour) with a grid that shows the bivariate relationships for `sepal-length`, `sepal-width`, `petal-length`, and `petal-width`. Sometimes species really highlights differences, but other times it is clear that there's a linear relationship across species. Notice that I use a different kind of visualisation for the variables in the upper right and the lower left.

```
fig = sns.PairGrid(df, hue="species", height=1.5)

fig.map_upper(sns.scatterplot)
fig.map_diag(sns.kdeplot)
fig.map_lower(sns.kdeplot)
fig.add_legend()

plt.show()
```

Figure 9.11 is a pair plot and it is very information dense, but I think really revealing. On the diagonals are the univariate distributions across species. Notice that in this case, the univariate distributions tend to be normally distributed. Some distributions have much higher peaks than others, like the setosa's `petal-width`, which is very tightly distributed, unlike the virginica's `sepal-length` which is very widely distributed. I have shown the bivariate relationships in two ways: as a kernel density estimation (KDE) plot and a scatter plot. The upper right set of scatter plots are the transpose (i.e. flipped on their side) version of the lower left ones. The scatter plots are useful for helping us imagine a trend line through the data. So for example, there seems to be a linear relationship across all flowers between `petal-length` and `petal-width`. However, for many of the

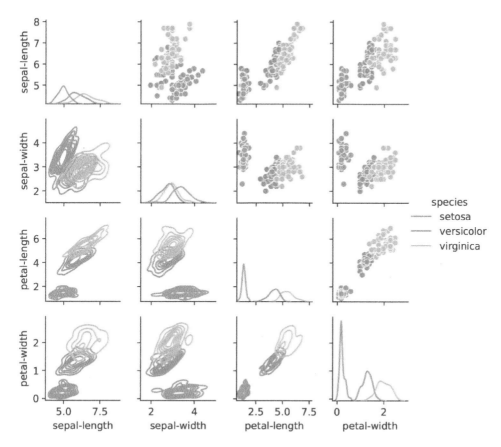

Figure 9.11 Pairgrid showing a variety of bivariate plots concerning flower measurements, grouped by flower species

other relationships it seems that there *is* a pattern, but just like Anscombe's quartet it is not very linear. The KDE plots show us the density of points in the plane. For example, it appears that there's a coherent relationship between `sepal-width` and `petal-length` but the relationship is not just linear. Rather, it is *flower-specific*. This shows us that we do not simply want to look for correlations between variables (or trend lines that characterise variables). Sometimes we want to look for clusters of observations that seem really similar.

Let's now look at the same iris data, but instead of showing a visual representation of the data, let's show a visual representation of a metric, namely the correlation between two distributions (Figure 9.12). Note that correlations are symmetric, so the values in the upper and lower triangles will reflect that.

```
sns.heatmap(df.corr(),vmin=-1,vmax=1,annot=True)

plt.show()
```

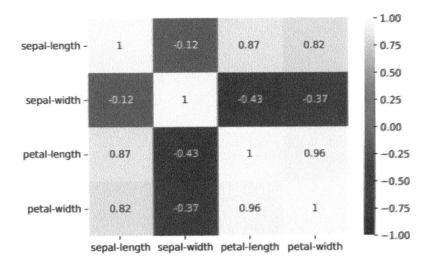

Figure 9.12 Heatmap of correlations between four measurements of flowers

The heatmap shows some interesting patterns as well. Most notably, the sepal width seems to be negatively correlated with much of the rest of the chart. However, this is somewhat of an illusion. As we can see from the pair plot, it's more the case that the sepal width *clusters* for the different flowers. So that means that there's a coherent relationship for each of the different flowers, but if we put them in the same bucket, it makes it look like it's a negative relationship rather than three distinct relationships, one for each flower species. See below how I disentangle that relationship by doing correlations per species.

```
tot_corr = stats.pearsonr(df["sepal-width"], df["petal-length"])

print(f"For all data combined:\t corr = {tot_corr[0]:.3f},",
      f"sig = {tot_corr[1]:.3f}")

for flower in df["species"].unique():
    corr = stats.pearsonr(df[df["species"]==flower]["sepal-width"],
                          df[df["species"]==flower]["petal-length"])

    print(f"For species {flower}:\t corr = {corr[0]:.3f},",
          f"sig = {corr[1]:.3f}")
```

```
For all data combined:      corr = -0.428, sig = 0.000
For species setosa:         corr = 0.178, sig = 0.217
For species versicolor:     corr = 0.561, sig = 0.000
For species virginica:      corr = 0.401, sig = 0.004
```

For each of the subgroups the correlation is positive. In one case (setosa) the correlation is both small and noisy ($p = 0.217$). However, the correlation is significant for both versicolor ($p < 0.001$) and virginica ($p = 0.004$). The original negative correlation, then, is an example of a 'suppression relationship', where the original data shows one relationship or no relationship at all but when adding a third variable, the relationship is revealed. I take the notion of a relationship being suppressed or spurious from the *elaboration model*, which is an approach to considering systematically how a third variable can help to understand the relationship between two prior variables. It is discussed in Chapter 15 of Babbie's incredibly thorough book, *The Practice of Social Research* (2020).

9.5.4 Comparing distinct groups

The above example motivates us to think not just about comparing two distributions but comparing two groups as subsets from the same distribution. To compare different groups we tend to want to say whether the two groups are meaningfully distinct. In a statistical sense, we have numerous tests for this. We have already noted the chi-squared test, which looks for differences between expected and observed values. To this we can add the *t-test* and the *one-way analysis of variance*.

t-test

A *t*-test looks at two different distributions and, based on their size, expected value, and dispersion, considers whether the two distributions are really distinct. This is important because whenever you have two groups with a distribution of values, the average is going to be at least slightly different between the two groups. Imagine two sets of posts on Instagram, one from a politician for one party, one for a politician from the other. The first politician gets an average of 34 likes (with a standard deviation (SD) of 20) on their 50 posts, the second gets an average of 28 likes (SD = 10) on their 20 posts. Of course 34 is more than 28, but in statistical terms, is it really that big a difference? The first account had a slightly higher score but the standard deviation was twice as high, meaning we may assume that the average was more noisy. A *t*-test compares the means of the two distributions, taking into account the size of the samples and dispersion in addition to the mean. In this case, the two distributions would not be considered statistically significant.

```
stats.ttest_ind_from_stats(mean1=34.0, std1=20, nobs1=50,
                           mean2=28.0, std2=10, nobs2=20)
```

```
Ttest_indResult(statistic=1.2753736993876346, pvalue=0.20651699514080454)
```

Now in terms of attention, the first politician still had more likes overall since they had more posts each with as many likes. Further this example is a little facetious because with posts on social media sites, the distributions tend to look a little more skewed, with perhaps most posts getting a small number of likes and a few posts getting a huge number of likes. In such cases, a *t*-test might not be ideal, since it compares the mean values, and the mean values would be really unrepresentative with highly skewed data. You might consider first transforming the data or using a *nonparametric* test, such as the Mann–Whitney *U*-test (a.k.a. Wilcoxon rank-sum test), which works similarly to a *t*-test except that it uses the rank order of the data rather than the values. It's also worth noting that *t*-tests can take into account whether the two distributions concern different groups ('independent samples *t*-test': `scipy.stats.ttest_ind()`) or repeated/related measurements of the same group ('paired samples *t*-test': `scipy.stats.ttest_rel()`).

Here is where visualisation can really help. By visualising your distributions you can get a better sense of how skewed they are. Generally, for tests concerning the mean, the test will be more accurate the closer the data is to normally distributed. So *t*-tests work better on normally distributed data than on heavily skewed data. Incidentally, so do regressions, although there are considerably more assumptions for regressions and diagnostics available. As some data on the web is *extremely* skewed, this will require some extra care. I recommend De Vaus (2002) for a clear discussion of many different instances of data to compare, with some guidance on which test to use in the right circumstances. There will not be much mention of some of the issues we see with online data, such as power laws, but it is otherwise really clear. Power laws are interesting because they represent distributions so skewed that the mean does not really describe either the many small numbers or the few very big numbers. This is like the number of links coming into a site. On the one side would be my website with very few links coming in. On the very same web is Amazon with tons of links coming in. Stumpf and Porter (2012) offer an engaging if mathematical discussion about this.

Analysis of variance

An analysis of variance (ANOVA) is like a *t*-test but for multiple groups. With this test we want to establish whether multiple groups are distinct from each other. The test focuses on whether there is a statistically significant difference in the means of the different groups. Extending our example above, imagine we have four politicians on Instagram, each with their own number of likes per post. An ANOVA can say whether there is a difference among them. However, it would take a post-hoc test to check if specific pairs are different from each other.

Just as *t*-tests can be independent or paired samples, there are multiple flavours of ANOVA. They tend to permit more complex tests, such as looking at group differences when you have multiple response variables. For example, imagine we have both the number of likes and the number of comments. Then we might use an approach called *multiple analysis of variance* (MANOVA). We might also want to think about considering a covariate in the model, such as time before the election, since posts nearer to the election might get more interest generally; that would be an example of an *analysis of covariance* (ANCOVA).

Note that, just as with the *t*-test, there is still interpretation to be done on whether a difference is substantively significant. These tests tend to do more to disprove a difference between groups that vary slightly than to prove a difference that is very obvious from visualisation or simple metrics. To show groups visually, there are a variety of approaches.

We can return to the iris dataset, as we had three different groups referring to the three different kinds of flowers. Notice that in one of the measurements above, `sepal-width`, it does not seem like there was a big difference between the three distributions. Let's look closer at those distributions using a box plot (Figure 9.13).

```
sns.boxplot(x=df["species"], y=df["sepal-width"])

plt.show()
```

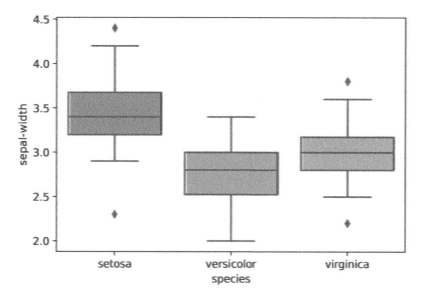

Figure 9.13 Box plot of flower measurements, grouped by flower species

A box plot is a useful means of showing multiple distributions side by side. The top and bottom of the rectangular box contain the middle 50% of the distribution. The remainder is contained within the T above and the inverted T below the box with some small exceptions: the diamonds in Figure 9.13 represent outliers, typically points three standard deviations from the mean or more.

By looking at the chart, I would surmise that setosa has significantly wider sepals than the other two. If we did an ANOVA, would we find it to be significantly different? There are a few ways to do an ANOVA in Python, but the simplest is probably in `scipy.stats`. Here we simply feed in n distributions and it will report the F-value and the p-value. The F-value refers to the difference between the groups, which is then used to calculate the p-value based on sample size.

```
x = df.groupby("species")["sepal-width"].apply(list)
```

```
stats.f_oneway(x["setosa"],x["versicolor"],x["virginica"])
```

```
F_onewayResult(statistic=49.160040089612075, pvalue=4.492017133309115e-17)
```

So it appears that they are very much distinct as groups, given the p-value. The mean difference between the groups is calculable and worth reporting.

9.5.5 Summary

While this chapter covers a lot of ground, it is yet overwhelmingly brisk with both statistics and visualisations. In both cases, there are dedicated resources that are likely deeper and more eloquent than this chapter. There are also resources that are more encyclopedic as well. I hope that this chapter has provided something a little novel in between. My goal was threefold:

- To provide examples of how to visualise one or more distributions in such a way that options like opacity and line style are used to illustrate a claim about data
- To provide examples of univariate and bivariate analyses that can complement visualisation to help us appreciate how much of the picture we should have expected by chance
- To communicate how visualisations and statistics can both be used to articulate some difference between what we expect and what we observe. They tend to have slightly different uses, but they work well together.

All too often in work by those who are just learning, the visualisation itself is taken as evidence of a difference. But because we can crop *x*- or *y*-axes, show trend lines without confidence intervals, and normalise data in all kinds of ways, it is possible to make more of a relationship than is really there. By combining a visualisation with some statistics, we can really emphasise a point about a difference, or step back and realise that while a difference is visible, it might not be meaningful.

There was a secondary goal more directly concerning Python. This chapter demonstrated a variety of features of plotting using both matplotlib and seaborn. Python's main visualisation package is matplotlib. When you import matplotlib.pyplot as plt then you get a plt object. Seaborn uses these objects implicitly, so if you use seaborn, this gives you access to a plt object for things like plt.show(). A plot includes one or more figures. plt manages many features of the plot, such as how to show what is on the figure, to add more details such as plt.text, to save the figure, and to instantiate a grid of subplots if you are trying to present more than one figure. Often it is tricky to know whether a feature of a plot requires you to reference the plot (plt), the figure (e.g., histplot), or the axis that contains the plot (ax). It gets less tricky with experience. Reading the matplotlib documentation can be useful, as can exploring a variety of questions about matplotlib on online forums such as Stack Overflow.

 ## Further reading in visualisation

- *Visualize This: The FlowingData Guide to Design, Visualization, and Statistics* by Yau (2011) provides page after page of clear insight into the relationship between stats and visualisation using a variety of exciting and interesting charts.
- *The Visual Display of Quantitative Information* by Tufte (2001). As this chapter combines statistics and visualisation there are many places to go for further reading. Tufte's work is cantankerous, lucid, and original. It is a classic. All his work since then has been particularly insightful in helping us consider how claims can be made or undermined by poor visualisations. His short book on how PowerPoint fails us is also a riot (Tufte, 2003).
- *Exploratory Data Analysis* by Tukey (1977). A thorough, brilliant, and coherent book on how to think through early data exploration. If I have been economical in this chapter it is only to carve out more time for you to have a browse of this book. He said everything in that book could be done with a pen and a pencil. In a way, the rest of the recommendations are just us trying to do the same thing in a different way. This book is also a kindred spirit in the interest in abductive thinking, though he doesn't refer to it by name.

- *Seaborn: Statistical Data Visualization* by Waskom (2021). This article explains the core concepts behind `seaborn`. I feel it is also worth reading the online documentation (https://seaborn.pydata.org/api.htm). I rarely enjoy documentation, but the `seaborn` team do a great job of not only articulating how to use the package but also why to use certain features. It is very readable and recommended, especially when discussing colour.
- *GGPLOT2: Elegant Graphics for Data Analysis* by Wickham et al. (2022). Yes, it's for R. But it is no surprise to see Wickham mentioned again here. There is much to learn from GGPLOT2's approach of layering data, even if you do not understand R. The writing is clear and the entire book is available online (https://ggplot2-book.org/).

 ## Extensions and reflections

- Before visualising some real data, try plotting collections of a few more random number generators. You can get many of these from `numpy.random`. Here are a few to try: `.normal()`, `.binomial()`, `.poisson()` and `.power()`. These all come from very different statistical generating processes and will show up as different shapes when plotted on the same figure. When viewing a shape of a real distribution it will be useful to think about how it might relate to these shapes depending on the circumstance. Getting a feel for this can involve both the maths used to produce the distribution but also the visual shape or statistical measures for that distribution. Explore how to change the scale from linear to log scale to see if it makes a difference. You can try this with `ax.xscale("log")`.
- If you have a look at how I built a linear regression model, you can see that there is space to add more columns of data. This becomes the start of multivariate regression. This is a huge and complex topic but worth exploring. I provide some resources for more statistics work in Chapter 15.
- In the next chapter I will introduce a dataset from Stack Exchange, the people who did Stack Overflow. I do not plot a lot of descriptive statistics in that chapter, as I leave that for you. It would be good for you to try out visualising the distributions seen in that chapter.

PART IV

SOCIAL DATA SCIENCE IN PRACTICE: FOUR APPROACHES

10
CLEANING DATA FOR SOCIALLY INTERESTING FEATURES

━━━━━━━━ Learning goals ━━━━━━━━

- Distinguish between data as streams of text and numbers and the kinds of social information that are represented by (and can be extracted from) this data
- Understand how to filter a dataset down meaningfully, such as by accounting for *structural missing data*
- Use built-in methods for cleaning data such as `to_datetime` and `to_numeric` which handle missing data and irregular formatting
- Reshape lists of data (such as tags) into a workable form
- Understanding what constitutes a regular expression and how to build one for simple text.

Happy families are all alike; every unhappy family is unhappy in its own way.

Tolstoy (1977, p. 1)

Data from the world doesn't always come in the shape that you'd like – a nice tidy table of data, with all the columns properly formatted. These tidy tables are the happy families of data science. Yet, it's the unhappy, messy data of the world that keeps things interesting. After the quote, this has been sometimes called the 'Anna Karenina' principle in ecology and other disciplines (https://en.wikipedia.org/wiki/Anna_Karenina_principle). In general it speaks of how good systems require a number of interrelated matters to all work together. Just one of these subsystems failing can spill over into the others. For data analysis, this is pretty acute. If your data is poorly encoded, has endemic issues with missing data, or is not in the shape you want, for example, it is just too difficult to make reliable and scientific claims. Most datasets that people practise with have already been sanitised or preprocessed in some way. As such, when going into the real world students and researchers can be sometimes overwhelmed at the many ways in which data simply fails to get into the form we need ('It was so much simpler in the tutorial!', they exclaim). So instead of leaving that to the reader for *after* the book, I decided to tackle this issue head on while thinking about the many forms of socially relevant data that might be embedded in online or trace data.

This cleaning data task will foreshadow the four approaches to social data science that I explore in the remainder of Part IV. These are on natural language processing, time-series data, social network analysis, and geographic information systems. Many of the techniques we need to explore data in each of these domains first requires us to clean (often unstructured) data in a methodical way.

In this chapter we will be looking at unstructured text, such as Wikipedia pages, tweets, or blog entries. We will see that embedded in this unstructured text are markers of social structure. For example, we can take characters that represent dates and turn them into a 'date format' so we can ask how many days since Sunday, 1 September 2019, or how often something occurs in a given week.

As data refers to measurements, social data science would thus be a science of the measures of social life. The social world is not merely about people, but about people *in their social contexts*. How are these contexts arranged? What do these contexts mean? How do such contexts affect the way people understand the world, and understand themselves?

As an example of a context, think of a train journey. It has a departure and arrival time, as well as a specific location of departure and arrival. There are roles on the train, such as driver, train manager, and passenger. Some passengers are known to each other, whereas others are not (meaning that the people represent a social network, however sparse). Train managers will communicate in a specific language, or set of languages, and they will expect certain forms of communication and behaviours, such as asking to see a ticket, or announcing the next stop. Each of these things can be encoded and thus measured in relation to other similar things. For example, we can ask which journeys take longer, which trains have more staff, which trains have more fraud, crowding in the aisles, or sufficient features for accessibility. We can also ask whether this varies over time, over space, by language?

We can similarly think about this on social media as well. A tweet has a send time, a sender, their followers, and often a location and a device from where it is sent. There are tweet conventions such as retweeting and @mentioning others. Thus, with some care we can reconstruct a lot of social life by reading these signals and asking questions about them. Knowing when a tweet was sent can help you learn about the sender, but also about the diffusion of information.

Data as a form of social context

Contexts as articulated here tend to have the following properties:

- *Temporality*. Time is not just a series of incrementing numbers. It represents the periodicity of the cosmos (such as the rotation of the Earth around the Sun), durations between events, and a whole host of social conventions, such as daylight saving, timezones, and marking the common era as starting roughly two millennia ago. It probably comes as no surprise that clocks were initially spread to synchronise the schedules of trains, thereby allowing much more complex and efficient logistics between stations (Zerubavel, 1979).
- *Spatiality*. Geography is similarly structured data. We measure place in terms of coordinates relative to the Earth, but also relative to boundaries humans have established and asserted. Some of these boundaries, such as those around Kashmir and Palestine, are contested, others are stable and well defined. While the Internet might seem like no place, it is thoroughly suffused with the same inequalities, cultural differences, and variations that we would expect outside the internet – all you need to do is look for them (Graham and Dittus, 2022).
- *Social relationships*. Interestingly, much like spatial boundaries, it turns out that establishing social relationships is contested and extremely tricky. Some relationships are related to genetic similarity (or assumed genetic similarity). Others are based on the social context, such as people who are co-attending a concert or school. Some social boundaries are vague and subjective, like establishing who is your best friend. Despite all the complexities of establishing different kinds of roles and relationships, there are still many forms of structured social data that suggest a relationship. This could be the patterns of messages between people at an office, the connections people provide on LinkedIn or Facebook, or the patterns of speech as measured through some sensor data. In this chapter we will not cover social relationships as a network directly, but will do so in Chapter 13, which gives some example techniques for building social networks.
- *Language*. Language is not simply a random set of grunts and screeches. It is highly structured, culturally dependent, and highly distinct among different speakers. Written language uses characters, glyphs, or symbols to represent words and utterances.

Not everyone uses the same language, nor do people use it in similar or even consistent ways. If we get on a train in China we might not expect someone to ask for a ticket in Spanish. Yet, among Chinese speakers there might be cues that the ticket taker is from one province or city compared to another. When I moved to the UK, I discovered a variety of these subtleties, like the use of 'take away' as equivalent to 'to go' in North American vernacular.

- *Regular or expected patterns of behaviour or communication.* Finally, regular or expected patterns of behaviour are worth considering in the transition between unstructured and structured text. For example, consider an email address. It always has an @ symbol, some characters to the left and right. Email clients, web browsers, and chat apps now all seem to be able to auto-detect things like emails and URLs. How do they know to do this if they have (presumably) never seen the address before? Because it is a regular pattern of text. Other regular patterns might be more abstract, like a name using a salutation, such as 'Mr.', 'Mr', 'Mrs', 'Mx', 'Miss', 'Master', or 'Dr.' in front of a name.

Before we get to some of the ways that Python can extract information from unstructured text, let's have a look at a brief example that contains all of the things we discussed above – an email message:

```
MIME-Version: 1.0
Date: Mon, 12 Aug 2019 16:10:31 +0100
Message-ID: <--------@example.com>
Subject: Example mail
From: Bernie Hogan <bernie.hogan@example.com>
To: Bernie Hogan <bernie.hogan@oii.ox.ac.uk>
Content-Type: multipart/alternative; boundary="000000000000d195ca058fecec49"


--000000000000d195ca058fecec49
Content-Type: text/plain; charset="UTF-8"


Dear reader,

This is an example mail message. It was sent from the Radcliffe Camera at
Oxford. You can see the time it was sent in the header, as well as who
it was sent to. Geography does not come by default with an email message
but the previous sentence has some geographical features that could be
extracted.

Best wishes,
Bernie

Dr Bernie Hogan
Senior Research Fellow, Oxford Internet Institute
Research Associate, Department of Sociology
University of Oxford
https://www.oii.ox.ac.uk/people/profiles/bernie-hogan
```

```
--000000000000d195ca058fecec49
Content-Type: text/html; charset="UTF-8"
Content-Transfer-Encoding: quoted-printable
```

<div dir=3D"ltr">Dear reader,=C2=A0<div>
</div><div>This is an example m=ail message. It was sent from the Radcliffe Camera at Oxford. You can see t=he time it was sent in the header, as well as who it was sent to. Geography= does not come by default with an email message but the previous sentence h=as some geographical features that could be extracted.=C2=A0<br clear=3D"al=l"><div><div dir=3D"ltr"><div dir=3D"ltr"><div><div dir=3D"ltr"><div><div dir=3D"ltr"><di=v>
</div><div>Best wishes,</div><div>Bernie
</div><div>
</div><di=v>Dr Bernie Hogan
Senior Research Fellow, Oxford Internet Institute
<=/div><div>Research Associate, Department of Sociology
</div><div>Univers=ity of Oxford
<a href=3D "https://www.oii.ox.ac.uk/people/profiles/bernie-hogan" target=3D"https://www. oii.ox.ac.uk/people/profiles/bernie-hogan"   </a></div></div></div></div></=div></div></div></div></div></div>

```
--000000000000d195ca058fecec49--
```

Recall above that we described five kinds of text we can use to bring context to social information: time, location, relationships, language, and regular expressions. Where can we see these in the text?

1 *Language and character sets*. This email message was sent in English. However, you should note that some of the features like the words 'date' and 'Content-Type' will be in English even if the message is not. Notice that the message is there twice. The bottom message is all a wall of text embedded with codes and tags like `<div dir=3D"ltr">`. These are HTML codes for formatting the message. This is because Gmail sends the message in both plain text and HTML. The email reader on the other side will choose which one to display. In this chapter we will look at how to strip out HTML from a blob of text. For more involved text processing and encoding matters, see Chapter 11.

2 *Time*. The time here has a date and is in the following format: `Date: Mon, 12 Aug 2019 16:10:31 +0100`. In a section later in this chapter we will unpack this phrase using a date parser. Later in Chapter 12 we will be looking at how to plot data temporally.

3 *Geography*. We don't know where exactly this message was sent from, except for the fact that it was written in the email. There it is said 'the Radcliffe Camera at Oxford'. Being able to detect that programmatically is very difficult. For example, there is an Oxford, Ohio, which is home to another university, Miami University. In fact, according to Wikipedia, there are 25 Oxfords in America in different states. So how would we know which one I was referring to in the message above? (Trick question – I was referring to the Oxford in the UK.) That's where it gets tricky. We plot spatial data in Chapter 14 on geography.

4 *Social relationships*. These can be extracted from structured or unstructured text. Here it is pretty structured. There is a message from one account (example.com) to another account (oii.ox.ac.uk). It gets more difficult when you have to infer things like who replied to whom in threaded conversations. We will introduce strategies for asking about relationships in Chapter 13 on social networks.

5   *Regular expressions.* This message employs some standard formatting. In that sense it is not strictly unstructured, but it is not in the form we need, either. However, every email we encounter downloaded from a single email provider should have consistent formatting that we can use to extract text. For example, not only does the message have a date in a parsable format, the date is on its own line with `Date:` in front of it and a return character afterwards. Parsing the actual date information is part of establishing temporality, but knowing where to look for that date is a matter of regular expressions. We will explore regular expressions more fully below.

In general, the more standardised the data is, the easier it is to move from unstructured to structured. Dates are relatively standard, but not rigorously so. For example, Twitter reports dates as `Mon Aug 12 16:10:31 +0100 2019` whereas emails from Google will format dates as `Mon, 12 Aug 2019 16:10:31 +0100`. Notice the slight differences? They are similar, but they are not the same and will need their own parsers to be created. How might we make them entirely standard? We can convert them to a standardised time format before storing them. For example, in both cases they convert neatly to `1565629831` in Unix time. Unfortunately, Unix time is so standard that it is just a series of numbers and thus really difficult for humans to comprehend meaningfully.

 A sustained example for cleaning: Stack Exchange

To provide an example of how to clean data, we first of course need data! For the remainder of this book, except in niche circumstances, we will be drawing heavily on a single dataset, the data dump of the archives of Stack Exchange (https://www.archive.org/download/stackexchange). Stack Exchange is pretty attractive here for a number of reasons. First, it is freely available with a generous Creative Commons licence. Second, it is a real living dataset. This is a place where many people ask and answer many questions about a whole host of topics. Thus, it is likely to still be up and running years after this book is published. Third, the largest Stack Exchange, Stack Overflow, is likely to be an indispensable resource for you when exploring other topics related to programming. But there are many other stack exchanges such as the one for statistics, Cross-Validated (https://stats.stackexchange.com/), data science (https://datascience.stackexchange.com/), and even one for pets (https://pets.stackexchange.com/), though it is not very active. Thus, learning how to characterise the site will also help you engage this useful resource.

In addition to being a useful question-and-answer site, Stack Exchange is also a viable site for social research. We can examine which topics are popular, whether this changes over time, what language is associated with popular or unpopular content, what is the variety of content and what sort of inequalities appear in voting – such as whether there are any of the pre-existing gender biases commonly seen in programming cultures (Vedres and Vasarhelyi, 2019).

While the main Stack Exchange (Stack Overflow) is multiple gigabytes of data, there are many others that are (merely) in the megabytes. In this chapter we will use the Movie Stack Exchange, which is a little less than 100 MB. This is the sort of size and scale that makes it a tad too large for spreadsheets but still workable on a desktop or laptop (i.e. a local) machine. All of the Stack Exchange data dumps follow a similar schema, which they have posted, of course, in a Meta Stack Exchange post (https://meta.stackexchange.com/questions/2677/). You can find the data for the Movie Stack Exchange from the Internet Archive (https://archive.org/details/stackexchange). Note that if you are using a different (more recent) version of the export than the one I've used here, the counts for the data will be a little different, but the logic should be exactly the same. You can also check on the GitHub archive for this chapter for updates about data collection.

The Stack Overflow data comes as XML. We will use the approach we saw in Chapter 4 on getting data into XML using `xmltodict`. Recall that `xmltodict` takes an XML file and produces a dictionary. The tag names become the keys and what's between the tags becomes the value. Additionally, `xmltodict` processes the tag attributes so that they become their own key–value pairs. The way to tell if a key refers to a tag or an attribute is whether the variable has an @ at the beginning of it.

To get a sense of the XML data on the Movie Stack Exchange we can peek at the data by reading the first few characters. This might be preferable to opening the file in a browser window or a text program since it is very large. We can give `read()` a numerical argument. That will be taken as the number of characters to read. Let's read the first 1000.

```python
from pathlib import Path

# I just unzipped the file within the data folder.
data_dir = Path().cwd().parent / "data" / "movies.stackexchange.com"

print(open(data_dir / "Posts.xml").read(1000))
```

```
<?xml version="1.0" encoding="utf-8"?>
<posts>
  <row Id="1" PostTypeId="1" AcceptedAnswerId="2776" CreationDate="2011-11-
30T19:15:54.070" Score="31" ViewCount="7679" Body="&lt;p&gt;Some comedians /
actors are given creative freedom to improvise at times when producing a new film.
Is there any evidence that Vince Vaughn or Owen Wilson improvised in any scenes,
diverging from the script in the film &amp;quot;Wedding Crashers&amp;quot;?&lt;/
p&gt;&#xA;" OwnerUserId="11" LastEditorUserId="94442" LastEditDate="2022-02-
12T21:59:39.633" LastActivityDate="2022-02-12T21:59:39.633" Title="To what
extent were the actors in Wedding Crashers improvising?" Tags="&lt;wedding-
crashers&gt;" AnswerCount="2" CommentCount="0" ContentLicense="CC BY-SA
4.0" />
  <row Id="2" PostTypeId="2" ParentId="1" CreationDate="2011-11-30T19:37:10.510"
Score="14" Body="&lt;p&gt;According to the &lt;a href=&quot;http://www.imdb.com/
title/tt0396269/trivia&quot;&gt;trivia on IMDb&lt;/a&gt;, Owen Wilson and Vince
Vaughn im
```

We can see that the file simply has a tag called 'posts' and that it has rows. Each row has the bulk of the data inside attributes of the XML. This is pretty different from the XML that was seen in Chapter 4 coming from Wikipedia, where virtually no data was stored in the attributes. Nevertheless, we can still work with this data, and do so easily.

```
import xmltodict

xml_data = open(data_dir / "Posts.xml",'r').read()

stack_dict = xmltodict.parse(xml_data)
print(type(stack_dict))

<class 'collections.OrderedDict'>
```

To get a sense of the data structure, I normally try to peek inside. First we check whether it is a list or dictionary at the top. Based on the output string above, the data should now be an ordered dictionary. By examining the keys for that dictionary, we can discover that the top-level dictionary only has one key, posts. Here you can see I asked for the keys, got them, then got a second key called row. But the value for row isn't a dictionary, it's a list of tags. Let's see that and print the first row.

```
print(stack_dict["posts"].keys())
print(type(stack_dict["posts"]["row"]))

odict_keys(['row'])
<class 'list'>

display(stack_dict["posts"]["row"][0])

OrderedDict([('@Id', '1'),
             ('@PostTypeId', '1'),
             ('@AcceptedAnswerId', '2776'),
             ('@CreationDate', '2011-11-30T19:15:54.070'),
             ('@Score', '31'),
             ('@ViewCount', '7679'),
             ('@Body',
              '<p>Some comedians / actors are given creative freedom to
improvise at times when producing a new film. Is there any evidence that
Vince Vaughn or Owen Wilson improvised in any scenes, diverging from the
script in the film &quot;Wedding Crashers&quot;?</p>\n'),
             ('@OwnerUserId', '11'),
             ('@LastEditorUserId', '94442'),
             ('@LastEditDate', '2022-02-12T21:59:39.633'),
             ('@LastActivityDate', '2022-02-12T21:59:39.633'),
             ('@Title',
              'To what extent were the actors in Wedding Crashers improvising?'),
             ('@Tags', '<wedding-crashers>'),
             ('@AnswerCount', '2'),
             ('@CommentCount', '0'),
             ('@ContentLicense', 'CC BY-SA 4.0')])
```

And it seems we have a lot of rows.

```
print(len(stack_dict['posts']['row']))
```

```
61184
```

Since we have converted the XML to a dictionary, we can now use `json_normalize()` to get the Stack Exchange data right into a table. That's when the cleaning really starts.

```
import pandas as pd
```

```
stack_df = pd.json_normalize(stack_dict["posts"]["row"])
```

10.2.1 Quick summaries of the dataset

Recall from Chapter 3 there are several different ways to show quick summaries of the dataset (such as `info`, `describe`, `shape`, and `len`). Each indicates a different perspective on the data inside. Neither is really sufficient on its own. The first, `info` summarises the column types in the dataset.

```
stack_df.info()
```

```
<class 'pandas.core.frame.DataFrame'>
RangeIndex: 61184 entries, 0 to 61183
Data columns (total 22 columns):
 #   Column                  Non-Null Count   Dtype
---  ------                  --------------   -----
 0   @Id                     61184 non-null   object
 1   @PostTypeId             61184 non-null   object
 2   @AcceptedAnswerId       13049 non-null   object
 3   @CreationDate           61184 non-null   object
 4   @Score                  61184 non-null   object
 5   @ViewCount              21504 non-null   object
 6   @Body                   61184 non-null   object
 7   @OwnerUserId            59408 non-null   object
 8   @LastEditorUserId       38375 non-null   object
 9   @LastEditDate           39037 non-null   object
 10  @LastActivityDate       61184 non-null   object
 11  @Title                  21504 non-null   object
 12  @Tags                   21504 non-null   object
 13  @AnswerCount            21504 non-null   object
 14  @CommentCount           61184 non-null   object
 15  @ContentLicense         61184 non-null   object
 16  @ParentId               35380 non-null   object
 17  @FavoriteCount          11729 non-null   object
 18  @LastEditorDisplayName  903 non-null     object
 19  @ClosedDate             2040 non-null    object
 20  @OwnerDisplayName       1939 non-null    object
 21  @CommunityOwnedDate     66 non-null      object
dtypes: object(22)
memory usage: 10.3+ MB
```

This summary is useful in some ways. First it indicates the number of non-null entries, which is particularly interesting since we see a few places where same numbers reappear. We will revisit that below in considering missing data. It also shows the memory footprint of this data, which is considerable but not overwhelming for modern computers. but unfortunately the dtype is an unhelpful object. Are we referring to a list? a string? a datetime object? Before we answer that question, I quickly want to remove the @ symbol from the front of the variable names. They came down this way because they were attributes of a tag. That's a feature of xmltodict, not a feature of the data, so we can remove it.

```
stack_df.columns = [i.replace("@", "") for i in stack_df.columns]
```

We can print the first row using stack_df.loc[0]. Doing that will reveal a variety of data types which we should probably change from a generic string into a meaningful variable type.

```
stack_df.loc[0]
```

```
Id                                                      1
PostTypeId                                              1
AcceptedAnswerId                                     2776
CreationDate                      2011-11-30T19:15:54.070
Score                                                  31
ViewCount                                            7679
Body                  <p>Some comedians / actors are given creative ...
OwnerUserId                                            11
LastEditorUserId                                    94442
LastEditDate                      2022-02-12T21:59:39.633
LastActivityDate                  2022-02-12T21:59:39.633
Title                 To what extent were the actors in Wedding Cras...
Tags                                    <wedding-crashers>
AnswerCount                                             2
CommentCount                                            0
ContentLicense                               CC BY-SA 4.0
ParentId                                              NaN
FavoriteCount                                         NaN
LastEditorDisplayName                                 NaN
ClosedDate                                            NaN
OwnerDisplayName                                      NaN
CommunityOwnedDate                                    NaN
Name: 0, dtype: object
```

A quick inspection reveals a number of places where we should probably alter the data. For example:

- CreationDate should be a datetime object
- Body still includes lots of HTML, and this will hinder some text analysis parsers

- Tags, which is a string representing a collection of tags of the form `<tag1><tag2>`. - these could be treated as a list and used more effectively
- AnswerCount and other counts should be integers.

Moving through all the variables we want (or in this case, perhaps all the variables in the table), we can now start to develop a plan. The rest of the chapter will now proceed as follows:

- Setting an index
- Considering missing data
- Cleaning up strings and numbers
- Cleaning up HTML
- Cleaning up lists in cells
- Cleaning up dates
- Extracting text with regular expressions.

These are the basis of data cleaning but they are not the end. More specialist tasks, such as detecting details in language, networks, and geography, are given their own chapter later. While we show time here in a superficial way, we will also elaborate on that in a later chapter as well. I could specify that this is 'the data analysis workflow' but the truth is that it really changes between different data sources even if there are a few commonalities such as focusing on an index and missing data. Instead, this should be treated as a learning exercise and an example that could go differently if you are collecting data from a different platform or API.

Setting an index

I identified 10 columns that seem to have numbers in them. However, several of them end with Id: Id, PostTypeId, AcceptedAnswerId, OwnerUserId, LastEditorUserId, and ParentId. I will keep these as strings since they do not represent a count, per se, just a unique identifier that increments with each new user account. By keeping them as strings, we can also use them as indices without worrying about mixing up the position index (e.g., the fourth row) and the label index (index == "4").

In this table, the column Id is a unique identifier that refers to each post or reply. Since this is unique per row and is related to the post itself, I will make this the index. The index will then be a label rather than an arbitrary number.

```
stack_df.columns
```

```
Index(['Id', 'PostTypeId', 'AcceptedAnswerId', 'CreationDate', 'Score',
       'ViewCount', 'Body', 'OwnerUserId', 'LastEditorUserId', 'LastEditDate',
       'LastActivityDate', 'Title', 'Tags', 'AnswerCount', 'CommentCount',
       'ContentLicense', 'ParentId', 'FavoriteCount', 'LastEditorDisplayName',
       'ClosedDate', 'OwnerDisplayName', 'CommunityOwnedDate'],
      dtype='object')
```

```
stack_df.set_index('Id', inplace=True)
```

Notably, Id works well as a string. You can insert that value into an HTML string as follows:

```
https://<Exchange_Name>.stackexchange.com/questions/<Id>
```

Then by navigating to that page, you will get the question as it is seen on the web rather than as a row in our table. So to look at the first question, you can navigate to https://movies. stackexchange.com/questions/1.

Handling missing data

Missing data is a nuisance, but it is often unavoidable. In the example above we got a lot of NaN values just within the top five rows. Then when we printed the type of the row it seems that we saw lots of 'float' types. These are actually not floats in the traditional sense of 3.1415 or 42.0. They are actually almost entirely np.nan characters.

Our choices now are to:

1   Understand and filter structural missing data versus missing completely at random (MCAR) data.
2   Delete rows with missing data. This would be referred to as deleting data 'listwise'. The alternative (deleting data 'pairwise') means to ignore it 'on demand', leading to models with different variables having different numbers of cases.
3   Impute the data (i.e. make a guess as to what it should be).
4   Ignore the data and hope for the best.

The first strategy is about how some data will never be recovered because it is 'structurally' missing. For example, if you do not own a car and a survey has a CarColour variable, then it will be missing as a logical necessity: no car, no car colour. However, if you said 'yes, I own a car but I'm not telling you its colour', then you have MCAR data. In the first case, the only thing to do is to ensure that your models do not require data that is structurally unavailable. In the second case, you have the choice of either deleting the rows that have missing data, guessing what the data would be, or finding a way to work around the data. Saunders et al. (2006) give a cogent discussion on missing-data strategies. More recent work has gone into estimating and imputing data using machine learning predictions. A slightly more in-depth approach is found in Chapter 25 of the very thorough and engaging text by Gelman and Hill (2007) on regression.

Let's take an example from our stack_df DataFrame by exploring one of the variables where the cell was NaN: OwnerDisplayName.

```
len(stack_df["OwnerDisplayName"].unique())
```

417

```
stack_df["OwnerDisplayName"].unique()[0:5]
```

```
array([nan, 'user35', 'user223', 'user315', 'spugsley'], dtype=object)
```

It is clear that this data is not a float at all! It is string data, but np.nan was in the first row. Now we have a decision to make:

1 Keep the missing as np.nan and have an uneven column but clearly demarcated missing values.
2 Replace np.nan with "" (i.e. the empty string).
3 Replace np.nan with pd.NA, the generic pandas missing data object.
4 Replace np.nan with some flag such as "missing".

In this case, I'll go for option 2. No username can be "", so it serves as both an easy flag to check for missing data and a way to ensure that if we do something like stack_df["OwnerDisplay'Name"].lower() it will not give us an error (e.g., AttributeError: 'float' object has no attribute 'lower').

```
stack_df["OwnerDisplayName"].fillna("",inplace=True)
```

Why do you think I used stack_df["OwnerDisplayName"].fillna() and not just stack_df.fillna()? Because I don't want to fill in the np.nan values for the other columns right now. We might want to replace some of these columns with a different value (such as 0 or pd.NA).

```
type(stack_df["OwnerDisplayName"][0])
```

```
str
```

 ## Cleaning numeric data

Recall that numeric data can broadly be classed into two types, 'infinitely divisible numbers' and 'counts'. Numbers that are infinitely divisible can have a decimal place. We tend to refer to them as float, as we use floating-point arithmetic to characterise the number. We use float64 to indicate that the number will be stored with 64 bits. Count numbers are meant to be whole numbers. We store these as int (for integer), or sometimes int64. It is not likely that you will come across a count in social science research large enough to reach the 64-bit size limit of (something like 3×10^{38}, depending on how it is stored). Yet, it is still worth noting that while the number system itself is infinite, the amount of computing resources available is not.

We can change a string into a number using 'casting' or 'formatting'. Casting changes the type of the number, whereas formatting simply changes its presentation. There is the basic Python way of casting, x = int(x), but there is also a pandas way, which we have previously seen in Section 2.2.2 using `x.astype(int)`. While `int(x)` will throw an error if you give it a string it cannot convert (e.g., `int("tomatoes")`), the two more involved methods (`x.astype(int)` and `pd.to_numeric(x)`) both have an optional parameters such as `errors={co-erce|ignore}` which can be used to handle such instances. Below, let's first make a list of all the `int` and `float` columns in the table. Then we can convert them for further analysis.

```
# I use [:5] for brevity. You can remove it to see all of the columns.
stack_df[stack_df.columns[:5]].head()
```

Id	PostTypeId	AcceptedAnswerId	CreationDate	Score	ViewCount
1	1	2776	2011-11-30T19:15:54.070	31	7679
2	2	NaN	2011-11-30T19:37:10.510	14	NaN
3	1	814	2011-11-30T19:41:14.960	29	1898
4	1	120	2011-11-30T19:42:45.470	59	3648
6	1	21	2011-11-30T19:44:55.593	16	8074

Through some exploring of this table, I have assessed that there are five columns that are currently strings that should be converted into numbers: `Score`, `ViewCount`, `AnswerCount`, `CommentCount`, and `FavoriteCount`. For these, I'll use the `pd.to_numeric()` method with the `errors="coerce"` flag to turn bad data into missing data.

```
for col in ["Score", "ViewCount", "AnswerCount",
            "CommentCount", "FavoriteCount"]:
    stack_df[col] = pd.to_numeric(stack_df[col],errors="coerce")

print(stack_df['Score'].mean())
```

```
7.281544194560669
```

Before we move on, let's have a quick look at how many missing data points we have for each of these different counts. We can count the NaN values to do this. Or rather, by using `x.count()` rather than `len(x)` we get a report of only the *valid* (i.e. non-missing) rows and not all rows.

```
stack_df.describe().style.format("{:0.2f}")
```

	Score	ViewCount	AnswerCount	CommentCount	FavoriteCount
count	61184.00	21504.00	21504.00	61184.00	11729.00
mean	7.28	7319.47	1.65	1.56	1.02
std	11.74	28508.51	1.45	2.42	1.65
min	-24.00	9.00	0.00	0.00	0.00

25%	1.00	383.00	1.00	0.00	0.00
50%	4.00	1306.00	1.00	1.00	1.00
75%	9.00	4817.75	2.00	2.00	1.00
max	324.00	1497835.00	19.00	31.00	39.00

```
tot = len(stack_df)

for col in ["Score", "ViewCount", "AnswerCount",
            "CommentCount","FavoriteCount"]:
    print(f"Missing rows for {col}:", tot - stack_df[col].count())
```

```
Missing rows for Score: 0
Missing rows for ViewCount: 39680
Missing rows for AnswerCount: 39680
Missing rows for CommentCount: 0
Missing rows for FavoriteCount: 49455
```

The fact that ViewCount and AnswerCount both have exactly the same number of missing data suggests that the data is likely missing structurally. By exploring the data and the other columns (even just visually) you should be able to figure out which rows are missing for structural reasons (and what those reasons are).

 ## Cleaning up web data

A lot of data comes from or through the web. Being comfortable with the web, HTML, and web technologies is an important skill in social data science. Often we play up the statistical elements of data science, but that tends to happen once we have the data. Getting the data often involves interfacing with the web in some way, whether it is just using a URL to download an existing dataset, or crawling the web and collecting data as you go. The Stack Exchange dataset can teach us a lot about the challenges that web data can throw up.

The Body column, where the comments are written, is stored as HTML. You will see it sometimes includes URL links, clever HTML formatting, and tags like </p> which mean 'end of paragraph'. We can use this HTML to see how to strip HTML from text from the web.

```
# Remember to set `Id` to the index (and remove the @symbols)
# if you get an error here.
stack_df.loc["2","Body"]
```

```
'<p>According to the <a href="http://www.imdb.com/title/tt0396269/
trivia">trivia on IMDb</a>, Owen Wilson and Vince Vaughn improvised the
"Lock it up!" banter. As I understand it, that also means the other scenes
did not - or only slightly - diverge from the script.</p>\n'
```

10.6.1 Encoding

Fortunately, `xmltodict` is smart enough to handle some encoding issues for us. However, there are some times when instead of seeing "Body=<p>Some comedian/actors are...", we see Body="<p>Some comedian/actors are.... The latter case is what is referred to as *encoded* text. This means that it is converted to a format that the computer can understand, but not necessarily one that a human can understand. There are many forms of encoding, from HTML encoding like that example, to Unicode encoding, which allows a computer to interpret emojis and a multitude of other characters, particularly international characters. Dealing with encoding and decoding can be a real trial. We are going to sidestep it for now using the built-in methods of `pandas`, but you can see a more thorough discussion of encoding and decoding at the beginning of Chapter 11.

10.6.2 Stripping HTML from text

Although `xmltodict` helped to decode the HTML text, so that < turns into <, the actual HTML tags are still present in the text. If we want to read that text, look at a distribution of words, or examine other advanced analytics, we should strip out the HTML tags first.

Below we will use Beautiful Soup in order to extract the text from the HTML. Unlike `pd.to_numeric()`, the `bs4.BeautifulSoup()` method does not deal so easily with missing data, so we will place this parser inside a function and wrap it in a `try`/`except` clause (as an example of 'duck typing' mentioned in Chapter 1).

Previously when we saw Beautiful Soup (to parse XML data) we wanted to treat the soup as an object and ask for things encased in tags, like (`soup.findall("a")`). In this case, we will be using the soup to extract the text *between* the tags with `soup.text` rather than focus on the tags themselves.

You should also notice that I did not simply replace the old data with the cleaned-up text. I chose instead to create a new column, despite this leading to a larger memory footprint. As we are removing the HTML from `Body` here, we are thus removing data. Therefore this time around I create a new column in case we want to revisit this HTML data later. Also notice that below I don't use the HTML parser (`html.parser`). Instead I use the generic XML parser, `lxml`, which will get rid of tags and extract text from either XML or HTML.

```
# Warning - this might take a few seconds to a minute to complete.
import bs4

def robustParse(text):
    try:
        return bs4.BeautifulSoup(text, "lxml").text.replace("\n"," ")
    except:
        return None

stack_df["CleanBody"] = stack_df["Body"].map(robustParse)


display(stack_df[["Body", "CleanBody"]].head())
```

	Body	CleanBody
Id		
1	\<p\>Some comedians / actors are given creative ...	Some comedians / actors are given creative fre...
2	\<p\>According to the \<a href="http://www. imdb.c...	According to the trivia on IMDb, Owen Wilson a...
3	\<p\>In his Star Wars Episode 1 \<a href="https:.../	In his Star Wars Episode 1 review/analysis, Mi...
4	\<p\>I'm a big fan of the Pink Panther movies (t...	I'm a big fan of the Pink Panther movies (the ...
6	\<p\>At the end of the movie, adult Jack (Sean P	At the end of the movie, adult Jack (Sean Penn...

10.6.3 Extracting links from HTML

Having clean data might be good for some text processing later, but it also gets rid of some things that might actually be interesting, such as URLs. This is one of the reasons why it is so important to be non-destructive when we are cleaning data.

Let's return to the original Body with the HTML data in there. How many of these comments link to external sources? In Chapter 4 on file types we explored a relatively cheap way to do this (by detecting :// in text) when examining a Wikipedia page. Alas, when things are cheap you often get what you pay for. By spot-checking the data (i.e. using data scepticism) we can determine that many of those links were messy or interestingly were in fact links *inside* other URLs, like https://web.archive.org/web/20051001053723/http://www.milliondollarhomepage.com/.

Just looking for http will pick up both cases above, but it might pick up some false positives as well. If we want to be strict about it, we can use Beautiful Soup to parse the page as HTML and then we can use the same sort of approach we used in the previous chapter to detect the URLs in the Wikipedia page. Only this time we are going to do it for ~54,000 snippets of text rather than one long single page.

```
# Notice that this will, like above, take a moment to run:
def returnLinks(text):
    try:
        soup = bs4.BeautifulSoup(text, 'html.parser')
        return [x['href'] for x in soup.find_all('a')
                if 'href' in x.attrs and "://" in x.get('href')]
    except:
        return None


# Let's make a new column with a list of all URLs found
stack_df["ListUrl"] = stack_df["Body"].map(returnLinks)


stack_df["ListUrl"].head()
```

```
Id
1                                                                    []
2              [http://www.imdb.com/title/tt0396269/trivia]
3              [https://redlettermedia.com/mr-plinketts-star-...
4              [http://www.imdb.com/title/tt0352520/, http://...
6                                                                    []
Name: ListUrl, dtype: object
```

10.7 Cleaning up lists of data

The `ListUrl` column shares something in common with the tags column. Both really are collections of multiple elements in a single cell. The tags data has not been cleaned yet. To remind you, the tags data looks something like:

```
<plot-explanation><analysis><ending><the-tree-of-life>
```

We could convert it into a list pretty easily by chopping off the first and last characters and then splitting the rest by `"><"`. Let's do that first:

```python
def splitTags(text):
    if type(text) != str:
        return []
    elif len(text) == 0:
        return []
    else:
        return text[1:-1].split("><")

print(stack_df["Tags"][4],end="\n\n")

stack_df["ListTags"] = stack_df["Tags"].map(splitTags)
print(stack_df["ListTags"][4])

<plot-explanation><analysis><ending><the-tree-of-life>

['plot-explanation', 'analysis', 'ending', 'the-tree-of-life']
```

Now we have many tags for every one row. If we wanted to have a dataset where we have one row for each tag (or each link) for each comment, we could `explode` the data as we saw in Chapter 5 on merging. However, before proceeding down that route, I wanted to pause here and use the tags data to help make sense of the entire dataset. First, let's count how many tags are there per row. Since `ListTags` is a column with a list, we can create a `Series` that counts the number of tags in that column, then use `value_counts()`. I'm going to do that in one line of code below:

```python
stack_df["ListTags"].map(len).value_counts().sort_index(ascending=True)
```

```
0      39680
1       4779
2      11264
3       4480
4        861
5        120
Name: ListTags, dtype: int64
```

In this version, 39,680 rows did not have a tag. Look above and you might see that specific number appear elsewhere in the data. It's the number for the missing data for ViewCount and AnswerCount. It seems that actually this table is really multiple classes of data in one, such as question data and answer data. We can see that clearly by doing a value_counts() of PostTypeID. But we are going to go a little further and use what's called a 'crosstab' to reveal some features.

```
pd.crosstab(stack_df['PostTypeId'],stack_df['ListTags'].map(len))
```

List Tags	0	1	2	3	4	5
Post TypeId						
1	0	4779	11264	4480	861	120
2	35380	0	0	0	0	0
4	2137	0	0	0	0	0
5	2137	0	0	0	0	0
6	21	0	0	0	0	0
7	5	0	0	0	0	0

crosstab (short for cross-tabulate) is a like value_counts() but on two or more axes. This allows us to see the subgroups of the data. In this case, it appears there's quite a correlation. If PostTypeId == 1, then there are between one and five tags. If PostTypeId > 1 then there are no tags. Looking at the schema for the Stack Exchange exports (https://meta.stack-exchange.com/questions/2677/), we can see that multiple types of content could be in the Posts.xml dataset, six of which occur herein:

- '1' = Question
- '2' = Answer
- '4' = Tag wiki excerpt
- '5' = Tag wiki
- '6' = Moderator nomination
- '7' = 'Wiki placeholder' (really description of an election).

In fact, going further into the documentation, you can see that someone has helpfully repro-duced the connections between all the tables (not just posts.xml) as a schema diagram (https://sedeschema.github.io/), which can help identify how to link the different tables together (or what keys to use in each table to do so).

Due to different kinds of posts in the same data, we now have identified some structural missing data. For example, if a post is not a question then it cannot have a tag. Thus, if we wanted to convert the tag data to long format, we might want to first remove all the rows with structurally missing data. So below I first report the number of non-missing rows. Then I embed that mask (stack_df['Tags'].notna()) in an explode() statement (introduced in Chapter 5 on merging for turning wide data into long data).

```
print(len(stack_df[stack_df["Tags"].notna()]))
21504
```

```
longtag_stack_df = stack_df[stack_df["Tags"].notna()].explode("ListTags")
display(longtag_stack_df[["ListTags",
                          "Body",
                          "Score",
                          "OwnerUserId"]].head(10))
```

	ListTags	Body	Score	OwnerUserId
Id				
1	wedding-crashers	\<p>Some comedians / actors are given creative ...	31	11
3	analysis	\<p>In his Star Wars Episode 1 \<a href="https:/...	29	41
3	star-wars	\<p>In his Star Wars Episode 1 \<a href="https:/...	29	41
4	comedy	\<p>I'm a big fan of the Pink Panther movies (t...	59	22
4	the-pink-panther	\<p>I'm a big fan of the Pink Panther movies (t...	59	22
6	plot-explanation	\<p>At the end of the movie, adult Jack (Sean P...	16	34
6	analysis	\<p>At the end of the movie, adult Jack (Sean P...	16	34
6	ending	\<p>At the end of the movie, adult Jack (Sean P...	16	34
6	the-tree-of-life	\<p>At the end of the movie, adult Jack (Sean P...	16	34
10	plot-explanation	\<p>Frank Costello the mob boss, one of the mai...	21	11

Because we have transformed the data from long to wide, longtag_stack_df has multiple indices with the same ID, up to five rows (since there were up to five tags in the original (stack_df). If you want to have a unique index here, you can simply use the RangeIndex() method shown earlier, but I would also recommend keeping this existing index as a column in your data with a name like QuestionId.

```
longtag_stack_df['QuestionId'] = longtag_stack_df.index
longtag_stack_df.index = pd.RangeIndex(len(longtag_stack_df))
display(longtag_stack_df[["ListTags",
                          "QuestionId",
                          "OwnerUserID",
                          "Score"]].head(6))
```

	ListTags	QuestionId	OwnerUserId	Score
0	wedding-crashers	1	11	31
1	analysis	3	41	29
2	star-wars	3	41	29
3	comedy	4	22	59
4	the-pink-panther	4	22	59
5	plot-explanation	6	34	16

10 ● 8   Parsing time

There are several columns in the Stack Exchange data that appear to express a specific time. They are presently stored as strings. This includes `CreationDate`, `LastEditDate`, `LastActivityDate`, `ClosedDate`, and `CommunityOwnedDate`. Transforming the data from a string to a `datetime` object can be done the easy way or the hard way. Here we can use the easy way, which is `pd.to_datetime(<Series>)`. This method does a very reliable job of parsing a string and checking for the various elements that make up the date. However, if dates are stored inconsistently (e.g., '2020-10-23' in one row and 'June 20, 2021' in another row), then `pandas` might give inconsistent results.

Sometimes you will need to be more specific when managing time (i.e. the 'hard way'). For example, you might want to parse a string yourself or print one that shows the date in a specific format, such as YYYY-MM-DD. In Python there are a standard set of codes for elements of time, such as a year (%Y), month (%B), day (%D). In Chapter 12, I discuss these codes and show how to use them to parse dates, print dates, manage details like timezones, and resample data within a time period (for charts of daily or monthly frequencies).

```
for col in ["CreationDate", "LastEditDate", "LastActivityDate",
            "ClosedDate", "CommunityOwnedDate"]:
    stack_df[col] = pd.to_datetime(stack_df[col])
    print(f"Number of missing for {col}: ",
          len(stack_df)-stack_df[col].count())
```

```
Number of missing for CreationDate:  0
Number of missing for LastEditDate:  22147
Number of missing for LastActivityDate:  0
Number of missing for ClosedDate:  59144
Number of missing for CommunityOwnedDate:  61118
```

From simply reporting the number of missing data points we can learn a little more about how this forum works. All of the posts appear to have a `CreationDate` and a `LastActivityDate`. There do not seem to be the same number of missing values for multiple columns, so I do not think there are many structural zeros. To understand why a post might have a `ClosedDate` we might want to look at the posts or read the documentation. But now, most importantly, we have five columns in their appropriate format.

To get started on querying by time, simply append .dt to a Series of datetime objects. Then you can append month, hour, or year to slice data down to that month, hour, or year. Observe below how I slice down to 2015, to October (which includes all the years), and in the range referring to one specific day (in this case 'Super Pi Day', March 14, 2015 or 3/14/15 when printed in North American date formatting). Notice that a day is a range since the posts were not created exactly at midnight of 2015-03-14.

```
# Slice by time 1: By Year
year = 2016
cyear = len(stack_df[stack_df["CreationDate"].dt.year == year])
print(f"There were {cyear} posts created in {year}")
```

```
There were 9549 posts created in 2016
```

```
# Time slicing: For one specific day
t1 = '2015-03-14'; t2 = '2015-03-15'
mask = (stack_df["CreationDate"]>= t1) & \
       (stack_df["CreationDate"]< t2)
```

```
print(f"There were {len(stack_df[mask])} posts made between",
      f"{t1} and {t2}")
```

```
There were 22 posts made between 2015-03-14 and 2015-03-15
```

```
type(stack_df["CreationDate"][0])
```

```
pandas._libs.tslibs.timestamps.Timestamp
```

10.9 Regular expressions

Regular expressions are ways that we can specify patterns in text and thereby ask for text according to this pattern rather than for specific characters. This is like a generalisation of the time parser above. In the previous section, we were able to parse strings representing datetimes because they were formatted consistently. The columns did not include Thu, Thursday, Thurs, Jeudi, Donnerstag, etc. They all included the three-letter English abbreviation Thu if it was a Thursday and Mon if it was a Monday. We can say then that the datetime string was *regularly* expressed: it has a consistent pattern that we can denote with *metacharacters* or codes that represent groups of characters. Above, the symbol for day of the week in our datetime parser was %a. Datetime is its own special form of a regular expression, so codes like %M mean minute.

In general regular expression work there is another set of codes for things like 'digit' and 'whitespace'. For example, notice the patterns in these pieces of text:

```
bernie.hogan@oii.ox.ac.uk
bernie.hogan@example.com
steve@apple.com
```

Of course, these are all email addresses. They have some characters including periods, an @ symbol, and some more characters (again including periods). As it turns out, trying to catch every possible variation of email is difficult as there are many possible patterns to catch. However, we can get part of the way there with the examples we have above.

You can use regular expressions for all kinds of tasks, not just detecting email addresses. In the example below we can look for 'new guitar' or 'new drum' by really looking for the pattern new <word>. And the code for a word character in regular expressions is \w. First, let's look for new <word> in some example text, then we will try that on the Stack Exchange data. Then we will look at a couple more complex regular expressions before summarising the chapter.

```
list_Comments = [ "I wanted a new guitar for Christmas, not a new sweater",
                  "I always knew trombones were not for me",
                  "Woohoo! New drums for my kit.",
                  "What to do with my new bass?"]

import re

pattern = re.compile(r"new \w")
for comment in list_Comments:
    print(pattern.findall(comment))

['new g', 'new s']
['new t']
[]
['new b']
```

The results suggest this might need a little finesse. It seems like the regular expressions pattern picked up the word 'new' and a single character from the subsequent word. The reason is that regular expressions tend to only match a single character unless you pair it with a 'greedy' wildcard character. There are two: * for 'one or more' and + for 'zero or more'. So if we want one or more characters in the word, we would use \w* instead of just \w. Observe:

```
pattern = re.compile(r"new \w*")
for comment in list_Comments:
    print(pattern.findall(comment))

['new guitar', 'new sweater']
['new trombones']
[]
['new bass']
```

We missed a couple issues here. We missed New drums because it has an uppercase N. We also picked up new trombones when in fact it was knew trombones and thus not exactly what we were looking for. So how about we tweak it just a little more? We will use the code \b which looks for the boundary of a word and a non-word so that we distinguish new from knew. We also use the re.IGNORECASE argument to attend to n and N. If we wanted to be very fussy and just look out for n and N but the rest stay lower case, we could have used a group [] and placed both letters within it: r"\b[nN]ew \w*".

```
pattern = re.compile(r"\bnew \w*",re.IGNORECASE)
for comment in list_Comments:
    print(pattern.findall(comment))


['new guitar', 'new sweater']
[]
['New drums']
['new bass']
```

10.9.1 Further learning for regular expressions

Here is a partial list of the regular expression codes. There are also many online cheat sheets for regular expressions. Below is a code snippet that checks for the first match of a given metacharacter. You can see in the table below what is the 'first match' of that metacharacter in the example below (Happy Birthday: It's 21 time!).

Table 10.1 Regular expression metacharacters and what they detect from an example phrase

Code	Meaning	First match
\w	any word character	H
\W	any non-word character	
[abc]	any character contained in the string	a
[^abc]	any character *except* those contained	H
\s	any whitespace character	
\S	any non-whitespace character	H
\d	any digit	2
\D	any non-digit	H
*	match zero or more of the previous code	na
+	match one or more of the previous code	na
.	match any character	H

```
# Try the various codes yourself for the text in the example
pattern = "\w"
text = "Happy Birthday: It's 21 time!"
```

```
if re_match := re.compile(pattern).search(text):
    print(re_match[0])
```

H

For practising regular expressions, I am a huge fan of *Regex 101* (https://regex101.com). This site provides an online regular expression tester with lots of additional help. It gives you a place to type in some blob of text, enter a regular expression pattern, and see explanations for why it would or would not match. If you head over there, type the following pattern where it says: 'Insert Regular Expression Here':

```
[\w\.]+@[\w\.]+
```

And in the text below, type the following:

```
Email1: bernie.hogan@oii.ox.ac.uk
Email2: bernie.hogan@example.com
Email3: steve@apple.com
These are emails I found @ "From Social Science to Data Science".
Try below to write a broken email that will still be picked up, such as: .@.
```

You will see that it picks up not just the three emails but also .@.. Can you make it avoid the last one?

10.9.2 Regular expressions and ground truth

Regular expressions are an incredibly tricky part of dealing with data. It is often useful to outsource this task, but sometimes you might need to build your own – for example, if you want to detect a specific word or phrase in a larger corpus while managing things like slight differences in spelling/punctuation. You might need to parse text and there is no readily available parser – for example, at present I could not find a good parser to turn Telegram texts into structured data but I highly anticipate one will appear.

Consider the challenge in parsing email. A dedicated site for regular expressions has some text on this (https://www.regular-expressions.info/email.html). It suggests the following is the lightweight way to collect virtually all email addresses. It does not seem very lightweight to me. It still it might struggle with some very rare but valid cases:

```
email_pattern = "\A[a-z0-9!#$%&'*+/=?^_'{|}~-]+(?:\.[a-z0-9!#$%&'*+/=?^_'{|}~-
]+)*@(?:[a-z0-9](?:[a-z0-9-]*[a-z0-9])?\.)+[a-z0-9](?:[a-z0-9-]*[a-z0-9])?\z"
```

One of the big challenges in this exercise is that you do not necessary know if you got it right or if your regular expression missed something. This is the issue of managing *false positives* (e.g., `"knew trombones"` for `r"new <word>"`) and *false negatives* (e.g., `"New drums"` not picked up because of the upper case N). These are two very important issues in classification, a task that is very similar to what we are doing here. In both cases, we often make an assumption that there exists a *ground truth* for this sort of data.

Ground truth data is data where we are confident in the label or classification of that data before analysis. So in the Stack Exchange data, we have the ground truth of whether a post is a question or an answer. In fact, in Chapter 11 we classify the posts as question or answer and see what we can learn. But what if we have new data that is not labelled? That is where things get tricky. The more complicated the regular text is, the more complicated the regular expression that is required to detect all valid instances. Take, for example, a paper of my own with colleagues on Wikipedia (Graham et al., 2014). We were tasked with determining which content on Wikipedia had latitude and longitude coordinates. But these could have been done in dozens of different styles (and languages). The resulting code is available online (https://github.com/oxfordinternetinstitute/Wikiproject/). The parser, primarily built by Medhat, comes in at over 500 lines of code. Compared to prior work, we found a larger (and not entirely overlapping) set of coordinates, owing to the extensive care we put into the regular expression. The work was considerable and actually took months to cross-check and be confident in, but the reward was an ability get a clear estimate of where in the world is represented on Wikipedia and thus help us understand why some regions are underrepresented. Along the way, we were always trying to balance the collection of false positives with the many (often systematically) missing pages with improperly formatted coordinates in them.

Storing our work

It is a good exercise to take all of the different cleaning approaches that we discussed here, refactor them and then put that in a function or script for future use. We might then use that function to clean a different Stack Exchange dataset. It might have arguments for whether we are parsing a `Posts.xml` or a `Users.xml`, or ways to determine if we want to parse the tags, etc. For our purposes, we should now store the data we have produced so that we can reuse it later.

The next three chapters (on networks, language, and time) will make use of `stack_df`. So if you want to follow along, you should store that data as a file for later use rather than expect to parse it all over again.

```
import pickle

with open(Path.cwd().parent / "data" / "movies_stack_df.pkl",'wb') as fileout:
    fileout.write(pickle.dumps(stack_df))
```

10 11 Summary

The above approaches indicate that when we import data into a table there is still an awful lot of cleaning work to be done to get it into a shape that works for analysis. Recall that above we first got the data into a rectangular shape. Then in order we looked at: index, missing data, proper column data types, reshaping as necessary, and extracting meaningful data (like with regular expressions).

These tasks may seem relatively dull and again far from social science theories, but they are anything but. Virtually all these columns were markers of some element of social life, from the voting to establish quality to the propensity for some people to attract replies while others do not. Our questions then can start to focus on some interesting aspects of social structure. Furthermore, we now get to apply some of the logic of expectations and observations discussed in Chapter 8.

 Further reading

- *Practical Python Data Wrangling and Data Quality* by McGregor (2021). This is a relatively recent book that does an extensive job of considering what signifies quality data and how to sanitise it. It goes through some of the same concepts as this book, but from a very different angle. I especially like the considerations in Chapter 6 on assessing data quality, where McGregor goes into detail with real data about ways to assess data quality issues using concepts such as completeness and timeliness. These sorts of concerns should help shape the bounds of your analyses.

 Extensions and reflections

- The chapter moved through one specific example and then used a pickle at the end to serialise the data for use in later chapters. Try to take all the different steps in the chapter and create a function that does them all. You will know it was done correctly when the `DataFrame` from the pickle matches the `DataFrame` from the function. There is a similar exercise on the book's GitHub page which you can use to compare with your function.
- Consider how to make that function more general. For example, in the Stack Exchange data export there is also a `Users.xml` file which has different columns, but could still be converted to numbers, `datetime` objects, and text. How could the function handle the different column names and types?
- Try to extract email addresses from the `Body` text. Are there any to be found? Did you need to look in a link or use a regular expression? Now seek out a different phrase related to the movies which might conform to a regular pattern and see if you can detect it in multiple different posts. You might want to look for a date, something with numbers (like a movie or its sequel), or a specific URL.

11
INTRODUCING NATURAL LANGUAGE PROCESSING: CLEANING, SUMMARISING, AND CLASSIFYING TEXT

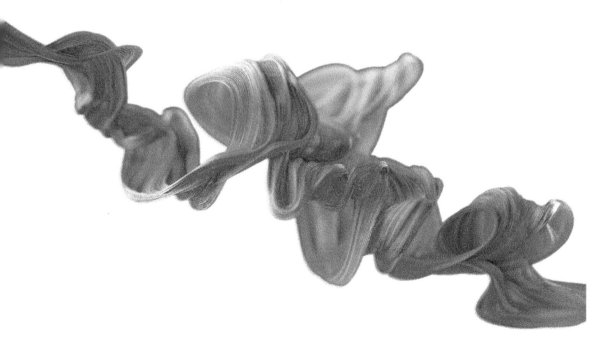

━━━━━━━━━ **Learning goals** ━━━━━━━━━

- Distinguish between decoded visual characters and encoded bytestreams
- Discover strategies for breaking a string of text into words in English
- Consider how to eliminate potentially redundant characters and words
- Show how text can be scored using an example sentiment analysis package
- Explore keywords extracted using TF-IDF
- Explore keywords extracted using a classifier (naïve Bayes).

 Reading language: Encoding text

For many tasks, we will want to transform *language* into *data*. Language is one of the key ways in which humans communicate. As we can appreciate, however, language is not data per se. Language carries information, undoubtedly, but information isn't data either. We might think of information as the resolution of uncertainty (Shannon, 1948). Text, however, is data. Text is an *encoding* of language. It doesn't carry all of the meaning of language, but it also has a number of meaningful features of its own that are worth considering. Text is used in ways that also don't strictly count as language as we would casually understand it. Text can contain measurements. Also, text, unlike language prior to recording media, can be divorced from *context*. More recently, we can encode audio, but we still need to either have a direct analogue mapping (for things like vinyl records and cassettes) or some form of means of encoding the audio signal into digital data (for things like streaming audio and compact discs).

Since the encoding of language has taken place within a variety of historical and cultural trajectories, it represents a highly diverse set of expressions. Depending on your experience with languages around the world, you might be surprised at how cumbersome the management of text can be. Some pretty standard concerns for languages are as follows:

- Am I only going to be collecting data in English? Do I know how to filter in or out other language?
- Are the characters used to represent my language available in a text encoding? These days Unicode has done much to resolve this, but some people will still compromise on words like 'cote' instead of 'côté' as a technological convenience.
- Do the technologies I use support the use of such an encoding by default? For example, the interfaces for selecting Chinese ideograms or Korean language boxes are not as direct as the QWERTY keyboard. Some languages are not supported physically at all, such as Canadian Aboriginal syllabics, used to encode a variety of First Nations languages. I have trouble finding an actual keyboard offering it, only a soft keyboard mapping, virtual keyboard, or some plastic overlay.
- How to manage the presentation of languages that run in different directions from English (and Python, which is implicitly in English)? Hebrew and Arabic run from right to left. Far Eastern languages such as Japanese and Chinese are sometimes represented from top to bottom.

11.1.1 Key definitions in text

To address issues with language, we first have to ensure that we can correctly read the text that represents that language. Text on your computer is comprised of a number of different elements, all of which work together to produce the symbols that we view and analyse to reconstruct language. Below is some terminology that we can use to distinguish the technical aspects of text representation.

- *Characters*. These are the individual symbols that we string together to make something meaningful. These symbols are understood culturally and linguistically, for example knowing that 'a', 'a' `(monospaced)`, and 'A' all refer to the same alphabetical character.
- *Glyphs*. These are the actual visual representations of the characters. They change from font to font and from system to system. So in the example above, a, A, and a are the same character, but are shown using different glyphs.
- *Font*. The set of glyphs representing characters, such as Helvetica and Courier.
- *Character points*. Each character you see on a screen rendered in a font has a character point. In ASCII there are the initial 128 such points, whereas in Unicode there are millions. Many of these character points aren't used yet.
- *Bytestrings*. When the computer reads some encoded fonts it is reading bytestrings. When it decodes these it turns them into glyphs on the screen. The collections of bytestrings that are stored and read by the computer are *bytestreams*.
- *Encoding*. A technology for mapping characters in a variety of languages, literally termed a *character encoding*. Prior to Unicode there was the introduction of a variety of encodings other than ASCII, such as Latin-1, KOI-7 (https://en.wikipedia.org/wiki/KOI-7), and ISO-8859-1. Unicode tends to be associated with two specific encodings: UTF-8 and, less commonly, UTF-16.
- *Unicode*. The namespace of the Unicode character map managed by the Unicode Consortium (https://en.wikipedia.org/wiki/Unicode_Consortium) under the Institute of Electrical and Electronics Engineers. Note that this means we can have both standard and non-standard Unicode as the empty cells on the character map get occupied (e.g., by combinations to represent skin tones 👋 👋 👋 👋 👋 👋 ; same-sex families 👪 👪 and non-binary people emojis 🧑 vs. 🧑 vs. 🧑). These often get adopted as official standards.
- *UTF-8 and UTF-16*. Specific implementations of the Unicode character map encoding. UTF-8 uses variable width 8-bit (1-byte) code units. The first 128 characters correspond to ASCII, the rest represent various character sets in Unicode. UTF-16 uses one or two fixed-width 16-bit code words. Thus, UTF-16 is a different approach, not a doubling of the UTF-8 code space.
- *Hex codes*. Hex is a term for codes in base 16. It's used by systems instead of base 10 for some encoding tasks as it more easily represents the underlying binary but in a more condensed form. It uses `0, 1, …, 9, a, b ,…, f` to represent 0, 1, …, 16. So 27 in base 10 would be 1b in base 16 or hex. When we see the bytestring from UTF, we will see hex codes:

```
hex(27)
```

```
'0x1b'
```

In Python, text is stored in the computer in bytestreams. These are how the computer uses some basic letters and numbers to construct the text you see. A Unicode bytestream, if you were to see it directly, would look more like `b'\xf0\x9f\x98\x82'` than 😂. You typically will not be exposed to bytestreams directly, but it does happen when files are not encoded or decoded properly. When you want to *encode* text you turn it into a bytestring or character point for the computer to store. When you want to read a character, the computer will *decode* that bytestring and show you the glyph associated with that character. We are encoding for the computer, which will map said codes on to characters in a character map, then find the glyph associated with that character from a font set to display as a letter.

```
print("a",ord("a"))
```

```
a 97
```

```
# 0 through 32 do not show up below or are whitespace, so they are omitted
for i in range(33,127): print(chr(i),end="")
```

```
!"#$%&'()*+,-./0123456789:;<=>?@ABCDEFGHIJKLMNOPQRSTUVWXYZ[\]^_`abcdefg
hijklmnopqrstuvwxyz{|}~
```

Remember when dealing with any Unicode matters that encoding (e.g., `<text>.encode("utf-8")`) means coding it for a computer's use, taking the thing we read and turning it into the code points for the computer, and decoding (e.g., `<text>.decode("utf-8")`) means turning bytes of data (e.g., `b'\xf0\x9f\x91\x8d'`) into the appropriate glyph for our use 👍. The glyph is the specific visual representation of a character and not the code point. Of course, it is worth noting that glyphs can vary between systems. Following Miller et al. (2017), we might consider how these differences can be large enough to affect visual understanding.

11●2 From text to language

Recall that the goal of using text is typically to understand language. Natural language processing (NLP) and the related domain of computational linguistics can make use of a vast array of signals in language as data. Some of these are particularly hard to manage computationally (like the stance of a speaker when they use a lot of negatives), but others are quite straightforward (whether a word is a noun or a verb).

The most basic NLP work is more literal. It tends to involve the regularisation of text (with 'A' and 'a' referring to the same character) or assume some homogeneous feature of text (i.e. that a word has a measurable and consistent 'sentiment'). Specialist approaches beyond the scope of this book will be able to add considerable nuance to this picture as we learn from not just grammatical conventions but statistical distributions of text. We use TF-IDF scores as a taster of that. More involved approaches tend to make use of machine learning techniques. Recently, transformer models have been popular tools. They are models trained on huge volumes of text that can be used to predict sensible combinations of words. Using such models, one can not only check grammar and predict autocorrect but also compose essays and converse. Due to many successes in computational linguistics, it is now possible to create chatbots that are virtually indistinguishable from human strangers based on such sophisticated language models (Warwick and Shah, 2016). We will only get a taster of that here as the goal will be to make sense of a corpus, not build a bot.

Below we will work with the `stack_df` that we created in Chapter 10. At the end of the chapter we pickled that data, so we can load the cleaned data below. The website for this book also has a notebook for downloading and processing the most recent version of the Stack Exchange on the Internet Archive. You can run it to create a similar pickle file if needed.

```
import pickle
from pathlib import Path

data_dir = Path().cwd().parent / "data"
pickle_file = data_dir / "movies_stack_df.pkl"

if pickle_file.exists():
    stack_df = pickle.load(open(pickle_file ,'rb'))
    print(stack_df.shape)
else:
    print("Please download and clean the Stack_df data as done in Chapter 10",
          "The data is available from",
          "https://archive.org/download/stackexchange")
```

(61184, 24)

11 3   A sample simple NLP workflow

Natural language processing concerns itself with interpreting the meaning in text. Thus, we move from distributions of words to the semantics of words from those distributions. This is a domain that has seen and will continue in the coming years to see rapid growth. Every conference, it seems, will introduce a new machine learning model to detect or infer some aspect of language and meaning from text. The goal in the second half of this chapter will be more modest. We will introduce four tools for NLP workflows that will hopefully get you on your way:

- *Text cleaning* approaches (stemming, lemmatisation, stop words, metatext)
- *Sentiment analysis* as a text summarisation technique
- *TF-IDF* as an information retrieval technique
- *naïve Bayes classifier* as a way to learn from text and classify texts.

These four approaches can really help to provide some meaningful descriptions of a text or ways of distinguishing texts pretty quickly. Note that classification is one of the most active areas of research in machine learning and that naïve Bayes is it itself a very old and simple approach. More recent approaches are much more complex but tend to be far hungrier with data and processing, such as transformer models.

In this chapter I'll be using the Python library `nltk` or the natural language toolkit. This library comes with the Anaconda distribution of Python and so it is pretty reliable to get up and running. That said, other compelling libraries exist and are worth checking out, such as spaCy (https://spacy.io), which extends a lot of `nltk`. Later on when I prepare the data for the naïve Bayes classifier you will see that `nltk`'s version is not quite the easiest to work with.

11.3.1 Preprocessing text

In Chapter 10 we cleaned a dataset in a way that converted strings and floats into more meaningful types, such as lists (using `split()`), HTML-free text (using `bs4`), numbers (using `pd.to_numeric()`), and `datetime` objects (using `pd.to_datetime()`). We will now need to do some further processing in order to make some statistical claims about the data. These steps are often considered preprocessing. They would be the first part of a 'pipeline' that takes the raw data in a `DataFrame` (or simpler structure like a list of documents) and transforms it first into the right chunks and then performs some analysis on the data.

Much of this approach here relies on a 'bag of words' approach. A 'bag of words' is a simplified way of thinking of a text as an unstructured collection of words. So with the sentence 'It was the best of times, it was the worst of times', we can split the text and look at the distribution of words without much concern for their order. In further work, you will see people employ more complex preprocessing that includes things like *n*-grams (numbers of word pairs, word triplets, etc.) or complete phrases. Below when we talk about multiple texts we will call them documents regardless of whether they refer to tweets, posts, comments, headings, etc.

Word tokenisation

Splitting a document into unique words and punctuation marks is referred to as 'tokenisation'. The simplest way to do this in English is by space. This is pervasive in most languages derived from Latin. Other languages have other means of tokenisation, depending on the context of words or their arrangement. For some languages where spaces are not as relevant, this can be a considerable challenge to get right across dialects and everyday speech. For example, AraBERT uses the recent BERT neural network models to improve Arabic tokenisation as well as word prediction (Antoun et al., 2020). Even within English, there are still some choices to make and simply splitting by space is insufficient. Observe:

```
import pandas as pd

s = "It was the best of times, it was the worst of times"

pd.Series(s.split(" ")).value_counts()

was     2
the     2
of      2
It      1
best    1
```

```
times,   1
it       1
worst    1
times    1
dtype: int64
```

From the `value_counts()` we can see some of the inadequacies of such a mechanistic approach. First, it includes punctuation. Notice that `times` and `times,` were considered separate. Second, it is case-sensitive when the meaning of words might not be, so `It` and `it` were counted separately.

We can resolve the punctuation and case issues mechanistically as well, but we want to pause here and be a bit thoughtful. Do `Mother` and `mother` mean the same thing? Capitalisation both refers to syntax and semantics, since title case is reserved for proper nouns but it also occurs at the start of sentences. Thus, using `lower()` might conflate these. This issue is not easily remedied using simple approaches, so we have to treat it, for now, as an edge case.

In order to break up the document, we can do tokenisation. A tokeniser usually does not rely on a single rule, but a number of them in concert (often through algorithms based on regular expressions). Below I use a conventional one that splits out punctuation and parts of words separately.

```
from nltk.tokenize import wordpunct_tokenize
```

```
result = wordpunct_tokenize(s)
pd.Series(result).value_counts()
```

```
was     2
the     2
of      2
times   2
It      1
best    1
,       1
it      1
worst   1
dtype: int64
```

Notice it handled the comma but not the case sensitivity. We can do that ourselves by first passing `s.lower()` rather than `s`, so long as we are comfortable with the risks of clobbering proper nouns. To keep the apostrophes with the text you can use `word_tokenize()` instead of `wordpunct_tokenize()`. And `nltk` has more complex tokenisers to explore as well.

Stop words

Notice that the text above included a number of words that typically are not very informative, like `it` and `was`. These are called *stop words* (Nothman et al., 2018). It is common, but not necessary, to remove stop words before further statistical processing. Note that sometimes there are theoretically meaningful reasons to keep stop words in. For example, in my own work on men's issues online (LaViolette and Hogan, 2019), when classifying the pro- and anti-feminist groups, the inclusion of 'her' and 'she' was actually informative as the anti-feminist group tended to use these pronouns much more than expected.

Generally, however, our analyses are greatly simplified by the removal of stop words. Below, observe that I load the `stopwords` package, set it to English, and then use a list comprehension to filter the words from the corpus.

```python
import nltk
# nltk.download("stopwords")
from nltk.corpus import stopwords

stopWords = set(stopwords.words('english'))

result_filtered = [word for word in result
                   if (word.lower() not in stopWords) and word.isalpha()]

pd.Series(result_filtered).value_counts()

times     2
best      1
worst     1
dtype: int64
```

From the result we are left with the words `times` (twice), `worst`, and `best`. Notably, writing 'times times best worst' in a search engine will still almost certainly get the quote from Dickens. This suggests to me that we have zeroed in on some useful information while removing some details (and sadly most of the lyricism).

Stemming and lemmatisation

Words in English, like in many languages, have alternative variations for different contexts. Typically verbs are conjugated, so that 'jump', 'jumps', 'jumping', and 'jumped' all refer to variations on the verb 'jump'. There are also modifications such as plurals for nouns. Filtering down to the core of these modifications is called *stemming*. There are a number of stemmers available. `PorterStemmer` is a conventional one. As there is not much to stem in that Dickens phrase, I'll make up another one for illustration purposes.

```python
from nltk import PorterStemmer

text = '''After running for office, his campaign office ran a huge tab
for the victory party. But with finances officially in trouble, his
finance officer ran away stating "it was a good run"!'''

tokens = wordpunct_tokenize(text)
```

```
tokens_filtered = [word.lower() for word in tokens
                    if (word.lower() not in stopWords) and word.isalpha()]

porter = PorterStemmer()
stemlist = [porter.stem(t) for t in tokens_filtered]

pd.Series(stemlist).value_counts()

offic       3
run         2
ran         2
financ      2
campaign    1
huge        1
tab         1
victori     1
parti       1
offici      1
troubl      1
away        1
state       1
good        1
dtype: int64
```

Notice that the stemmer isn't perfect by any means. For example, 'ran' is the past tense of 'run', which was not picked up, but it did pick up on 'run' versus 'running'. One of the challenges with stemming is that sometimes the words that are stemmed actually do mean something different. Thus a more cautious approach might be to use *lemmatisation* rather than stemming. This approach is a little more involved, but it uses some context around the words to more faithfully gauge what should be the 'root' version. Notice in the list that the stem for some words is a bit peculiar, such as officer and office being stemmed as offic but officially as offici. Lemmatisation can avoid that but it does take up more resources. That said, it can often use parts of speech to infer some important variations of words and also report the human-readable root rather than the stem.

```
# nltk.download('wordnet')
# nltk.download('omw-1.4')
from nltk.stem import WordNetLemmatizer

wlemma = WordNetLemmatizer()

lemmadf = pd.DataFrame(tokens_filtered, columns=["Word"])
lemmadf['Lemma'] = lemmadf["Word"].map(
                    lambda word: wlemma.lemmatize(word, pos="v"))
lemmadf[:12].style.hide(axis="index")
```

Word	Lemma
running	run
office	office
campaign	campaign
office	office
ran	run
huge	huge
tab	tab
victory	victory
party	party
finances	finance
officially	officially
trouble	trouble

Lemmatisation seems a little better but it is not perfect either. In this case, it distinguished the three `offic*` as different words, but it combined the multiple meanings of 'ran', 'run', and 'running' as 'run'. Also notice that we considered derivations based on 'parts of speech' with the `pos` parameter. In this case, I suggested that we should consider conjugating verbs using `pos='v'`. There are other parts of speech options worth investigating that might work better in other circumstances.

With the extraneous text sifted and the words made consistent, it is then possible to do some analyses where we give the document itself a score, compare or classify documents, or consider some interesting features of the words in a collection of documents.

 ## NLP approaches to analysis

Below are three introductory approaches to the analysis of text in NLP. The first shows how to 'score' a document, in this case using the VADER sentiment analyser. The second gives words scores based on a popular keyword retrieval algorithm. The third classifies documents using the frequency of words in the document. For each you will notice that most of the challenge is in getting the data in the right shape. So below, notice how I use a number of tricks for reshaping data from a `Series` into the sort of form each algorithm expects.

11.4.1 Scoring documents with sentiment analysis

Scoring documents will permit us to sort, sift, and classify documents according to the scoring criteria. We might want to ask if the scores of documents increase over time or correlate with some other variable related to the author of the document, the context, or some other measure. One way to score the documents is to use a sentiment analyser. These range from the most rudimentary bag of words approach to recent APIs based on neural networks, like Google's Perspective API (https://perspectiveapi.com).

The simplest sentiment analysis approach is to first assume each word has a score, so for example, 'smile' is 0.8 on the happy scale, and 'cloud' is 0. Then you count all the words that have a score and take the average. More complex approaches might take into account punctuation, ALL CAPS, repetition, and word order. This is the approach of VADER, a sentiment analysis package designed for tweets. It uses scores for specific words and some modifiers for grammar. The algorithm is pretty readable in their code and has been published in academic work (Hutto and Gilbert, 2014). Yet, it is not perfect, and it will not catch complex negations or local variants of words, as we show below.

VADER is inspired by an earlier package called `liwc` (pronounced 'Luke'), which has extensive sorts of text quantification beyond positive and negative (Tausczik and Pennebaker, 2010). The LIWC platform (https://www.liwc.app/) is worth checking out for the variety of scores possible beyond positive and negative, but it is unfortunately not for free.

```
try:
    import vaderSentiment
except ModuleNotFoundError:
    import sys
    !{sys.executable} -m pip install vaderSentiment
    import vaderSentiment
```

I will first use VADER on a few synthetic sentences to give you a sense of what makes it give a very high or low value.

```
from vaderSentiment.vaderSentiment import SentimentIntensityAnalyzer

analyzer = SentimentIntensityAnalyzer()

texts = ["Wow I'm feeling great today, the weather is lovely. HOORAY!!!",
         "I would be lying if I said this was a really bad day",
         "I would not be lying if I said this was a really bad day",
         "Hey bro! Those sick beats brought down the house!"]

for i in texts:
    print(i, analyzer.polarity_scores(i), sep="\n", end="\n\n")

Wow I'm feeling great today, the weather is lovely. HOORAY!!!
{'neg': 0.0, 'neu': 0.216, 'pos': 0.784, 'compound': 0.959}

I would be lying if I said this was a really bad day
{'neg': 0.375, 'neu': 0.625, 'pos': 0.0, 'compound': -0.8016}

I would not be lying if I said this was a really bad day
{'neg': 0.204, 'neu': 0.646, 'pos': 0.149, 'compound': -0.254}

Hey bro! Those sick beats brought down the house!
{'neg': 0.327, 'neu': 0.673, 'pos': 0.0, 'compound': -0.5972}
```

VADER's scores originally were based on data from labelled tweets (as a form of 'ground truth' as mentioned in the Chapter 10). Notice how the negation changes the scores of the second and third text. Also notice that the vernacular phrases 'bring down the house' and 'sick beats' are not classed as positive by VADER. Scoring those as positive might require a more complex model than VADER.

In many cases, whether you are using sentiment analysis, or something more complex like Google's Perspective API, you will be sending a function some text and returning a score. From there we again are likely to want to examine a distribution and compare them.

Below I show how to apply the sentiment analyser to a `DataFrame`. Recall that the results from the algorithm were a dictionary with four entries. There are thus a few ways to reshape that data. The way I do it below is to create a `Series` of results using a `map` statement. Since this is a `Series` of dictionaries, I borrow from `json_normalize()`, which turns the `Series` into a `DataFrame` with four columns (one for `neg`, `neu`, `pos`, and `compound`) and then I concatenate that `DataFrame` to the original one.

One important note here. For this book, you'll see that I sample 2000 rows and do the sentiment analysis on them. That's because this is slow and I wanted to simply show the technique. In published work, it might be prudent to use all the rows, or even use a *resampling* strategy (where you select the rows in small randomised batches).

```
sample_df = stack_df.sample(2000,random_state=12345).copy()

senti_sr = sample_df["CleanBody"].map(
    lambda text: analyzer.polarity_scores(text))

senti_df = pd.json_normalize(senti_sr)
senti_df.index = senti_sr.index

sample_df = pd.concat([sample_df, senti_df],axis=1)

display(sample_df[["CleanBody", "pos", "neg"]].head())
```

Id	CleanBody	pos	neg
74465	Season 4 episode 8: Alan at the psychiatrist s...	0.000000	0.000000
105929	No. It does not. Near the end of the film, Ana...	0.087000	0.071000
89621	It's not like Salazar and his crew are complet...	0.058000	0.110000
55084	Every now and again, we don't get through all ...	0.103000	0.062000
23203	I found a bit of information about the Nielsen...	0.052000	0.037000

With the raw material in hand, we can now start to think about how to use sentiment analysis to predict another measure. We might correlate it with another variable (e.g., does negativity correlate with a low score? Have comments become more positive over time?). We might check how the scores differ between different groups (e.g., are movies from one franchise associated with more positive content than movies from another?). Overall, I expect the signal from sentiment analysis to be noisy and faint even if it's a good starting point to think about how we evaluate text at scale.

11.4.2 Extracting keywords: TF-IDF scores

The approaches above took each blob of text as separate. Thus, the sentiment scores for one row of our table did not have an effect on the sentiment scores for another row. However, if we want to summarise some of the text, it might be useful to take into account some distributions across the rows.

A now classic approach to summarising key words (and particularly in information retrieval) is *TF-IDF*, or 'term frequency – inverse document frequency'. Term frequency measures how common a word is. That in itself might be revealing, but often generic words like 'the' and 'is' tend to show up at the top. By offsetting the term frequency by how many documents the word is in, the results tend to be more revealing (Jones, 1972). So if you run it on words from a series of political tweets, it will likely highlight 'left', 'right', 'voting', and some names of politicians and parties from that context.

Below I show how to employ the version of TF-IDF that is included in the popular Python package `scikit-learn`. More details about this version can be found in the package documentation (https://scikit-learn.org/stable/modules/feature_extraction.html).

We start again with the `Series CleanBody` from the smaller `sample_df`. To assess which words we want to include we now have to first preprocess the data. Then, similarly to above, once we get the scores, we will have to do some work to get them in a form we want. Below I have created my own preprocessor as a function. You will notice that a lot of these are also arguments for some algorithms. For example, `TfidfVectorizer` shown below has arguments for stop words and a custom tokeniser. When fine-tuned it will work a little faster than what I have below. Regardless, it does not hurt to specify exactly what you are doing in preprocessing. Also, I will reuse this function again in the section below on text classification.

```python
# As a convenience, all the imports needed for this function
import pandas as pd
from nltk.stem import WordNetLemmatizer
from nltk.corpus import stopwords
from nltk.tokenize import wordpunct_tokenize
from sklearn.feature_extraction.text import TfidfVectorizer

def clean_text(text, lower_case = True, stop_words = True,
               lemma = True, join_words = " "):

    if lower_case: text = text.lower()

    tokens = [x for x in wordpunct_tokenize(text) if x.isalpha()]

    if stop_words:
        tokens = [word for word in tokens
                  if word not in stopwords.words('english')]
    if lemma:
        tokens = [WordNetLemmatizer().lemmatize(word,pos='v')
                  for word in tokens]
```

```
    if join_words:     return join_words.join(tokens)
      else:                return tokens


documents = sample_df["CleanBody"].map(clean_text)
```

Notice that I again use the sample data, now as a preprocessed `Series` called `documents`. I am using a relatively simplified approach here where I create a matrix of words by documents. This will be a very large matrix. A lot of work goes into simplifying and minimising the calculation of large matrices in this sort of work. Some extensions of this work can be found in the `scikit-learn` documentation. For example, you can limit the number of features or otherwise fine-tune performance.

```
from sklearn.feature_extraction.text import TfidfVectorizer


vectorizer = TfidfVectorizer()


wordmat = vectorizer.fit_transform(documents).todense()
```

At this point we have a word matrix (`wordmat`). It is large and will have scores for each word in each document. These are then summed, so we have collection of scores per word (`.sum(axis=0)`). But this is a one-dimensional matrix, which, like a list, simply has a position. To make it useful, we can first get the list of words that correspond to each position (`vectorizer.get_feature_names_out()()`) and then use this to make a `Series`. However, one teensy issue is that a `Series` does not seem to like a one-dimensional matrix as input. So I use `<matrix>.A1` which transforms it into an array in the appropriate shape. Then we can query for the most distinct words. Have a look:

```
tfidf_scores = wordmat.sum(axis=0)


wordlist = vectorizer.get_feature_names_out()
top_words = pd.Series(tfidf_scores.A1, index=wordlist)


top_words.sort_values(ascending=False)[:10]
```

```
movie     40.471016
film      37.397752
would     34.719049
know      32.913460
one       32.505876
show      31.135298
like      30.643401
see       30.517230
time      30.006641
get       29.471909
dtype: float64
```

TF-IDF can become a baseline metric for later work. Imagine running it on a yearly basis – do the keywords change over the years? Or what about using it to classify different groups based on how commonly they use different words? TF-IDF comes with a number of caveats: what if documents are of different length, or what if you change the number of features or documents you consider? These should not discourage you, but invite you to think of how you can further refine your own analyses.

11.4.3 Text classification

A vast amount of work in data science involves classifying text. We might want to classify a specific word, sentence, or text blob. The classification itself might be based on statistical features of the text, human annotations, or black box features based on neural networks (King et al., 2017). The results of such a classification can figure in social science analysis either as a set of explanatory or response variables. Given the breadth of potential approaches, it would be challenging and trivialising to summarise them all here. But there are a few core distinctions with these models that are worth considering:

1   *A binary classification.* A binary classification would be the simplest text classification. Herein, we can think of words, sentences, or text blobs as having a true or false value, for example representing 'is this content hate speech?' A classic example of a binary classification is a naïve Bayes classifier, which will be shown below.

2   *A discrete or overlapping classification.* A discrete classification assigns text to either one class or another. An overlapping classification will give text some value of how much it links to some classification. So we might classify a tweet as being 0.6 in group 1, 0.8 in group 2, 0.1 on group 3. If we create some sort of cut-off, then we can often filter the documents from the overlapping groups into the group that best represents some cluster of documents. This is what we commonly see with latent Dirichlet allocation (LDA), an approach often associated with *topic modelling* (Blei et al., 2003). In LDA, each text blob is assigned to one mutually exclusive group but the number of groups is pre-determined.

3   *An inductive or trained classification.* Naïve Bayes and LDA are inductive classifiers. They do not make assumptions about the values of words and only work on their distributions in the documents you give them. Trained classifiers, on the other hand, work like the sentiment analysis scoring above. You take a document and, based on some external pre-training, make an assessment of whether this document should similarly be classified. In computer vision you can train on whether a photo has a face or not, but the face detection algorithm is already trained on previous faces (potentially poorly). Neural network approaches often involve pre-trained classifiers. In text classification, there is a lot of interest in the use of transformer models, as already mentioned above with respect to Arabic word tokenisation. TweetBERT, for example, has shown promise in use for models classifying tweets (Qudar and Mago, 2020) but this work is evolving rapidly (Kirk et al., 2021). Jurafsky and Martin (2021, Chapter 10) review a number of approaches to deep learning in NLP.

Text classification is not as common in social science as in other domains. I contend this is partially due to the emphasis in classification on *prediction* rather than *explanation*. Normally in text classification studies there is an interest in how to make the classification the best it can be. For example, in the case of hate speech, we might think of an advance that makes a classifier more effective. But that advance might be about a different algorithm that increases a goodness-of-fit metric (such as F_1 score). For some disciplines that is an innovation, but for others, the nature of hate speech or how to explain it using other measurable variables is more desirable. Within this discipline, I consider the paper by Röttger et al. (2021) to be an engaging look at how to compare text classifiers on the very challenging but relevant issue of hate speech. Thinking more broadly, Hofman et al. (2017) expand on the challenges of navigating prediction- and explanation-based approaches in data science and propose an integrated approach that shows theoretical promise.

Naïve Bayes classifier as an example

To run a naïve Bayes classifier we split our text into several groups. The goal of such a classifier is to have (in the binary case) some way of marking text as either 0 or 1. This might be text from two political parties, two subreddits, hate speech/not hate speech, etc. Often we split the data into multiple sets: a training set and a testing set (and sometimes a 'holdout' set, but not in naïve Bayes). We then feed the training data into the classifier. It associates some features (in this case some word counts) with the 0 class and some features with the 1 class. Then you can feed in new documents and it will predict whether they belong in the 0 or the 1 class. If the new documents are already labelled with 0 or 1 we can check how well our classifier did. If it did perfectly well, all the 0 texts will be in the 0 class and all the 1 texts will be in the 1 class.

From a research perspective, why would we classify if we already have labels?

- *Feature extraction.* Finding out which words are most distinctive between the two sets is interesting.
- *Scalability.* You might have 1000 things labelled but have a context with many thousands. This might be like labelling content in a politics forum. If your classifier is good then you might want to deploy it on a much larger scale.
- *Resampling differences.* If your classifier works better when you bias your sampling of documents in one way rather than another, then you can learn something about that bias (e.g., instead of a random sample, perhaps we preferentially sample the more upvoted content).
- *Comparing algorithms.* Admittedly not the most interesting in social science, but we might want to check some newer algorithm. For example, the words which are most distinctive might actually vary between algorithms as might the quality of the classification.

Below we will test whether we can tell if a blob of text is coming from a question or an answer in our Stack Exchange. In order to do this, we have to preprocess some data as well as partition our data into training and testing data. In this case, we want words as separate elements in a list per document. We also want to be able to distinguish the documents according to a label. In this case we will take question and answer from `PostTypeId`, and tokenise the body text to compare between questions and answers. Because of the expectations of the classifier we are using, we want to have the text as separate elements in a list per document rather than as a single string per document.

```
from nltk import NaiveBayesClassifier,classify


nbc_df = stack_df[(stack_df["PostTypeId"]=='1') |
                  (stack_df["PostTypeId"]=='2')] \
                 [["PostTypeId","CleanBody"]][:2000]
```

```
nbc_df["CleanTokens"] = nbc_df["CleanBody"].map(
                        lambda x: clean_text(x,join_words=False))
```

In addition to limiting to the first 2000 rows (a somewhat arbitrary choice), I will filter down to words that appear six or more times. There are over 12,000 unique words in the preprocessed corpus. Limiting it to more frequently used words should help simplify the calculation and remove some noise.

To filter the words, first I take the `Series` with all the body text split up as lists (`CleanTokens`) and combine it into one long list using (`nbc_df.["CleanTokens"].sum()`). Here I use `Counter` for the first time. It is like `value_counts()` but for lists. The result is a dictionary of the form `{<word1>:<count1>, <word2>:<count2>, ...}` so I turn it back into a `Series` and filter to `count >= 6`.

```
from collections import Counter

min_count = 6

all_words = pd.Series(Counter(nbc_df["CleanTokens"].sum()))

print(f"{len(all_words)} words in total.",
      f"{len(all_words[all_words >= min_count])} appear at least",
      f"{min_count} times.")

above_min_words = frozenset(all_words[all_words >= min_count].index)
```

```
12748 words in total. 3263 appear at least 6 times.
```

When I limit to six or more occurrences it gives us 3263 unique words, which is a lot (but it's worth trying with even more or other ways of grouping synonyms). Here's a tricky part for this algorithm. It excepts data of the form:

```
[(<{features}>,<group>),
 (<{features}>,<group>),
 ... ]
```

This again shows how much wrangling we need to do to manage this work. The `features` dictionary uses the `top_6words` as keys and `True` or `False` for whether they are in that document (done using `{i:i in set(x) for i in top5_words}`). This means we create a 3263-element dictionary in each row and we have 2000 rows. Then we also say whether the document is in the 0 or 1 group.

```
features = nbc_df["CleanTokens"].map(lambda x:
                   {i:i in set(x) for i in above_min_words})

print(nbc_df["PostTypeId"].value_counts())
feature_list = list(zip(features, nbc_df["PostTypeId"]))
```

```
2     1192
1      808
Name: PostTypeId, dtype: int64

train_set, test_set = feature_list[:1000], feature_list[1000:]
classifier = NaiveBayesClassifier.train(train_set)

print(classify.accuracy(classifier, test_set))
print(classifier.show_most_informative_features(5));

0.666
Most Informative Features
                  wiki = True              2 : 1      =        8.1 : 1.0
               anybody = True              1 : 2      =        7.2 : 1.0
             excellent = True              2 : 1      =        6.3 : 1.0
                  tone = True              2 : 1      =        6.3 : 1.0
               disease = True              1 : 2      =        6.2 : 1.0
None
```

The classifier has an accuracy of 0.67, which is not bad but not particularly impressive. If you cynically guessed `"PostTypeId" == 2` for all of them, you would get an accuracy of 1192/2000 = 0.60. Perhaps more data would make the classifier more effective, or perhaps questions and answers do not substantially differ in the propensity to use different words. Further, naïve Bayes is not known to be the best classifier, with others such as random forests, support vector machines, and logistic regression approaches all having their advantages. Finally, it's worth noting that we not only did a naïve Bayes classification, we did it on a naïve sample – the first 2000 valid rows. If we filtered the rows down in more meaningful ways, we might find it easier to classify highly upvoted and highly downvoted content.

Having said that, even without much of an impressive showing, we can still see some interesting things in the most informative features. `wiki` is eight times more common in an answer than a question while `anybody` is seven times more common in a question than an answer. But this is just the start of a journey in natural language processing.

11.5 Summary

This chapter started by distinguishing text as characters which can be encoded for computers, and language which has meaning and structure for humans. I discussed how we often need to clean text in order to make use of it, which might involve considering different encodings (such as Unicode) and ways of breaking up text (tokenising). Then we considered how to reduce noise by removing common words and ensuring words that have the same meaning but different syntax (like 'jump', 'jumps', and 'jumped') are all counted similarly using either stemming or lemmatisation. Then with these words in hand, we looked at a few approaches to gathering information from data in natural language processing.

The first approach was to score the text. This is usually done by taking existing scores for specific words on some meaningful axis. A prevailing axis is 'sentiment', so we might score a text as having really negative sentiment or really positive sentiment. This approach is often superficial but can have some use. Then we showed how to use TF-IDF scores (essentially a complex way of counting the frequency of words) to extract keywords. These are usually helpful in describing text. Finally, we used a classifier to *learn* which words to expect in one group as opposed to another. The classifier then reported on which words were really likely to distinguish one kind of text (a question) from another kind of text (an answer). The results were not great, but they were a start.

This is the first of a number of chapters demonstrating core data science skills, the next being time-series, networks, and geography. To me, the discussion in every one of these chapters is too brief. But my hope is that it helps tame some of the more formidable aspects of trying to make a quantitative claim from existing data.

From here, you might want to extend this work by thinking of more involved approaches to classification and prediction, such as word embeddings (which looks at similarities between words), transformer models (or predicting text from a pre-trained corpus), LDA (to group text in separate thematic bins), and support vector machines (to classify text with more nuance than naïve Bayes). I want to think of this as a place to get you started and to appreciate the scale of both the challenge and the opportunities.

Further reading

- *Speech and Language Processing* by Jurafsky and Martin (2021) is available online (https://web.stanford.edu/~jurafsky/slp3/). The first stop on any NLP journey could easily be this book. You will notice that many of the topics covered in this chapter appear in the earlier chapters of this book. But it definitely goes very quickly further into the mathematics of this sort of work as well as applications with a variety of machine learning models. It's a challenging book, but it is more than equally rewarding. Jurafsky also runs an excellent online course on these materials which is worth seeking out. The new edition is forthcoming as of this writing, but the resources are online in draft form, including new work in Chapters 10 and 11 on transfer learning approaches like BERT and GPT. The resources on linear algebra at the end of Chapter 3 would be a good primer for the maths in here.
- *Natural Language Processing with Python* by Bird et al. (2009). A slightly more lightweight (and admittedly older) book than the current Jurafsky and Martin text, but the website has all the text and has updated the code to Python 3 (https://www.nltk.org/book/). This book offers potentially a gentler introduction to those who find the linear algebra of Jurafsky and Martin a bit intimidating.
- The Python docs on how to use Unicode (with lots of little examples) are really useful (https://docs.python.org/3/howto/unicode.html). Admittedly Unicode is tedious and boring. But I think that the Python documentation has done an admirable job of explaining how Unicode works. Notably, Python 3 was a major shift from Python 2 to 'Unicode everywhere'.

Extensions and reflections

- Download data from elsewhere where you can identify two pools of reasonably balanced size. Explore classifiers for these two pools, starting with naïve Bayes as noted above. For example, select two subreddits or two sets of tweets pulled from Twitter, using the details in Chapter 7. For example, collect 1000 post titles on two slightly different subreddits (such as r/politics and r/worldnews). What words are especially distinct between the two groups? Are these highly discerning words found among the top scoring words using TF-IDF scores? What is the model accuracy comparing your chosen two groups? How does this differ with sample size? That is, what if you double the sample size by comparing 2000 post titles per subreddit instead of 1000 titles): does the model become more accurate?

- Extend this further by extending the range or the diversity of your exploration. For example, take a third subreddit or hashtag and determine if it easier to distinguish this third from the first or the second (i.e. for which comparison, subreddit 3 versus subreddit 1, or 3 versus 2). You could expand this further by comparing text from news sites or blogs.

- Combining the skills in this chapter with those in the next chapter on time, create a moving window for some data, such as a collection of blog entries, tweets, or reviews on a site. What happens when you compare the top words from a TF-IDF score as you move through time?

- Explore the limits of a text summary with the community or group that produced it. Consider generating a summary of an online community and sharing it with that community, for example using TF-IDF to indicate the key phrases. Would they think that these phrases accurately reflect their community? Do they see it as succinct or oversimplifying?

12

INTRODUCING TIME-SERIES DATA: SHOWING PERIODS AND TRENDS

- Parse time from textual data, including the eccentricities of daylight savings and Unix time
- Use a `datetime` index to slice and filter to specific time periods
- Resample data temporal data to get counts per day, per week, or per year
- Discover periodic trends by grouping by temporal resolutions (daily, weekly, monthly, etc.)
- Use a moving window to eliminate noise from a trend.

Introduction: It's about time

This chapter concerns the use of temporal information in Python. Time is one of the fundamental organising principles of society, and as such we are likely to see time emerge in a variety of analyses. By using time we can explore the popularity of something in a moving window or count the frequency of activity per day or per week. We can calculate the average time since something happened (such as the time since a post got a reply) or filter to a specific period and compare data in that period to data in another period.

In theoretical work in the social sciences there is a distinction between time as a physical concept and social time. Time as a physical concept (sometimes called Earth time or natural time) is about the relative rhythms of the universe. On human scales, the only real natural rhythms we tend to focus on are the day and the year. We can nevertheless establish a generally consistent measurement of time which we apply to social life through conventions. These include dividing the year into 12 months, or roughly 52 weeks, as well as having a single reference point for time across most all societies and a rational basis for the second (Zerubavel, 1982). Time around the clock is especially important for some forms of social coordination, although online its effects are more diffuse as people from multiple timezones interact.

The distinctions between natural time and social time is manifested in Python. There is a separate library for `time` as unit of measurement, where we can pause for *n* seconds or measure how long it takes some calculation to complete, and `datetime`, which manages many of the conventions of social time, for example taking a specific timestamp and formatting it, calculating the difference between that and another timestamp, or converting it to a different time depending on the timezone. Below we are mainly concerned with dates and how we can leverage timestamps in `pandas` to plot activity over time (from 2015 to the present) and over periods (like activity over the day or over the week). We also can make use of the `calendar` library which includes the words for various time periods in most widely used languages.

In many cases we will want to look not only at *when* things happened (which in `pandas` is a `Timestamp` object representing a *timestamp*) but also at *how long between* things happening. If how long between refers to a range between two specific times, like the time between 25 December 1999 and New Year's Day 2000, then it is a specific *timespan*. If it is a general measurement of the difference between two times, like a '2 hour' difference, then it is a *timedelta*. A period is a regular interval like day, week, or year. `pandas`, `matplotlib`, and Python generally all have ways of considering and wrangling data based on times, timedeltas, periods, and timespans. Each one of these measurements can prompt or be included in a variety of useful research questions, but that depends on having the data in the right form. Thus, for the remainder of this chapter we will be discussing how to wrangle, parse, format, and aggregate temporal data. We will not be doing any statistical modelling in this chapter, but I do point to resources for future work in topics such as difference-in-difference regressions and ARIMA models that depend on temporal data.

12.2 Dates and the `datetime` module

Dates have a variety of representations. We think of time in a cyclical sense of years, weeks, and months. These have meaning for humans. Computers tend to use a different representation of time, often called 'Unix' time. This is a long integer number that started at 0 on 1 January 1970. That specific date (or at the stroke of midnight, that specific 'datetime') is referred to as 'epoch'. Much of what we see in Python output involves the computer converting datetimes from their Unix representation to a more readable and manageable representation. Below I record a 'now' from when I was writing this book. When we print now, we can see it either in a string readable format, a collection of tags as in a *timetuple*, or in Unix time. Note that Unix time is in seconds since epoch so it's not actually as granular as time as stored in Python.

```
from datetime import datetime
import calendar

now = datetime.now()

print(now)
print(now.timetuple())
print(calendar.timegm(now.timetuple()))

2022-05-10 07:58:44.518171
time.struct_time(tm_year=2022, tm_mon=5, tm_mday=10, tm_hour=7,
tm_min=58, tm_sec=44, tm_wday=1, tm_yday=130, tm_isdst=-1)
1652169524
```

Notice above that when we printed `now()` it included a decimal to the highest level of precision available. Also notice that when we printed it as a timetuple it included a number of periods as key–value pairs but also `tm_isdst=1` (referring to 'is daylight savings, yes or no'). This is because there still exists the notion of daylight savings time, which is not equally followed around the world but can really mess with work across timezones if not considered. For example, if I see three posts from 10:30pm, they might be almost a day apart, if one each one is from New Zealand, the UK, and Hawaii. When data has no timezone information, it typically (but not necessarily) refers to Coordinated Universal Time (UTC). However, if there is a timezone or timezone offset in your data, you really ought to use it to create a standardised set of time coordinates for all rows.

12.2.1 Parsing time

Below I will use an example tweet in order to show how we can parse time, using both the 'easy' and 'hard' ways.

```
# Taken from https://developer.twitter.com/en/docs/tweets/data-dictionary/
overview/tweet-object.html

tweet = {
  "created_at":"Thu Apr 06 15:24:15 +0000 2017",
  "id": 850006245121695744,
  "id_str": "850006245121695744",
  "text": "1/ Today we're sharing our vision for the future of the Twitter API
platform!nhttps://t.co/XweGngmxlP",
  "user": {},
  "entities": {}
}

print(type(tweet['created_at']),tweet['created_at'])

<class 'str'> Thu Apr 06 15:24:15 +0000 2017
```

This is an example 'tweet' object. If you query historical tweets, they sometimes come as JSON with a lot of details including a `created_at` parameter. When JSON reads this it treats the `created_at` value as a string. Previously, we parsed that string into a `datetime` object in pandas using `to_datetime()`. First, let's do that again:

```
import pandas as pd

pd.to_datetime(tweet["created_at"])

Timestamp('2017-04-06 15:24:15+0000', tz='UTC')
```

Now let's inspect this `Timestamp` object. It appears to be a tuple, with the first element being the time (represented by Python as `2017-04-06 15:24:15+0000`. The second element is the timezone, which in this case is UTC. How did `pandas` know that it was UTC – did it just guess? No, it parsed the time using a regular expression oriented towards time. It's very handy to know how to do this manually even if it is possible *most of the time* to have `pandas` manage it.

Recall that regular expressions use 'metacharacters' such as \w to mean any word character or \d to mean a digit. Python has some standardised metacharacters for time as well (be careful, as they mean different things in a regular expression and when parsing time). Below are just a few of these alongside their value in the above tweet. For a fuller set you can either check the documentation or check out a website that lists these as a cheatsheet (https://strftime.org).

Table 12.1 Time-specific metacharacters for marking datetime periods

Code	Description	In tweet
%a	Weekday as locale's abbreviated name	Thu
%b	Month as locale's abbreviated name	Apr
%d	Day of the month as a zero-padded decimal number	06
%H	Hour (24-hour clock) as a zero-padded decimal number	15
%M	Minute as a zero-padded decimal number	24
%S	Second as a zero-padded decimal number	15
%z	UTC offset in the form ±HHMM	+0000
%Y	Year with century as a decimal number	2017

So we can see that as a string, `"created_at":"Thu Apr 06 15:24:15 +0000 2017"` can be coded semantically as `Weekday Month Date 24hour:minute:seconds +time-zonehours year`, which we can code explicitly in metacharacters as `%a %b %d %H:%M:%S %z %Y`. If we place that sequence of metacharacters inside either `datetime.strptime()` or `pd.to_datetime()`, then it will parse dates with precisely that format regardless of day or year. This method is more fragile than leaving `pd.to_datetime()` empty and letting pandas guess, but there are many instances where knowing these metacharacters will come in handy later. One reason is when you want to customise how you print timestamps. For this, you can send a timestamp and the desired sequence of metacharacters to `datetime.strftime()` (notice the `f` for format rather than `p` for parse).

```
tweet_date = "Thu Apr 06 15:24:15 +0000 2017"
print(f"The original date was formatted as: {tweet_date}")

tweet_stamp = datetime.strptime(tweet_date, "%a %b %d %H:%M:%S %z %Y")
print("We can format it differently, such as:",
    datetime.strftime(tweet_stamp, '%Y--%d--%b--%a %H and %M and %S %z'))
```

```
The original date was formatted as: Thu Apr 06 15:24:15 +0000 2017
We can format it differently, such as: 2017--06--Apr--Thu 15 and 24 and 15 +0000
```

`pd.to_datetime()` or `datetime.strptime` both return a timestamp. You can treat a timestamp as a timetuple, meaning you can query for temporal values by label, such as `year`, `month`, or `minute`.

```
print(tweet_stamp.year,tweet_stamp.month,tweet_stamp.day,sep="--")
```

```
2017--4--6
```

12.2.2 Timezones

Since `tweet_stamp` is a timestamp, we can compare it to other timestamps, ask if it falls within a range, and make use of other features of a `datetime` object, such as `strftime()`. But we have to be careful to ensure we compare it also to timezone-aware data. By default, `now()` is not timezone-aware. Thus, when trying to get the difference between that timestamp and now it will throw an error. See below how I added `timezone.utc` and this solved the issue.

```python
from datetime import timezone

try:
    print(datetime.now() - tweet_stamp)
except:
    print("Cannot subtract timezone-aware from non-aware data")
    print(datetime.now(timezone.utc) - tweet_stamp)
```

```
Cannot subtract timezone-aware from non-aware data
1859 days, 15:35:26.902178
```

12.2.3 Localisation and time

By default, Python assumes English names for dates. However, you can set a locale flag for other languages. Details about this are in the Python documentation under `locale` (https://docs.python.org/3/library/locale.html). Generally speaking, you would set this using a flag such as `locale.setlocale(locale.LC_ALL, '<the locale code>')`. If Python is assuming English and you are on a different locale on your operating system, it is often simply enough to type `locale.setlocale(locale.LC_ALL, '')` which will ensure your Python uses the system default. Up until recently, different operating systems used different locale codes. More recently, in Windows as well as Mac and Linux, there appears to be some unification towards the codes, as seen below.

We can use the `calendar` module to demonstrate locales. This will also illustrate how to produce a list of labels for time ranges like a list of all days of the week. For this, we draw upon the `calendar.day_abbr` and `calendar.week_abbr` objects.

```python
import locale
from calendar import day_abbr

locale.setlocale(locale.LC_ALL, 'fr_FR.UTF-8') # French
print([day_abbr[i] for i in range(7)])

locale.setlocale(locale.LC_ALL, '') # Local (English)
print([day_abbr[i] for i in range(7)])
```

```
['Lun', 'Mar', 'Mer', 'Jeu', 'Ven', 'Sam', 'Dim']
['Mon', 'Tue', 'Wed', 'Thu', 'Fri', 'Sat', 'Sun']
```

You can see that `day_abbr` is not merely a list of days in English, but a localised day object. `month_abbr` works in the same way except with the 12 months of the year. The locale change will also show up in `strftime()`.

 Revisiting the Movie Stack Exchange data

The Movie Stack Exchange has a number of temporal columns that we can use in our analyses. Recall that in Chapter 10 we used `pd.to_datetime()` so now our columns should already be timestamps that we can work with. First I load that data in memory using the pickled file.

```
import pickle
from pathlib import Path

data_dir = Path().cwd().parent / "data"
pickle_file = data_dir / "movies_stack_df.pkl"

if pickle_file.exists():
    stack_df = pickle.load(open(pickle_file ,'rb'))
    print(len(stack_df))
else:
    print("Please download and clean the Stack_df data as done in ",
          "Chapter 10. See https://archive.org/download/stackexchange")
```

```
61184
```

```
print(stack_df["CreationDate"][0], type(stack_df["CreationDate"][0]))
```

```
2011-11-30 19:15:54.070000 <class 'pandas._libs.tslibs.timestamps.Timestamp'>
```

When we cleaned these columns in Chapter 10 we did not spend any time visualising the data. Below, I will make extensive use of visualisations to help characterise some temporal features. First let's use `histplot` from `seaborn`. This should automatically chunk up the data by time and present some meaningful ticks along the x-axis.

```
import matplotlib.pyplot as plt
import seaborn as sns
%config InlineBackend.figure_format = 'svg'

sns.histplot(stack_df["CreationDate"])

plt.show()
```

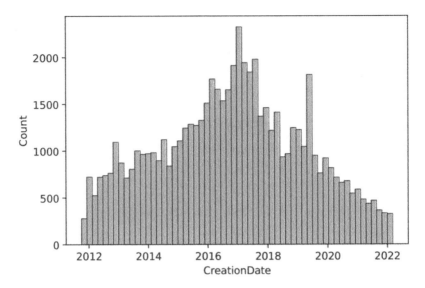

Figure 12.1 Distribution of number of posts created from 2012 to 2022 on the Movie Stack Exchange

As shown in Figure 12.1, seaborn chunked up the data in a way that looked like about five or six bins per year, but they were not entirely clear. Nevertheless, it is more granular than merely one bin per year. Notice the spike in early 2019? If we had coarser data (such as binned by year) we might miss a spike like that. On the other hand, if we make things too granular the plot will get very noisy. Selecting the right level of temporality or granularity is generally useful with time-series data. Below are some approaches to help.

12.4 `pandas datetime` feature extraction

From a timestamp you can extract specific temporal features like `year` or `month`. For a `Series` you can also do this. You might expect that if the `Series` is full of timestamp objects you could just say `df["CreationDate"].year` to get a `Series` of years. That's close, but not quite how it is done. You must instead employ an *accessor object*. The accessor object syntax allows you to access a part of the original object for all elements in the `Series`. For `datetime` objects, the accessor object is `<Series>.dt`. When you append this to a `Series` you can then query for regular periods like `year`, `month`, `day`, `hour`, `second`. Below I create a `Series` of just the year for `"CreationDate"` and print five random rows.

```
result = stack_df["CreationDate"].dt.year
display(result.sample(5, random_state=12345))
```

```
Id
74465     2017
105929    2019
89621     2018
```

```
55084      2016
23203      2014
Name: CreationDate, dtype: int64
```

The accessor object is really handy if you want to create (on demand) a column in your `DataFrame` to represent some coarsened version of a timestamp. Once you have a column coarsened by an accessor object then you can begin to explore periodicity by summarising that column. Compare the plot in Figure 12.2 that uses data by year instead of the `histplot` in Figure 12.1.

```
stack_df["CreationDate"].dt.year.hist()

plt.show()
```

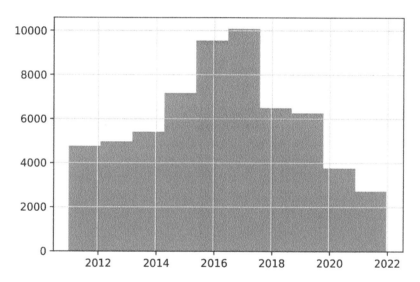

Figure 12.2 Distribution of number of posts created from 2012 to 2022 on the Movie Stack Exchange, coarsened to year

Some temporal measurements are sequential, like years, and others are periodic, like months. We will never have another 2020 (perhaps thankfully), but next year will have an October. Using the accessor object by period type allows us to look generally at which periods are more or less active. Thus, if we use `dt.month` over multiple years we will get the counts for all Octobers and all Junes using `value_counts()`. Then we can look to see if there appear to be periodic trends by month (or seasonally).

```
month_vals = stack_df["CreationDate"].dt.month.value_counts().sort_index()
month_vals.index = [calendar.month_abbr[x] for x in month_vals.index]

month_vals.plot(kind="bar");

plt.show()
```

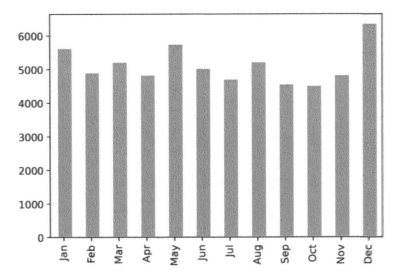

Figure 12.3 Distribution of number of posts created from 2012 to 2022 on the Movie Stack Exchange, grouped by month

Figure 12.3 shows that generally there appears to be a bit of an uptick in December, which would coincide with the Christmas blockbuster movies. They seem to be popular in this forum. In Figure 12.4 I do the same thing for hours.

```
hour_vals = stack_df["CreationDate"].dt.hour.value_counts().sort_index()
hour_vals.index = [ f"{x}h" for x in hour_vals.index]
hour_vals.plot(kind="bar")

plt.show()
```

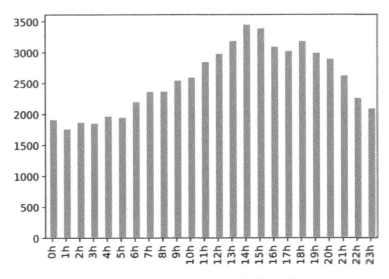

Figure 12.4 Distribution of number of posts created on the Movie Stack Exchange, grouped by hour of post creation

Posts on the Movie Stack Exchange appear to rise at around the 10th hour, peak around the 15th hour, and keep descending until the 1st hour. Want to guess why I say the 10th, 15th, and 1st rather than 10:00, 15:00, and 01:00? "CreationDate" is not timezone-aware. It is not the time on the clock for the user, it is the time on the clock for the server, and that time is set to UTC. It is likely that most users of the Stack Exchange are located in North America, which is 5–8 hours behind UTC most of the time. So the uptick at 10am is just after the start of the day in the UK and before most people rise in North America. The peak at 14h UTC is 9am on the Eastern seaboard (New York, Boston, Toronto), suggesting that many people check this site first thing in the morning.

Since the .dt returns a timestamp, we can also say .strftime() and have the new Series be a formatted string representing the timestamp. As an example, see below how I create a Series of string-formatted dates that are day plus three-letter month code.

```
stack_df["CreationDate"].dt.strftime("%d %b").sample(5,random_state=12345)
```

```
Id
74465       08 Jun
105929      27 Dec
89621       11 Jun
55084       06 Jun
23203       19 Jul
Name: CreationDate, dtype: object
```

Resampling as a way to group by time period

Earlier when I mentioned resampling I described it as a statistical approach where we repeatedly sample from the larger DataFrame and get an average result from the sample results or check how different sampling might lead to different biases. In this case, we mean resampling as an approach to creating a DataFrame of regular periods. Here resampling our data by time is much like a groupby operation, as if we are going to group by year or group by day. This is especially useful if we want to compare a frequency between different days or years.

When we use df.resample(<interval>,on=<datetime_col>), we transform a DataFrame with one timestamp per row into one with even temporal intervals for the rows. So if we resample by day with a dataset that ranges from 2010 to 2019, we will end up having 365 × 10 = 3650 rows, once for each day from the start of the decade until the end. Resampling is really useful when you want to have normalised plots over time. For example, you might want to discover not just how many posts were made, but whether the average score of those posts is going up or down over time. Resampling is effectively what Twitter is doing when you query for counts of tweets as seen near the end of Chapter 7.

In order to resample, we will want to first identify the column upon which we will resample. It should be a datetime column. Later we will relax this requirement by having a datetime index for our data. The first argument in the resample() method is called the 'rule'. This is how we are going to resample our data. Then we need some aggregating operation, just like with a groupby operation.

```
stack_df.resample('M', on="CreationDate").sum().head(5)
```

CreationDate	Score	ViewCount	AnswerCount	CommentCount	FavoriteCount
2011-10-31 00:00:00	52	950	1	7	0
2011-11-30 00:00:00	825	322076	66	51	28
2011-12-31 00:00:00	9585	3237967	552	637	245
2012-01-31 00:00:00	5179	1767587	309	480	129
2012-02-29 00:00:00	3331	3256564	250	401	92

When we aggregate using sum(), then, we get the sum of all the scores *within* that specific date range. We can use a variety of aggregation functions such as sum, mean, min, max, first, last, std, and median. So, for example, if we wanted the maximum value per year then we could resample('Y', on='CreationDate').max(), which will give us the top score for that year. Unless you specify which variables to aggregate, the new DataFrame will have resampled columns for all numeric variables. If we only want to aggregate one or a handful of columns, it's advisable to do a mask first and then resample like so:

```
display(stack_df[["CreationDate","Score"]]
        .resample('Y',on="CreationDate")
        .max().head())
```

CreationDate	CreationDate	Score
2011-12-31 00:00:00	2011-12-31 21:26:23.347000	199
2012-12-31 00:00:00	2012-12-31 22:45:58.037000	221
2013-12-31 00:00:00	2013-12-31 23:40:50.410000	175
2014-12-31 00:00:00	2014-12-31 22:30:25.773000	118
2015-12-31 00:00:00	2015-12-31 19:26:07.840000	124

In contrast to the plots above, if we wanted to force the chart to have one bin for each month, we could resample to month and then plot that. Figure 12.5 shows a histogram with the default options compared to two plots using resampled data. I adjust the labels and the layout accordingly.

```
fig, (ax1,ax2,ax3) = plt.subplots(3,1)

sns.histplot(stack_df["CreationDate"],
             ax=ax1).set_xlabel(None)#.set_ylabel(None)
ax1.set_ylabel(None)

stack_df[["CreationDate"]].resample('Y',
    on="CreationDate").count().plot(ax=ax2,legend=False).set_xlabel(None)
ax2.set_ylabel("Count")

stack_df[["CreationDate"]].resample('M',
    on="CreationDate").count().plot(ax=ax3,legend=False)
```

```
plt.tight_layout()

plt.show()
```

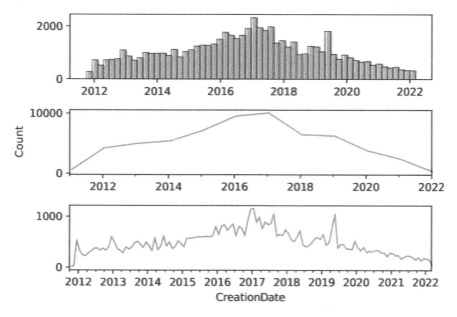

Figure 12.5 Comparing post frequency over time using a histogram and two coarsened distributions, one by month and one by year

The rule for resampling tends to be a period, including standard periods such as year (Y), month (M), week (W), day (D), hour (H), minute (Min), second (S). The resampler can do this for multiples of these periods, such as 'every 2 weeks' or 2W. Perhaps month is a bit too granular for our data, for example. In that case we can resample to 3 months at a time. Simply append 3 in front of M in the rule. Making a plot more or less granular allows us to see trends at different temporal resolutions.

12.6 Slicing and the datetime index in pandas

If we have a datetime column in our data then we can slice by dates. We can slice at a variety of resolutions, such as down to the year or month. These work pretty similarly to other slices that can be used to create a mask.

```
time_mask = (stack_df["CreationDate"] >= '2015-03-14') & \
            (stack_df["CreationDate"] < '2015-03-15')

stack_df.iloc[:,:5][time_mask].head()
```

Id	PostTypeId	AcceptedAnswerId	CreationDate	Score	ViewCount
32102	2	NaN	2015-03-14 00:21:42.027	3	NaN
32105	2	NaN	2015-03-14 00:47:27.420	0	NaN
32112	2	NaN	2015-03-14 04:58:13.863	2	NaN
32113	1	32115	2015-03-14 05:12:25.473	7	4245.0
32115	2	NaN	2015-03-14 06:19:47.067	8	NaN

```
# Counting posts within a two-year range
mask2 = (stack_df["CreationDate"] >= '2015') & \
        (stack_df["CreationDate"] < '2017')

print(len(stack_df[mask2]))
```

```
16719
```

Although we can make use of any `datetime` column in a `DataFrame` for temporal slicing and grouping, there are some advantages to having the index as a `datetime` object itself. For example, rather than slicing we can use `.loc` and use all kinds of temporal indices. Just be careful not to clobber a meaningful index. In this case, since the index is an `Id` variable, I first copy that into its own column.

```
time_df = stack_df.copy()
time_df['Id'] = stack_df.index
time_df.set_index('CreationDate',inplace=True)
time_df[["Id","CleanBody","Score"]].sample(5, random_state=1984)
```

CreationDate	Id	CleanBody	Score
2014-05-21 14:15:35.293	19564	It's hard to tell, but I be...	1
2016-03-22 11:04:48.730	50609	Donovan is an insurance lawyer. The CIA chief...	-2
2013-04-06 16:29:02.760	10845	I could not understand the significance of the...	6
2017-08-11 20:24:33.400	78673	In the 2014 movie Magallanes, the female lead...	1
2014-09-21 10:49:33.227	24752	The Matrix, as Morpheus explains, is styled on...	21

Below we can see the use of `.loc` to query for rows by month and even by range. This also gives us access to a nicer syntax than a long and unwieldy slice/mask. Compare

```
mask = (stack_df["CreationDate"] >= '2015-03-14') & \
       (stack_df["CreationDate"] < '2015-03-15')

stack_df[mask]
```

to

```
time_df.loc["2018-03-14":"2018-03-15"]
print(len(time_df.loc["2015-06"]),
      len(time_df.loc["2015-07"]),
      len(time_df.loc["2018"]),
      len(time_df.sort_index().loc["2018-03-14":"2018-03-15"]),sep="\n")
```

607
600
6496
30

12●7 Moving window in data

Above we have used resample to create distinct and separate aggregations. So we have one for 14 March 2015 and one for 17 March 2015, etc. But as we saw from the time plots, some of this data is very noisy as some days might be more popular than others regardless of the general trends. In order to *smooth* the noise in the data, we can create a moving window that averages some duration including dates before and after the specific date. This is called *rolling* the data.

time_df["Score"] has a value for each post. If we want a rolling average score, then we can select a window for how many rows we want in our window. We need to have enough data on either side of the row in order to create that window. So if we want a seven-row rolling average we can say <Series>.rolling(7). However, we can set whether we want our row at the beginning, the middle or the end of that seven-row rolling average. If we say center=True then we need three rows of data first. This is because we cannot calculate an average of seven rows with our row in the middle until the fourth row.

In the following example we create a rolling average for the mean value of Score. If we plot the mean score by day, it will be very noisy, but by using a rolling window we can see whether the average score is trending upwards or downwards. As an intuition, I would say that it is trending downwards since we can upvote all the past posts, meaning that the earliest posts might benefit from the passage of time and the opportunity to get more upvotes. Doing a rolling window is much easier when our data has a datetime index.

```
time_df["Score7d"] = time_df["Score"].rolling(7, center=True).mean()
time_df[["Score","Score7d"]].head(8).style.format({"Score7d":"{:.2f}"})
```

CreationDate	Score	Score7d
2011-11-30 19:15:54.070	31	NaN
2011-11-30 19:37:10.510	14	NaN
2011-11-30 19:41:14.960	29	NaN
2011-11-30 19:42:45.470	59	25.43
2011-11-30 19:44:55.593	16	28.00
2011-11-30 19:51:44.350	8	31.86
2011-11-30 19:53:23.387	21	42.57
2011-11-30 20:03:48.037	49	36.29

Thus we now have a column with a seven-row moving window that starts on row 4 and keeps going. However, a seven-row window is not a *seven-day* window. To get a moving window across a time period we combine the resampling above with the rolling here so that one row equals one day. One nice thing about resampling with `datetime` indices is that it cleanly handles the different lengths of months and other fussy calendar details. Note that because we are resampling, we are aggregating the data and thus will need a new `DataFrame`.

```
time_df_mnth = time_df[["Score", "CommentCount"]].resample('M').mean()
display(time_df_mnth.head(5))
```

CreationDate	Score	CommentCount
2011-10-31	26.000000	3.500000
2011-11-30	24.264706	1.500000
2011-12-31	17.949438	1.192884
2012-01-31	16.083851	1.490683
2012-02-29	13.707819	1.650206

In the resulting `time_df_mnth` DataFrame we can see that the resampling ended on the final day of each month, such as 31 December 2011 and 29 February 2012, thereby highlighting the ability to correctly resample by actual months and not just 30-day periods.

12.7.1 Missing data in a rolling window

There might be some days in the dataset that are missing or have no data for some other reason. If there's an `np.nan` in the rolling window, it might make the score `np.nan` for the entire window. Figure 12.6 shows three rolling windows based on data that has been resampled by day. Notice that the gaps get more severe the larger the window.

```
daily_df = time_df[["Score"]].resample('D').mean()

daily_df["Score7d"] = daily_df["Score"].rolling(7, center=True).mean()
daily_df["Score30d"] = daily_df["Score"].rolling(30, center=True).mean()
daily_df["Score60d"] = daily_df["Score"].rolling(60, center=True).mean()

fig, (ax1,ax2,ax3) = plt.subplots(3,1)

daily_df["Score7d"].plot(ax=ax1, legend=True, sharex=ax3)
daily_df["Score30d"].plot(ax=ax2, legend=True, sharex=ax3)
daily_df["Score60d"].plot(ax=ax3, legend=True)
```

```
ax3.set_xlabel("Average score of posts over time")
plt.tight_layout()

plt.show()
```

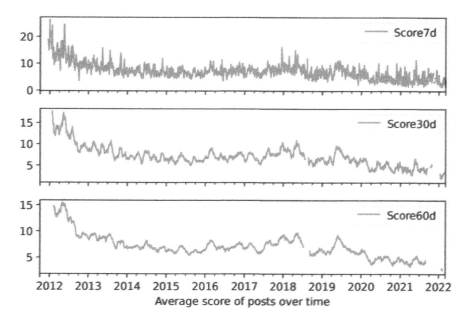

Figure 12.6 Comparison of frequency of posts created across three different-sized rolling windows: 7, 30, and 60 days

As we can see, the `np.nan` values propagated into the rolling average. So all it took was a single absent value to knock out a chunk of time in mid-2018 and again in late 2021. We can tolerate missing data by setting a `min_periods` option within the `rolling()` method. By default `min_periods` is the same as the window size, meaning that if there is one period missing, then it returns a missing value. If instead we take a minimum of 55 periods in a 60-day window this will smooth over this issue.

Also, I will use this as an opportunity to show a different syntax for commands that allows a tidy break across lines. To do this, simply wrap the command in () and start each line at the periods:

```
(daily_df["Score"]
 .rolling(60, center=True, min_periods=55)
 .mean()
 .plot(legend=True,ylabel="Average post score", xlabel="year"));

plt.show()
```

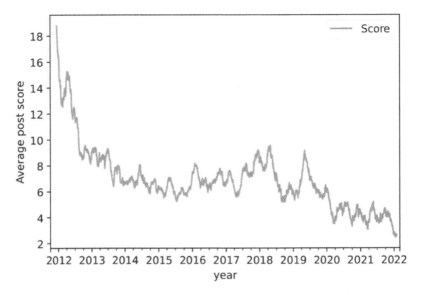

Figure 12.7   Line plot showing rolling window for average number of posts, with a small tolerance for a gap in the data

Compared to the charts above, Figure 12.7 does not have the gaps in 2018 and 2021. Instead, we have a smooth rolling average that shows the score was highest in the first year but then stabilised on average around 2014 and continued that way until about 2019 once the community starts to lose interest in this site.

12.8   Summary

This chapter has expanded on the notion of time as a concept for measurement and structuring of social life. As time has become more standardised, it has led to systems which we can use in programs, like Unix time, and UTC as a global time standard with timezones. These times are represented in data in a variety of formats which we can parse or format with Python. Usually, we can get away with `pd.to_datetime` but we can also use metacharacters and `strptime()` for detailed work. Parsing a date converts it to a `datetime` or related `pandas.timestamp` object. These objects can be queried using a syntax that allows for date ranges. When used as the index for a `DataFrame`, it allows even easier filtering by time.

Grouping by time period is a good way to see trends and periodicity. When we group rows by time period (e.g., days or months) we can *resample*, which allows us to aggregate statistics. This way we can get a count per period, but also a maximum, minimum, etc. A resampled `DataFrame` can then be plot to show trends over time quite clearly. The axis for these figures can be tuned as the code demonstrated. When we have counts over time we can plot them but they are sometimes noisy. Thus, I showed how we can *smooth* time using a moving window using the `rolling` method. That window can also handle some missing data with the `min_periods` parameter. Plotting this data on different levels of granularity can reveal different kinds of spikes or trends.

Further explorations

Time is a very deep concept generally. Thus it is no surprise that it is also a deep concept in pandas. In this preliminary chapter on time-series we did not even get into some of the more interesting notions in the statistics of time-series data. Instead of listing specific books below, instead I wanted to highlight here a number of future approaches you might apply now that you have data in some time-series format.

Some places to go from here:

- *ARIMA models.* These are used for time-series forecasting by extrapolating from data. They are like an extension of the `rolling` above but done in a thoughtful way that uses past data to forecast future data. One repository of helpful Jupyter notebooks for ARIMA models in Python can be found at https://github.com/marcopeix/time-series-analysis.
- *Granger causality.* This is a form of hypothesis testing that suggests whether fluctuations in one time-series predict variations in another time-series. It is not actually a true form of causality but one that takes correlations and leading/lagging indications to suggest how one variable can predict another (Toda and Yamamoto, 1995). Implementations for Granger causality exist in Python, but are mainly relegated to blog plots (https://towardsdatascience.com/3226a64889a6).
- *Difference-in-difference regressions.* This is a form of hypothesis testing that uses a 'natural experiment' to establish whether we can establish a causal relationship between the change and the outcome. It looks at how a difference in one time-series, perhaps an event or discontinuity, led to some observable and consistent difference in another time-series or distribution. Ensuring that the effect is robust in such a case is not always straightforward (Bertrand et al., 2004). Nevertheless, being able to articulate a discontinuity in data and explore its possible outcomes is both theoretically sensible and worth considering carefully. There's nothing particular about these models relative to other regression models for Python. It is more about the research design leading to the data. Extensive web videos and blogs about resources in Python exist for these models.
- *Fourier transformations.* These are approaches to detecting periodicity in a time-series. The periodicity might be as simple as a sine wave representing seasonality or a complex wave function that repeats in data. Usually, researchers want to detect if there is some periodicity that is like seasonality. This is a slightly different approach to ARIMA and seasonal ARIMA, however, based on signal detection. Again, this is another case where there exist mainly blogs showing these approaches in Python (https://towardsdatascience.com/292eb887b101).

To explore causality in more depth, I would start with Pearl and Mackenzie's accessible *The Book of Why* (2018) and then move on to Pearl's statistical work. His tome, *Causality* (Pearl, 2009), is an extensive overview of causal inference.

Yet even in the absence of these more complex tests and approaches, you now have at your disposal a way to characterise data somewhat effectively over time and thus wield time and temporality in your analyses. Used carefully, it can be the start of a compelling series of insights about time and about the social systems that operate through time.

Extensions and reflections

- The further explorations section above provided some interesting models, each of which might have an online tutorial or approach that you can reproduce or apply to the Stack Exchange data above.
- For the Stack Exchange data, explore the issue of *granularity* by using the `game-of-thrones` tag. Despite the fact that it was a television show, it figures heavily in the Movie Stack Exchange archives. Plot the frequency of the tag over time. When you do this on different time scales, what does it reveal? (*Hint*: the show's ending was considered unsatisfying by many fans, leading to considerable online engagement; but over what time scale?) Look at how many of these posts were made and try to determine if *Game of Thrones* was responsible for the peak in the data seen in Figure 12.1 on counts by `CreationDate`. There is an exercise related to this on the course GitHub page.
- Yasseri et al. (2012) note that there are clear circadian and weekly patterns for Wikipedia, but that these show different trends across the world. For example, in countries where the religious day is on Saturday rather than Sunday, this shows up in the editing patterns. There are Stack Exchanges for different religions. Do these show similar patterns of editing? Recall above that if you plot by `.dt.hour` it will be all 24 hours, or for `.dt.week` it will be for all weeks.

13

INTRODUCING NETWORK ANALYSIS: STRUCTURING RELATIONSHIPS

- Appreciate that networks have distinct types (e.g., directed or undirected, uniplex or multiplex, unweighted or weighted)
- Be able to create and modify a network object in Python using `networkx`
- Understand how to make a network plot
- Understand how to create a subplot of only the largest component and why
- Be able to generate a network from thread replies on Stack Exchange.

 Introduction: The connections that signal social structure

Networks are a huge component of data science work, but they operate in different ways in different fields. In general, network methods are used when we can identify a specific relation between two discrete identities. That's pretty abstract, but here are some examples in different fields:

- Friendships between people
- Trade between countries
- Replies to a comment
- People who share an interest in a musical artist
- Links between webpages.

Some of these relations are more *distinct* than others. A reply to a comment is an identifiable object. It is very clearly distinct. A lot of trace data involves very distinct relationships, like links on webpages or replies to comments. A lot of other social science work still relies on self-reports of 'people with whom you discuss important matters' (McPherson et al., 2006). These are not as distinct. As such they are subject to some interpretation and some recall bias, as pointed out by Bearman and Parigi (2004) in their superlatively titled 'Cloning Headless Frogs and Other Important Matters: Conversation Topics and Network Structure'. Yet, they tend to be considered meaningful to people and for some networks are considerably easier and clearer than more ambiguous signals from trace data (Gilbert and Karahalios, 2009).

The reason, then, for utilising online and trace data is not because it provides a more 'accurate' picture of social structure. It can provide a more unobtrusive picture, one at a larger scale, or one with more data. But the question of whether it is more accurate will rely in part on what we are trying to predict with that data. If everything we need to know about a conversation comes from how long the thread is or how diverse the participants are, then it is probably not an interesting thread. That being said, online and trace data do allow for some pretty amazing opportunities to study group cohesion (Traud et al., 2011), how one's social position can change depending on context and contagion dynamics (Centola, 2010; Vicario et al., 2016).

In this chapter I focus on networks created from social behavioural data. For the most part, this chapter is focused around considerations for the *creation* of a network and the application of simple descriptive statistics to networks. As in the previous two chapters, I will use the `stack_df` pickle created at the end of Chapter 10 to demonstrate these concepts after some toy examples. We will not get very far into network analysis. But that's by design. There are now extensive resources for reading about, measuring and analysing social networks, some of which I mention in the further reading section below. What I want you to come away with is a sense that you can get the network in Python and start exploring and analysing it. Then it will be up to you to discover the many potential ways forward.

13.1.1 Doing network analysis in Python

Network analysis concerns the particular relationships between entities. This means we have to denote both the entities, which we will call *nodes*, and the relationships, which we will call *edges*. A graph G is thus described as the set of nodes V and the set of edges E where an edge e_{ij} refers to the relationship between nodes v_i and v_j. Why v_i and not n_i, if we call them nodes? Network analysis is an amalgam of maths, statistics, sociology, anthropology, and social psychology (and more)! Nodes actually go by many names including *actor*, *point*, *dot*, and *vertex*. The term 'vertex' comes from maths and we tend to retain this nomenclature when using mathematical symbols.

There are a handful of social network analysis packages for Python. The most commonly used ones to my knowledge are `networkx` and `igraph`. As `networkx` is installed with Anaconda and we will be using it here for convenience. It is worth noting, however, that language choice is an important aspect of network analysis work. While I tend to prefer Python, many people in social network analysis will use R for their research. In R there are far more packages for network modelling, such as `sna` (Butts, 2020), `RSiena` (Ripley et al., 2021), `goldfish` (Stadtfeld et al., 2017), `egor` (Krenz et al., 2022), and `statnet` (Hunter et al., 2008), which are all popular and powerful tools for statistical work in networks. That being said, if you are comfortable collecting and wrangling the data in Python, it is often possible to then import the data into R and then use libraries needed there. Again, as we have seen in past chapters, often the complex part is getting the data into the shape that the algorithm expects, and thereafter much of the work is just careful model specification.

Below, we will be using `networkx`, which has a wide number of network analysis methods and a relatively simple syntax. To ensure that `networkx` is installed, you should first import it (as `nx` by convention).

```
import networkx as nx
print(nx.__version__)
```

```
2.7.1
```

Creating network graphs

A *network* is a conceptual object representing social structure. Some people use the term 'network' in loose and metaphorical ways while others use it more strictly. A *graph* is a mathematical representation of a network. Here, we tend to use 'graph' and 'network' interchangeably, but it is worth noting that networks are actually more abstract. It is challenging to define everything that goes into a friendship and thus a friendship network. Even if you have everyone's communication pattern, you do not really have the sentiment and the contexts that will prompt future communication. But the assumption is that by using a network in a formal sense as a *graph*, we can draw upon many insights from graph theory, mathematics, and the computation of graph features (such as layouts). These can then help us make sense of a social system or at least highlight some of its patterns. To do this, however, requires that we specify quite precisely what the relations mean (and if we are not cautious, maybe too precisely to be meaningful).

Graphs exist in `networkx` as Python objects. To create an empty graph, you can initialise it using `g = nx.Graph()`. If you print the graph you get a basic summary of the number of nodes and edges as well as the graph type (discussed below).

```
g = nx.DiGraph(name="Demo")
print(g)
```

```
DiGraph named 'Demo' with 0 nodes and 0 edges
```

13.2.1 Selecting a graph type

`networkx` expects you to specify a few key features of the `Graph` object at the outset, the main ones being whether the connections are directed or not (a `Graph` versus a `DiGraph` object) and whether there is only one kind of relationship between nodes or two (a `Graph` versus a `MultiGraph` object). By implication, you can also have a `MultiDiGraph` object. Conceptually all of these represent graphs if they are nonetheless different objects in Python for different kinds of graphs. Here are examples of how you might use all four different graph objects:

- A friendship between two people, Isaac and Jan, could be represented by a `Graph` object, since we often consider friendship symmetric. Undirected relations are often 'states', such as on or off ($e_{ij} = e_{ji}$).
- If we want to have a separate link for whether Isaac and Jan are friends (yes), workmates (no), and/or kin (no), we can do this with a `MultiGraph`. Therein $e_{ijf} = e_{jif}$, where f means friend but $e_{ijf} \neq e_{jiw}$ where w means a work tie.
- Imagine the friends send messages to each other. This is a directed relation. This means we would want one edge for the flow of messages from Isaac to Jan, e_{ij}, and one for the messages sent by Jan in return, e_{ji}. These we can contain in a `DiGraph`.
- Imagine we want to have different edges for Facebook messages versus text messages versus calls. Perhaps Isaac never calls Jan, he only texts, but sometimes Jan calls him. Thus we would have $e_{ijc} = 0$, $e_{ijt} = 1$ for Isaac and $e_{ijc} = 0$ for Jan. This we can handle in a `MultiDiGraph`.

Typically, if you are doing work with existing data, you would be most concerned with representing your data faithfully, considering how it was originally structured. So that means messages sent would be represented as a directed network since there's meaning to the difference between Isaac sent a message to Jan and Jan sent a message to Isaac. In social media work, a `MultiDiGraph` might be relevant for whether people like each other's tweets versus retweet them.

You can convert networks from one kind to another but you will possibly lose precision. Imagine if there is only a message from Isaac to Jan, but not from Jan to Isaac. If we convert the network to undirected (i.e. from `DiGraph` to `Graph`), should the one-way edge be included? For what it's worth, `nx.to_undirected(<DiGraph>)` will only include reciprocal edges by default, but that can be altered. The important thing is to understand which one would be more meaningful in your case.

13.2.2 Adding nodes

A graph requires nodes. These can either be added first before adding any edges or they can be recovered from the edges. Look below how I create one network with and without the node list. What is the difference in the second network?

```
nodes = ["Ali","Barb","Cam","Dot"]
edges = [("Ali","Barb"),
         ("Barb","Cam")]

g1 = nx.Graph()
g1.add_nodes_from(nodes)
g1.add_edges_from(edges)
print(f"{g1}:",g1.nodes)

g2 = nx.Graph(edges)
print(f"{g2}:", g2.nodes)

Graph with 4 nodes and 2 edges: ['Ali', 'Barb', 'Cam', 'Dot']
Graph with 3 nodes and 2 edges: ['Ali', 'Barb', 'Cam']
```

Notice that the second graph, g2, would be missing Dot since they were not featured in any edge. Dot in this instance would be considered an *isolate*.

13.2.3 Adding edges

Undirected and directed

In a `Graph` object, an edge is just two nodes in a collection (usually a tuple, like `"Ali"`, `"Barb"`). In a `Graph`, adding (`"Ali"`,`"Barb"`) is the same as adding (`"Barb"`,`"Ali"`). In a `DiGraph`, the order matters. Observe this in the following code:

```
edges_list = [("Ali","Barb"),
              ("Barb","Cam"),
              ("Cam","Barb")]
```

```
g = nx.Graph(edges_list, name = "undirected")
dg = nx.DiGraph(edges_list, name = "directed")

print(g, dg, sep="\n")

Graph named 'undirected' with 3 nodes and 2 edges
DiGraph named 'directed' with 3 nodes and 3 edges
```

Multiplex

In a `MultiGraph`, the edge has a third parameter stipulating the edge type. Yet, the same distinction between undirected and directed persists. Perhaps in this case below, 1 represents friendship and 2 represents work ties. Online, for a `MultiDiGraph` we might say that edge type 1 represents retweeting content and 2 might mean liking content.

```
mult_edges = [("Ali","Barb",1),
              ("Barb","Cam",1),
              ("Barb","Cam",2),
              ("Cam","Barb",1)]

try: g = nx.Graph(mult_edges)
except: print("Not a valid edge list for uniplex graphs.")

mg = nx.MultiGraph(mult_edges)
mdg = nx.MultiDiGraph(mult_edges)

print(mg, mdg, sep="\n")

Not a valid edge list for uniplex graphs.
MultiGraph with 3 nodes and 3 edges
MultiDiGraph with 3 nodes and 4 edges
```

13.3 Adding attributes

The graph itself as well as nodes and edges can all have attributes assigned as key–value pairs. Below, observe how I query for a single node and a single edge. Then for each of these I can add an attribute. In the examples we can query for a node using `g.nodes[]`, not `g.nodes()`. This is a syntax matter. Recall that we use `[]` as an 'indexer'. With a `DataFrame`, we have `df[]`, `df.loc[]` and `df.iloc[]` as indexers. Here we have `g.nodes[]` and `g.edges[]` as indexers.

For any graph g, the syntax `g[<label>]` will actually query for nodes. For example, `g["Ali"]` will return that specific node and a list of other nodes to whom `Ali` is connected. It is a view of the structure of the network. This means that we cannot use `g[<attribute>]` for graph-level attributes, like the name of the graph. Instead we use `g.graph[<attribute>]`. For node attributes, we can use `g.nodes[<node_label>][<attribute>]` and for edges we can use `g.edges[<node1_label>,<node2_label>][<attribute>]`. See these below:

```
g = nx.DiGraph([("Ali","Barb"),("Barb","Cam"), ("Cam","Barb")],
                name="label example",
                demovar="demo_1")

g.nodes["Ali"]["weight"] = 32
g.edges["Ali","Barb"]["type"] = "friend"
g.edges["Ali","Barb"]["weight"] = 30

print("g:\t\t\t",g)
print("g.graph:\t\t", g.graph)
print("g['Ali']:\t\t", g["Ali"])
print("g.nodes['Ali']:\t\t",g.nodes["Ali"])
print("g.edges['Ali','Barb']:\t", g.edges["Ali","Barb"])
```

```
g:                        DiGraph named 'label example' with 3 nodes and 3 edges
g.graph:                  {'name': 'label example', 'demovar': 'demo_1'}
g['Ali']:                 {'Barb': {'type': 'friend', 'weight': 30}}
g.nodes['Ali']:           {'weight': 32}
g.edges['Ali','Barb']: {'type': 'friend', 'weight': 30}
```

13.3.1 Working with distributions of attributes: The case of degree

Above I entered a value for weight for `Ali` as a node-level attribute. I also entered two edge-level attributes for ("Ali","Barb"): ["weight"] = 30 and ["type"] = "friend". Normally, however, you would expect to have an attribute for every node or every edge. For example, in this network, we might be interested in the *degree connectivity*. This is a pretty standard measure in network analysis, with a number of variations depending on circumstance. The *degree* counts the number of edges connected to a node. If the network is directed, as we have above, the *in-degree* and *out-degree* count the number of edges coming *in* and going *out*, respectively. The total degree count for a directed networks is the sum of the in-degree and out-degree scores. Below we can calculate the degree scores for our example network:

```
print(g.degree(),g.in_degree(),g.out_degree(),sep="\n")
```

```
[('Ali', 1), ('Barb', 3), ('Cam', 2)]
[('Ali', 0), ('Barb', 2), ('Cam', 1)]
[('Ali', 1), ('Barb', 1), ('Cam', 1)]
```

Notice that these were all lists. Each element of the list was a tuple with node name and value. We can then attach those values as data to our nodes. However, a graph object is not like a `DataFrame`. You cannot currently say `g.nodes["deg"] = g.degree()` and have it match the nodes and add the data. Instead, you must iterate through each node and match it or iterate through each result and assign it. Since the result comes back as a list, I will iterate through it and assign each result in turn.

```
for node_id,score in g.out_degree():
    g.nodes[node_id]["out-degree"] = score
```

```
for node_id,score in g.in_degree():
    g.nodes[node_id]["in-degree"] = score
```

Nodes often have values that come from elsewhere. If we have a simple text file with a list of everyone's names (or node_id) and a value, it is easy to wrangle that data into a network object. It assumes that the node_id is the *key* to merge in data. Below is a simple DataFrame with the same names and some node attributes:

```
import pandas as pd

node_data = {"Ali":{"age":32,"travel":"cycling"},
             "Barb":{"age":28,"travel":"walking"},
             "Cam":{"age":43,"travel":"bus"}}

display(df) = pd.DataFrame.from_dict(node_data,orient="index")
display(df)
```

	age	travel
Ali	32	cycling
Barb	28	walking
Cam	43	bus

Now to get those attributes into the nodes in the network object, we have to iterate through each object.

```
for index, val in df["age"].items():
    g.nodes[index]["age"] = val

g.nodes["Ali"]["age"] # Just spot checking
```

32

networkx networks can be clumsy at times for storing data but they are useful for performing network-specific operations, such as filtering a network based on who is connected. That said, I prefer to store my data in DataFrame objects where possible, such as one for nodes and another for edges. To get the attributes from a graph object into a DataFrame is pretty straightforward, since the nodes are stored much like the node_data I showed above.

```
display(pd.DataFrame.from_dict(g.nodes,orient="index"))
```

	weight	out-degree	in-degree	age
Ali	32.0	1	0	32
Barb	NaN	1	2	28
Cam	NaN	1	1	43

Then you can do a lot of merging and managing of the node details with the extra feature of pandas. Then you would return to the network and assign an attribute if you need it for a specific purpose.

Plotting a graph

There are many ways to render a network as an image. We can do this in Python, in specialised software such as Gephi (https://gephi.org), or using frameworks such as d3.js or sigma.js in JavaScript. networkx has a way to plot graphs but it is not especially optimised. This is because networkx appears lately to have become more of a library for various kinds network objects, with more specialist libraries taking on optimised versions of other tasks. Then what is the use of networkx? Graphs are effectively constructions of relationships between entities, but to work with them on a computer we need to formalise that data. By creating a relatively Pythonic way to manage nodes, edges, and their attributes, this can become a base for things like taking data from one format and cleanly converting it to another (such as exporting to a file format like GraphML), or working smoothly with other packages like community for community detection. In the case of network visualisation, for more sophisticated and finely tuned layouts, you might turn to a different package such as pygraphviz, which, like community, will work well with networkx objects.

One of the nice things about this system is that once you navigate which parts can be optimised by different libraries you can also start to see how to combine these parts. For example, while we are drawing 'in networkx', we are actually drawing in matplotlib and so we can use matplotlib features to draw titles, have a legend, or compare two plots side by side.

First I will do a very simple drawing of a network with four nodes. It will be like a triangle with one line extending from one side. Then I will mention network generators and draw a generated network.

```
g = nx.Graph([("a","b"),("b","c"),("c","a"),("a","d")])
print(g)


Graph with 4 nodes and 4 edges

import matplotlib.pyplot as plt
%config InlineBackend.figure_format = 'svg'

nx.draw_random(g,with_labels=True)

plt.show()
```

Figure 13.1 is not a very exciting graph. Often interesting features in networks show up in larger graphs, including randomly generated graphs. In fact, randomly generated graphs help us establish a baseline for comparison for other observed graphs. One of the classic random networks is the Erdős–Rényi graph (Newman, 2018), often also called a *binomial* graph. This is a really basic graph where every edge between two nodes exists with some probability, *p*. So the number of nodes and probability are parameters. Interestingly, the graph will still probably look very 'networky' to you in a way that a grid would not. In this case, I use 50 nodes and a probability of 0.05. Since there are (50×49)/2 possible edges, we should expect there to be approximately 0.05 (50×49)/2 ≈ 61 edges in the graph.

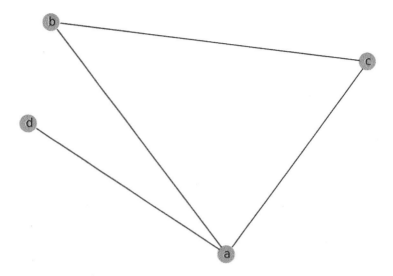

Figure 13.1 Random layout of simple four-node graph

```
g = nx.generators.binomial_graph(50,.05,seed=1979)
print(g)

Graph with 50 nodes and 60 edges

pos = nx.spring_layout(g)

nx.draw_networkx_nodes(g,pos,node_size=20)
nx.draw_networkx_edges(g,pos,edge_color="grey")
plt.axis("off")
plt.show()
```

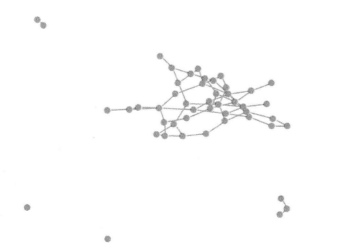

Figure 13.2 Random binomial graph (*n* = 50) with a 0.05 probability of connection between any two nodes, leading to a large component and some islands

That large connected blob in the centre of Figure 13.2 is the largest connected component. Often the network will not be fully connected. In an undirected network if you want to filter down to that network (as in Figure 13.3) you can use the following syntax:

```
largest_comp_nodes = max(sorted(nx.connected_components(g),
                         key=len, reverse=True))
lcc = g.subgraph(largest_comp_nodes)

nx.draw_networkx_nodes(lcc,pos,node_size=20)
nx.draw_networkx_edges(lcc,pos,edge_color="grey")
plt.axis("off")
plt.show()
```

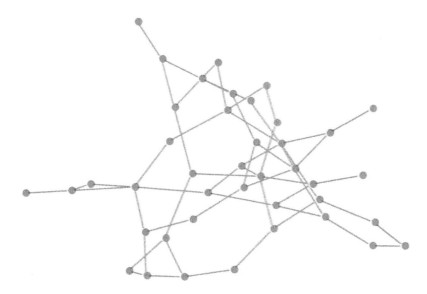

Figure 13.3 The largest connected component of a random binomial graph

Notice how we have kept the same position values. pos is really just a dictionary. If the node is not in there the program will throw an error, but if extra keys are in the dictionary they are ignored. This can be used to preserve a position across multiple views of a network.

13.4.1 Considering layouts for a graph

All graphs require a layout to be perceived visually. Since most graph layouts are planar (i.e. they extend in two dimensions), they consist of x and y coordinates for the nodes. Layouts are calculated first as a set of x and y coordinates and then applied to the layout. Sometimes these positions can be slow to calculate and so fine-tuning is recommended. For small graphs the calculations are generally fast. For larger graphs in Python, matplotlib should still be able to visualise a lot of objects, but you might want to investigate other algorithms for assigning the x and y coordinates that are more efficient than the built-in layout algorithms in networkx.

The `spring` algorithm in `networkx` is a layout algorithm that iterates through the nodes, starting from random and adjusting them to settle into a relative positioning that should reveal some structure. This algorithm is a version of the classic Fruchterman–Reingold 'force-directed' algorithm (Fruchterman and Reingold, 1991). Force-directed algorithms use simple heuristics such as 'keep nodes that are connected close together, but not too close' and 'keep nodes that are not connected further apart'. These heuristics are applied to each node iteratively. At first a random graph will start to clump or cluster and then with many iterations it tends to settle into a stable pattern. If your network has some underlying structure to it, this process often leads to well-connected groups of nodes being laid out near each other, with that familiar 'blobby' network look.

Below I will stick with the classics and demonstrate the algorithm using a built-in dataset, Zachary's Karate club data (Zachary, 1977). This was friendship data on a Karate club that split into two clubs shortly after data collection. Half the members went to the new club and half remained. By drawing the node attributes as colours and laying out the graph using a `spring` layout, we can see how the structure of friendships clearly presaged the split.

```
kg = nx.karate_club_graph()
print(kg)
print(kg.nodes[0])


Graph named "Zachary's Karate Club" with 34 nodes and 78 edges
{'club': 'Mr. Hi'}
```

Earlier I used `nx.draw_spring(<graph>)`, which used the defaults and combined a lot of steps into one. Below I will separate out some of these steps to help make the network clearer. The steps are:

1   Calculate a node positions using a layout algorithm.
2   Apply the layout to the nodes.
3   Apply the layout to the edges.
4   Apply the layout to the node labels.

In this case, I want to do step 2 twice, once for the nodes from one Karate club, with one node colour, and once with the nodes from the other club, in a different colour. First I have to get a list of who is in which club. I do that as a dictionary with the club name as key and a list of node_ids as the values.

```
from collections import defaultdict

clubs = defaultdict(list)
for node in kg.nodes:
    clubs[kg.nodes[node]["club"]].append(node)

for club, members in clubs.items():
    print(f"Club {club} has {len(members)} members")
```

```
Club Mr. Hi has 17 members
Club Officer has 17 members

pos = nx.spring_layout(kg)

nx.draw_networkx_nodes(kg.subgraph(clubs["Mr. Hi"]), pos,
                       node_color="lightgrey")

nx.draw_networkx_nodes(kg.subgraph(clubs["Officer"]), pos,
                       node_color="darkgrey")

nx.draw_networkx_edges(kg,pos)

nx.draw_networkx_labels(kg,pos,
                        font_size=6)
plt.show()
```

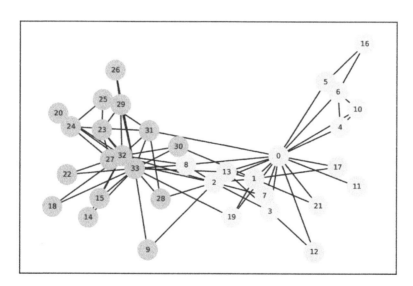

Figure 13.4   Sociogram of Zachary's Karate club data, highlighting two groups which would subsequently split

Almost magically, all the dark and light grey nodes are placed on their sides of the picture in Figure 13.4. This of course is a prototypical example, and the clusters will not always show up so obviously (or be so obvious) in many networks.

13.5   Subgroups and communities in a network

In the interest of brevity, I cannot dive in to the huge number of ways to describe or model a network. However, one specific technique has really captured a lot of people's attention and is a good extension to see at this point. This is *community detection*, which is a way of assigning nodes to groups called 'communities' (Porter et al., 2009). A 'partition' is a set of communities for the whole network. So we can create a partition for the Karate club network and then check whether the algorithm picked up everyone who actually went to either club.

13.5.1 A goodness-of-fit metric for communities

Rather than selecting communities randomly or strictly according to some attribute, such as which club they were in, community detection algorithms tend to want to maximise some goodness-of-fit criterion. A common one is *modularity*, which is a measure of whether edges mainly fall within communities or between them (Newman, 2006). If the score is 0, then, compared to a random network, the edges do not really fall preferentially within or between the communities. If the score is above 0 then the edges are more commonly found within communities, and if the score is below 0 then the edges mainly fall between the communities. A score over 0.30 usually means the communities are relatively distinctive. Because of the way the score is calculated, we do not get a *p*-value the way we would with some of the other measures we have seen.

Below I will run a built-in community detection metric on the Karate club data and then report the modularity score.

```
import networkx.algorithms.community as nx_comm

greedy_comm = nx_comm.greedy_modularity_communities(kg)

for c,i in enumerate(greedy_comm):
    print(f"Community {c} has {len(i)} members")

Community 0 has 17 members
Community 1 has 9 members
Community 2 has 8 members
```

So, interestingly, it picked up three groups rather than two. But they seem to number precisely 17 and 17 (8 + 9). Let's check the modularity for the community detection algorithm and also for a partition from the club names.

```
greedy_mod = nx_comm.modularity(kg, greedy_comm)
print(f"Using an algorithm, modularity was: {greedy_mod:0.2f}")

attr_mod = nx_comm.modularity(kg, list(clubs.values()))
print(f"Using the clubs, modularity was: {attr_mod:0.2f}")

Using an algorithm, modularity was: 0.41
Using the clubs, modularity was: 0.39
```

It seems that splitting one of the clubs even further produced a better modularity score. Oh dear, perhaps one of the clubs would be due for a second split! As the community solutions are themselves just a list of nodes for each community, we can do the same as above and visualise them separately by colour, but for brevity I leave that to you.

 ## Creating a network from data

There are many ways to create networks from data. As long as we can identify a relationship between two nodes, we can start to build a network of such nodes. The relationship can be indirect (like posts in the same forum) or direct (replies to one's comment). It can be behavioural (person 1 retweets person 2), self-reported (person 1 nominates person 2 on a survey), or it can be declarative (person 1 follows person 2).

From the data we have shown so far from Reddit, Wikipedia, the World Wide Web, and Stack Exchange, it is clear that there are ways to make a variety of network datasets. As most textbooks tend to focus on the *analysis* of the networks, I wanted to use this opportunity walk through the creation of a network dataset from existing data. I hope this helps you envision how to create your own datasets as well as look for existing data online. This will also help consolidate some of the data wrangling skills on merging and aggregating tables in Chapter 2 with the Stack Exchange data in its cleaned format from Chapter 10. Once created, we will only briefly query and visualise a part of the data. I then defer for further analysis to many of the other extensive textbooks for thinking about social network analysis or network science ways of querying, transforming, and analysing this data which I mention in the further reading section below.

```
import pickle
from pathlib import Path

data_dir = Path().cwd().parent / "data"
pickle_file = data_dir / "movies_stack_df.pkl"

if pickle_file.exists():
    stack_df = pickle.load(open(pickle_file ,'rb'))
    print(len(stack_df))
else:
    print("Please download and clean the Stack_df data as per Chapter 10.",
          "See data from https://archive.org/download/stackexchange .")
```

61184

Currently, we have a list of posts, which we can access using (stack_df["PostTypeId"] =='1') and a list of answers (stack_df["PostTypeId"] =='2'). In theory, if we filter down to just the answers, then we can make a set of links from the user who wrote the answer to the user who wrote the question. This is a 'reply' network. In order to build it we need to fill in some data. In the row with the answer is a column called ParentId (which is missing for the questions, but shows the root question for all the answers). That's the identifier for the question, not the user who wrote the question. So below I do some wrangling and merging. When I do, we get a second OwnerUserId, but this one will have a suffix to denote that it is the owner of the question as `OwnerUserId_q`. This will still result in a very big network and not one that is easily visualised, but we will get to see some subsets of this network below.

```
question_mask = stack_df.PostTypeId =='1'
answer_mask = stack_df.PostTypeId =='2'

# Only questions have tags and I will want them later.
thin_df = stack_df[question_mask][["OwnerUserId","ListTags"]]

answer_df = stack_df[answer_mask].merge(thin_df,
          left_on="ParentId",right_index=True,
          how="left", suffixes=["","-q"])

# Remove deleted accounts where only content remains
answer_df.dropna(subset = ["OwnerUserId","OwnerUserId-q"],inplace = True)

display(answer_df[["OwnerUserId","ParentId","OwnerUserId-q"]]
          .sample(5,random_state=1984))
```

Id	OwnerUserId	ParentId	OwnerUserId-q
98210	55668	98209	71749
55170	23541	55162	16095
35184	20356	35175	7955
41382	8071	41381	326
104659	34317	104642	76914

To recap, I created a new `DataFrame` called `answer_df`. The rows are the answers. Each one has a `ParentId` which is the index of the question to which this answer is a reply. I wanted the user who wrote that question in the row. So I merged two columns of data from the question `DataFrame` (`OwnerUserId` and `ListTags`, for later). Here the index is `Id`, so I match that to `ParentId` in the `answer_df`. We now have a `DataFrame` with one column, `OwnerUserId`, which we can use as the *from* node and one called `OwnerUserId_q` which we can use as the *to* node. These should go in `networkx` in a list of edge pairs. To do this, I use the `zip` command.

```
stack_edgelist = list(zip(answer_df["OwnerUserId"],
                     answer_df["OwnerUserId-q"]))

g = nx.DiGraph(stack_edgelist)
print(g)

DiGraph with 14054 nodes and 29101 edges
```

This is a large graph by human social network standards. And yet, the Movie Stack Exchange is a small network by platform standards. Some of the techniques that might be useful for small networks will be computationally slow or intractable for larger networks. For example, it will take a long time to generate a layout of this network, and some community detection algorithms might take some time. Research continues on how to do sound statistical estimation on large networks (networks with more than a few hundred nodes might be considered large).

For the rest of this chapter, I wanted to consider some methodological choices in constructing a network that might not have been obvious. Some of these choices help us understand how better to consider our data and thereby facilitate some meaningful expectations to which we can observe and compare with real data.

13.6.1 Whole networks versus partial networks

A whole network is a network with a meaningful boundary that helps to articulate the shape of the network. A whole network is a conceptual distinction, not a technical one. That is, once we have a graph, we can think of it as a single 'network'. But did the inclusion criteria for that network signify a meaningful boundary? In social network analysis, things like a 'school classroom' might be a clear distinction for a whole network since it is a meaningful boundary. However, this network also has a meaningful *exclusion criterion* in that it is not customary to include the teacher in the class network. So, revisiting the Stack Exchange data, is `answer_df` a whole network? Not yet, for several reasons.

1 *Unanswered questions.* If there is a user who only wrote a question that was never answered, the question author would not show up in our final `answer_df`, since we merged using `how="left"`. Using a `"left"` join meant we preserved all the answers, but if we did an outer join, then we would have a `Series` of rows for each of the questions that did not get an answer. They would have many missing values but we could still create a list of these users and add them as `node_ids` in our network.

2 *Technical accounts.* While we only looked at the `Posts.xml` data, if we were to look into the `Users.xml` data we would see that several user accounts refer to moderators or automated accounts. We might want to delete these from our data, just as a teacher would not be in a class network. Other work on whether an account is a bot or meets some other exclusion criteria might also be worth considering.

3 *Deleted accounts.* People have a right to be forgotten and it is common for users to delete their data as well as to unlink their data from content that will persist (Mayer-Schönberger, 2011). This means we will have some gaps in our network compared to the true network of question writers and answer writers. The latter issue is not something we can reasonably solve. Furthermore, doing so might raise ethical issues. It is for this reason that we have not stored a version of the Stack Exchange data but prefer you download a fresh copy, nor have I used the specific screen names in the data where possible.

Is it necessary to have a whole network? Maybe or maybe not, depending on the question. If the question compares individuals in the network, it is often less severe than if the question is about the whole structure of the network. In the latter case, if a few high-profile users delete their accounts, then it would be a bit of a challenge to disentangle which questions belonged to which user, and perhaps thereafter create gaps in the structure that are difficult to account for (Costenbader and Valente, 2003; Kossinets, 2006).

Partial networks are a reasonable methodology so long as you are clear about the *inclusion* or *exclusion* criteria for the network. For example, you can create a network of links between Wikipedia pages and follow the links on these pages. In practice you cannot follow the links for ever. One approach is to use stopping criteria, so that if a linked page includes a concept or term, such as 'climate change' the program follows the links on that page. If a linked page does not mention the desired term, then the program stops. In the case of this network, you might want to compare the subgraphs of questions and their answers for different kinds of questions or perhaps different topics. Since we have imported `ListTags` we can mask by some tag and then create a smaller graph (or get those `OwnerUserId` values and use them for a subgraph). For example:

```
tag = "dialogue"
tag_mask = answer_df['ListTags-q'].map(lambda x: "dialogue" in x)
len(answer_df[tag_mask])
```

```
1336
```

So now instead of using the entire `answer_df` you can use the subset and compare it to other subsets.

13.6.2 Weighted networks

A network can take virtually any Python object as an attribute, but *weight* takes on a special importance since edges are often more or less significant depending on some weighted value. In the case above, we have a network from question users to answer users. But we did not think of the weights. What if some people are particularly inclined to answer the questions of specific others? This means that when we zipped up the data the same edge might be in there multiple times. First let's check if that's really the case:

```
print(len(stack_edgelist))
print(len(pd.Series(stack_edgelist).unique()))
```

```
33278
29101
```

So it appears that there are at least a few thousand non-unique edges, meaning that someone answered someone else's questions more than once. Let's make that the weight value. In this case, I will use `value_counts()` to count the number of times an edge occurs and then I will take that result and map it on to the network. Then I will filter down the network to where a weight is greater than 4 and plot the network. The result is shown in Figure 13.5.

```
weight_ser = pd.Series(stack_edgelist).value_counts()
wg = nx.DiGraph(name="Weighted Directed Reply Graph")
```

```
ebunch = []
for nodes,weight in weight_ser.items():
    if weight >= 5 and nodes[0] != nodes[1]:
        ebunch.append((nodes[0],nodes[1],weight))

wg.add_weighted_edges_from(ebunch)
print(wg)

DiGraph named 'Weighted Directed Reply Graph' with 115 nodes and 222 edges

filter_graph = wg.subgraph([node for node,val in wg.degree() if val > 2])

pos = nx.spring_layout(filter_graph)
nx.draw_networkx_nodes(filter_graph,pos,alpha=0.4)
nx.draw_networkx_edges(filter_graph,pos,edge_color="lightgrey")
nx.draw_networkx_labels(filter_graph,pos,font_size=6)

plt.show()
```

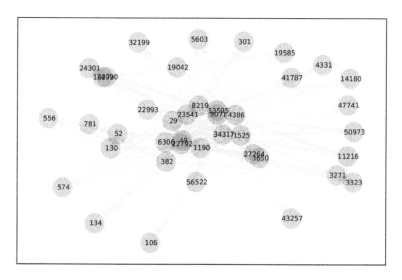

Figure 13.5 Sociogram of Movie Stack Exchange posters who reply to each other and have used the tag `dialogue`

So I have really sculpted a network from the data using a few structural features and some weights. We took only those nodes who had replied to each other four or more times. Then I further filtered the graph so that there were no self-loops (people replying to themselves) and that the nodes had to have more than one degree (meaning either two people had to answer more than four times, or they had to both send to or receive from two different people more than four times). This is an *operationalisation* of community activity. In a research paper, I would explore in detail why I think four replies is a good number or I might choose a different number or filter in a different way.

13.6.3 **Bipartite networks**

A common approach in network analysis is to create networks of two sets of nodes where each set refers to a different type of object. In social network analysis, you will sometimes hear of 'affiliation graphs' or 'co-citation networks'. These both have this feature. An affiliation graph describes a network where one set of nodes (such as people) have co-associated in the other set of nodes (such as parties, departments, tags). So we could create a graph of university students where level 1 is the students and level 2 are the classes. Then we can make use of this graph to see which students are taking a similar profile of classes or which classes seem to attract a similar profile of student.

With the Stack Exchange data we can create lots of bipartite networks. All we need is a set of overlapping categorical attributes. For example, we could have a network that links people to the tags they use to answer questions. Then, by reducing these tags down, we can learn which tags are 'co-similar'. To say they are co-similar does not mean they mean the same thing, it means that they connect to the rest of the graph in similar ways.

Below I will create a bipartite network of users (who ask questions) to tags used to describe these questions. Then we use this data to create a 'projection' that will allow us to see which tag nodes are similar to each other. I will select the tags that have been featured the most to limit the nodes in our network. So admittedly it will be a partial network, but hopefully with fewer tags it will not be so noisy.

```
stack_df[question_mask][["OwnerUserId","ListTags"]].head()
```

Id	OwnerUserId	ListTags
1	11	['wedding-crashers']
3	41	['analysis', 'star-wars']
4	22	['comedy', 'the-pink-panther']
6	34	['plot-explanation', 'analysis', 'ending', 'the-tree-of-life']
10	11	['plot-explanation', 'the-departed']

In this case, the data is in 'wide format', meaning one row per 'from' node with many 'to' nodes. We want each 'from' and 'to' node pair to have its own row. We can use explode to convert this data to long format.

```
tags_df = (stack_df[question_mask][["OwnerUserId","ListTags"]]
            .explode("ListTags").dropna())

display(tags_df.head())
```

Id	OwnerUserId	ListTags
1	11	wedding-crashers
3	41	analysis
3	41	star-wars
4	22	comedy
4	22	the-pink-panther

```
print(tags_df.shape)
```

```
(43259, 2)
```

Now we can do the same as above to create a network. However, this time we will have two sets, as there should only be numbers in the first set and only words with no spaces in the second. We can check that the sets are not overlapping in the `DataFrame` first just to make sure.

```
in_common = set(tags_df["OwnerUserId"]) & set(tags_df["ListTags"])
print(f"The sets have {len(in_common)} elements in common")
```

```
The sets have 0 elements in common
```

```
top40_tags = list(tags_df["ListTags"].value_counts().index[:40])
tag_filtered_df = tags_df[tags_df["ListTags"].map(lambda x: x in top40_tags)]
print(f"All rows: {len(tags_df)}")
print(f"Rows counting only top 40 tags: {len(tag_filtered_df)}")
```

```
All rows: 43259
Rows counting only top 40 tags: 22434
```

I chose the top 40 somewhat arbitrarily since I figured 40 nodes would be clear in an image on the screen. I first filter `tags_df` down to these top 40 and then build the network since it is easier to filter using a `DataFrame` and it is nice to have smaller networks to work with.

```
bp_tag_list = list(zip(tag_filtered_df["OwnerUserId"],
                       tag_filtered_df["ListTags"]))
```

```
tagg = nx.Graph(bp_tag_list)
print(tagg)
```

```
Graph with 5828 nodes and 12258 edges
```

So this bit below is new. We will first separate the graph into two sets automatically. You can check first if this is possible with `bp.is_bipartite(g)`.

```
from networkx.algorithms import bipartite as bp

bp.is_bipartite(tagg)

True

bp_lvl1,bp_lvl2 = nx.bipartite.sets(tagg)
print(len(bp_lvl1),len(bp_lvl2))

lvl2g = bp.weighted_projected_graph(tagg, bp_lvl2)
print(lvl2g)

5788 40
Graph with 40 nodes and 780 edges

nx.draw_spring(lvl2g)

plt.show()
```

The plot is shown in Figure 13.6.

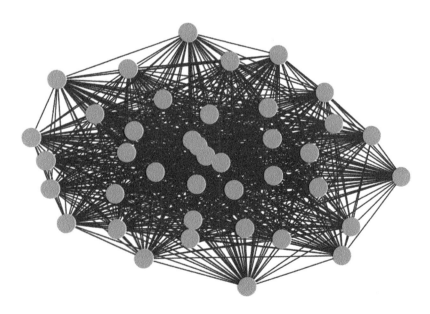

Figure 13.6   Sociogram of the co-used tags within the Movie Stack Exchange

Part of the problem with bipartite projection is that it seems every node is connected to almost every other node. But in reality the nodes have differing weights depending on how frequently the two tags appeared together. So for the final network in Figure 13.7, I filter down the weights so that tags had to co-occur at least 50 times and then plot the network with some extra aesthetics. I could filter these at the `draw_networkx_edges`, but then all the nodes would still be considered for the layout, so I will do a subgraph first.

```
keep_list = []
for edge in lvl2g.edges:
    if lvl2g.edges[edge]["weight"] >= 50:
        keep_list.append(edge)

print(len(lvl2g.edges), len(keep_list))

780 107

lvl2g_sub = lvl2g.edge_subgraph(keep_list)

pos = nx.spring_layout(lvl2g_sub)

nx.draw_networkx_nodes(lvl2g_sub,pos,node_color="lightblue",alpha=0.3)
nx.draw_networkx_edges(lvl2g_sub,pos,edge_color="lightgrey")
nx.draw_networkx_labels(lvl2g_sub,pos,font_size=8)

plt.show()
```

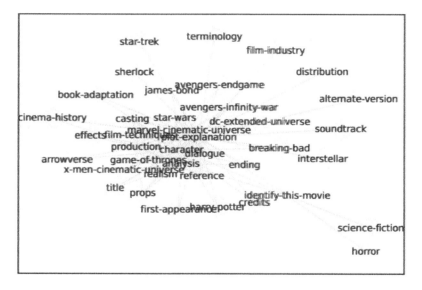

Figure 13.7   Sociogram of a subset of the co-used tags within the Movie Stack Exchange

From here there is so much left to do. For example, we might want to label the tags as to whether they are franchises to see which of these are the most central, or examine such a network across multiple Stack Exchanges. We might look at the weighted degree or other centrality measures to see who is the best connected, or do a *k-core composition* to see what is the core of the most nodes connected to each other. Since this network looked very much like a 'core–periphery' network with a single dense core, I do not think that community detection is useful here. But that says something in itself: there are not multiple clusters of tags for different discussions. Rather, some tags seem to be especially central in binding the network together. If we did this on the very large Stack Overflow, which concerns programming and coding languages, might we find similar commonalities, or perhaps the tags will be clustered by programming language. I will leave this to you to explore.

Before we conclude, it is worth showing how to save a network in a common format for storage and then how to read the same graph back into `networkx`. I do this using GraphML, which is an XML standard for network graphs and can be read by most popular network analysis programs.

```
nx.write_graphml(tagg, data_dir / "bipartite_tagdata movie stack.graphml")
newg = nx.read_graphml(data_dir / "bipartite_tagdata movie stack.graphml")
print(newg)
```

```
Graph with 5828 nodes and 12258 edges
```

 Summary

Social network analysis is a widely used paradigm to help understand and represent social structure. In technical terms this entails creating graphs based on people (or accounts, etc.) and some relationship between them. The graphs can include additional information about the nodes and the edges. Sometimes these attributes act as weights that can be used to do things like resize nodes or filter edges.

In the statistical modelling of networks, there is an interest in assessing how a network compares to some random baseline. We can get a random baseline using a graph generator. One important metric that uses a random baseline is modularity. It compares whether node assignments into separate groups lead to more edges within groups than the baseline. Modularity theoretically ranges −1 to +1, with 0 meaning there's no bias towards more edges within a group and values above 0 meaning more of a group. The Karate club network had a modularity of around 0.4. This was for both the 'ground truth' partition of who went to which club and the community detection partition which suggested three groups (two actually being subsets of one of the clubs).

Deferring to other texts on the ways to describe and analyse networks, I chose instead to show some details on how to visualise a network as well as how to wrangle data from the Stack Exchange into a network. In doing so, I featured a number of wrangling approaches which provided different perspectives on the dataset. This included looking at the user reply network, a weighted reply network as a subset, and a tags affiliation network.

The further reading section below lists some resources for collecting and analysing social network data. Unfortunately, none of them are in Python, but the `networkx` routines for doing many of the tasks featured therein are available. However, this far in the book, I do not think that we need to be stubborn about the use of Python. I think it is a useful language to wrangle and reshape data. In doing so, it can allow us greater access to the sorts of data we might want to explore. However, if there are some things that are only available elsewhere, then see if you can manage. You might be able to get your data in the shape you need here in Python and then port only the final desired network over to the program you need, whether it is in R, MatLab, or JavaScript.

I want to end with a plea here to consider social theory in this work. These networks are not mere maps for a *very large* community detection as is often seen online. Structural features such as the amount of reciprocity or closure can have a considerable consequence on how a network feels and develops. They come from past work observing people, describing their behaviour and their systems. Many of the most interesting structural features are not even obvious from a sociogram like those above. But getting a full picture of how nodes interact might effectively involve such sorts of metrics regardless of whether they show up in a sociogram. Pre-dating many of the packages we use and even the languages themselves, I think Wellman's 'Structural Analysis: From Method and Metaphor to Theory and Substance' (Wellman, 1988) inspires here. It captures the idea that these networks represent a paradigm for understanding social behaviour. Networks show how our activities and attitudes are not covariates for a regression that treats cases as independent. Rather, behaviours and features of users can directly affect each other and can be seen as an overall structure representing a social system. Similarly, when collecting data, researchers can sometimes be convenient or ambiguous about their boundary. This is known as the boundary specification problem (Laumann et al., 1989). It persists because of its challenges and the many ways in which network data is both constructed and expressed (Perry and Roth, 2021).

Further reading

Network science and social network analysis have both seen some excellent texts over the last few years. These would scarcely be in Python, but they often discuss the important conceptual issues involved in collecting and analysing the data.

For a clear perspective on social network analysis, my go-to reference is *Analyzing Social Networks* (Borgatti et al., 2018). I have yet to see the new edition with R (and new co-author Filip Agneessens), but I have taught with the previous editions of this book. I think that it does an excellent job of describing some features of social networks that are apparent when you measure them systematically but might be difficult to spot in everyday life or intuitively. They elucidate why concepts such as closure, reciprocity, and equivalence might make a difference to a social networks and how to make clear claims using a bevy of statistical approaches such as exponential random graph models (ERGMs) and the quadratic assignment procedure (QAP).

A book that uses a more diverse ensemble of networks and examples, being an exemplar of network science, is Newman's *Networks* (second edition, 2018). This book shows a wide array of network metrics and approaches, with some relatively mathematical descriptions of key approaches. Newman has had a hand in many of my favourite approaches to networks, such as modularity, assortativity, and community detection. This book covers these and many more topics that I mentioned only very briefly in this chapter (such as network generators and co-citation networks).

For a variety of ways that networks have been linked to approaches in data science, I like a now slightly out-of-date book called *Programming Collective Intelligence* by Segaran (2007). It starts to show how ideas from what was emerging in network science and statistics were becoming what we now consider to be machine learning. The code for this book is in Python. Also from O'Reilly Press, there is an excellent text not too far from this one called *Mining the*

Social Web. Its third edition is by Russell and Klassen (2019). It pre-dates Twitter v2 API and thus illustrates how much these APIs change so quickly, but in each of the three editions there are some interesting examples of how to use data in a networked way, whether it was with clustering LinkedIn contacts or collaborations on GitHub. This is in addition to the many other creative examples that introduce a number of data science methods in each chapter alongside a specific platform or medium. The code for this book is in Jupyter notebooks on GitHub (and also written in Python).

Extensions and reflections

- In Chapter 7 on APIs, we saw how to collect data from Twitter. A classic approach is to search for a hashtag, generally a niche one, and then build a network of who retweets whom with that hashtag. You can get the nodes from the Twitter author ID and build links using the `in_reply_to_userid` field in the tweet. If the hashtag is for a specific conference, festival, or community, you will likely see cohesion and some interesting clustering. This is because these people are likely to use the hashtag as part of means to organise their shared online identity. They may retweet each other or mention each other.

- There was little said in this chapter about key network metrics such as betweenness and closeness centrality. If you are comfortable with the Python thus far, running these commands should not be challenging by exploring the `networkx` documentation. But it will be important to determine what they mean for their network. Construct a network using Reddit replies. For example, take all the people who replied to the most recent 100 posts. This would be a person-to-post network. Project it so that you can see which posts are most strongly connected (implying the same users reply to any two posts that are strongly connected). Use resources like Agneessens et al. (2017) and Borgatti (2005) to help consider how to build the network.

- The standard community detection measures in `networkx` are not as flexible as some others which have become more relevant lately. Two in particular stand out: the Leiden method (Traag et al., 2019) and InfoMap (Rosvall et al., 2009). These allow for greater use cases, like taking into account weighted directed networks and some element of overlapping community structure. Both are available in Python. These are additional installs but the up-to-date instructions would be available online for both. InfoMap in particular has an extensive and engaging website (https://www.mapequation.org/) to facilitate its use. In Python there is also the really interesting `cdlib` library. This library facilitates the testing and comparing of community detection methods as well as plotting them and reporting on goodness-of-fit statistics. The repository includes Jupyter notebook tutorials (https://github.com/KDDComplexNetworkAnalysis/CNA_Tutorials) for comparing community detection algorithms that can be run directly in the browser via Google Colab. Install `cdlib` on your instance of Python/Jupyter and compare the solutions of the different aforementioned algorithms. Use `cdlib`'s methods to simplify the drawing of nodes in communities. In particular, try the `viz.plot_community_graph()` method featured in the visualisation section of the `cdlib` tutorial. It allows you to summarise a very large graph into the connections between the much smaller number of communities discovered.

14

INTRODUCING GEOGRAPHIC INFORMATION SYSTEMS: DATA ACROSS SPACE AND PLACE

Learning goals

- Understand how a map means a projection of data into a coordinate space
- Appreciate how projecting a sphere onto a plane leads to warping
- Make a map with a default shapefile as well as shapefiles downloaded from the web
- Understand how to show differences within a distribution on a map using `mapclassify`
- Be able to link together data from different sources using shared geoidentifiers.

 ## Introduction: From space to place

Geography is an important and pervasive aspect of computational social science. While much work on data science takes place with data from the internet, sensors, or surveys, all data (as it is drawn from phenomena) is structured in some way as data is defined by measurement. Geography is a quintessential structured constraint. We can physically only be in one place at one time. Places have their own logics, their own cultures, and their own ways of being described or addressed. As those in geography tend to note, there is a difference between space and place (Graham and Dittus, 2022). Where space refers to the three-dimensional area containing or defining physical boundaries, place is a cultural construction. This distinction is relatively important for social data science, as we will have measurements of both *place* and *space* and sometimes it can be tricky to arbitrate between them. For example, we might have data with latitude and longitude, which are spatial coordinates. But then we want to take that point and assign it to a place.

Below we will use Python's powerful but difficult-to-install `geopandas` package to represent both space and measurements of places associated with that space. Our goal here is modest and generally descriptive. Geographic information systems (GIS), noogeography, data cartography and more are all expert means of engaging in scholarly work at the nexus of geographic data science and social science. I will point to some readings to go further in this at the end of the chapter. Nevertheless, we can actually get pretty far in a single chapter by focusing on some of the basics of plotting and maps in Python.

First, however, we ought to talk generally about what is spatial data and particularly spatial data on the surface of a sphere (e.g., the surface of the Earth). Then we will get to show how different maps of this space have different levels of detail. Finally, we will apply some data to our maps and observe how we can represent this data visually. This is just scratching the surface of geographic work but it should hopefully be a good starting point for building intuitions and embarking on your own spatially infused data science work.

 ## Kinds of spatial data

Spatial data refers to measurements of space. Now this space need not be real and it need not be on Earth. We can think of spatial distances between characters in video games or in virtual spaces. What defines spatial data is that objects are associated with coordinates within a coordinate reference system. We can use different systems for different shapes. Imagine taking a piece of paper and trying to assign every 1 cm square its own reference. You might start at one corner, call that corner 'top left' and then count in 1 cm units until you get to the right-hand side in one direction. Then count in 1 cm units in the other direction and call that the bottom. So now if you say 'colour in the square that's 3cm from the top and 4cm from the left', you will know where to fill in the colour. Now imagine someone comes by and suggests they do the same thing, but they have a rule with inches rather than centimetres. They will be able to make fewer, larger squares with inches than with centimetres. But what if they are asked to colour the square that's 3 cm from the top and 4 cm from the left? The squares don't quite overlap! Thus the first thing to consider with coordinates is that they have different resolutions. The more granular the resolution the more detailed a square we could colour. But if the units of measurement are different, such as miles and kilometres, then we have to not only convert distance, but then link the points from one unit to another. A large amount of work to be done with geospatial data really comes down to this issue: you have some point, line, or shape in one system of measurement or coded in some way and you'll need to convert it to another.

What differentiates geospatial data from merely geometry is that it tends to be in reference to real objects in three-dimensional space, like the Earth or a city. With geospatial data we often have to contend with the fact we want to represent space in some flat two-dimensional way, like a rectangular map, yet the data itself refers to coordinates on the surface of the planet which is pretty close to being a sphere (actually an 'oblate spheroid' or a squished sphere). To convert from a shape with one dimension to one with another dimension, we tend to call this a 'projection'. By projecting our data into some shape, we can visualise our data in space in relation to other shapes (like seeing Canada as just north of the United States of America), or we can use some visual variables (Roth, 2017) to signify something about these shapes and points (like seeing that Chongqing in China is the most populous municipality in the world, but Tokyo is still the largest urban area).

14.2.1 From a sphere to a rectangle

To think about how we apply a coordinate system to the Earth let's use the example of an orange (the fruit), which like the Earth is generally spherical. For this orange metaphor, I extend the engaging materials from the online code tutorial at Data Carpentry (https://datacarpentry.org/organization-geospatial/03-crs/).

Imagine the part of the orange that was previously connected to the tree (the pit) as the 'top' of the orange. We will call that the North Pole. Then consider the point on the orange furthest from this pole. On the orange it's often called the navel, but we will imagine it is the South Pole. Imagine sticking a pencil through the orange and then twirling it. You are rotating the orange around its axis, as well as potentially making a juicy mess. In theory we could have stabbed the poor orange anywhere and had the pencil come out the other side and twirled it, but the pit and the navel seemed like sensible choices. Why? Because the orange is organised around the pit and the navel. It's not just that we find one point and call it north and another south, but that when we open the orange up we see segments, often called orange slices, that appear to rotate around this main axis. Now an orange might have a almost a dozen segments. For the Earth, we could imagine carving up the globe into 360 segments. Why 360? Because it is a number that divides into many useful smaller numbers. And we traditionally use 360 for degrees from geometry. Each wedge then represents some range of longitude as we rotate around the axis.

If we wanted to mark somewhere on the planet, we would first then want to identify which wedge it falls in. We have, for historical reasons, suggested that we start our first wedge somewhere that includes the middle of England – Greenwich, in fact – which also helps us with respect to timekeeping (Zerubavel, 1982). Now if we happen to be in Greenwich and can identify which way is north (and lucky for us, there's a pretty bright star in the sky, Polaris, which if you look in its direction also happens to be north), then we can also identify east and west. That is, if we are in Greenwich, facing the North Star, and start walking to our left, we will be going west, leaving Greenwich, heading towards Ireland, the Atlantic and North America. If we instead walk to our right, we will be heading east, first towards western then eastern Europe, then towards Eurasia, China, and Japan. Either way, when we get halfway around the globe we will be in the Pacific Ocean. Each 1/360 turn around the Earth will be a degree. And we will say from Greenwich that heading left will be 0 to 180 degrees West and heading right will be 0 to 180 degrees East.

While some landmarks in the world are directly east or west of Greenwich, some would require us to either go up or down a little on our journey. For this up or down, which we call *latitude*, we also need to define a 0 and then mark things relative to 0. In keeping with the notion of nice numbers to work with, by convention we use 180 degrees. The middle point, around the Equator (meaning equal distance from the North and South Poles) is going to be 0. Going closer to the North Pole will be up to 90 degrees North. Going closer to the South Pole will be 90 degrees South.

With these slices in hand we can now mark points around the globe using a latitude and longitude coordinate system. The handy thing about this is that we can now draw squares on a grid to represent both which wedge and how far from the Equator. The problem, though, is that a 1° longitude by 1° latitude square actually covers a lot more ground near the Equator than near the North Pole. This is what has been known as the 'trouble with Greenland' issue. When you make each 1° × 1° square of our globe equal to 1° × 1° square on paper, things near the poles seem much larger than they really are. To explain this issue, we can return to our orange. Take the pencil out and then try to peel the orange. But don't break the peel, leave it all in one piece. How exactly should we flatten it so that we get a decent rectangle? In geospatial terms, when we take the points on the sphere with 360° longitude and 180° latitude and then arrange them on that 360° × 180° rectangle we are employing a projection. There's no ideal projection, but some do a better job of conveying the scale of different shapes on the globe or the distance between any two points on the globe.

While much is often made of how different projections give a distorted view of the size of some parts of the world, I think that the main story is that we have now carved the world up according to some coordinate system. This allows us to synchronise our sense of where objects are, to transform these points on a globe to those on a rectangle, and thereby unify how we describe places as being mappable entities in space.

14.2.2 Mapping places onto spaces

Projections in geography mean that we are taking some abstract reference system and imposing it on the world. But the projections are mathematical abstractions, like a cube or a grid. When we project them on to the world we need to establish some reference points or conventions. This is the act of mapping the world. In this book we have previously seen mapping in a more mathematical sense. We would take some value from a `Series` and then use some function or dictionary to give us a different result. This would often take the form `df["Series"].map(lambda x: func(x))`. Mapping in the conventional sense, then, is not actually that different from what we have been doing in `pandas`. We are translating some spatial entity from one domain (measurements from reality) to another (a coordinate reference system) using some operation. Then we use the results in the CRS to represent the spatial entities in reality.

If we use the `geopandas` library in Python we can get a sense of this mapping using one of their example datasets. `geopandas` comes with a dataset called `world` as one of its three defaults. It's not very high resolution but when you view it you will definitely identify it as the world from other such representations. Note that `geopandas` is an additional installation from Anaconda.

Installing geopandas

Depending on your operating system configuration, installing `geopandas` and the related libraries might be easy or very complicated. On Windows the installation instructions on the `geopandas` website appeared to be successful for me. On a Mac OSX computer I have found the most success through a different approach, which was to first install GDAL (the Geospatial Data Abstraction Library) through `brew` using these two commands in sequence in the terminal:

```
brew install gdal --HEAD
brew install gdal
```

You will first need to install `homebrew`. Then once these two are installed, use `pip` to install the following packages *in order*: `pyproj`, `mapclassify`, `Fiona`, `Shapely`, and finally `pip install geopandas`. I have had limited success using `conda`. If everything is working out you should be able to `import geopandas` with no errors. These instructions are liable to change. Check in with the book's GitHub repository to see if there are more updated instructions.

```
import geopandas
import matplotlib.pyplot as plt
%config InlineBackend.figure_format = 'svg'

world = geopandas.read_file(geopandas.datasets.\
                    get_path('naturalearth_lowres'))
```

```
world.columns = [x.replace("_","-") for x in world.columns]
print(world.columns)
```

```
Index(['pop-est', 'continent', 'name', 'iso-a3', 'gdp-md-est', 'geometry'],
dtype='object')
```

```
world.plot()
plt.show()
```

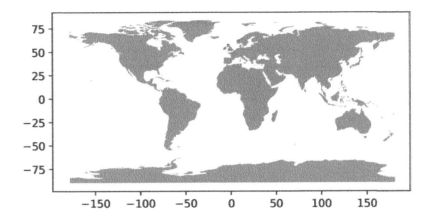

Figure 14.1 Plot of the world using the default geopandas shapefile

The image in Figure 14.1 certainly looks identifiable as the countries of the Earth. Admittedly the aesthetics are a little plain, but we can tune this up later. Notice that the x-axis goes from −180 to 180. These are the longitude coordinates of the Earth. The prime meridian goes through Greenwich in the UK at 0 and the Equator goes through the y-axis at 0.

Notice how Antarctica is a stretched-out blob at the bottom. That's because in this coordinate system, we have had to stretch the area down there to fit this projection. You might also notice by the name of the file, naturalearth_lowres, that the file is low-resolution. So, for example, if we have a look at the United Kingdom, we will see that it omits or smoothes over entire parts of the country (Figure 14.2).

```
world[world['iso-a3'] == "GBR"].plot()
plt.show()
```

This is very much not a high-resolution map of the United Kingdom. Close up it looks a little more like the logo from the London 2012 Olympics. But from this we can still learn a few things. First, note that world was a geopandas dataset. The world had a column in it called iso_a3 and we used that column to get a row for the United Kingdom of Great Britain and Northern Ireland using the three letters GBR. This is the three-letter (alpha-3) ISO code for the United Kingdom. All countries and territories around the world have both a two- and three-letter code. An index of these can be found on Wikipedia among other places (https://en.wikipedia.org/wiki/List_of_ISO_3166_country_codes). When data has one of these codes we can use it to link data to that country.

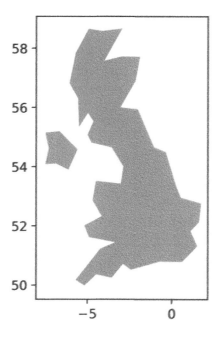

Figure 14.2 Plot of Great Britain using the default geopandas shapefile, highlighting the low resolution

14.2.3 Introducing the geopandas GeoDataFrame

Now this is not just any DataFrame, it's a GeoDataFrame. The difference is that a GeoDataFrame has columns dedicated to geometry. Looking at the first few rows of world, we can see that it has a geometry column. Let's look below at that column and a couple others from the DataFrame.

```
world[["name", "iso-a3", "gdp-md-est", "geometry"]].head()
```

	name	iso-a3	gdp-md-est	geometry
0	Fiji	FJI	8374.0	MULTIPOLYGON (((180 -16.06713266364245, ...
1	Tanzania	TZA	150600.0	POLYGON ((33.90371119710453 -0.950000000...
2	W. Sahara	ESH	906.5	POLYGON ((-8.665589565454809 27.65642588...
3	Canada	CAN	1674000.0	MULTIPOLYGON (((-122.84 49.0000000000001,...
4	United States of America	USA	18560000.0	MULTIPOLYGON (((-122.84 49.0000000000001...

In the geometry column are rows titled POLYGON and MULTIPOLYGON. These are using latitude and longitude coordinates as boundaries of the shapes. Other kinds of shapes to be found in a geometry column would be POINT and LINESTRING and multiples thereof.

As a GeoDataFrame, Python treats the geometry column differently. There is usually only one geometry column in a GeoDataFrame, but there could be multiples in which case only one is the active column. With that column we can ask questions of the geometry that allow us to link place to space. In the DataFrame we can see that there are two numerical columns, pop_est and gdp_md_est. These represent values we can show on the map. Drawing liberally from the tutorial provided by the authors of geopandas (https://geopandas.org/en/stable/docs/user_guide/mapping.html), let's make a map that plots the gross domestic product (GDP) per capita. We will also mask Antarctica from the DataFrame, which will then alter the shape of the map (Figure 14.3).

```
world['gdp-per-cap'] = world['gdp-md-est'] / world['pop-est']

world_na = world[world.name!="Antarctica"]

world_na.plot(column='gdp-per-cap')

plt.show()
```

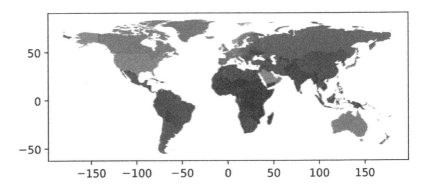

Figure 14.3 Choropleth map of the world by GDP per capita illustrating difficulties in seeing small wealthy countries on map

Admittedly this is not particularly effective without a legend. But as noted in the geopandas tutorial, the generic legend does not play nice with this figure (but try for yourself by adding the legend=True parameter above). So instead, we have to manage a few things. The first is to get the dimensions of the axis (divider = make_axes_locatable(ax) below), then we can add a legend to one side with the right height (Figure 14.4). It's not the only form of legend, as we shall see below, but it is a start.

```
from mpl_toolkits.axes_grid1 import make_axes_locatable
fig, ax = plt.subplots()

divider = make_axes_locatable(ax)

cax = divider.append_axes("right", size="5%", pad=0.1)

world_na.plot(column='gdp-per-cap', ax=ax, legend=True, cax=cax);
plt.show()
```

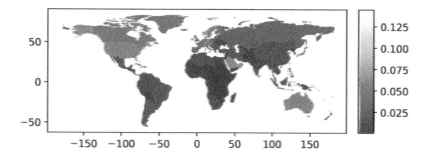

Figure 14.4 Choropleth map of the world by GDP per capita with well-contained legend showing wealth disparity

You might also notice that this map uses the `viridis` colour scheme. The authors of `matplotlib` have created a helpful essay on this colour scheme and its advantages (https://bids.github.io/colormap/). One thing to note on the legend is that the colours go very light, whereas it is hard to see a lightly coloured country on the map. If we look in the `DataFrame` for the countries with the highest GDP per capita, we can see they are generally small countries, so seeing them on a large map of the Earth would be difficult.

```
world_na.sort_values("gdp_per_cap")\
    [["name", "iso_a3", "pop_est", "gdp_md_est", "gdp_per_cap"]].tail()
```

	name	iso-a3	pop-est	gdp-md-est	gdp-per-cap
128	Luxembourg	LUX	594130	58740.0	0.098867
86	Kuwait	KWT	2875422	301100.0	0.104715
84	United Arab Emirates	ARE	6072475	667200.0	0.109873
23	Fr. S. Antarctic Lands	ATF	140	16.0	0.114286
85	Qatar	QAT	2314307	334500.0	0.144536

14.2.4 Splitting the data into intervals using `mapclassify`

Qatar, the United Arab Emirates, Kuwait, and Luxembourg are all very small in area compared to these other countries. This suggests that there might be a better approach through binning available. Instead of a continuous gradient on a legend, we can have a map with some intervals based on aggregating the data. There are many ways to create cutpoints in a distribution to create intervals. A fair number of these are available in a separate package called `mapclassify`. If this package is installed with `geopandas`, then we can use it even without importing it. Simply call the `scheme` parameter in the `plot()` statement. This tells `mapclassify` how to partition the data to highlight differences in a distribution that we can render on a map. It's called `scheme` because the differences are usually binned in relatively small numbers of bins and we would use a colour palette (or colour scheme) to distinguish the bins. These become the basis of the very popular *choropleth* map (Jenks and Caspall, 1971). 'Choro' means 'region' (from a Greek root).

In Figure 14.5 I use `scheme='quantiles'` to create a choropleth map with bins including equal numbers of countries. And I also use a slightly different, simpler colour gradient in yellow-green.

```
world_na.plot(column='gdp-per-cap',
              scheme='quantiles',
              cmap='YlGn',
              legend =True);

plt.show()
```

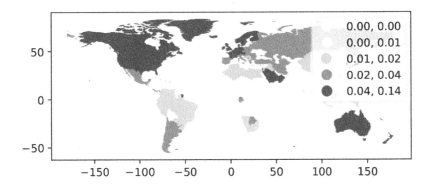

Figure 14.5   Choropleth map of the world by GDP per capita with well-contained legend split by quantiles

Now we can see a lot more distinction between the different sets of countries. Whether these distinctions are the right ones to make is another matter. Are we trying to explain some feature or claim, and are we using the map to annotate this claim? Or are we trying a more predictive approach where we are trying to maximise some distinction? There's an extensive discussion in geography about how best to cut a distribution based on its geometric properties (Jiang, 2013). Simply binning the data into five buckets might obscure some extreme differences between the bins or otherwise group together rows that are likely to be qualitatively distinct in some manner.

Below, in a practical example on Covid-19 rates in England, we will look at different ways of cutting the distribution using a simple `mapclassify` algorithm that splits the data in to 5 even buckets. Later we show a smarter approach that is more careful with where it cuts the data. To use the `mapclassify` library it on its own (instead of inside a `plot` statement):

```
import mapclassify as mc

print(mc.Quantiles(world["gdp-per-cap"], k=5), sep="\n\n")
```

```
Quantiles

   Interval        Count
-----------------------------
[0.00,  0.00]  |     36
(0.00,  0.01]  |     35
(0.01,  0.02]  |     35
(0.02,  0.04]  |     35
(0.04,  0.20]  |     36
```

Admittedly this is still a bit hard to read as a table since the interval is truncated. Here the measurement is GDP per capita in millions of US dollars, which is not really well normalised. But the classifier provided five groups of roughly 35 countries each. We can tweak this with some parameters such as the number of groups (for most classifiers). With quantiles it is k. You can either pass that as a parameter to mc.Quantiles(y=<distribution>,k=<n>) or when plotting you just pass k as in

```
world_na.plot(column='gdp-per-cap', scheme='quantiles', k=8)
```

14.2.5 Plotting points

We can plot points in a similar way to shapes as long as we have a GeoDataFrame. It uses the geometry column (or another GeoSeries column if that has been set) to find the points and plot them on a map. Here we can take the cities data from geopandas, which is just a list of world capitals and their latitude/longitude coordinates as points (typically in the centre of the city); see Figure 14.6. Each city is a polygon in its own right, but at this scale we use a point to denote the city.

```
cities = geopandas.read_file(
    geopandas.datasets.get_path('naturalearth_cities'))

cities.head()
```

	name	geometry
0	Vatican City	POINT (12.45339 41.90328)
1	San Marino	POINT (12.44177 43.93610)
2	Vaduz	POINT (9.516669 47.13372)
3	Luxembourg	POINT (6.130003 49.61166)
4	Palikir	POINT (158.15007 6.91664)

```
ax = world_na.plot()

cities.plot(marker = "*", color = "black", markersize = 5, ax=ax)

plt.show()
```

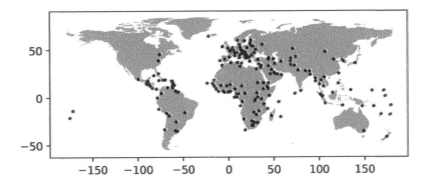

Figure 14.6 Map of the world, with points for capital cities

 3 **Creating your own** `GeoDataFrame`

A `GeoDataFrame` is an extension of a `DataFrame` except that it has one active `GeoSeries` column, called `geometry`. Thus, to create a `GeoDataFrame`, you merge a `GeoSeries` with a `DataFrame`.

If you do not have a `GeoSeries` at the ready, but you do have longitude coordinates, you can set them yourself. For example, to place Jim Henson, creator of the Muppets, on the map, we might first note that he was born in Greenville, Mississippi. By looking up Greenville (admittedly from Wikipedia), I noticed that the geocoordinates for the city were (33.398, –91.048). So I created a `GeoSeries` with one row using `geopandas.point_from_xy()` and then combined this with the `DataFrame` that included the name as the new `GeoDataFrame`.

```
import pandas as pd

landmarks = pd.DataFrame({"name":["Greenville"],
            "lat":[33.398],"long":[-91.048]})

gdf = geopandas.GeoDataFrame(landmarks,
        geometry=geopandas.points_from_xy(landmarks.long,landmarks.lat))

display(gdf)
```

	name	lat	long	geometry
0	Greenville	33.398000	-91.048000	POINT (-91.048 33.398)

```
ax = world_na.plot(color="grey")

gdf.plot(color="black", ax=ax)

plt.show()
```

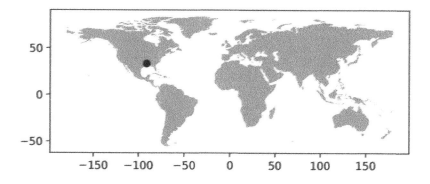

Figure 14.7 Map of the world, highlighting a user-defined point from a `GeoDataFrame`

The result is plotted in Figure 14.7.

14.3.1 Loading your own maps

For many tasks the low-resolution world map with geopandas will not be sufficient, particularly when trying to represent subnational divisions. To work with another map, you would first need a shapefile. A shapefile stores the vectors that represent the location, boundaries, and some related information for a specific geographic region. There is not a universal one-stop repository for shapefiles, nor a single package that draws upon a worldwide index of them. This is because there might be very detailed shapefiles of a city, region, or place that a particular government or agency keeps and updates for their records.

Nevertheless, perhaps the closest to a worldwide set of shapefiles for administrative areas like countries, provinces, and municipalities would be the GADM project (https://gadm.org), or the Database of Global Administrative Areas. The top level of GADM is a country and, depending on the country, there might be two or three lower divisions such as provinces or states.[1] I have already copied the entire zipped shapefile for the UK into my data folder. geopandas reads shapefiles as easily as pandas reads CSV. With a well-formatted shapefile geopandas will turn it into a `DataFrame` with multiple elements each becoming a row for their own polygon, line, or point. The following code generates Figure 14.8.

```
from pathlib import Path
data_dir = Path.cwd().parent / "data"
gbshp = geopandas.read_file(data_dir / "gadm36_GBR_shp" / "gadm36_GBR_1.shp")
gbshp.plot()

plt.show()
```

---

[1]Shapefiles are freely available from https://GADM.org but not for commercial use. Thankfully we have permission to include some of them here for educational purposes. They are available from the book's GitHub page.

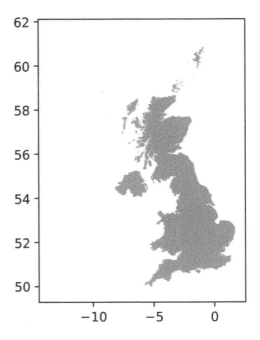

Figure 14.8   Higher-resolution shapefile of the UK from GADM

One challenge with shapefiles, especially at the subnational level, is that the codes that are used in order to indicate the various regions might not be the ideal regions for whatever analysis you are doing, just like having a government report on 1 inch by 1 inch squares, but you only have a shapefile for 1 cm by 1 cm squares. For example, the data from the UK local authority divisions uses LPA21CD as the field names which should be merged in with other data, yet other files might use slightly different shapes or regions, such as the reporting by a local hospital board.

The GADM project is an attempt to create a unified key for such shapefiles across countries by using the ISO code and decimal points to signify the subregions. As the UK has four constituent countries, each one will have its own administrative regions. We loaded the shapefile at region 1 which is just these countries, but if we load it at a lower level we can see more granularity.

```
gbshp = geopandas.read_file(data_dir / "gadm36_GBR_shp" / "gadm36_GBR_3.shp")

gbshp.columns = [x.replace("_","-") for x in gbshp.columns]

print(gbshp.columns)

Index(['GID-0', 'NAME-0', 'GID-1', 'NAME-1', 'NL-NAME-1', 'GID-2', 'NAME-2',
       'NL-NAME-2', 'GID-3', 'NAME-3', 'VARNAME-3', 'NL-NAME-3', 'TYPE-3',
       'ENGTYPE-3', 'CC-3', 'HASC-3', 'geometry'],
      dtype='object')
gbshp[["NAME-1","GID-3","NAME-3","geometry"]].sample(5,random_state=7)
```

	NAME-1	GID-3	NAME-3	geometry
220	England	GBR.1.66.1_1	Nottingham	POLYGON ((-1.21835 52.90842...
295	England	GBR.1.103.1_1	Torbay	POLYGON ((-3.57106 50.48154...
391	Wales	GBR.4.8.1_1	Conwy	POLYGON ((-3.51270 53.31681...
357	Scotland	GBR.3.6.1_1	Dumfries and Galloway	MULTIPOLYGON (((-3.97972 54...
384	Wales	GBR.4.1.1_1	Anglesey	MULTIPOLYGON (((-4.48695 53...

What is interesting is when we can merge in statistics that can be layered over such a map. The OxCOVID19 project is an example of a data repository with statistics keyed to GADM (Mahdi et al., 2021). It links Covid-19 statistics around the world at the subnational level using these GADM codes. The database of Covid-19 statistics is freely available either through a database connection or through GitHub. Here I will use a static database accompanying this chapter in case the URL or data changes over time. The database shows statistics for Covid-19 infections in the UK. By creating a column of data and then merging it with the gbshp GeoDataFrame, I can then create a choropleth related to Covid-19.

14.3.2 Linking maps to other data sources

The shapefile on its own produces some nice maps at differing levels of detail. However, these shapes are generally more interesting when we use them to represent differences geographically. We can do that through the use of points or colour-coded regions. As an example of work by colour-coded regions, the OxCOVID project has been collecting public health statistics and a variety of other related indicators, all of which are keyed to GADM regions. Thus, we can take a table (either queried through their database or downloaded as a static file) and merge in the data to our shapefile.

```
covid_df = pd.read_csv(data_dir / "covid19db-epidemiology-GBR_PHE.csv.bz2")

print(len(covid_df))
display(covid_df.loc[0])

260119

source                  GBR_PHE
date                 14-09-2021
country          United Kingdom
countrycode                 GBR
adm_area_1              England
adm_area_2            Hampshire
adm_area_3              Gosport
tested                      NaN
confirmed                6949.0
recovered                   NaN
dead                      158.0
```

```
hospitalised                        NaN
hospitalised_icu                    NaN
quarantined                         NaN
gid                    ['GBR.1.38.5_1']
Name: 0, dtype: object
```

Although the first row was from the most recent data in this version of the table, `14-09-2021`, some data exploration will reveal that this table has many more time periods than the most recent. For example, above I used `len` to discover that there are 260,119 rows, and so we will have to filter the data down to the most recent reporting date. I do that and check that we have the same number of regions as we do in the shapefile for England.

```
cdf = covid_df[covid_df.date=="14-09-2021"].copy()
print(len(cdf),len(gbshp[gbshp['NAME-1'] == "England"]))
```

```
315 326
```

It appears that we have more regions in the shapefile (326) than in OxCOVID (315). But this is only because we have not properly parsed the `gid` column. When that column is imported from the CSV it has in it a list, but the list is literally printed as `"['element1',...]"` as a string, which we have to first turn into a list. When we do that, we can see that some rows have multiple GIDs associated with them, but if we count them all up we get 326 just like in the shapefile. To first turn the literal string representing a list into a list object we can use the built-in abstract syntax (`ast`) library.

```
import ast

try:
    cdf.gid = cdf.gid.map(ast.literal_eval)
    print(len(cdf.gid.sum()))
except ValueError:
    print("You can only convert the data once")
```

```
326
```

These 326 GIDs are spread around 315 rows. But since they are stored in a column in a list we can use `df.explode()`. But that copies each value into a new row. So the number of confirmed cases for three GIDs will be assigned to each of the three new rows. This means the confirmed cases will be triple-counted. To avoid this, I first select the measures I want (`confirmed`, `dead`). Then before I run `explode` I divide these columns by the length of the list of GIDs. Then I run `explode`. The sum of `confirmed` cases in the original `DataFrame` should then equal the number in the exploded `DataFrame`, even though the exploded `DataFrame` has 326 rows instead of 315.

```
cdf["lengids"]= cdf.gid.map(len)
cdf["ndead"] = cdf["dead"] / cdf["lengids"]

cdf["nconfirmed"] = cdf["confirmed"] / cdf["lengids"]
cdf_ex = cdf[["gid","ndead","nconfirmed"]].explode("gid")

# Some data integrity checks
print(len(gbshp[gbshp["NAME-1"] == "England"]) == len(cdf_ex))
print(cdf["confirmed"].sum() == cdf_ex["nconfirmed"].sum())
```

```
True
True
```

In the cases where we had to split the row into two or three, I understand that it is not accurate to assume that the three GIDs all had even numbers of cases or fatalities, but in the absence of more data it is better than triple-counting. However, there is still an issue with our data – it is not *normalised*. We can now plot the number of confirmed or dead per region, but the regions have different populations, different areas, and differential access to wealth and health care. If we want to make a map of where Covid-19 had the greatest impact, perhaps the number of fatalities would drive home the point. But if some areas have considerably more people, then this will only dilute the point. Instead of merging in population, which we would need to acquire at this granular scale from another source, we can normalise by the number of confirmed cases. This gives us the case–fatality ratio (CFR). Showing the CFR can give us clues to consider where Covid-19 was most deadly, although we need not be too confident (Spychalski, Błażyńska-Spychalska and Kobiela, 2020). Maybe the places where Covid-19 *seems* to be the most deadly are places where people simply did not test as commonly. But holding that thought for now, let's calculate and then have a look at the CFR for England.

```
cdf_ex["cfr"] = cdf_ex['ndead'] / cdf_ex['nconfirmed']

print(cdf_ex["cfr"].describe())
```

```
count    326.000000
mean       0.020349
std        0.005692
min        0.008807
25%        0.016426
50%        0.019581
75%        0.023528
max        0.045195
Name: cfr, dtype: float64
```

```
cdf_ex["cfr"].plot(kind="hist");
plt.show()
```

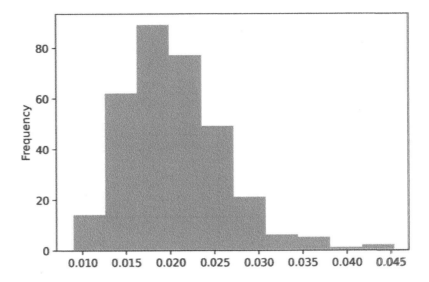

Figure 14.9 Distribution of case-fatality ratio by UK subnational region

The plot in Figure 14.9 shows that the CFR is a relatively normal distribution with a bit of a right skew. The average was at 0.02. Death counts for Public Health England refer to the fact that the person tested positive for Covid-19 within 28 days of death, not necessarily that they died of Covid-19 complications. That said, it appears that across the regions, roughly 2% of those who tested positive died within 28 days. Yet, that ratio has a pretty considerable range from 1% to 4.5%

If we want to map the rates, we would want to classify them in some way to see the colours more effectively. Let's view the quantiles of `mapclassify` and compare them to a more thoughtful approach, due to Fisher and Jenks, that considers where the distribution changes notably. For both the default is five groups.

```
fig, ax = plt.subplots()

cdf_ex["cfr"].plot(kind="hist",bins=20,
                   color="lightgrey",label="Case-Fatality Ratio")

res_fj = mc.FisherJenks(cdf_ex.cfr)
ax.axvline(res_fj.bins[0],color="black",label="Fisher Jenks")
for i in res_fj.bins[1:]:
    ax.axvline(i,color="black")

res_q = mc.Quantiles(cdf_ex.cfr)
ax.axvline(res_q.bins[0],linestyle=":",color="red",label="Quantiles")
for i in res_q.bins[1:]:
    ax.axvline(i,linestyle=":", color="red")
```

```
ax.legend()

plt.show()
```

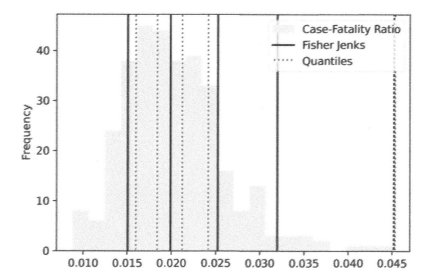

Figure 14.10 Case-fatality ratio distribution overlaid with multiple classifications showing differences in how algorithms split the data

Figure 14.10 plots the result.

I placed the quantiles in there using dotted lines and the Fisher–Jenks solution in solid black. As can be noted, the Fisher–Jenks solution does not have as even a distribution as five quantiles of equal numbers of regions. That said, looking at the distribution, it seems to more fairly chunk together regions with qualitatively similar CFR scores. We will use Fisher–Jenks as our scheme for the map. But first we must merge in our data from `cdf_ex` into `gbshp`.

```
eng_covid_df = gbshp.merge(cdf_ex,
                   left_on="GID-3",right_on="gid")

ax = eng_covid_df.plot(column="cfr",
          scheme="fisher_jenks", legend=True)

leg = ax.get_legend()
leg.set_bbox_to_anchor((0., 0.5, 1.5, 0.))
ax.set_axis_off()

plt.show()
```

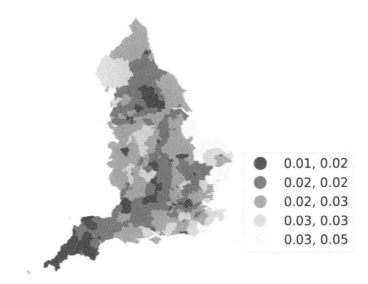

Figure 14.11 Choropleth map of case-fatality ratio using Fisher-Jenks cutpoints at the subnational level

The map in Figure 14.11 is not conclusive by any means, but it does highlight that CFR does indeed have some spatial autocorrelation. Notice that the yellow areas, which are especially extreme, are all clustered around the East of England. This was an area hard hit by one of the early variants of Covid-19. Beyond this, one might want to investigate some geospatial analyses of such things as investment in hospitals, distance to hospital, and the spread of specific variants, in order to get a fuller picture of why the distribution looks the way it does. Try to make a different map with either cases or deaths on their own, however, and you'll see a very different picture, one that is not normalised by population per region but is more a reflection of the population differences between the different regions than differences in the outcomes of Covid-19.

14.4 Summary

Geography is an exemplary case for computational social science since it involves both social science questions of power and culture in who defines a place alongside computational needs for mapping and coordinate systems. In this chapter, I have briefly introduced the coordinate system for the Earth, followed by an introduction to geopandas. Difficulties in installing geopandas might put some people off. But if you can get it working, then you can use a GeoDataFrame much like you would use a regular DataFrame. The main difference is that a GeoDataFrame has a column for geometry which includes shapely objects such as a LINE, POINT, or MULTIPOLYGON.

I demonstrated how to create a new GeoDataFrame with a single row (with a point for Greenville, Mississippi). Then I showed how to import shapefiles that are more granular than the default world map. With these shapefiles I was able to plot a map of Great Britain that was more detailed than the default. It was also at a scale where I could link external data using GADM codes as keys between the shapefile and the Covid-19 data. I highlighted how we could use some interesting features though *normalisation* and how we can be thoughtful about how our partitions reflect underlying distributions and not just bins of numbers.

With the skills in this chapter, I hope you will consider not merely using maps, but using them effectively, with clear selective presentation of geographic features and thoughtful divisions in the data.

 Further topics and reading

Hopefully this chapter has whetted your appetite for more mapping and geographic information system features within computational social science. I further hope it makes you feel a little more comfortable with one of Python's most active and engaging packages for geographic work. From here there are many extensions that lead either back to geographic information systems or forward to data science work. Below are a few extensions to this work that you might enjoy. Many of these are featured in the online book *Geographic Data Science with Python* (https://geographicdata.science/book/intro) by some of the foremost experts in GIS generally (Rey et al., 2020).

- *Spatial joins.* A spatial join takes shapes and determines if they overlap or cross each other. For example, if you are given the latitude and longitude coordinates, for example 48°57′25″N 54°36′32″W, then you would determine whether this is in a given city or a given country. This might be from sensor data or photo data where you map how photos of the world are concentrated in certain places. There has been a lot of interesting work in the last decade using user-generated data linked to geocodes (Quercia et al., 2014; Zook and Graham, 2007).
- *Geocoding.* Geocoding enables you to take generic names such as 'Oxford, UK' and assign a geographic entity to the name. If we are dealing with a world-scale map, then perhaps having a POINT for Oxford would be sufficient. If we are dealing with Oxfordshire county, maybe we want to code Oxford as a POLYGON. Nowadays, it is common to use third-party services to get a 'best guess' for the geocoordinates such as Google Maps or OpenStreetMap. The library geopy can take in text data and output geographic coordinates. One remarkable paper on the challenges of geocoding and dealing with Justin Bieber fans is Hecht et al. (2011).
- *Spatial autocorrelation regressions.* In standard regressions each row is independent, but in a spatial autocorrelation model we account for the fact that nearby neighbours would have a higher influence on some region than faraway regions.
- *Distance calculations as feature extraction.* The distance between points can tell you how far away something is. However, distance can be a tricky thing to calculate. For example:
  - *Euclidean distance* is the direct shortest path between two points in space. This might be fine for a gamma ray but most humans cannot easily pass through the Earth.
  - *Haversine distance* is the distance 'as the crow flies', which is the shortest path along the surface of a sphere.
  - *Manhattan distance* is the distance when we only move at right angles. It gets its name from the idea of travelling in Manhattan, where you have to zig-zag through city blocks.
  - *Practical distance* is the distance one might actually travel across a route such as by driving or walking, since these have to abide by roads.

Each of these distance metrics might have its own relationship to data depending on the research question. Geography is a very interesting contrast to social data science in so far as there are not only many resources for very technical work, but also a number of very thoughtful books on how the use of data about space has political, social, and cultural implications.

- *Code/Space* (Kitchin and Dodge, 2014) and *Rethinking Maps* (Dodge et al., 2009) are excellent places to get started on a critical approach to geography that is fully suffused with understandings akin to data science and questions about operationalisation and power.
- *The Visualisation of Spatial Social Structure* by Dorling (2012) is an explosion of ideas about how different presentations of maps can have different interpretations of social inequality. It is thorough and creative. Dorling's books tend to effectively use maps to display inequality generally, but this one is particularly methodical as in introduction to different ways of conveying this information visually.
- Graham and Dittus (2022) have recently published an engaging book, *Geographies of Digital Exclusion*, that clarifies how online spaces and offline spaces play off each other. It is suffused with arguments from both big data and anthropology and is a real culmination of Graham's ideas over the past decade and a half (though in full disclosure I collaborated on some of these ideas along the way).

Extensions and reflections

- When is geography relevant to online communities? Or rather, how wide a boundary should we expect for any community? For many languages around the world there are both regions where this language is commonly spoken and regions where it is less commonly spoken. How might we understand from social data whether we are seeing a community as a diaspora or as a nation?
- Geographic information as data is collected by a variety of actors, from national governments to online platforms (think Google Maps or Apple Maps) and community efforts (such as OpenStreetMap). When comparing these different sources through the lens of representation, what do we discover? Will the Google API give us more local businesses than OpenStreetMap? Whose results change more rapidly? When political turmoil happens can we detect it in the map data somehow?
- `mapclassify` was able to split up the data using a variety of approaches from simple quantiles to one that seems to capture distinct bends in the distribution such as Fisher-Jenks. Although the algorithms were driven by cartography, these can be used for binning distributions beyond choropleths. Try using `mapclassify` on other distributions we have encountered to come up with meaningful cutpoints and compare some other variables between these bins.
- When we collect data on some platforms such as Twitter, it can come with geographic information. In this book we have used the Movie Stack Exchange due to its accessibility and scope. Explore the `Users.xml` table to see people's self-reported location. Explore the use of `geopy` to map these locations onto geocodes. Then report on where these users are from. Has this changed over time? Is it different for different Stack Exchanges?
- You may recall well back in Chapter 4 on file types that we downloaded an Excel table from the World Bank. That table also used ISO codes in one of the columns, so with some

wrangling we could merge in values from the World Bank into our `world DataFrame`. Try to create multiple plots of different measurements in the data. Each one should show a different colour map of values by country from the World Bank data.

- Perhaps the most ambitious culmination of these skills might be to reproduce Hans Rosling's magnificent Gapminder program showing how, across the world, extreme poverty has been receding over the twentieth century. This has been done in interactive visualisations such as Bokeh, which is a library in Python for interactive graphics (https://demo.bokeh.org/gapminder). That URL also links to Rosling's electrifying TED talk, reasonably titled 'The Best Stats You've Ever Seen'.

15
CONCLUSION: THERE (TO DATA SCIENCE) AND BACK AGAIN (TO SOCIAL SCIENCE)

There is so much more that I could have put in this book and yet this version took me several years to put together. So I hope that, rather than seeing this as the end of the book, you will think of it as the start of the journey in social data science. With the skills demonstrated herein you should be able to collect, represent, analyse, and interpret social data, particularly data collected from a variety of places online. From this work, there are a huge number of ways you can make scientific or research claims.

One of the places to go after this book is further towards data science, but what exactly does that mean? Many things to many people, but generally it refers to several of the following:

- Machine learning based approaches to prediction and explanation. These approaches use an expanded version of the logic of precision and recall to determine whether we can accurately predict something. Work in this domain is expanding rapidly. For this, you might want to look at technologies such as `tensorflow and PyTorch` for machine learning prediction and `opencv` for computer vision. One classic textbook in this field is *The Elements of Statistical Learning*, which is an engaging next step after this book (Hastie et al., 2009). It is not written in Python, but the good news is that an ambitious community has reproduced all the code and figures in Python. See for example, Gaskov's GitHub repository (https://github.com/empathy87/The-Elements-of-Statistical-Learning-Python-Notebooks).
- Pipelines for automated data and analysis. There are ways to set up a program to download data from an API in real time, or at periodic intervals. This data is then 'ingested' and processed. These pipelines can help us understand interaction on a website, goods in an inventory, or anywhere else where data is constantly churning. Many of the books in this domain focus on specific technologies such as Microsoft Azure or AWS. They can be a bit dry, but I hope that they offer you the potential for work that is itself exciting.
- Dashboards and greater user experience features. Using Python technologies like `flask` and `dash`, you can present figures from a `DataFrame` on a dashboard that allows views of the data at a glance. Combined with pipelines for data from APIs, you can build really engaging ways to monitor data.

However, let's not forget that there is a wealth of social science approaches that can benefit from these newfound skills in wielding data. The social sciences have many of their own highly specialised and engaging approaches. For example:

- Statistical analyses within econometrics. In econometrics, time-series analysis is very sophisticated, with notions of Granger causality and difference-in-difference models to help understand change over time.
- Statistical estimation of networks. Within social network analysis there are methods that not only describe a network, but also estimate the probability of seeing a network like this by chance (e.g., exponential random graph models). Other models seek to estimate change over time. As Chapter 13 demonstrated, there are a multitude of ways to shape data to make it amenable to network analysis.
- Computational linguistics. This is a huge field that crosses computation and linguistics (and the social sciences broadly). Within it there are now some really incredible models for predicting words, checking which words co-associate, and examining change.

And then there is the wealth of work at the intersections of these domains, such as the incredibly exciting emergent community in fairness in AI, centred around the Fairness, Accountability, and Transparency (FAccT) conference. This field makes excellent use of these sorts of tools to interrogate sociotechnical systems, legal and regulatory regimes, and critique algorithms or online computational practices. I highlighted several texts to consider in this domain in Chapter 6. To this I would also add the online text by Barocas et al. (2019) which goes through some critical issues in assessing bias and especially bias in online spaces and data analysis. One of the most cohesive recent books on this topic is Crawford's magisterial *Atlas of AI* (2021). Crawford throws into sharp relief the people and the processes that can run with data science approaches to really exert power in the physical world in ways productive, exploitative, and environmentally destructive. This can be coupled nicely with Zuboff's thought-provoking *The Age of Surveillance Capitalism* (2019), which focuses keenly on the economic logics behind such technologically-driven exploitation.

Many of the works described above and the books mentioned in Chapter 1 such as *Data Feminism* (D'Ignazio and Klein, 2020) should act as an antidote to the notion that 'big data is the new oil', a vulgar and triumphant phrase that misunderstands both what can be done with data science and why. But below I would like to highlight two critical reasons why I take issue with that phrase.

The first is that, via the undeniable march of climate change, we can now recognise that oil is not simply consumed and transformed into energy. It leaves waste behind in the form of carbon dioxide, wreaking havoc on our planet. I do not like the idea that our data analysis itself leaves behind undue waste choking up the environment. Also, to make this metaphor less abstract, consider the paper 'On the Dangers of Stochastic Parrots' by Bender et al. (2021) which takes a very critical look at the carbon impact of training large-scale models among other issues with a big-is-better mindset.

The second reason is that we are not apart from the data we measure. These practices are literally about how *we*, as people, encode the world. Considering who gets to encode, who is or is not encoded, and what our encodings do to the behaviour of others is a key concern now. There is no 'best' way to sort a newsfeed or predict when to remind someone to check for news. These are algorithmic processes that intervene rather than merely reflect. Data, in my view, is more like a garden. We cannot simply extract from a garden if we want it to survive. We must nurture it, give back, take what we need and at the right time. We must be patient. Also, a garden is not wildflowers. When we tend the garden it becomes more orderly. The datafication of society has led, from clock time to longitude, to the world being more orderly (Schäfer and van Es, 2017). Data is not taken from society, it is only circulated and produced within, often in ways that reinforce inequality locally and globally (Graham et al., 2015; Noble, 2018).

My one hope is that the takeaway is not simply some strong skills in Python, but a respect for the detailed and intensely artful decisions that go into scientific work of encoding life as data. Some of these decisions concern how we think 'beyond the interface'. This tends towards questions we can answer of online data by understanding how to capture data through APIs or other creative online sources. Some decisions concern how we can best normalise data, clean out noise from a trend, or select a set of words. The most delicate decisions concern operationalisation. These are where we make scientific claims based on measurements of phenomena. With greater tools comes not only greater power, but also greater responsibility to ensure that you are measuring the concept you seek and not excluding, biasing, or marginalising in the process.

If the goal is to see the world at different scales, it is quickly followed by the goal of knowing how to tell the world what you have seen. In that, we must be careful to keep our results well presented with fair comparisons and clear details of how we got from our raw data to our claims. And then when doing so, we can relish, if only for a minute, a feeling of confidence that our claims are part of the sum total of human knowledge. And maybe then those claims will be superseded with newer claims as we continue to understand, represent, and critique our own continually changing world.

REFERENCES

A'Hearn, B., Peracchi, F., and Vecchi, G. (2009). Height and the normal distribution: Evidence from Italian military data. *Demography*, 46(1), 1–25. https://doi.org/10.1353/dem.0.0049

Agneessens, F., Borgatti, S. P., and Everett, M. G. (2017). Geodesic based centrality: Unifying the local and the global. *Social Networks*, 49, 12–26. https://doi.org/10.1016/j.socnet.2016.09.005

Anscombe, F. J. (1973). Graphs in statistical analysis. *The American Statistician*, 27(1), 17–21. Retrieved from http://www.jstor.org/stable/2682899

Antoun, W., Baly, F., and Hajj, H. (2020). AraBERT: Transformer-based model for Arabic language understanding. Preprint, arXiv:2003.00104. Retrieved from http://arxiv.org/abs/2003.00104

Archer, M. (2003). *Structure, Agency and the Internal Conversation*. Cambridge: Cambridge University Press.

Austin, J. L. (1975). *How to Do Things with Words*. Oxford: Oxford University Press.

Babbie, E. (2020). *The Practice of Social Research* (15th edn). Boston, MA: Cengage.

Barocas, S., Hardt, M., and Narayanan, A. (2019). *Fairness and Machine Learning*. https://fairmlbook.org.

Bateson, G. (2000). *Steps Towards an Ecology of Mind*. Chicago: University of Chicago Press.

Bearman, P., and Parigi, P. (2004). Cloning headless frogs and other important matters: Conversation topics and network structure. *Social Forces*, 83(2), 535–557.

Bechmann, A., and Nielbo, K. L. (2018). Are we exposed to the same 'news' in the news feed? An empirical analysis of filter bubbles as information similarity for Danish Facebook users. *Digital Journalism*, 6(8), 990–1002. https://doi.org/10.1080/21670811.2018.1510741

Bender, E. M., Gebru, T., McMillan-Major, A., and Shmitchell, S. (2021). On the dangers of stochastic parrots: Can language models be too big? In *FAccT '21: Proceedings of the 2021 ACM Conference on Fairness, Accountability, and Transparency* (Vol. 1, pp. 610–623). New York, NY: Association for Computing Machinery. https://doi.org/10.1145/3442188.3445922

Benkler, Y. (2002). Coase's penguin, or, Linux and the nature of the firm. *Yale Law Journal*, 112(3), 369–446.

Bertrand, M., Duflo, E., and Mullainathan, S. (2004). How much should we trust differences-in-differences estimates? *Quarterly Journal of Economics*, 119, 249–275. https://doi.org/10.1162/003355304772839588

Bird, S., Klein, E., and Loper, E. (2009). *Natural Language Processing with Python: Analyzing Text with the Natural Language Toolkit*. Sebastopol, CA: O'Reilly.

Blei, D. M., Ng, A. Y., and Jordan, M. I. (2003). Latent Dirichlet allocation. *Journal of Machine Learning Research*, 3, 993–1022.

Borgatti, S. P. (2005). Centrality and network flow. *Social Networks*, 27(1), 55–71.

Borgatti, S. P., Everett, M. G., and Johnson, J. C. (2013). *Analyzing Social Networks*. Thousand Oaks, CA: Sage.

Borgatti, S. P., Everett, M. G., and Johnson, J. C. (2018). *Analyzing Social Networks* (2nd edn). Los Angeles: Sage.

Brisset, N. (2016). Economics is not always performative: Some limits for performativity. *Journal of Economic Methodology*, 23(2), 160–184.

Buolamwini, J., and Gebru, T. (2018). Gender shades: Intersectional accuracy disparities in commercial gender classification. In S. A. Friedler and C. Wilson (eds), *Proceedings of the 1st Conference on Fairness, Accountability and Transparency* (pp. 77–91). PMLR. Retrieved from https://proceedings.mlr.press/v81/buolamwini18a.html

Butler, J. (1989). *Gender Trouble: Feminism and the Subversion of Identity*. New York: Routledge.

Butts, C. T. (2020). *sna: Tools for Social Network Analysis*. Retrieved from https://cran.r-project.org/package=sna

Cairo, A. (2011). *The Functional Art: An Introduction to Information Graphics and Visualization*. Berkeley, CA: New Riders.

Card, S. K., Mackinlay, J. D., and Shneiderman, B. (1999). *Readings in Information Visualization: Using Vision to Think*. San Diego, CA: Academic Press.

Centola, D. (2010). The spread of behavior in an online social network experiment. *Science*, 329, 1194–1197. https://doi.org/10.1126/science.1185231

Cha, M., Haddadi, H., Benevenuto, F., and Gummadi, K. P. (2010). Measuring user influence in Twitter: The million follower fallacy. *Proceedings of the 4th International AAAI Conference on Weblogs and Social Media (ICWSM)*, (pp. 10–17). Menlo Park, CA: Association for the Advancement of Artificial Intelligence. Retrieved from http://www.aaai.org/ocs/index.php/ICWSM/ICWSM10/paper/download/1538/1826

Chandrasekharan, E., Pavalanathan, U., Srinivasan, A., Glynn, A., Eisenstein, J., and Gilbert, E. (2017). You can't stay here: The efficacy of Reddit's 2015 ban examined through hate speech. *Proceedings of the ACM on Human-Computer Interaction*, 1 (CSCW), 1–22. https://doi.org/10.1145/3134666

Costenbader, E., and Valente, T. W. (2003). The stability of centrality measures when networks are sampled. *Social Networks*, 25(4), 283–307.

Crawford, K. (2021). *Atlas of AI*. New Haven, CT: Yale University Press.

D'Ignazio, C., and Klein, L. F. (2020). *Data Feminism*. Cambridge, MA: MIT Press.

De Vaus, D. (2002). *Analyzing Social Science Data: 50 Key Problems in Data Analysis*. Thousand Oaks, CA: Sage.

Dodge, M., Kitchin, R., and Perkins, C. R. (2009). *Rethinking Maps*. London: Routledge.

Dorling, D. (2012). *The Visualization of Spatial Social Structure*. Chichester: John Wiley & Sons.

Dubois, E., and Blank, G. (2018). The echo chamber is overstated: The moderating effect of political interest and diverse media. *Information, Communication and Society*, 21(5), 729–745. https://doi.org/10.1080/1369118X.2018.1428656

Durkheim, E. (1982). *Rules of Sociological Method* (W. D. Hall, Trans.). New York: The Free Press.

Edwards, L., and Veale, M. (2017). Slave to the algorithm: Why a right to an explanation is probably not the remedy you are looking for. *Duke Law & Technology Review*, 16, 18.

Emirbayer, M., and Mische, A. (1998). What is agency? *American Journal of Sociology*, 103(4), 962–1023.

Eslami, M., Karahalios, K., Sandvig, C., Vaccaro, K., Rickman, A., Hamilton, K., and Kirlik, A. (2016). First I 'like' it, then I hide it: Folk theories of social feeds. In *Conference on Human Factors in Computing Systems – Proceedings* (pp. 2371–2382). New York, NY: Association for Computing Machinery. https://doi.org/10.1145/2858036.2858494

Franzke, A. S., Bechmann, A., Zimmer, M., and Ess, C. M. (2019). *Internet Research: Ethical Guidelines 3.0 Association of Internet Researchers*. Retrieved from https://aoir.org/reports/ethics3.pdf

Friendly, M. (2008). A brief history of data visualization. In *Handbook of Data Visualization* (pp. 15–56). Berlin: Springer. https://doi.org/10.1007/978-3-540-33037-0_2

Fruchterman, T. M. J., and Reingold, E. M. (1991). Graph drawing by force-directed placement. *Software: Practice and Experience*, 21(11), 1129–1164.

Gaver, W. W. (1991). Technology affordances. In *CHI '91: Proceedings of the SIGCHI Conference on Human Factors in Computing Systems*, 79–84. New York, NY: ACM. https://doi.acm.org/10.1145/108844.108856

Gelman, A., and Hill, J. (2007). *Data Analysis Using Regression and Multilevel/Hierarchical Models*. Cambridge: Cambridge University Press.

Gilbert, E., and Karahalios, K. (2009). Predicting tie strength with social media. In *CHI '09: Proceeding of the Twenty-Seventh Annual SIGCHI Conference on Human Factors in Computing Systems*. New York, NY: ACM. https://doi.acm.org/10.1145/1357054.1357304

Gillespie, T. (2010). The politics of 'platforms'. *New Media and Society*, 12(3), 347–364. https://doi.org/10.1177/1461444809342738

Gillespie, T. (2021). *Custodians of the Internet: Platforms, Content Moderation, and the Hidden Decisions that Shape Social Media*. New Haven, CT: Yale University Press.

Gleick, J. (2011). *The Information: A History, a Theory, a Flood*. London: Fourth Estate.

Golbeck, J., Robles, C., and Turner, K. (2011). Predicting personality with social media. *Conference on Human Factors in Computing Systems – Proceedings* (pp. 253–262). New York, NY: ACM. https://doi.org/10.1145/1979742.1979614

Goodfellow, I., Bengio, Y., and Courville, A. (2016). *Deep Learning*. Cambridge, MA: MIT Press.

Graham, M., and Dittus, M. (2022). *Geographies of Digital Exclusion*. London: Pluto Press.

Graham, M., Hogan, B., Straumann, R. K., and Medhat, A. (2014). Uneven geographies of user-generated information: Patterns of increasing informational poverty. *Annals of the Association of American Geographers*, 104(4), 746–764. https://doi.org/10.1080/00045608.2014.910087

Graham, M., Straumann, R. K., and Hogan, B. (2015). Digital divisions of labor and informational magnetism: Mapping participation in Wikipedia. *Annals of the Association of American Geographers*, 105(6), 1158–1178. https://doi.org/10.1080/00045608.2015.1072791

Granovetter, M. (1973). The strength of weak ties. *American Journal of Sociology*, 78, 1360–1380.

Haig, B. D. (2015). Commentary: Exploratory data analysis. *Frontiers in Psychology*, 6(August), 1–2. https://doi.org/10.3389/fpsyg.2015.01247

Hale, S. A. (2012). Net increase? Cross-lingual linking in the blogosphere. *Journal of Computer-Mediated Communication*, 17(2), 135–151. https://doi.org/10.1111/j.1083-6101.2011.01568.x

Hallinan, B., Brubaker, J. R., and Fiesler, C. (2020). Unexpected expectations: Public reaction to the Facebook emotional contagion study. *New Media and Society*, 22(6), 1076–1094. https://doi.org/10.1177/1461444819876944

Hastie, T., Tibshirani, R., and Friedman, J. (2009). *The Elements of Statistical Learning* (2nd edn). Berlin: Springer. Retrieved from https://hastie.su.domains/Papers/ESLII.pdf

Hayles, N. K. (1999). *How We Became Posthuman: Virtual Bodies in Cybernetics, Literature, and Informatics*. Chicago, IL: University of Chicago Press.

Healy, K. (2015). The performativity of networks. *European Journal of Sociology*, 56(02), 175–205.

Healy, K. (2017). Fuck nuance. *Sociological Theory*, 35(2), 118–127. https://doi.org/10.1177/0735275117709046

Hecht, B., Hong, L., Suh, B., and Chi, E. H. (2011). Tweets from Justin Bieber's heart: The dynamics of the location field in user profiles. In *Proceedings of the SIGCHI Conference on Human Factors in Computing Systems* (pp. 237–246). New York, NY: ACM.

Heft, H. (2001). *Ecological Psychology in Context: James Gibson, Roger Barker, and the Legacy of William James's Radical Empiricism*. Mahwah, NJ: Lawrence Erlbaum Associates.

Henrich, J., Heine, S. J., and Norenzayan, A. (2010). The weirdest people in the world? *Behavioral and Brain Sciences*, 33(2–3), 61–83. https://doi.org/10.1017/S0140525X0999152X

Hofman, J. M., Sharma, A., and Watts, D. J. (2017). Prediction and explanation in social systems. *Science*, 355(6324), 486–488. https://doi.org/10.1126/science.aal3856

Hogan, B. (2010). The presentation of self in the age of social media: Distinguishing performances and exhibitions online. *Bulletin of Science, Technology & Society*, 30(6), 377–386. https://doi.org/10.1177/0270467610385893

Hogan, B. (2017). Online social networks: Concepts for data collection. In N. Fielding, R. Lee, and G. Blank (eds), *The SAGE Handbook of Online Research Methods* (2nd edn, pp. 241–258). Thousand Oaks, CA: Sage.

Hogan, B. (2018). Social media giveth, social media taketh away: Facebook, friendships, and APIs. *International Journal of Communication*, 12, 592–611. Retrieved from http://ijoc.org/index.php/ijoc/article/view/6724

Hogan, B. (2022). *Introducing Python in Jupyter*. Retrieved from https://github.com/berniehogan/introducingpython

Hogan, B., and Wellman, B. (2014). The relational self-portrait: Selfies meet social networks. In M. Graham and W. H. Dutton (eds), *Society and the Internet: How Networks of Information and Communication are Changing Our Lives* (pp. 53–66). Oxford: Oxford University Press.

Humphries, L. (1970). *Tearoom Trade*. London: Duckworth.

Hunter, D. R., Handcock, M. S., Butts, C. T., Goodreau, S. M., and Morris, M. (2008). ergm: A package to fit, simulate and diagnose exponential-family models for networks. *Journal of Statistical Software*, 24(3), 1–29. https://doi.org/10.18637/jss.v024.i03

Hutto, C. J. and Gilbert, E. (2014). VADER: A parsimonious rule-based model for sentiment analysis of social media text. In *Eighth International AAAI Conference on Weblogs and Social Media* (pp. 216–225). Retrieved from https://www.aaai.org/ocs/index.php/ICWSM/ICWSM14/paper/viewPaper/8109

Jenks, G. F., and Caspall, F. C. (1971). Error on choroplethic maps: Definition, measurement, reduction. *Annals of the Association of American Geographers*, 61(2), 217–244. https://doi.org/10.1111/j.1467-8306.1971.tb00779.x

Jiang, B. (2013). Head/tail breaks: A new classification scheme for data with a heavy-tailed distribution. *The Professional Geographer*, 65(3), 482–494.

John, P., Smith, G., and Stoker, G. (2009). Nudge nudge, think think: Two strategies for changing civic behaviour. *Political Quarterly*, 80(3), 361–370. https://doi.org/10.1111/j.1467-923X.2009.02001.x

Jones, K. S. (1972). A statistical interpretation of term specificity and its application in retrieval. *Journal of Documentation*, 28(1), 11–21.

Jung, C. (1921). *Psychologische Typen*. Zurich: Rascher Verlag.

Jurafsky, D., and Martin, J. H. (2021). *Speech and Language Processing*. Retrieved from https://web.stanford.edu/~jurafsky/slp3/

Kahneman, D. (2011). *Thinking, Fast and Slow*. London: Penguin. Retrieved from https://books.google.co.uk/books?id=oV1tXT3HigoC

Kahneman, D., and Tversky, A. (1979). Prospect theory: An analysis of decision under risk. *Econometrica*, 47(2), 263–291. Retrieved from http://www.jstor.org/stable/1914185

King, G., Lam, P., and Roberts, M. E. (2017). Computer-assisted keyword and document set discovery from unstructured text. *American Journal of Political Science*, 61(4), 971–988. https://doi.org/10.1111/ajps.12291

Kirk, H. R., Vidgen, B., Röttger, P., Thrush, T., and Hale, S. A. (2021). Hatemoji: A test suite and adversarially-generated dataset for benchmarking and detecting emoji-based hate. Preprint, arXiv:2108.05921. Retrieved from http://arxiv.org/abs/2108.05921

Kitchin, R., and Dodge, M. (2014). *Code/Space: Software and Everyday Life*. Cambridge, MA: MIT Press.

Kossinets, G. (2006). Effects of missing data in social networks. *Social Networks*, 28(3), 247–268.

Kozlowski, A. C., Taddy, M., and Evans, J. A. (2019). The geometry of culture: Analyzing the meanings of class through word embeddings. *American Sociological Review*, 84(5), 905–949. https://doi.org/10.1177/0003122419877135

Kramer, A. D. I., Guillory, J. E., and Hancock, J. T. (2014). Experimental evidence of massive-scale emotional contagion through social networks. *Proceedings of the National Academy of Sciences*, 111(24), 8788–8790.

Krenz, T., Krivitsky, P. N., Vacca, R., Bojanowski, M., and Herz, A. (2022). egor: Import and analyse ego-centered network data. Retrieved from https://cran.r-project.org/package=egor

Laumann, E. O., Marsden, P. V., and Prensky, D. (1989). The boundary specification problem in network analysis. *Research Methods in Social Network Analysis*, 61(8).

LaViolette, J., and Hogan, B. (2019). Using platform signals for distinguishing discourses: The case of men's rights and men's liberation on Reddit. In *Proceedings of the International AAAI Conference on Web and Social Media*, 13(1), 323–334. Retrieved from https://ojs.aaai.org/index.php/ICWSM/article/view/3357

Lessig, L. (2000). *Code and Other Laws of Cyberspace*. New York: Basic Books.

Lomborg, S. (2013). Personal internet archives and ethics. *Research Ethics*, 9(1), 20–31. https://org/10.1177/1747016112459450

Lomborg, S., and Bechmann, A. (2014). Using APIs for data collection on social media. *The Information Society*, 30(4), 256–265. https://doi.org/10.1080/01972243.2014.915276

MacKenzie, D., Muniesa, F., and Siu, L. (eds). (2008). *Do Economists Make Markets? On the Performativity of Economics*. Princeton, NJ: Princeton University Press. https://doi.org/10.1515/9780691214665

Mahdi, A., Błaszczyk, P., Dłotko, P., Salvi, D., Chan, T. S., Harvey, J., et al. (2021). OxCOVID19 Database, a multimodal data repository for better understanding the global impact of COVID-19. *Scientific Reports*, 11(1), 1–11. https://doi.org/10.1038/s41598-021-88481-4

Malik, M. M., and Pfeffer, J. (2016). Identifying platform effects in social media data. In *Proceedings of the International AAAI Conference on Web and Social Media*, 10(1), 241–249. Retrieved from https://ojs.aaai.org/index.php/ICWSM/article/view/14756

Margetts, H., John, P., Hale, S., and Yasseri, T. (2015). *Political Turbulence: How Social Media Shape Collective Action*. Princeton, NJ: Princeton University Press.

Marres, N. (2017). *Digital Sociology: The Reinvention of Social Research*. Malden, MA: Polity Press.

Martin, J. L. (2010). Life's a beach but you're an ant, and other unwelcome news for the sociology of culture. *Poetics*, 38, 228–243. https://doi.org/10.1016/j.poetic.2009.11.004

Mason, S., and Singh, L. (2022). Reporting and discoverability of 'Tweets' quoted in published scholarship: Current practice and ethical implications. *Research Ethics*, 18(2), 93–113. https://doi.org/10.1177/17470161221076948

Mayer-Schönberger, V. (2011). *Delete: The Virtue of Forgetting in the Digital Age*. Princeton, NJ: Princeton University Press.

Mayer-Schönberger, V., and Cukier, K. (2013). *Big Data: A Revolution that Will Transform How We Live, Work, and Think*. Boston, MA: Houghton Mifflin Harcourt.

McAuliffe, W. H. B. (2015). How did abduction get confused with inference to the best explanation? *Transactions of the Charles S. Peirce Society: A Quarterly Journal in American Philosophy*, 51(3), 300–319.

McConnell, E., Néray, B., Hogan, B., Korpak, A., Clifford, A., and Birkett, M. (2018). 'Everybody puts their whole life on Facebook': Identity management and the online social networks of LGBTQ youth. *International Journal of Environmental Research and Public Health*, 15(6), 1078. https://doi.org/10.3390/ijerph15061078

McGregor, S. E. (2021). *Practical Python Data Wrangling and Data Quality*. Sebastopol, CA: O'Reilly.

McKinney, W. (2012). *Python for Data Analysis*. Sebastopol, CA: O'Reilly.

McLevey, J. (2021). *Doing Computational Social Science*. Los Angeles: Sage.

McPherson, J. M., Smith-Lovin, L., and Brashears, M. (2006). Changes in core discussion networks over two decades. *American Sociological Review*, 71(3), 353–375.

Metaxa, D., Park, J. S., Robertson, R. E., Karahalios, K., Wilson, C., Hancock, J., and Sandvig, C. (2021). Auditing algorithms: Understanding algorithmic systems from the outside in. *Foundations and Trends® in Human–Computer Interaction*, 14(4), 272–344. https://doi.org/10.1561/1100000083

Miller, H., Kluver, D., Thebault-Spieker, J., Terveen, L., and Hecht, B. (2017). Understanding emoji ambiguity in context: The role of text in emoji-related miscommunication. In *Proceedings of the International AAAI Conference on Web and Social Media*, 11(1), 152–161. Retrieved from https://ojs.aaai.org/index.php/ICWSM/article/view/14901

Mittelstadt, B. D., and Floridi, L. (2016). The ethics of big data: Current and foreseeable issues in biomedical contexts. *Science and Engineering Ethics*, 22(2), 303–341. https://doi.org/10.1007/s11948-015-9652-2

Musgrave, A. (2011). Popper and hypothetico-deductivism. In D. M. Gabbay, S. Hartmann, and J. Woods (eds), *Handbook of the History of Logic, Volume 10: Inductive Logic* (pp. 205–234). Amsterdam: Elsevier.

Newman, M. (2018). *Networks*. Oxford: Oxford University Press.

Newman, M. E. J. (2006). Modularity and community structure in networks. *Proceedings of the National Academy of Sciences*, 103, 8577–8583.

Nissenbaum, H. (2009). *Privacy in Context: Technology, Policy, and the Integrity of Social Life*. Palo Alto, CA: Stanford University Press.

Noble, S. U. (2018). *Algorithms of Oppression*. New York, NY: New York University Press.

Nosrat, S. (2017). *Salt, Fat, Acid, Heat*. New York, NY: Simon & Schuster.

Nothman, J., Qin, H., and Yurchak, R. (2018). Stop word lists in free open-source software packages. In *Proceedings of Workshop for NLP Open Source Software (NLP-OSS)* (pp. 7–12). Association for Computational Linguistics. https://doi.org/10.18653/v1/W18-2502

O'Neil, C. (2016). *Weapons of Math Destruction: How Big Data Increases Inequality and Threatens Democracy*. New York: Crown Publishers.

Pager, D. (2007). The use of field experiments for studies of employment discrimination: Contributions, critiques, and directions for the future. *Annals of the American Academy of Political and Social Science*, 609(1), 104–133. https://doi.org/10.1177/0002716206294796

Pariser, E. (2011). *The Filter Bubble: What the Internet Is Hiding from You*. New York, NY: The Penguin Press HC.

Pearl, J. (2009). *Causality*. Cambridge: Cambridge University Press.

Pearl, J., and Mackenzie, D. (2018). *The Book of Why*. New York, NY: Basic Books.

Peirce, C. S. (1878). How to make our ideas clear. *Popular Science Monthly*, 12, 286–302.

Perry, B. L., and Roth, A. R. (2021). Commentary, On the boundary specification problem in network analysis: An update and extension to personal social networks. In M. L. Small, B. L. Perry, B. A. Pescosolido, and E. B. Smith (eds), *Personal Networks: Classic Readings and New Directions in Egocentric Analysis* (pp. 431–443). Cambridge: Cambridge University Press.

Pioli, M. R., Ritter, A. M. V., de Faria, A. P., and Modolo, R. (2018). White Coat Syndrome and Its Variations: Differences and Clinical Impact. *Integrated Blood Pressure Control*, 11: 73–79. https://doi.org/10.2147/IBPC.S152761

Porter, M. A. P., Onnela, J.-P., and Mucha, P. J. (2009). Communities in networks. *Notices of the AMS*, 56(9), 1082–1166.

Puschmann, C., and Burgess, J. (2014). Metaphors of big data. *International Journal of Communication*, 8, 1690–1709.

Qudar, M. M. A., and Mago, V. (2020). TweetBERT: A pretrained language representation model for Twitter text analysis. Preprint, arXiv:2010.11091. Retrieved from http://arxiv.org/abs/2010.11091

Quercia, D., Lambiotte, R., Stillwell, D., Kosinski, M., and Crowcroft, J. (2012). The personality of popular Facebook users. In *Proceedings of the ACM 2012 Conference on Computer Supported Cooperative Work* (pp. 955–964). New York, NY: ACM. https://doi.org/10.1145/2145204.2145346

Quercia, D., Schifanella, R., and Aiello, L. M. (2014). The shortest path to happiness: Recommending beautiful, quiet, and happy routes in the city. In *Proceedings of the 25th ACM Conference on Hypertext and Social Media* (pp. 116–125). New York, NY: ACM.

Rajkumar, K., Saint-Jacques, G., Bojinov, I., Brynjolfsson, E., & Aral, S. (2022). A causal test of the strength of weak ties. *Science*, 377(6612), 1304–1310. DOI: 10.1126/science.abl4476

Rey, S. J., Arribas-Bel, D., and Wolf, L. J. (2020). *Geographic Data Science with Python*. Jupyter Book. Retrieved from https://geographicdata.science/book/intro.html

Riach, P. A., and Rich, J. (2004). Deceptive field experiments of discrimination: Are they ethical? *Kyklos*, 57(3), 457–470. https://doi.org/10.1111/j.0023-5962.2004.00262.x

Rieder, B., Abdulla, R., Poell, T., Woltering, R., and Zack, L. (2015). Data critique and analytical opportunities for very large Facebook pages: Lessons learned from exploring 'We are all Khaled Said'. *Big Data & Society*, 2(2), 2053951715614980. https://doi.org/10.1177/2053951715614980

Ripley, R. M., Snijders, T. A. B., Boda, Zs., Vörös, A., and Preciado, P. (2021). *Manual for SIENA version 4.0* [Technical report]. Oxford: University of Oxford, Department of Statistics; Nuffield College. Retrieved from https://www.stats.ox.ac.uk/~snijders/siena/RSiena_Manual.pdf

Robbins, R. J. (1995). *Database Fundamentals* [Technical report]. Retrieved from http://www.esp.org/db-fund.pdf

Rosvall, M., Axelsson, D., and Bergstrom, C. T. (2009). The map equation. *European Physical Journal: Special Topics*, 178(1), 13–23. https://doi.org/10.1140/epjst/e2010-01179-1

Roth, R. E. (2017). Visual variables. In D. Richardson, N. Castree, and M. F. Goodchild (eds), *International Encyclopedia of Geography: People, the Earth, Environment and Technology, Volume 14: U–Z*. Hoboken, NJ: John Wiley & Sons.

Röttger, P., Vidgen, B., Nguyen, D., Waseem, Z., Margetts, H., and Pierrehumbert, J. B. (2021). HATECHECK: Functional tests for hate speech detection models. In *Proceedings of the 59th Annual Meeting of the Association for Computational Linguistics and the 11th International Joint*

Conference on Natural Language Processing (Volume 1: Long Papers), pages 41–58, Online. Association for Computational Linguistics. https://doi.org/10.18653/v1/2021.acl-long.4

Rowley, J. (2007). The wisdom hierarchy: Representations of the DIKW hierarchy. *Journal of Information Science*, 33(2), 163–180. https://doi.org/10.1177/0165551506070706

Russell, M. A., and Klassen, M. (2019). *Mining the Social Web* (3rd edn). Sebastopol, CA: O'Reilly.

Salganik, M. J. (2019). *Bit by Bit: Social Research in the Digital Age*. Princeton, NJ: Princeton University Press.

Sanderson, G. (2016). *Essence of Linear Algebra*. https://www.3blue1brown.com/topics/linear-algebra

Sandvig, C., Hamilton, K., Karahalios, K., and Langbort, C. (2014). Auditing algorithms: Research methods for detecting discrimination on internet platforms. *Data and Discrimination: Converting Critical Concerns into Productive Inquiry*, 22, 4349–4357.

Sandy, C. J., Gosling, S. D., and Durant, J. (2013). Predicting consumer behavior and media preferences: The comparative validity of personality traits and demographic variables. *Psychology & Marketing*, 30(11), 937–949. https://doi.org/10.1002/mar.20657

Saunders, J. A., Morrow-Howell, N., Spitznagel, E., Doré, P., Proctor, E. K., and Pescarino, R. (2006). Imputing missing data: A comparison of methods for social work researchers. *Social Work Research*, 30(1), 19–31. https://doi.org/10.1093/swr/30.1.19

Schäfer, M. T., and van Es, K. (eds). (2017). *The Datafied Society: Studying Culture through Data*. Amsterdam: Amsterdam University Press. Retrieved from http://www.jstor.org/stable/j.ctt1v2xsqn

Segaran, T. (2007). *Programming Collective Intelligence: Building Smart Web 2.0 Applications*. Sebastopol, CA: O'Reilly.

Shannon, C. E. (1948). A mathematical theory of communication. *Bell System Technical Journal*, 27(3), 379–423. https://doi.org/10.1002/j.1538-7305.1948.tb01338.x

Solove, D. J. (2008). *Understanding Privacy*. Cambridge, MA: Harvard University Press.

Spychalski, P., Błażyńska-Spychalska, A., & Kobiela, J. (2020). Estimating case fatality rates of COVID-19. *The Lancet Infectious Diseases*, 20(7), 774–775. https://doi.org/10.1016/S1473-3099(20)30246-2

Stadtfeld, C., Hollway, J., and Block, P. (2017). Dynamic network actor models: Investigating coordination ties through time. *Sociological Methodology*, 47(1), 1–40. https://doi.org/10.1177/0081175017709295

Stevens, S. S. (1946). On the theory of scales of measurement. *Science*, 103(2684), 677–680. https://doi.org/10.1126/science.103.2684.677

Streri, A., De Hevia, M. D., Izard, V., and Coubart, A. (2013). What do we know about neonatal cognition? *Behavioral Sciences*, 3(1), 154–169. https://doi.org/10.3390/bs3010154

Stumpf, M. P. H., and Porter, M. A. (2012). Critical truths about power laws. *Science*, 335(6069), 665–666. https://doi.org/10.1126/science.1216142

Sugiura, L., Wiles, R., and Pope, C. (2017). Ethical challenges in online research: Public/private perceptions. *Research Ethics*, 13(3–4), 184–199. https://doi.org/10.1177/1747016116650720

Sweeney, L. (2002). *k*-Anonymity: A model for protecting privacy. *International Journal of Uncertainty Fuzziness and Knowledge Based Systems*, 10(5), 557–570. Retrieved from http://citeseerx.ist.psu.edu/viewdoc/download?doi=10.1.1.163.9182{\&}rep=rep1{\&}type=pdf

Tanner, J. M. (1981). *A History of the Study of Human Growth*. Cambridge: Cambridge University Press.

Tausczik, Y. R., and Pennebaker, J. W. (2010). The psychological meaning of words: LIWC and computerized text analysis methods. *Journal of Language and Social Psychology*, 29(1), 24–54. https://doi.org/10.1177/0261927X09351676

Tiwari, S. (2020). *Face Recognition with Python, in Under 25 Lines of Code*. Retrieved from https://realpython.com/face-recognition-with-python/

Tiwari, S. (2021). *Python for Scientists and Engineers*. Victoria, British Columbia: Leanpub.

Toda, H. Y., and Yamamoto, T. (1995). Statistical inference in vector autoregressions with possibly integrated processes. *Journal of Econometrics*, 66(1–2), 225–250.

Tolstoy, L. (1977). *Anna Karenina* (1901 trans. by Constance Garnett). London: Pan Books.

Traag, V. A., Waltman, L., and van Eck, N. J. (2019). From Louvain to Leiden: Guaranteeing well-connected communities. *Scientific Reports*, 9(1), 1–12. https://doi.org/10.1038/s41598-019-41695-z

Traud, A. L., Kelsic, E. D., Mucha, P. J., and Porter, M. A. (2011). Comparing community structure to characteristics in online collegiate social networks. *SIAM Review*, 53(3), 526–543.

Tubaro, P., Ryan, L., Casilli, A. A., and D'Angelo, A. (2021). Social network analysis: New ethical approaches through collective reflexivity. *Social Networks*, 67(2), 1–8. https://doi.org/10.1016/j.socnet.2020.12.001

Tufte, E. R. (2001). *The Visual Display of Quantitative Information* (2nd edn). Cheshire, CT: Graphics Press.

Tufte, E. R. (2003). *The Cognitive Style of PowerPoint: Pitching Out Corrupts Within* (2nd edn). Cheshire, CT: Graphics Press.

Tukey, J. W. (1977). *Exploratory Data Analysis*. Reading, MA: Addison-Wesley.

Tyler, J. R., Wilkinson, D. M., and Huberman, B. A. (2003). Email as spectroscopy: Automated discovery of community structure within organizations. In *Communities and Technologies: Proceedings of the First International Conference on Communities and Technologies, c&t 2003* (pp. 81–96). Dordrecht: Kluwer Academic Publishers.

VanderPlas, J. (2016a). *A Whirlwind Tour of Python*. Sebastopol, CA: O'Reilly . Retrieved from https://jakevdp.github.io/WhirlwindTourOfPython/

VanderPlas, J. (2016b). *Python Data Science Handbook*. Sebastopol, CA: O'Reilly.

Vedres, B., and Vasarhelyi, O. (2019). Gendered behavior as a disadvantage in open source software development. *EPJ Data Science*, 8(1), 25.

Velleman, P. F., and Wilkinson, L. (1993). Nominal, ordinal, interval, and ratio typologies are misleading. *The American Statistician*, 47(1), 65–72. Retrieved from https://www.jstor.org/stable/2684788

Vicario, M. D., Bessi, A., Zollo, F., Petroni, F., Scala, A., Caldarelli, G., et al. (2016). The spreading of misinformation online. *Proceedings of the National Academy of Sciences of the United States of America*, 113(3), 554–559. https://doi.org/10.1073/pnas.1517441113

Viner, J. (1932). Cost curves and supply curves. *Zeitschrift für Nationalökonomie*, 3(1), 23–46. https://doi.org/10.1007/BF01316299

Wachter, S., Mittelstadt, B., and Floridi, L. (2017). Why a right to explanation of automated decision-making does not exist in the general data protection regulation. *International Data Privacy Law*, 7(2), 76–99.

Warwick, K., and Shah, H. (2016). Can machines think? A report on Turing test experiments at the Royal Society. *Journal of Experimental and Theoretical Artificial Intelligence*, 28(6), 989–1007. https://doi.org/10.1080/0952813X.2015.1055826

Waskom, M. L. (2021). Seaborn: Statistical data visualization. *Journal of Open Source Software*, 6(60), 3021.

Wellman, B. (1988). Structural analysis: From method and metaphor to theory and substance. In B. Wellman and S. D. Berkowitz (eds), *Social Structures: A Network Approach* (pp. 19–61). Cambridge: Cambridge University Press.

Wickham, H. (2011). The split-apply-combine strategy for data analysis. *Journal of Statistical Software*, 40(1), 1–29. Retrieved from http://www.jstatsoft.org/v40/i01/

Wickham, H. (2014). Tidy data. *Journal of Statistical Software*, 59(10), 1–23. Retrieved from https://vita.had.co.nz/papers/tidy-data.pdf

Wickham, H., and Grolemund, G. (2017) *R for Data Science*. Sebastopol, CA: O'Reilly. Retrieved from https://r4ds.had.co.nz/

Wickham, H., Navarro, D., and Pedersen, T. L. (2022). *GGPLOT2: Elegant Graphics for Data Analysis*. Berlin: Springer.

Williams, M. L., Burnap, P., and Sloan, L. (2017). Towards an ethical framework for publishing Twitter Data in social research: Taking into account users' views, online context and algorithmic estimation. *Sociology*, 51(6), 1149–1168. https://doi.org/10.1177/0038038517708140

Yasseri, T., Sumi, R., and Kertész, J. (2012). Circadian patterns of Wikipedia editorial activity: A demographic analysis. *PLoS ONE*, 7(1), 1–8. https://doi.org/10.1371/journal.pone.0030091

Yau, N. (2011). *Visualize This: The FlowingData Guide to Design, Visualization, and Statistics*. Indianapolis, IN: Wiley Publishing.

Zachary, W. W. (1977). An information flow model for conflict and fission in small groups. *Journal of Anthropological Research*, 33(4), 452–473.

Zerubavel, E. (1979). Private time and public time: The temporal structure of social accessibility and professional commitments. *Social Forces*, 58(1), 38–58.

Zerubavel, E. (1982). The standardization of time – a sociohistorical perspective. *American Journal of Sociology*, 88(1), 1–23.

Zerubavel, E. (1998). *Social Mindscapes: An Invitation to Cognitive Sociology*. Cambridge, MA: Harvard University Press.

Zimmer, M. (2010). 'But the data is already public': On the ethics of research in Facebook. *Ethics and Information Technology*, 12(4), 313–325. https://doi.org/10.1007/s10676-010-9227-5

Zook, M., and Graham, M. (2007). Mapping DigiPlace: Geocoded Internet data and the representation of place. *Environment and Planning B: Planning and Design*, 34(3), 466–482. Retrieved from http://www.geospace.co.uk/files/b33111.pdf

Zuboff, S. (2019) *The Age of Surveillance Capitalism*. London, UK: Profile Books.

Zwitter, A. (2014). Big Data ethics. *Big Data and Society*, 1(2), 1–6. https://doi.org/10.1177/2053951714559253

INDEX